THE WORLD'S RELIGIONS

THE
WORLD'S
RELIGIONS

Understanding the living faiths

Consultant Editor

Dr. Peter B. Clarke

Reader's Digest

Published by The Reader's Digest Association Limited

LONDON · SYDNEY · CAPE TOWN

The World's Religions
Published by The Reader's Digest Association Limited,
Berkeley Square House, Berkeley Square, London W1X 6AB

A Reader's Digest Book
Produced by Marshall Editions Limited

The credits and acknowledgments that appear on page 220 are
hereby made a part of this copyright page.

Printed in the United States of America

ISBN 0 276 42116 7

Editor: **James Harpur**
Assistant Editor: **Lindsay McTeague**
Research: **Malcolm Day**

Picture Research: **Elizabeth Loving**
Art Director: **David Goodman**
Design Assistant: **Glenda Tyrrell**

Editorial Director: **Ruth Binney**
Production: **Barry Baker**
                   Janice Storr

Authors
Consultant Editor
    Dr. Peter B. Clarke, King's College, University of London

Religion in the Modern World
    Dr. Peter B. Clarke

Judaism
    Rabbi Dr. Albert H. Friedlander, Westminster Synagogue, London

Christianity
    Rev. Dr. Charles Elliott, Dean of Trinity Hall, Cambridge

Islam
    Dr. Peter B. Clarke

Zoroastrianism
    Sarah Stewart, M.A., School of Oriental and African Studies,
    University of London

Hinduism
    V.P. Kanitkar; Dr. W. Owen Cole, West Sussex Institution of
    Higher Education, Chichester, England

Jainism
    Dr. N. Shah, President, Jain Samaj, Europe; Dr. W. Owen Cole

Buddhism
    Peggy Morgan, Senior Lecturer in Theology and Religious Studies,
    Westminster College, Oxford

Sikhism
    Piara Singh Sambhi; Dr. W. Owen Cole

China's Religious Tradition
    Professor T.H. Barrett, Professor of East Asian History, School of
    Oriental and African Studies, University of London

Shinto
    Dr. John Breen, Lecturer in Japanese Studies, School of Oriental and
    African Studies, University of London

Micropedia
    Dr. Peter B. Clarke

Contents

Introduction   6

Religion in the   8
Modern World

Judaism   16

Christianity   40

Islam   84

Zoroastrianism   120

Hinduism   124

Jainism   144

Buddhism   148

Sikhism   172

China's Religious   176
Tradition

Shinto   196

Micropedia   202

Bibliography   212

Index   214

Acknowledgments   220

The decorative panels that introduce each religion here and in their respective sections use motifs important to each faith. They are as follows: Judaism, the seven-branched candlestick, or menorah; Christianity, the cross; Islam, the crescent moon and star; Zoroastrianism, a fire altar surrounded by divine wings; Hinduism, the sacred syllable Om; Jainism, the saint Mahavira; Buddhism, the wheel of the law; Sikhism, the Khanda symbol – the circle and the double-edged sword flanked by two swords; China's Religious Tradition, the symbol for yin and yang; Shinto, a ceremonial shrine gateway, or torii.

Introduction

FROM THE DAWN OF CIVILIZATION, religion has played an indispensable role both in people's private lives and in the realm of society. In prehistoric times, evidence from Stone Age cave paintings of animals suggests religious rituals may have been used to ensure the success of hunting. A similar need to invoke a supernatural agency was felt in later agriculture-based communities, whose prayers and rituals were designed to ensure an abundant harvest or sufficient rainfall to make the ground fertile.

Religion is concerned with the fundamentals of human existence, attempting to address crucial questions and issues such as the creation of the world, the meaning of life, survival after death, ethical living and personal happiness. Religion has never been solely a cerebral affair, concerned only with abstract ideals. It has been and continues to be the lifeblood of societies all over the world, providing communities with meaningful rituals, colourful festivals and pilgrimages to sacred places, many of which are described and illustrated on the pages of this volume.

Although religion has its dark side and can be used to bolster intolerance and unbridled nationalism, its power to inspire acts of charity and great works of art is unrivalled. Illuminated manuscripts, music, paintings, statues, poetry, mosques, cathedrals and temples – many examples of which appear in this book – are just some of the cultural high points of civilization.

This book introduces the great living faiths of the world and explains how these religions arose, how they developed and what their basic rites, rituals and beliefs are. The religions are introduced and outlined from their beginnings to the present, with maps to show the distribution of their adherents worldwide or to chart crucial moments in their history. Dates are given as B.C.E. (Before Common Era) and C.E. (Common Era) – a form acceptable to different religions – which are equivalent to B.C. and A.D., respectively. Special features on topics such as death and the afterlife, saints and scholars, and forms of worship complement the main narrative, focusing on the more human and colourful aspects of religion.

Apart from the major living religions, a number of important smaller religious movements, sects and philosophies are outlined in the micropedia. There is also a select bibliography for further reading.

In the late 20th century, a time of increasing population shifts, global travel and pluralistic, multifaith societies, there is a greater need than ever to understand the religions, and therefore the ethical ideals and culture, of the various communities that make up a particular society. This book is a starting point for such an understanding.

A Trappist monk concentrates on his studies in St. Joseph's Abbey, Massachusetts. Founded by Armand de Rancé (1626–1700) at the abbey of La Trappe, France, the Trappist order is a branch of the Roman Catholic Cistercians.

The elegant minaret of a mosque in Jeddah, Saudi Arabia, is mirrored in the reflecting glass of a skyscraper. The image frames a centuries-old symbol of Islam within a futuristic, secular context. Although religion may be as old as humankind itself, it faces perhaps its greatest challenge in the late 20th century.

Whether in the east or west, mainstream religions such as Islam, Christianity and Buddhism must confront problems posed by the power and influence of new technologies, pluralistic societies, a population explosion, ecological and environmental issues, and a host of other concerns.

8

Religion in the Modern World

WHEN FRIEDRICH NIETZSCHE (1844–1900), the German philosopher, pronounced "God is dead! God remains dead!" through the character of a madman in his book *Joyful Wisdom*, he seemed to sum up the prevailing spirit of his age. During the 19th century, the progress of science and the rise of industrial societies in the west led many thinkers to believe that religion was indeed coming to an end. Science, with its ability to explain so many of the mysteries of existence, would, they argued, convince people that they did not need to look to God for guidance.

Toward the end of the 20th century, however, it could be said that in many parts of the world both God and religion are in excellent health. In India, for example, millions of Hindus worship their various gods, such as Vishnu and Shiva, participate in flamboyant and colourful religious festivals, and make pilgrimages to sacred places such as Varanasi (Benares) on the Ganges. In Sri Lanka, Southeast Asia, Japan, Korea and elsewhere, millions of Buddhists go about their daily lives trying to follow the precepts attributed to Gautama Buddha, whose ethical and spiritual teachings form the basis of their religion. And in Islamic countries of the Middle East, northern Africa and other parts of the world, Muslims lead God-centred lives, with Islam pervading every aspect of society, from personal behaviour to public institutions.

In the west, the status of religion is complex. In most of Europe, the number of adherents of the traditional Christian denominations, such as the Catholic Church, has declined. But in the United States, the traditional churches still retain sizable followings. Catholicism continues to hold its own, missionary movements are growing, especially those connected with Protestant churches, and Pentecostalists thrive in some regions.

Nor is religion in the west confined to Christianity. Islam, largely through the influence of Muslim immigrants, is increasing in both Europe and North America, and Buddhism is expanding in both these continents. The years since World War II have also witnessed the birth of many new religions, offering a wide variety of spirituality to those disenchanted with old forms of Christian worship. Some of these new religions, such as Transcendental Meditation (p.207), have become well known and well established.

Decline in the west
Apart from Nietzsche, other thinkers of the 19th century scrutinized the notion of God and the place of religion in society. Some, such as the German revolutionaries and thinkers Karl Marx (1813–83) and Friedrich Engels (1820–95), developed the theory of religion, now called "projectionist", which was first proposed by the philosopher Ludwig Feuerbach (1804–72). According to this theory God was not an objective reality independent of human beings; on the contrary, God was a creation of the human mind, a figment of the imagination. People simply projected on to this "illusion" human qualities, such as compassion, that they regarded as ideal.

But what gave rise to this "illusory" God in the first place? For Marx and Engels it was clear. They believed that the alienation ordinary working people suffered in capitalist societies made them turn to religion for comfort. Religion was "the opium of the people", a drug that soothed their pain. Once capitalism had been destroyed, they said, religion would be discarded. However, their prediction appears to have been at least partially disproved by the rugged survival of religion in the former bastions of communism in eastern Europe and what was the Soviet Union.

By contrast, the distinguished French scholar and sociologist Emile Durkheim (1858–1917) did not believe that God could be so easily dispensed with. Durkheim proposed that God was a product of society and that when a society worshipped God, it was actually worshipping a projection of itself. Put simply, God is society worshipping itself. By this he meant that when communities gather on important occasions they naturally give rise to collective sentiments and rituals which take on a sacred character and a life of their own, independent of those who created them. In this way, a rich store of symbols, rituals and beliefs emerge which bond people together. Moreover, religion understood in this way is eternal, since it is a product of society and will, therefore, survive as long as there are human communities.

The general feeling that religion was in decline continued into the present century. Sigmund Freud (1856–1939), the founder of psychoanalysis, for example, was concerned about the effect on society the demise of religion would have. In *Civilization and its Discontents* and *The Future of an Illusion*, Freud stressed that although religion could have its negative and destructive aspect, it helped to make civilization possible. Without it, Freud argued, life in society would be impossible unless everyone was educated to behave morally.

Secular societies and the search for unity
In the west in the 20th century, the loss of religious influence over society, or secularization, that became evident with the Age of Enlightenment (pp.72–73) in the 18th century has continued. However, in the early 1990s, religious trends are complex and do not necessarily reflect a straightforward decline in belief or spirituality.

In western Europe, many people, although nominally Christian, have to all intents and purposes left the old established Christian denominations. In Sweden and Denmark, for example, less than five percent of the population participates in church worship regularly,

Religion in the Modern World

and the situation is similar elsewhere. In France, once the foremost Catholic country in Europe, if the decline in churchgoing continues, there will soon be more practising Muslims than Catholics. There are, however, exceptions: in Malta, the Republic of Ireland and, to a lesser extent, Italy, Catholicism remains strong.

In the United States, 50 percent of the adult population still practises religion of some type regularly, and certain Christian denominations, such as Catholicism, continue to grow. However, many people have become disenchanted with traditional forms of worship and have been drawn to what are often perceived as the more "spiritual" religions of the east, such as Zen Buddhism.

Along with the general decline in traditional church practice in western Europe and elsewhere, there has been an erosion of distinctions between churches. This has helped what is known as the ecumenical movement (pp.82-83) – the pursuit of unity among churches. In the modern era, the movement goes back to the early years of the 20th century. It was stimulated by the International Missionary Conference in Edinburgh, Scotland, in 1910, at which Protestant Christians sought to increase understanding and cooperation among themselves. Other churches joined the movement later, and attempts have since been made to include other denominations, such as the Catholic Church, and other religions, such as Judaism and Islam.

This ecumenical tendency and the desire for dialogue with non-Christian religions were reflected in the Catholic Church's Second Vatican Council (1962–65), which spoke favourably for the first time in centuries about Islam. The Council recognized Islam's holy scripture, the Qur'an, as being revealed by God and therefore authentic. In this way, it prepared the ground for initial dialogue with Muslims and with other non-Christian religions.

Christian revival

Although many established churches in the west are in decline, they continue to gain ground in other parts of the world. And, ironically, as Christianity directs its zeal more toward the third world, religions such as Islam, Buddhism and Hinduism, as well as movements derived from them, are making a significant impact in the west.

The Christian missionary movement is a global success story even though an estimated 70 countries are closed to all foreign missionaries. In the United States, there are almost 800 Protestant agencies, supporting some 70,000 overseas representatives. Since about 1980, while the number of European missionaries has remained more or less the same, the number of American Protestant missionaries has risen by 80 percent. Much of this output emanates from California, which has the largest concentration of Protestant missionary organizations in the world.

Modern Christian missionaries often come from prosperous churches and benefit from the latest technology, as did their 19th-century counterparts, who used lantern slides and gramophones in the field. Modern resources include literally millions of computers, fleets of vehicles and aircraft, television and radio stations with a combined total of over a billion listeners, and the printing and dissemination of some 22,000 books and four billion tracts a year. There is also a thriving industry of gospel music, records, tapes, videos and films.

Epitomizing this hi-tech approach to missionizing is Campus Crusade for Christ (p.202), founded in the late 1940s for the purpose of evangelizing college students throughout North America. In

time, it extended its work overseas. Large, rich and optimistic, Campus Crusade uses the most up-to-date cinema technology to convey its message.

The impact of American and other missions, while often impressive, is perhaps not as profound as might be expected. In Africa, for example, although Christianity, like Islam, is expanding, it is also being adapted to local customs, such as polygamy, and often in ways disapproved of by Christians, particularly evangelical Protestants. Since about 1930, thousands of African Independent churches (p.74) have emerged on the continent, with their own distinctive rituals and structures which are not always consistent with mainstream Christian practices.

Sometimes the success of a Christian mission is at the expense of another church. In Latin America, for example, Protestant Christianity has made deep inroads into what was primarily Catholic terrain. Various denominations, mainly Pentecostal (p.82), have been gaining unprecedented numbers of converts, especially in Brazil, where, since 1960, the Catholic monopoly has been steadily eroded. Now, an estimated 20 percent of the country's 150 million people are Protestant. Also, across the Pacific, Pentecostalism is expanding as never before in South Korea.

A "Jesus Saves" sign on the Church of the Open Door in Los Angeles shines out like a beacon, proclaiming its neon message to the L.A. populace. One of the branches of the Christian church effectively rising to the challenge of the modern era is its evangelical wing. In the west, inner city decay and spiritually disaffected populations have provided a fertile seedbed for urban missions to grow.

Two French nuns sit among empty bath chairs at the healing shrine of Lourdes in southwestern France. Despite the general decline of mainstream Christianity in the country, as well as in the rest of western Europe, Lourdes continues to attract millions of pilgrims each year. The shrine commemorates the alleged appearances of the Virgin Mary to a peasant girl named Bernadette (1844–79) in 1858, and its waters are believed to effect miraculous cures.

Missionary movements in the 19th century made use of the latest technology, such as magic lanterns, to spread the gospel. In many cases, however, the most effective tool the evangelist had at his disposal was the power of his voice, as shown by the contemporary engraving (LEFT) in which a missionary in Africa preaches to local village people.

By contrast, modern evangelists have a wealth of hi-tech wizardry to further their aims. For example, to aid communication and impress audiences, the image of a preacher can be projected on to giant screens, as is shown here (RIGHT) in Crystal Cathedral, Orange County, California.

Many of the new religions to have taken root in North America and Europe in the 20th century have originated from India and other parts of Asia. One of the fastest-growing groups in the west is the Hindu Swaminarayana movement (p.207), members of which are shown gathered at a celebration (RIGHT) in India. Founded in the early 19th century, the movement appeals mainly to Indian immigrants.

A British Buddhist monk sits cross-legged in a meditation pose at a monastery in Sussex, southern England. Buddhism, a religion founded in India some 2,500 years ago, has an increasing number of adherents in the west. This is partly due to the influx of Asian immigrants, particularly to North America and western Europe, but also because many westerners, dissatisfied with mainstream Christianity, have found a more intimate, gentle spirituality in this eastern religion.

Religion in the Modern World

Innovation and change

Protestant Christianity is not the only success story in Latin America. Popular religions, such as Umbanda and Candomblé (p.211), based on African and Catholic belief and ritual, flourish in Brazil and are spreading to Argentina and beyond. Cuban Santería (p.211), which has a similar form and content to Umbanda and Candomblé, is also prospering and is widely practised by immigrant communities, mainly Hispanic and African-American, in Los Angeles, New York and elsewhere in North America.

Religious change and innovation have not been confined to the third world. Since the 1960s, Islam has greatly increased in the west. In the early 1990s, Muslims are estimated to constitute about two percent of the populations of Germany and France; one and a half percent of that of Britain. And in the United States, Muslims now number about six million, constituting, along with Buddhists, one of the fastest-growing religious communities in the United States.

Also, in the United States alone, it has been estimated that more than 3,000 new religions, some of which are listed on pages 202 to 211, have emerged since World War II. Western Europe and Japan are not far behind, and rough estimates suggest that followers of new religions worldwide number millions rather than thousands.

New religions in Japan, such as Soka Gakkai (Value Creation Society, p.208), mostly derive from indigenous Buddhist and Shinto traditions. Those in North America and Europe come mainly from the Indian subcontinent, Japan and other parts of Asia. A number, such as the Unification Church (p.210) – popularly known as the Moonies – and Scientology (p.210), are the creations of charismatic leaders. Many new religions promote the idea of a this-worldly paradise and market religion as if it were a "health-friendly" commodity, essential not only to personal well-being but also to ecological well-being, world peace and human survival.

The purpose of religion

With changing patterns of religion in the world – the increase of Christianity in the third world, the rise of eastern religions in the west – it may be asked what purpose religion plays in people's lives. What questions does it answer? What is its appeal?

Religion's function has been debated since the 19th century by various scholars, and one of the most interesting and influential theories was developed by Emile Durkheim. He thought religion had two main functions: "cognitive" and practical. By cognitive, Durkheim meant that religion makes the world intelligible to people, providing them with their notions of time and space, cause and effect, and the ability to think about and understand the nature of society and the world. In other words, religion is like philosophy and has a mental dimension that involves faith, ideas, dogma, theology and reason. That said, Durkheim, among others, felt that religion's ability to explain the everyday world had been largely taken over by science and secular philosophy.

With a giant banner bearing the image of Ayatollah Khomeini looming above them, crowds of Iranians pay homage to their country's spiritual and political leader after his death in 1989. In Iran, the Shiite form of Islam is predominant, and this, allied with nationalism, has fostered a strong sense of cohesion among the Iranian people. One of the purposes of religion, according to the French sociologist Emile Durkheim and others, is to unite people in a society, forging a unity born of shared ideals and norms of moral behaviour. Many commentators believe religion in the west has lost this unifying function.

Religion's practical function, helping people to conduct their lives, Durkheim believed, would continue to be of the utmost importance, a fact that he felt critics of religion often overlooked at great cost to society. He said that through its various rituals, religion releases energy within the committed followers of a religion in a particular community. This energy gives rise to a sense of security, happiness, belonging and inner strength. In this way, religion functions as a sort of social cement, uniting people of the same society, binding them together with a common set of ideas, norms of behaviour and duties. Durkheim was eager to emphasize this unifying element and spoke of religious beliefs and practices "*uniting into one moral community* [author's italics] called a Church all who adhere to them".

Many contemporary observers, however, think that religion has lost this unifying function. This is because modern society is so diverse and pluralistic that it is almost impossible for any one religion to hold it together. Also, many aspects of society, such as the economy, education, politics and the law, depend on technology and reason rather than belief in God for their functioning.

However, there are parts of the world where religion, sometimes combined with nationalism, fosters cohesion and unity. This is achieved, for example, by the Catholic Church in Poland and by Shiite Islam (pp.90–91) in Iran. On the other hand, in places such as the Lebanon and Northern Ireland, both suffering from internal strife, religion appears to bind some communities together, but to divide them from others within the same country.

Unity and identity

There are societies, particularly in the non-western world, such as Muslim Iran and much of rural Africa, where religion continues to serve as a "sacred canopy" overhanging the world. Both its explanatory and its unifying roles remain vitally important. And, in a rapidly changing world, religion in many places, especially Africa, Iran and Latin America, serves as a reassuring link with the past, which is often idealized as a glorious era: secure, meaningful, without evil and enjoying supernatural approval.

By contrast, in much of the western world, religion no longer explains the mysteries of existence nor, in many places, does it continue to function as a form of social cement. Nevertheless, many still participate in some form of religion, although this increasingly takes place in the private sphere, involving, for example, informal gatherings for prayer or meditation, sometimes in private homes. Indeed, there seems to be a paradox at the heart of modern society: the greater the influence of science and technology, the more people turn to religion – even if it takes a non-traditional form.

In the west in particular, religion still attempts to provide a sense of community and to cater for the development of the "total" person – the integration of the individual's public and personal, or outer and inner, lives. Much of modern daily life is fragmented and diverse. People encounter systems of faceless bureaucracy both in and out of the workplace and often need to specialize and conduct relationships based on impersonal criteria, such as client and customer. As a result, many have taken refuge in religion, particularly in its private form, because it can help to cater for their emotional, intellectual and spiritual needs.

As well as providing a sense of community, religion can often provide a sense of identity, as well as many of the benefits Durkheim highlighted: inner strength, purpose, meaning and a sense of

Religion in the Modern World

belonging. The Rastafarian movement (p.211), which developed in Jamaica, is one of the most striking examples in modern times of a religion creating an identity for its adherents. Religion served much the same function in the past and, to an extent, continues to do so for Catholics, Protestants and Jews in the United States, as well as for Hispanic and African-Americans. Moreover, for minority communities, religion can mediate between the individual and what is perceived as the ever more powerful state, offering protection for beliefs and practices that do not fully accord with the perceived core values of the dominant society.

The future of religion

How religion will fare in the future and, if it survives, what form it will take is difficult to predict. In the 1960s, some Christian theologians and social scientists predicted the end of Christianity by the year 2000. And there were other scholars, such as the American Paul van Buren, who claimed that the idea of a transcendent God, beyond the sphere of human existence, was meaningless to the modern secular person. They said that God had "withdrawn" altogether to allow people the space and scope to exercise responsible choice in their lives.

Those theologians who espoused this view were trying to emphasize the necessity of a faith centred on Jesus Christ that was appropriate to a world that had "come of age". Even those who were in disagreement suggested that new ways of thinking about God were essential if people in the modern world were to retain a belief in God. For example, in his controversial and best-selling book *Honest to God* (1964), the Anglican theologian Bishop John Robinson asked people to stop thinking of God as if he were an old man with a beard dwelling in the clouds who occasionally had to intervene in the world below.

Some years before Robinson's book was published, the American-born British poet and critic T.S. Eliot (1888–1965) believed that people had already lost faith in this traditional view of God. Eliot pointed out the uniqueness of this development in his play *The Rock*, in which he wrote, "men have left God . . . for no God; and this has never happened before. . . ."

But Eliot's prognostication does not seem correct. It could be argued, for example, that relatively few people "have left God". Well over 90 percent of North Americans say they believe in God, and the figure is much the same in western Europe. In England, for example, the number who profess to a belief in God is between 80 and 90 percent. There is also widespread adherence to other central tenets of Christianity, including the belief in Jesus as the Son of God and his resurrection from the dead.

What is interesting, however, is that less than 50 percent of people believe that Christianity is the only true religion. And this opens up the possibility for much more experimentation in the field of religion and for much greater movement between religions. Many people are not leaving God for no God, as Eliot imagined, but for new ways of understanding God and new forms of religion to suit their contemporary situation. This often, but not always, entails a rejection of older forms of religion or notions of God. But some new religions, such as the Hare Krishna movement and Soka Gakkai, would claim to be a continuation of old religious traditions, in this case Hinduism and Buddhism, respectively.

Increasing numbers of people in the west, it seems, are prepared to be less dogmatic and more open-minded and accept beliefs from a variety of traditions without too much concern about their consistency. Reincarnation, for example, is a non-Christian belief held by an estimated 25 percent of western Europeans, many of whom would also appear to believe in the resurrection of Jesus and other Christian tenets about the afterlife. The New Age movement (p.209), which draws on insights from many traditions, is perhaps the best example of this eclectic approach.

In the future, as communications increase contact and interaction between cultures on a global scale, people may well acknowledge a range of beliefs once considered totally incompatible and gain benefit from practices found outside their own religious traditions. Christians, for example, may increasingly practise Buddhist- and Hindu-style meditation. The openness to other religions, the perception of the relative nature of religious truth, and the readiness to experiment suggests that the movement toward eclecticism may gather momentum.

If new religions influenced by eastern traditions and the New Age movement can be taken as a guide to the future, religion in years to come may be shaped by concerns about self-identity and personal well-being and wholeness. This concern with the "self" does not necessarily reflect a narcissistic strain, but rather a belief that the world can be changed only through a change in individuals, not by organizations and governments.

In the future, religion will probably not be all of a piece. It is more likely that people will exercise choice in the matter of religion and view it as a "commodity". There will be more experimentation, with the result that lifelong membership of one particular faith could become much less common.

Durkheim wrote of the almost limitless capacity of humans for innovation when it came to religion. In the modern world, with the easy access to such a variety of religious traditions, the material is there to facilitate such innovation on an unprecedented scale.

Members of the Findhorn Community (p.209) in Scotland participate in a group meditation session. Many people in the west have embraced the more private forms of religion – small prayer or meditation groups, often conducted in a private home – as a more efficacious way of satisfying their emotional and spiritual needs.

A woman meditates outdoors within an "Aquarian Pyramid" in Boulder, Colorado, hoping to harness cosmic energy to promote a sense of well-being. New Age spirituality focuses strongly on self-realization and the harmonious relationship between people and their natural environment. New Age values and concerns, which run counter to much of the secular spirit of western industrialized societies, may point toward the path religion could take in the future.

A procession of Catholic bishops files across St. Peter's Square, Rome, looking like chess pieces on a board. Mainstream Christian denominations are experiencing mixed fortunes in the late 20th century. In much of western Europe, churches are in decline, with many people seeking out the more personal spirituality of eastern religions or New Age movements. However, Catholicism remains strong in Ireland and Italy, as well as in the United States, where its numbers are on the increase.

This powerful menorah – the seven-branched candelabra of Judaism – stands in front of the Knesset (Parliament) in Jerusalem. The menorah represents the days of the week and the Sabbath. It was used first in the Temple of King Solomon and, later, in synagogues. It is the national emblem of the state of Israel.

The joyous harvest festival of Sukkot is here celebrated in a Hasidic synagogue in New York. The festival commemorates the journey of the Israelites through the desert on their way to the Promised Land, and Jews traditionally make stalls out of leaves to symbolize the Israelites' tents.

During the service, the scrolls of the Torah are paraded around the building seven times, together with the lulav – palm branches, myrtle leaves, willow branches and a citron. Poetical prayers are chanted and, at the end of the service, the palm branches are beaten on the ground.

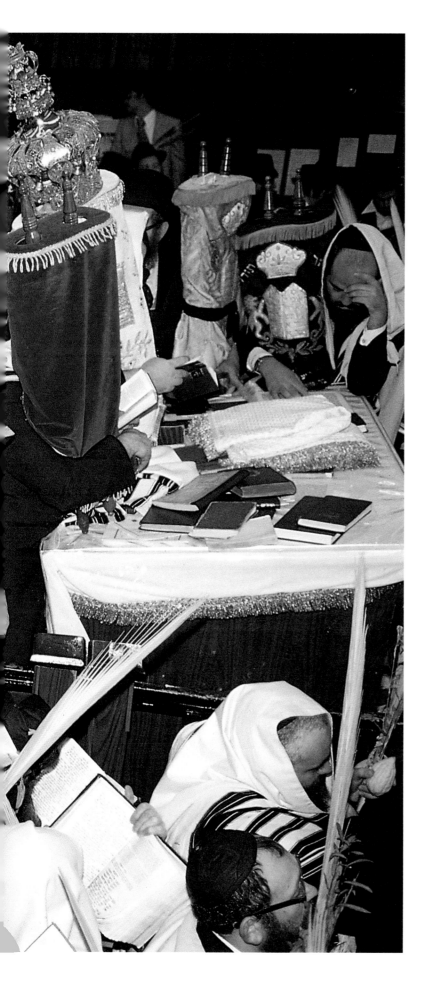

The Chosen People

THE RELIGION OF THE JEWISH PEOPLE – Judaism – was the first great faith to hold that there is only one God. This monotheism is not only its cornerstone but also that of Christianity and Islam, both of which derive much of their spiritual traditions from Judaism. Central to Judaism is the Hebrew Bible, known to Christians as the Old Testament, which tells of the origins and development of the Jewish people beginning from God's creation of the world. In the Bible, there is emphasis on the Jews being God's chosen people: ". . . you have been chosen by THE LORD your God to be his own people" (Deuteronomy 7:6).

However, even the Jews are not certain that they are a chosen people. "Chosen" for Jews means accepting a "covenant" with God to be God's witnesses, which may entail suffering, but does not mean superiority. The revelation contained in the Bible is accepted by most of the approximately 14.5 million Jews in the world today, but the interpretation of that text varies among the different branches of Judaism (p.18), which also differ in their observances of ancient customs and rituals.

Jews are broadly divided between Ashkenazi (German, Central European and Russian Jews) and Sephardi (Spanish, Portuguese, northern African, Greek, Italian, Ethiopian, Yemenite and Syrian Jews). Jews follow a similar life pattern which affirms their identity as a religious and cultural grouping; but they are *not* a race. Of the more than 3.5 million Jews in the state of Israel, it is possible to see blond Scandinavians, Slavic Russians, dark Yemenites, Indians and even Chinese and Japanese Jews. Converts are accepted; but there is no missionary movement within Judaism.

From biblical times, there has been a creative tension between Jews living in the land of Israel and those outside it – known as the Diaspora, or dispersion. Today, the most dynamic centres of Jewish life are in the state of Israel, founded in 1948, and in the United States. In the early 1990s, Israel was in a state of flux, with migrants arriving from a variety of countries, including Russia, the Balkans, Yemen and Ethiopia.

Outside Israel, the almost six million Jews living in the United States are the most supportive of Israel, although they are sometimes at odds with changes there. American Jews live in a relaxed relationship with their mainly Christian American neighbours, contributing to the culture of an often secular society. In terms of numbers, they have had more than their share of Nobel Prize winners for science, literature and peace, including Isidor Isaac Rabi, Isaac Bashevis Singer, Saul Bellow, Elie Wiesel and Henry Kissinger.

The Chosen People

However, what Jews in America view as symbiosis or a close, mutually beneficial association with the gentile (non-Jewish) community, Israelis see as assimilation, with loss of identity. As evidence, they point to the erosion of American Jewry, marked by 30 to 50 percent intermarriage with gentiles, lower synagogue membership and attendance, a low birthrate and some anti-Semitism. Many American Jews, however, reject this criticism.

Changes continue to take place in the United States. For example, Jews of the Orthodox Hasidic group (p.34) have formed close enclaves in New York City and other places, while Holocaust (p.37) studies rival black studies at universities. Population shifts continue: by 1990 there were more than half a million Jews in Los Angeles and just under two million Jews in New York, which is the centre of United States Jewry. And Jewish institutions such as Temple Emanu-El, the Union of American Hebrew Congregations, the Hebrew Union College-J.I.R. (Reform), the Jewish Theological Seminary (Conservative) and Yeshiva University (Orthodox) still flourish. American Jewry remains strong.

In Europe, however, the situation is different. The 2.2 million Jews living in Russia and the other former Soviet republics face an uncertain future, as they do in the Balkans. In France in the early 1990s, more than 600,000 Jews were faced with a rise in anti-Semitism stirred up by Jean-Marie Le Pen among others. Nevertheless, French Jews, whose numbers have been increased by Sephardi from Tunisia and Morocco, continue to develop their religious life.

The Jewish community in Great Britain, which totals about 300,000, has been declining in numbers, although the Leo Baeck College (which ordains women rabbis) has strengthened Reform and Liberal Judaism. Only 30,000 Jews live in Germany, but with the collapse of communist eastern Europe, thousands of Russian Jews have flocked to the country, and Berlin has now become a central and more prominent Jewish area.

Despite their varying fortunes, Jews all over the world are welded together by various factors. There is, for example, their faith as people of the Book, as well as more than 3,000 years of an ethical monotheism combined with ancient rituals and a sense of group identity. There is now the memory of the Holocaust, giving Jews the will to survive new adversity. And there is the state of Israel, a homeland to support the rebirth of Jewish life in its cradle.

The basic beliefs of Judaism are shared by all believing Jews and include the belief in the one and unique God, the creator of the universe, who is to be worshipped (Deuteronomy 6:4–5). The Ten

---

"And I shall maintain my covenant between myself and you, and your descendants after you, generation after generation, as a covenant in perpetuity, to be your God and the God of your descendants after you."

GENESIS 17:7

Commandments (Exodus 20) are the central code of conduct and should lead Jews to serve their neighbours as much as their families. Jews believe all humans are created with the capability to do right or wrong, but the *yetzer ha-tov* (the good inclination) can rule over the *yetzer ha-ra* (the evil inclination).

Some Jews continue to hold the belief that a messiah (*moshiach*, or "anointed one"), descended from the house of King David (pp.22–23), will come to establish God's kingdom on earth. Today, it is more common for Jews to believe in a "messianic age" of peace and harmony created by joint human efforts. Jews also

Branches of Judaism

The practices of Jewish life come from the Bible via the interpretations of Jewish law (*Halacha*), which is based on the Talmud (pp.28–29). However, the practice of orthodox law is changed by Progressive Jews – those of the Reform, Liberal and Conservative traditions (pp.34–35).

Reform and Liberal Judaism arose at the end of the 18th century and blended modern scholarship with the rejection of what was, to them, antiquated *Halacha*. Together with Conservative Judaism, which developed in the United States a century later, they adopted new customs, such as allowing men and women to sit together in synagogues, the use of more English in services, modified dietary laws and new prayers.

Israel's religious Jews are largely Orthodox, but the Progressive movement is growing. In the United States, Orthodox Jews are in the minority. In Britain, 25 percent of the (approximately) 300,000 Jews are Liberal or Reform. Jews are still one community, but there are growing tensions within Orthodox and Progressive Judaism.

believe in immortality and in the role of humans as "God's partners in creation", a task given in the Torah, or Pentateuch (pp.28–29), and reinforced through biblical rites and practices.

The lifestyle of the Jew stresses the home and the synagogue, and there are a number of rites that Jews undertake in their lives – for example circumcision, *bar mitzvah* and marriage. Circumcision is performed on the eighth day after birth – just as the patriarch Abraham (pp.20–21) was commanded by God to circumcise himself and his sons (Genesis 17:10–14) and, later, his youngest son Isaac when the boy was eight days old (21:4). A *mohel* (circumciser) performs this ritual in the home, hospital or synagogue.

A first-born boy may have a *pidyon ha-ben* ("redemption of the first born") ceremony on his 31st day, by which he is released from the biblical pledge of serving as a priest. Girls – and boys – are blessed and named in the synagogue in a modern ceremony. At the age of 13, a boy may formally become an adult member of the Jewish community by having a *bar mitzvah* ("son of the commandments") ceremony in a synagogue, when he reads from the Torah. In the Reform and Conservative traditions, girls can have a *bat mitzvah*.

Jewish weddings are colourful ceremonies and take place under a *chuppah* (bridal canopy) in the home or synagogue. A *ketubah*, the Hebrew wedding contract, is read after the ring ceremony, and a glass is broken at the end, a reminder of the destruction of Jerusalem and that life has sorrows as well as joys.

In the home, the Seder meal at the start of the Passover festival recalls the Exodus of the Hebrews from Egypt (pp.20–21). The Exodus becomes an ever present event through readings from a story or prayer book known as the Haggadah and by the children of the family asking four set questions about it, which are then answered by their father. The Friday evening meal welcoming the Sabbath with candles, wine and the *challah* (a special Sabbath loaf) makes every Sabbath a reassertion of Jewish identity.

A mohel, or ritual circumciser, officiates at a circumcision ceremony. This occurs on the eighth day after a boy's birth and can take place in a home, hospital or synagogue in the presence of the family.

An Israeli family gathers around the dinner table (OPPOSITE) on the eve of Passover, the festival that commemorates the escape of the Jews from Egypt. The various foods relate symbolically to the story of the Exodus.

Death as part of life

Orthodox and Progressive Jews believe in the immortality of the soul, and Orthodox Jews also believe in the resurrection of body and soul, and in a final judgment. There is no unanimous agreement about the nature of heaven and hell. Variant teachings of the transmigration of the soul and of heaven as a place where Jews can devote themselves totally to the study of scriptures abound. Few Jews believe in hell, and judgment is left to God. Jews live one world at a time, and a good deed is regarded as being its own reward – as the Talmud (pp.28–29) states, "do not be as servants . . . expecting a reward".

Mourning rites are patterned according to the Bible, moving from the expression of absolute grief to acceptance that death is part of life. The brief funeral, which is preceded by the chief mourners ritually cutting their garments (*k'riah*), takes place in a Jewish cemetery, such as that on the Mount of Olives (ABOVE) in Jerusalem. It usually involves burial, although Progressive Judaism permits cremation. The funeral is followed by *shivah*, which involves seven days of mourning in the home, when friends visit the bereaved family who are required to sit on low chairs as a mark of humility.

There is also *sh'loshim*, a period of 30 days after the funeral during which mourners must abstain from festivities or entertainments. Also, for a year after the funeral, the chief mourners should attend the synagogue daily to say *kaddish* (a memorial prayer glorifying God) before the gravestone is set with due ceremony.

On each *yahrzeit*, or anniversary, of the death, a 24-hour candle is lit in the home or synagogue, and the name of the deceased is recited at synagogues at various festivals during the year. Special prayers for the six million Jews who died during the Holocaust are also recited in April on Yom Ha-Shoa (Holocaust Memorial Day). Jews may remarry after the death of a spouse. Indeed, if there are no children to continue the tradition, some Jews would consider this a duty.

Toward the Promised Land

In about 1900 B.C.E., Abraham, whom Jews revere as their first great patriarch and the ancestor of the Hebrews, migrated with his family from the city of Ur in southern Mesopotamia. His mission was to find a new land and to found a new faith in Palestine, the heart of the Fertile Crescent curving from the Euphrates to the Nile. Here, Abraham established a Hebrew pattern of life that was patriarchal and based on a pastoral economy differing little from that of the neighbouring peoples.

However, in matters of religion, the Hebrews broke new ground: they rejected idols, and a covenant was made by God with Abraham. By this agreement, Abraham and all his descendants, including his son Isaac and grandson Jacob (who became known as Israel), would live in the presence of God and be circumcised. In return, God promised: "And to you and to your descendants after you, I shall give the country where you are now immigrants, the entire land of Canaan, to own in perpetuity...." (Genesis 17:8). Thus arose the concept of the "Promised Land", which bound the people to Canaan, or present-day Palestine, and still does today.

Some time during the late 17th century B.C.E., the children of Jacob-Israel followed their brother Joseph into Egypt, at a time when it was ruled by the Hyksos kings (c.1674–c.1567 B.C.E.), who were Semitic invaders from the desert. When the Hyksos were overthrown, Egypt became a land of bondage for the children of Israel, who struggled to maintain their faith in God in the face of myriad Egyptian deities.

About 250 years later, a leader named Moses took the children of Israel out of Egyptian slavery. Combining the roles of teacher, prophet, leader and general, Moses shaped his people in a unique way. His authority is such that he is attributed as author of the Torah, or Pentateuch (pp.28–29) – the first five books of the Bible – even though scholars debate whether he wrote all of the text.

The Torah describes the Exodus of the Israelites from Egypt and their wanderings in the desert. It is also the law book which unites the people in a covenant with God and presents the dynamic faith of Judaism – based

The first stage of Abraham's migration took him from Ur to Haran. Following a divine command, he journeyed to Egypt.

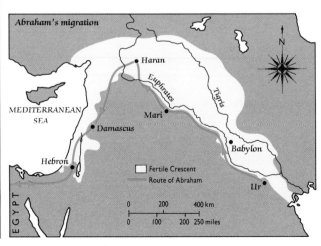

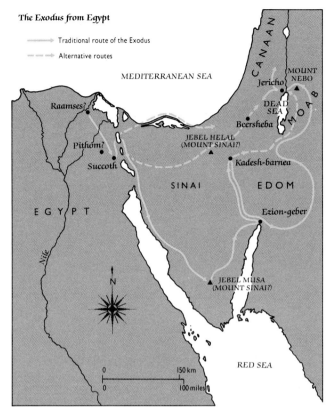

The Exodus from Egypt

→ Traditional route of the Exodus

⇢ Alternative routes

The route of the Exodus is difficult to establish, since many places named in the Bible cannot be located. The traditional route includes Jebel Musa (OPPOSITE INSET).

Moses leads the Israelites across the Red, or "Reed", Sea, whose waters miraculously part to allow them to pass, in this 15th-century Greek mural. Once they had reached safety, the waters flowed back, drowning the mounted soldiers Pharaoh had sent in pursuit to prevent the Israelites' flight.

on the belief in one God and a strong ethical code. In these accounts Moses is depicted as having human failings, struggling with himself and a people made rebellious by nomadic desert life. They quickly forgot the suffering of slavery and remembered only the plentiful food and water in the fertile Nile valley. Testament to Moses' leadership is that in 40 years of desert wanderings, the slaves who had fled from Egypt were changed from discontents challenging him into a confident people ready to enter Canaan, the Promised Land.

After his farewell address (Deuteronomy 33), Moses died and was buried in an unmarked grave, for there were to be no pilgrimages, no worship of a mere man and no "Mosaism" to challenge Judaism. For Jews, his imprint remains for all time, and they think of him as *Rabbenu* Moses – "our teacher Moses". With Moses' death, Joshua became the general and leader who brought the Israelites into the Promised Land.

Joined in a loose confederation of tribes governed by elders, the Israelites found new war leaders, known as judges, who were also religious figures. Some of them were built on legends – for example, Samson's name and the symbolism of his story liken him to a sun god.

Other judges included the great leader Deborah, who united the tribes against their enemies and whose military success is immortalized in the Song of Deborah (Judges 5). Only Deborah, the priest Eli and the prophet Samuel really "judged", that is, meted out justice. In the time of Samuel in the 11th century B.C.E., the people began to look for a king, despite being reminded that, unlike their neighbours, their king is God.

The Ten Commandments

Uttered by God to Moses (Exodus 20:1–17) in a dramatic moment on Mount Sinai, often identified with Jebel Musa (BELOW RIGHT), the Ten Commandments are ten statements that form the basis of the covenant between the Jewish people and God, as well as of the Jewish faith. The commandments, also called the Decalogue, or *Devarim* in Hebrew, can be summarized as follows:
1 I am THE LORD your God.
2 You shall have no other gods to rival me.
 You shall not make yourself a carved image.
3 You shall not misuse the name of THE LORD your God.
4 Remember the Sabbath day and keep it holy.
5 Honour your father and your mother.
6 You shall not kill.
7 You shall not commit adultery.
8 You shall not steal.
9 You shall not give false evidence against your neighbour.
10 You shall not covet.
Other civilizations have also had their decalogues, and an early Egyptian "Protestation of Guiltlessness" includes the phrases "I have not stolen ... I have not killed men ... I have not lied ... I have not committed adultery".

The famous code of Hammurabi, ruler of Babylon in the 18th century B.C.E., contains much legislation also found in the Bible, notably the *lex talionis*, the law of retaliation that limited the punishment to the crime – "an eye for an eye ... a life for a life".

In Hammurabi's code, the law was taken literally – if a neighbour's child fell over the parapet of your roof, your child was to be thrown as well. From the context of the Bible, however, it is clear that it is the *value* of an eye, rather than the eye itself, that was to be given.

Above all, the Decalogue was central to a covenant by which Israel served God by behaving in the right way, and by which humans could live together in a system opposed to primitive blood laws. Ancient blood feuds, particularly those involving accidental manslaughter, were ended by providing "cities of refuge", where the perpetrator could not be touched by the blood avenger.

The Haggadah, meaning "narration", is the set ritual for the recitation of the Exodus during the Seder meal at Passover. The book contains legends, proverbs and excerpts from the Bible.

Haggadahs, such as this 14th-century copy, are often richly illustrated. Here, the Egyptians' oppression of the Jews is symbolized in the top row which shows the Jews building cities for the Egyptians (left) and making bricks out of straw (right).

In the bottom row, Moses transforms his rod into a serpent as a sign of his power (right), following Pharaoh's refusal to grant him an audience. Moses later turned the Nile to blood (left) in the first of 10 plagues sent by God to persuade Pharaoh to allow the Israelites to leave Egypt.

21

Israel's First Kings

The first king of Israel, anointed by the prophet Samuel, was Saul (*c*.1021–1000 B.C.E.), a great warrior and a tragic, moody figure. Saul soon quarrelled with Samuel, and as a result the prophet chose as the king's successor a young man named David, son of Jesse, who served at the royal court. After the wounded Saul fell on his sword to avoid capture following the deaths of his sons Jonathan, Abinadab and Malchishua in battle against the Philistines, David was duly enthroned. He was well respected in his lifetime and, after his death, he fuelled the dreams of generations to come.

The Jewish belief in a future king, an anointed one, or messiah (from Hebrew *moshiach*), who would destroy his enemies and establish God's kingdom of righteousness, developed over a long period of time. David was a true leader who also possessed a religious dimension (he is credited with the authorship of the Psalms). And his reign, during which he defeated his enemies, enlarged the kingdom, and built the conquered city of Jebus into Jerusalem, "David's City", was deemed a model for the future. Thus it was thought that the messiah would be of David's seed.

Yet the Bible portrays David as human, with frailties, and not exempt from God's law. For example, when he committed adultery, he was confronted by the prophet Nathan, who pronounced God's judgment upon him. But David was a strong king and, by creating the city of Jerusalem, he united the tribes politically – just as Solomon's Temple would later unite them in their faith. And Jerusalem, the eternal city, would command Jewish loyalty ever after: "If I forget you, Jerusalem, may my right hand wither!" (Psalm 137:5).

Solomon (*c*.960–922 B.C.E.) inherited from David, his father, a strong central government, a sound fiscal administration, a trained army and the holy city. Under Solomon's rule, the Temple (*opposite*) became a national shrine, built, in line with David's plans, with great expense and forced labour.

Jewish tradition acknowledges Solomon as "the wisest of men", credited with writing much of the "wisdom" literature in the Bible, such as Proverbs and Ecclesiastes. However, his vast building projects alienated many people, even though his mercantile policies also enlarged the land. The success of Solomon's merchant fleet may have induced the Queen of Sheba (a country possibly located in southern Arabia or Ethiopia) to visit him and subsequently enter into a number of trade agreements with Israel.

Solomon inherited from his father David a strong and wealthy empire which had been gained through conquest. It included most of the habitable territory between Egypt, in the west, and northeastern Syria. Through trade, Solomon was able to exploit the strategic position of his kingdom, straddled as it was between Africa and Asia, and to consolidate his empire.

King David remains a central figure in Jewish life and thought. This 12th-century image from a Cypriot monastery emphasizes his royal aspect, without any suggestion of the frailties to which he, as a mere mortal, was subject. The warrior-king who created the first Jewish kingdom, David was also celebrated as both a poet and a talented musician.

David made Jerusalem into a great city and the capital of his empire. One of the earliest parts of the city in existence today, probably dating from David's time, is the pool of Siloam (FAR RIGHT), a water supply for centuries.

The allegiances of Solomon's merchant empire were often secured through marriages with other ruling houses, which explains the biblical reference to Solomon's 1,000 wives. Often, these women brought with them their household gods and priests, undermining basic Jewish practices.

Yet the great heritage transmitted by Solomon was a religious one. And it was symbolized by the magnificent Temple, which was to be a house of prayer for all people and the place where Israel would continually renew itself for many centuries.

David had given the people of Israel a vision of a kingdom which would endure and a future, ultimate king. Solomon had given them a house of God, knowing that "the heavens, the highest of the heavens, cannot contain you [God]" (1 Kings 8:27). The austere ethical monotheism was enriched by the pomp and ceremony of the Temple cult, even though it threatened to become a priestly monopoly. When the Temple fell – eventually to be succeeded by the democratic synagogue – what endured was the knowledge of a holy place in Jerusalem. That vision never died.

The Temple

Built by Solomon to unite the tribes of Israel in worship, the Temple also made Jerusalem the spiritual capital of the kingdom. In his prayer at the Temple's opening, Solomon declared: "Day and night may your eyes watch over this temple, over this place of which you have said, 'My name will be there'." (1 Kings 8:29).

The Temple's magnificent edifice was constructed according to local architectural style. The two freestanding columns, which are called Jachin and Boaz (1 Kings 7:21), and the three main divisions – the outer court, the inner holy place and the Holy of Holies (*ulam*, *hekhal* and *debir*) – became part of a ritual that continued to

be practised long after the Temple itself ceased to exist. The Holy of Holies was entered only by the high priest on the Day of Atonement (*Yom Kippur*), when he pronounced the ineffable name of God.

The Temple was destroyed in 586 B.C.E. by the Babylonians. Rebuilt about 70 years later by former Babylonian exiles, it was subsequently enlarged by Herod the Great in 19 B.C.E. and destroyed again by the Romans in 70 C.E. The remnant, the Western (earlier called the Wailing) Wall, is only part of the outer shell upon which Herod built his temple. Nevertheless, it is an object of veneration to the Jewish people and is seen as a place of pilgrimage, lamentation and prayer (RIGHT). Some Jews still place slips of paper with supplicatory prayers between the cracks of the immense stones.

This reconstruction of the Temple of Solomon is based on biblical accounts. Priests washed in the bronze "sea" (**2**), before slaughtering animals which had been cleansed in bronze basins on wheels (**8**). The animals were then sacrificed at the altar (**1**) as burnt offerings. Within the Temple, flanked by candelabra (**7**), stood

the golden altar of incense (**3**) and the gold table (**4**), on which 12 loaves were laid every Sabbath. In the Holy of Holies, the ark of the covenant (**6**), containing the stone tablets inscribed with the Ten Commandments, was guarded by two cherubim (**5**).

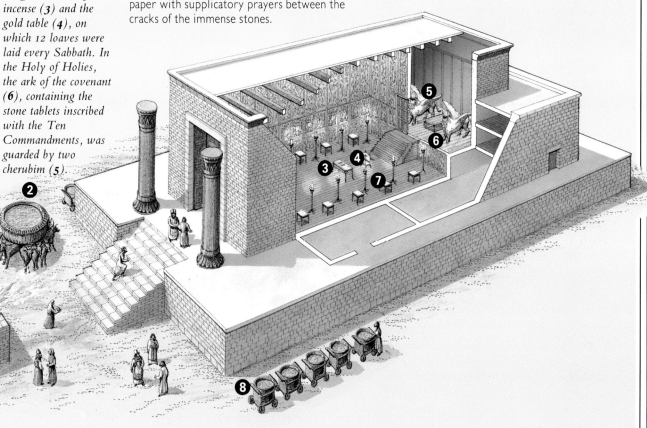

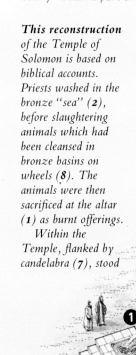

The Two Kingdoms

After the death of Solomon c.922 B.C.E. and the accession of his son Rehoboam, a rebellion led by a nobleman named Jeroboam split the Jewish nation in two. Jeroboam and 10 of the 12 tribes united to form the new kingdom of Israel. Located in central and northern Palestine, Israel was more powerful than the southern kingdom of Judah, which consisted of the two tribes of Judah and Benjamin, as well as the city of Jerusalem and the Temple (p.23).

Jeroboam set up golden calves in the cities of Dan and Bethel to rival the Temple cult of Jerusalem and, in time, Israel moved toward the worship of idols and created a new, royally appointed, priesthood. Contrary to the old vision of a law based on a covenant with God and a divine rule obeyed by kings, Israel's various rulers followed their own turbulent course. There were a number of murders and usurpations. Finally, in about 878 B.C.E., King Omri brought stability and wealth to Israel and established Samaria as its capital. Omri's son

The Daughters of Zion, a Romantic painting by the 19th-century artist Herbert Schmalz, depicts Jewish women exiled in Babylon watched over by the king and members of his court. For the Jewish exiles, Babylon with its splendid architecture, such as the Ishtar Gate, part of which is shown (ABOVE) in reconstruction, was a new pagan world with different values and customs. However, in accordance with Jeremiah's injunction, the Jews built houses, planted vineyards and prayed for the peace of their new city. Guided by spiritual leaders, such as Ezekiel, they maintained their vision of Zion. And the great prophet named by modern scholars Second Isaiah gave the Jews new teachings to prepare them for their eventual return to Jerusalem.

and successor Ahab married Jezebel, the daughter of the king of Tyre; their exploitation of the poor set the prophet Elijah against them.

By contrast, Judah, more isolated by mountains and poorer in resources, and governed by the descendants of David, had a quieter existence. However, both kingdoms were caught up in regional politics, as the armies of Egypt, Damascus and Assyria, a land lying to the east, marched across their territory in the eighth century. Israel, particularly during the Omrid dynasty and, later, the reign of Jeroboam II (c.783–741), was powerful and prosperous and enlarged its borders. But its prosperity was confined to the upper levels of society.

During the first half of the first millennium B.C.E., Jewish history becomes more the history of the prophets, charismatic figures who were more teachers of righteousness than foretellers of the future. Court prophets, such as Elijah and Elisha in Ahab's era, battled against the immoralities of kings and commoners. They also fought against the priests of the Phoenician god Baal and other cults, which had been introduced into Israel and were also present in Judah. They were followed by the great literary prophets whose teachings form a major part of the Bible (the distinction between "major" and "minor" prophets refers only to the length of the books included in the scriptures). Sometimes these prophets – Isaiah and Jeremiah, for example – gave political advice, but they always fought against social injustice.

Israel's end eventually came about as a result of Assyrian aggression. Samaria, the last independent province of Israel, fell in about 721 B.C.E., and the Assyrian king Sargon II deported more than 27,000 citizens. Israel ceased to exist, and the kingdom of the 10 tribes vanished from history.

The kingdom of Judah outlived Israel and remained loyal to David's descendants. The kings Asa (c.908–867) and Jehoshaphat (c.873–849) carried out judicial and religious reforms and tried to achieve security through alliances. Jehoshaphat's son Joram, for example, married Athalia, the daughter of Ahab and Jezebel. Judah's greatest religious reform was achieved centuries later in 621 by King Josiah. It was prompted by the discovery during renovation work on the Temple of the "Book of the Covenant" – probably the Book of Deuteronomy. Its teachings united the community.

By this time, the Babylonians, to the northeast, were on the verge of becoming a regional superpower. In 601, King Jehoiakin sided with Egypt against Babylon. In 597, the Babylonian king Nebuchadnezzar overran Judah and took many of its leaders to Babylon. When Judah rebelled again in 586, Zedekiah, the last king, was blinded and taken into captivity with many others, and Jerusalem and the Temple were destroyed. A former palace official named Gedaliah was appointed to govern the land. But when he was murdered by Jewish zealots, the Babylonian army returned and utterly ravaged the land, taking more captives to Babylon in 582. The history of Judah had come to an end.

Isaiah as portrayed by the Italian artist Michelangelo (1475–1564).

Prophets of Israel and Judah

A recurring theme in the history of the kingdoms of Judah and Israel was the conflict between the prophets, who claimed to set out and enforce God's laws, and the secular rulers, who tried to evade them. The prophets articulated for Israel its obligations according to its covenant with God and warned that evil actions result in an evil future. Four of the most important prophets during the two kingdoms period were:

Amos (c.783–741 B.C.E.) was active during the reign of Jeroboam II. He is known as the prophet of social justice because he censured Israel for exploiting the poor: "because they have sold the upright for silver and the poor for a pair of sandals, ..." (Amos 2:6). His prophecy that the king, the priests and the land would be destroyed was fulfilled by the destruction of Israel by the Assyrians.

Hosea (c.774–734 B.C.E.), known as the prophet of love, proclaimed that God could forgive Israel as Hosea himself had forgiven his wayward wife. Israel, too, was covenanted to God in marriage and had gone astray with foreign gods. He also demanded social justice from Israel.

Isaiah (c.742–701 B.C.E.), shown above, was a great courtier and statesman who advised King Ahaz of Judah not to join Israel and Damascus against Assyria. A brilliant poet, who used parables to express his meaning, Isaiah is regarded as the prophet of holiness, since the theme of God's holiness is a central part of his preaching. He exhorted the people to perform righteous actions in order to share in this holiness.

Jeremiah (fl. c.626–580 B.C.E.) was a priest who is sometimes regarded as the prophet of anguish. He said he was compelled by God to prophesy and speak of the destruction of Jerusalem, even though he claimed that he would have preferred to keep silent. He fought for the rights of slaves and the poor and also instructed the Jewish exiles in Babylon to pray for their new land and to remain true to their faith.

Liberation and Destruction

In 538 B.C.E., the destiny of the Jewish exiles in Babylon took a dramatic turn. King Cyrus of Persia (550–c.529) conquered the city and allowed the Jews to return to their homeland. Some did so immediately, and work later began on rebuilding the Temple, completed in 515. Others went back in about 458, led by Ezra the Scribe, who was later joined by Nehemiah, the Persians' appointee as governor of Judah. Together these two men rebuilt Jerusalem, with Ezra reinstituting the Torah (pp.28–29), the first five books of the Hebrew Bible, in a public reading. The sweeping social reforms that followed laid the foundations for a theocratic, or god-centred, state in which religious life continued to grow.

However, in the next century, Judah's stability was again threatened, by the Macedonian general Alexander the Great (356–323 B.C.E.), who conquered much of the Middle East, including Palestine. After Alexander's death, his generals and successors Ptolemy, in Egypt, and Seleucus, in Syria, battled over Palestine. In 198 B.C.E., the Seleucids gained control of Judea, as Judah was known to them, and the new Greek environment brought many Hellenistic practices and worship into the populace. Although there was some prosperity, there were increasing fears of a loss of Jewish identity.

In 167/6, Mattathias, a priest of the Hasmonean family, and his five sons, including Judah (nicknamed Maccabeus, probably meaning "the Hammer"), began a partly successful rebellion and liberated the land in 164. The Temple in Jerusalem was restored.

The Hasmonean family were now the rulers of Judea. In 161 B.C.E., Judah died and was succeeded by his brother Jonathan, while another brother, Simon, became high priest and hereditary ruler. Simon's son John Hyrcanus (c.135–104) enlarged the land, and his son Alexander Jannaeus (103–76) then extended the boundaries over almost the whole of Palestine. There were internal struggles as he confronted the growing influence of the Pharisees (*opposite*), who challenged the priestly authority assumed by the Hasmoneans.

Jannaeus's widow and successor, Salome Alexandra, who installed the Pharisees, achieved peace during her rule (76–67 B.C.E), but her two sons Hyrcanus and Aristobulus fought for supremacy. Hyrcanus gained the backing of Pompey, the Roman general and statesman, who, in 63, brought Jerusalem under Roman control and made Hyrcanus high priest. He appointed Herod Antipater, the governor of Idumea, as administrator.

Antipater's son, Herod, later known as the Great, eventually became Rome's puppet king and ruled from 37 to 4 B.C.E., enlarging the Temple and building other imposing structures, such as the fortress of Masada. On his death, his kingdom was divided among his three sons. However, before long, Rome intervened and Judea was ruled directly through Roman governors.

Roman soldiers carry off booty, including a candlestick, or menorah, from the sacked city of Jerusalem in this relief from the Arch of Titus in Rome. The city capitulated to the forces of Titus in 70 C.E., and the subsequent plundering of the Temple was one of the darkest moments in Jewish history. Even today, many Jews refuse to walk under Titus's arch because of its graphic depiction of Israel's subjugation.

Roman oppression led the Jews to hope for the coming of a messiah, an anointed one, to lead them to victory over their enemies. Eventually, the rumblings of resentment erupted into the great Zealot uprising of 66 C.E. Four years later, in 70 C.E., the Romans retook Jerusalem and destroyed the Temple. A remnant of Jewish resistance centred on the fortress of Masada but it, too, fell in 73. Jewish national independence had come to an end. But Judaism survived and developed in Yavneh (present-day Jamnia) on the Palestinian coast. Here, a Jewish religious academy founded by Rabbi Johanan ben Zakkai, who had fled besieged Jerusalem in 68, became the new Pharisaic centre for Jewish learning and a focus for scattered Jewish communities.

After the suppression of the last Jewish revolt, led by Bar Kochba, against the Romans in 135, Yavneh declined in prestige. But its place was taken by other academies in Galilee, such as Usha and Sepphoris, which continued the tradition of Jewish Scholarship.

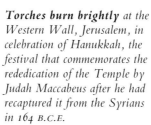

Torches burn brightly at the Western Wall, Jerusalem, in celebration of Hanukkah, the festival that commemorates the rededication of the Temple by Judah Maccabeus after he had recaptured it from the Syrians in 164 *B.C.E.*

The fortress of Masada (LEFT) *was the last Jewish stronghold to fall to the Romans. For Jews it is a symbol of heroism, and modern Israeli soldiers* (BELOW) *are sworn into service here.*

Jewish sects

At the beginning of the first century C.E., Judea was under Roman control. At this time, there were various Jewish groups who reacted to Roman rule and expressed their spirituality in different ways.

Pharisees: arose in the time of the Hasmoneans as a sect that was more representative of the people than the aristocratic Sadducees. They emerged as the dominant Jewish group after 70 C.E. Contrary to the priests, they stressed the holiness in all of life. They believed in the resurrection of the dead and their liberal interpretations of the Torah created a chain of new laws that became known as the Oral Law (later forming the Talmud, pp.28–29), as opposed to the Written Law – that is the Torah.

Sadducees: wealthy aristocrats and priests who backed Rome in return for its support of the Temple cult. They interpreted the Torah strictly, respecting its authority and therefore, for example, rejecting the notion of resurrection, but they gradually lost their influence in religion and politics. In 70 C.E., when the Romans destroyed the Temple, the focal point of the Sadducees' power, they practically disappeared.

Essenes: believed to have been based at Qumran in the Dead Sea region, they were a religious fellowship that led a strict communal life based on ascetic practices and rites of purification. According to one of the texts of the Dead Sea Scrolls, found near Qumran, not all the Essenes lived at Qumran – some may have lived as ordinary citizens throughout Judea.

Zealots: a general term for Jewish political activists fighting militarily and politically to liberate Judea from Rome. Members of its extreme wing were known as *sicarii* ("dagger-men"), a group which some scholars think was founded by Judas of Galilee in 6 C.E. to fight Rome. The Zealots had a distinctive religious dimension: they were passionate and uncompromising in their service to God.

Holy Scriptures

This rich design comes from the Duke of Sussex German Pentateuch, made in southern Germany in about 1300. It bears, in the centre, the Hebrew word eleh ("These"), the first word of the book of Deuteronomy. Much Jewish art uses calligraphy, and many Hebrew texts are enriched by illumination, governed by the biblical injunction not to make "graven images" of human figures in case they might be worshipped.

> I am the rose of Sharon,
> the lily of the valleys.
> As a lily among the thistles,
> So is my beloved among girls.
>
> SONG OF SONGS 2:1–2

The Jews are the people of the Book, meaning the Hebrew Bible, and their scriptures lie at the heart of their religion. Ezra the Scribe (pp.26–27) had established the Torah, or Pentateuch, as the constitution of Jewish life in a public reading in Jerusalem in about 458 B.C.E. Over time, the Jewish scriptures were eventually arranged into three sections through a process of canonization, or establishing scriptural authority. The Torah (Law), the Nevi'im (Prophets) and the Ketuvim (Writings) became the Hebrew Bible and were to determine future Jewish conduct and thought.

Inevitably, there were texts whose sacred status was questioned. They were examined at the end of the first century C.E. at an assembly of rabbis convened at Yavneh to determine the holy canon. The rabbis had no doubts about the Torah, written by Moses (pp.20–21) as God's revelation. And while many prophets had not produced their own written texts, their words, many of which had been recorded by others, were also deemed to be inspired by God.

The rabbis also grouped the historical writings with the prophetic texts and made a distinction between the Nevi'im Rishonim (the earlier prophets, namely Joshua, Judges, 1 and 2 Samuel, 1 and 2 Kings) and the Nevi'im Acharonim (the later prophets), Isaiah, Jeremiah and Ezekiel, also called the major prophets mainly because the texts were longer). The other prophets were included in the Book of the Twelve (minor) Prophets: Hosea, Joel, Amos, Obadiah, Jonah, Micah, Nahum, Habakkuk, Zephaniah, Haggai, Zechariah and Malachi.

Then the arguments began. The Ketuvim which are canonized are the Psalms, Proverbs, Job, Song of Songs,

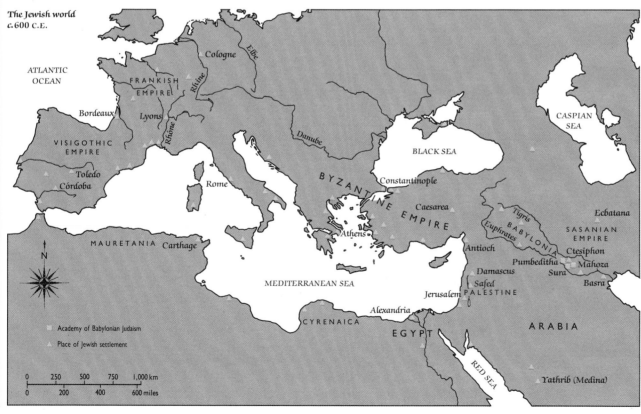

The Jewish world c.600 C.E.

- ▪ Academy of Babylonian Judaism
- ▲ Place of Jewish settlement

By about 600 C.E. the Jewish Diaspora was strongest in Babylonia, where religious academies continued to flourish. The Geonim, or academy leaders, had spiritual authority over the various Jewish settlements scattered around the Mediterranean. At this time, the Jews in Spain were suffering under severe legal restrictions, and the new religion of Islam was about to enter history.

Ruth, Lamentations, Ecclesiastes, Esther, Daniel, Ezra, Nehemiah, and 1 and 2 Chronicles. But many rabbis felt that the Song of Songs, with its erotic imagery, did not belong in a sacred book. However, the great rabbi Akiva ben Joseph (c.40–c.135) made the case that the symbolism was allegorical and that the book was not a love story between a man and woman, but between God and Israel, and the text was admitted to the canon.

A controversy also arose over the Book of Esther. It was pointed out that, unlike every other book in the Bible, it did not contain God's name. However, at one point in the book, Mordecai, Esther's cousin and foster father, tells her that help will come from *makom*, "another place". And *makom*, by the time of the rabbinic assembly, was one of the names used for God. Esther thus became part of the canon. The excluded books, including the books of the Maccabees and the Wisdom of Ben Sirach, were late writings, too recent to have acquired holy status. They became known as the Apocrypha ("hidden away"), outside the canon, but were still revered and used in the Jewish liturgy.

The Torah remained the foundation of Jewish law. After the destruction of the Temple by the Romans in 70 C.E., the rabbis had tried to utilize a law that had been written for different times and circumstances. They found it possible to reinterpret the text without having to change it. These new interpretations were called the Oral Law, since the rabbis did not want a rival for the Torah, the Written Law. However, around the year 200 C.E., Rabbi Judah the Prince (c.135–c.220) collected these interpretations into the Mishnah, where most new commentaries to the Torah became a new legal code.

From this time on, the Jewish academies in Palestine began to be superseded by those in Babylonia, such as Sura and Pumbeditha, where the Jews prospered under the Persian Sasanian rulers (pp.122–23). Over the next few centuries, Jewish scholars in both Babylonia and Palestine pored over every line of the Mishnah and produced an even larger text. Around 500, a Babylonian rabbi named Rav Ashi put this text, known as the Gemara ("completion"), together with the Mishnah, and this enormous collection was called the Talmud. A Gemara was also compiled in Palestine, but it never gained the importance of the Babylonian one.

This Torah *is protected by an embroidered mantle decorated with an embellished silver breastplate. The scroll itself is too sacred to touch, so a pointer, here hanging from the righthand finial, is used by the reader.*

Men and women (BELOW) *at Leo Baeck College in London examine classic texts in terms of their relevance to modern times. Archaeological findings and contemporary literary research are used in conjunction with rabbinic interpretations by these student rabbis, who will serve Reform and Conservative communities throughout the world.*

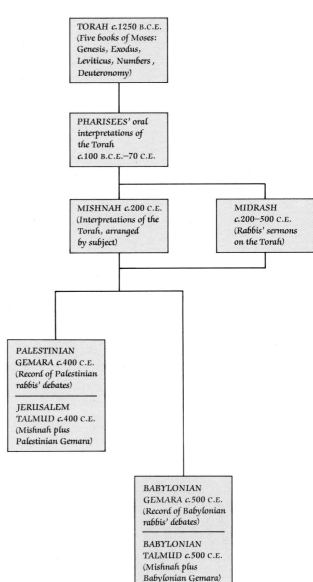

The development of the Jewish scriptures

TORAH c.1250 B.C.E. (Five books of Moses: Genesis, Exodus, Leviticus, Numbers, Deuteronomy)

PHARISEES' oral interpretations of the Torah c.100 B.C.E.–70 C.E.

MISHNAH c.200 C.E. (Interpretations of the Torah, arranged by subject)

MIDRASH c.200–500 C.E. (Rabbis' sermons on the Torah)

PALESTINIAN GEMARA c.400 C.E. (Record of Palestinian rabbis' debates)

JERUSALEM TALMUD c.400 C.E. (Mishnah plus Palestinian Gemara)

BABYLONIAN GEMARA c.500 C.E. (Record of Babylonian rabbis' debates)

BABYLONIAN TALMUD c.500 C.E. (Mishnah plus Babylonian Gemara)

The cornerstone of the Jewish Law is the Torah, which was first fully promulgated as the constitution of Jewish life by Ezra the Scribe. To make it relevant to changing circumstances, Pharisees made oral interpretations of this constitution from about 100 B.C.E. until the fall of Jerusalem in 70 C.E.

Later, in about 200, Rabbi Judah the Prince arranged these different oral interpretations into the Mishnah. Also, from then on, the collection of writings known as the Midrash came to be written down. The Midrash, sermons on the Torah, concentrated on ethical teachings through stories (Aggadah), whereas the Mishnah was concerned with the Law (Halacha).

Between 200 and 500, the Mishnah received its own commentary – the Gemara, which combined Aggadah with Halacha.

In about 500, Babylonian rabbis created the Babylonian Talmud by adding their Gemara to the Mishnah. Rabbis in Palestine had done the same, in about 400, to create the smaller Jerusalem Talmud.

The Golden Age of Spain

By about the middle of the seventh century, Muslim Arab conquests had changed the balance of power in the Mediterranean world. In the early eighth century, Muslim armies invaded Spain and defeated the Christian Goths, who had oppressed the Jewish communities there. Under Muslim rule, Sephardi Jews (pp.32–33), as those in Spain and Portugal were called, were generally given access to the professions and cultural life. For several hundred years they flourished.

Outstanding Jewish individuals during this golden age included Samuel ha-Nagid (993–1055), the general and vizier of the city of Granada and an important Hebrew grammarian and head of the Talmudic academy. Solomon ibn Gabirol (*c*.1022–*c*.1070) of Malaga celebrated God's rule of the world in his *Royal Crown*, which is still used in the synagogue liturgy; and his *Fountain of Life* influenced Christian theologians, who thought he was a member of their faith.

Moses ibn Ezra (*c*.1060–1139), a poet of delicate sadness, was overshadowed by his contemporary the great Yehudah ha-Levi (*c*.1075–1141) of Toledo, whose poems sang of the love of Zion and whose brilliant philosophic treatise *Kuzari* tells the story of the Khazar kingdom, in what is now the Ukraine, whose people chose Judaism as their state religion over Islam and Christianity. Ha-Levi portrayed Judaism as a religion of faith and the Jews as the "heart of the nations".

Ha-Levi's philosophy was influenced by the Muslim thinker al-Ghazali (p.98), and Islamic thought in general influenced the Jews. For a time, the two cultures were able to coexist harmoniously. But it did not last. By the time of Moses Maimonides (1135–1204), the greatest Jewish teacher of his age, Muslim attitudes toward the Jews had become more aggressive and intolerant. In Córdoba, Maimonides, then aged 13, and his family faced persecution from a fanatical Muslim group known as the Almohads. In 1159, they fled to Fez in Morocco, and six years later Maimonides made his way to Cairo. Here he worked as a physician at the court of Saladin, the great Muslim leader who fought in the Crusades (pp.56–57).

Through his writings, Maimonides built up a comprehensive structure of religious thought that helped to guide the lives of Sephardi Jewry. "From Moses to Moses there was none like unto Moses," the people said, comparing the sage of Córdoba with his great namesake (pp.20–21). Maimonides had not only mastered all of the Jewish tradition but he also knew Greek philosophy. He showed that faith was not opposed to reason. In his survey of rabbinic laws, he presented them in a rational manner. Reason is not everything: at the heart of life is the *sekel ha-poel*, the creative intellect which imposes form on life and also gives humans the faculty of prophecy. And reason builds its house upon the rock of faith.

During the 13th century, Spanish Christian armies began to reconquer Muslim Spain. Although Sephardi Jewish life continued to prosper for a while, growing religious intolerance eventually turned into active

King Carlos and Queen Sophia of Spain attend a ceremony of reconciliation in a synagogue in Madrid in 1992 in order to mark officially the revocation of the edict which proclaimed the Jews' expulsion from Spain 500 years ago. Jews made a significant impact on the culture of medieval Spain, but since their expulsion, they have been estranged from the country. The king's symbolic action is an important first step toward a reconciliation which a number of leading Jews in Europe are encouraging.

Maimonides' 13 principles

The greatest Jewish teacher of his time, Maimonides (BELOW RIGHT) wrote a number of important works. The most significant, many believe, was the *Guide to the Perplexed*, which tried to reconcile philosophy with religion. Many other works helped contemporary Jewish communities retain their faith under difficult circumstances. Still recited in synagogues today are his 13 principles of faith, which are the belief that:

1 God exists.
2 He is one in a unique and perfect sense.
3 He is immaterial and not to be compared to anything else.
4 He is eternal.
5 Prayer must be addressed to him alone.
6 God revealed himself to the prophets.
7 The prophecy of Moses is unique and superior to everything else.
8 Through Moses God gave the Jews the Torah.
9 God will never change or revoke the Torah.
10 God's providence observes people's outer and inner actions.
11 People are rewarded or punished as they deserve.
12 The Messiah will come, even if he is delayed.
13 The dead are resurrected.

persecution through the Inquisition (pp.62–63). In the 14th and 15th centuries, Jews began to leave Christian Spain for the more welcoming climate of Ottoman Turkey (pp.106–7).

In 1492, when the Christians retook Granada, the last Muslim stronghold in Spain, the decision was made to expel any Jews who had not been converted. And many *conversos*, or converts, often called *marranos* ("pigs") by the Spaniards because they longed to return to Judaism after their forced conversion to Christianity, also left for places such as the Netherlands, Turkey and Palestine. The golden age was over; but, elsewhere, Sephardi Jewish life continued to grow.

We suffer from evils which we inflict upon ourselves, and we ascribe them to God who is far from connected with them.

MOSES MAIMONIDES

The synagogue of Toledo dates from 1203 and shows the influence of Islamic Moorish craftsmen in its horseshoe arches. During medieval times, Toledo was the hub of Sephardi life and scholarship. But the Jewish community there was destroyed first by the Black Death in 1349 and later by persecutions by Christians in 1391. In 1411, the synagogue was converted into a church and named Santa Maria la Blanca. Now a national monument, the building still has a serenity that recalls its former religious life.

A reader leads the congregation from a raised pulpit in this 14th-century illumination showing a dignified service in a synagogue in northern Spain, possibly Barcelona. During the golden age of Spanish Jewry, Muslims and Jews lived together in peaceful cooperation, and some Jews served as high functionaries in the Moorish courts.

Kabbalah

The branch of Judaism known as the Kabbalah ("tradition"), concerned with secret, mystic truths, developed fully during the Middle Ages in southern France and Spain. Central to Kabbalists was the idea of God as the *En Sof* – the Endless, Infinite One. Their aim was to achieve communion with, rather than absorption into, the *En Sof*, who did not enter the world directly, but through a series of 10 emanations, or *sefirot* ("spheres"). Only through the *sefirot*, which make up inner reality, can God be understood and can people move toward God.

The most important Kabbalist text of the period was the *Sefer ha-Zohar* ("Book of Splendour") ascribed to Simeon ben Yochai of the second century C.E., but actually the work of Moses de León of Granada (c.1250–1305). The *Zohar* used the idea of the *sefirot*, which were visualized as an arrangement in the form of Adam Kadmon (Primordial Man), and which radiate from the *En Sof*, allowing people to retain its original light. The spark of divine goodness existed in everyone, but was enclosed by evil in the form of shells, which had to be broken to let the divine light shine out.

This doctrine was later developed by Moses Cordovero (1522–76) in Safed, Palestine, whose poem *Pardes* ("Orchard") combined the best of reason and mystical thought. The most renowned Kabbalist master was Isaac Luria (1534–72), who combined the system of the *sefirot* and the breaking of the shells (*shevirat ha-kelim*) with the concept of *zimzum* ("contraction"), which envisaged the Infinite *En Sof* "contracting" to make room for the finite world of creation.

This Kabbalistic engraving shows aspects of the Infinite One, at the top, emanating as interconnected spheres and reaching down toward humanity.

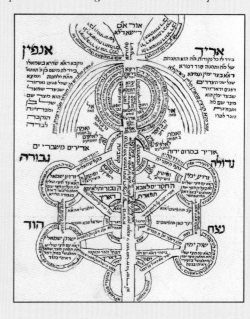

The Jews of Europe

By the Middle Ages, the Jewish Diaspora had become broadly divided into two areas: the Sephardi Jews of Spain, Portugal and the Mediterranean world and the Ashkenazi Jews of Germany and central Europe. Sephardi scholars wrote in Arabic, the legacy of their contact with Islam, and spoke a Spanish-Hebrew dialect called Ladino, while Ashkenazim wrote in Hebrew and spoke a German-Hebrew dialect called Yiddish. The Sephardi-Ashkenazi division still exists to a lesser degree in Jewish life today, with Ashkenazim forming more than 70 percent of Jews in the world.

Some Jewish scholars bridged the two traditions, including Rabbi Solomon ben Isaac (1040–1105), known as Rashi, whose works are studied to this day. Much later, Joseph Caro (1488–1575) wrote *The Prepared Table* as a guide to all of Jewish life. Printed in Venice in 1565, the book was geared to the Sephardi world, and Moses Isserles (c.1525–72) of Krakow in Poland added his *Mappah* ("tablecloth") to adjust it to Ashkenazi life.

Ashkenazi Jews suffered hardships in medieval Europe. The prevalent feudal system prevented Jews from working the soil, and Christian guilds closed ranks to keep them out of the crafts. Jews were forced into moneylending and peddling, and in the cities were made to live in cramped, self-contained areas known as ghettos. Persecution was common, particularly when the Crusades (pp.56–57) got underway from the 11th century onward. Several massacres of Jews took place, either before or during the crusades to the Holy Land, notably at the towns of Metz, Speyer, Worms, Mainz, Prague and York. Also, Jews suffered from widespread allegations of "ritual murder", which hinged on the scurrilous charge that they killed a Christian child for the baking of unleavened bread for the Passover festival.

In the 14th century, amid an atmosphere of rank hostility throughout much of Europe, Jews found a place of refuge in Poland during the reign of Casimir III, the Great, (1333–70). This tolerance continued under King Sigismund Augustus (1548–72), who granted Jews self-government in 1551. As a result, the Jewish Council of the Four Lands (Great and Little Poland, Lvov, Volhynia and Lithuania) was able to pass laws that created a prosperous and highly cultured community. Later, in the 17th century, this positive state of affairs changed, and the Jews one again became an impoverished and persecuted minority. They withdrew into Talmudic studies, where brilliant interpretation (*pilpul*) sometimes became an end in itself.

The Ashkenazi and Sephardi traditions in the Middle Ages were never sealed off from each other. However, Sephardi life was stronger around the Mediterranean, while Ashkenazi Jews were concentrated in central and eastern Europe. After the expulsion of the Sephardi from Spain in 1492, many took refuge in the Netherlands, while others went to lands of the Ottoman Empire.

The differences between Ashkenazim and Sephardim have now faded, but many distinctive customs and traditions still persist. For example, Ashkenazi-influenced western Jewry tends to emphasize the powers of rational thought, while eastern, Sephardi-dominated Jews seem to have a stronger mystical tradition.

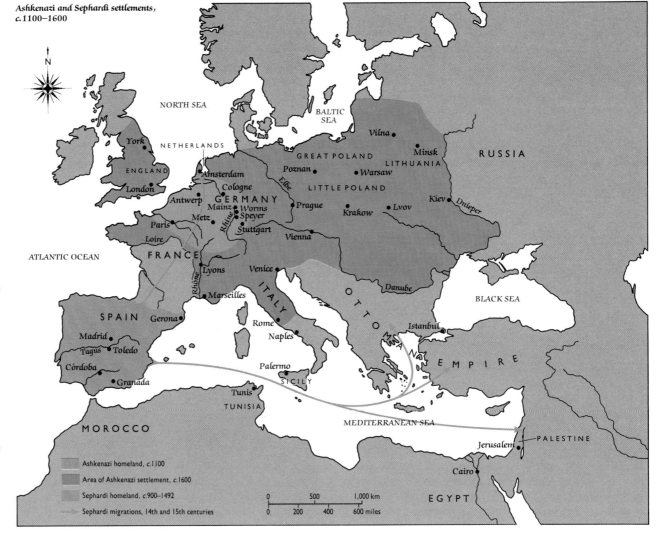

Ashkenazi and Sephardi settlements, c.1100–1600

Ashkenazi homeland, c.1100
Area of Ashkenazi settlement, c.1600
Sephardi homeland, c.900–1492
Sephardi migrations, 14th and 15th centuries

In Germany and central Europe, the Jews of the Middle Ages were often expelled from principalities and cities, and depended on important people to defend them. The most effective of these was Josel of Rosheim (c.1478–1554), a court Jew who had access to the Holy Roman emperors Maximilian I and Charles V. Josel fended off Catholic challenges to Jewish life, but was less successful in the case of Martin Luther (pp.60–61), leader of the Protestant Reformation, who, in his later years, was vehemently anti-Semitic.

Often, the Jews found solace from their hardships in mystic strivings, keeping alive the ardent hope that a descendant of King David (pp.22–23), a messiah, would free them from their enemies and create a better world. In the course of the 16th century, and in subsequent centuries, a number of messiahs (below) did appear. However, in the event, all turned out to be false, and they failed to have a lasting effect on the condition of the people. Jewish life continued much as it had before. The effect of living in a constant state of physical and psychological seclusion within the ghettos served to strengthen Jewish faith. Eventually, during the 18th century, Jews began to emerge from ghetto life into an outside world. They made great intellectual and cultural contributions, but that world still persecuted them.

A mob attacks the Jews of the Frankfurt ghetto in 1614 (BELOW). *The assault was led by a local baker, Vincent Fettmilch, who was executed by the city authorities for this crime. Within the ghetto, also shown in this 19th-century photograph* (LEFT), *Jews often found security in their close-knit family life, which compensated for their enforced isolation. Among the Jews who emerged from the ghetto were the Rothschilds, the great banking family.*

False messiahs

The Jews' ancient dream of a messiah who would free them from their sufferings brought a number of false claimants during the 16th century and after. For example, David Reubeni (c.1491–1535) appeared before Pope Clement VII in Rome as a messenger from a "secret Jewish kingdom in Africa" and was believed. One of his disciples was Solomon Molcho, a Portuguese Jew, who also came to think of himself as the Messiah. Both received popular support, but were finally killed by the Christian authorities as heretics, Molcho in 1532, Reubeni three years later.

The greatest false messiah was a Turkish Jew named Sabbatai Zvi (1626–76) (LEFT), whose spokesman, or prophet, Nathan of Gaza in Palestine built up a movement and an ideology around this charismatic figure. Sabbatai was believed to be the Messiah by a vast number of Jews all over Europe – in 1666, in excitement over the imminent coming of the messianic kingdom, the brokers of Amsterdam sold their stocks. Prayers for Sabbatai Zvi, the "Anointed of the Lord", were offered up in synagogues, and Jewish communities were torn apart by conflict between believers and doubters. Finally, the Sabbatai episode ended in anguish. He was given a choice by the sultan of Turkey: convert to Islam or be put to death. He converted. However, many Jews still believed in him, holding that he was only testing them. Indeed, there are still a few believers of Sabbatai Zvi today in Turkey and the Near East.

The Enlightenment

The Rothschilds of Europe

Mayer Amschel Rothschild
1744–1812

Amschel Mayer
1773–1855

Salomon Mayer
1774–1855

Nathan Mayer
1777–1836

Karl Mayer
1788–1855

James (Jacob)
1792–1868

Founded by Mayer Amschel Rothschild, the Rothschild dynasty became the greatest banking family in Europe. Mayer's sons established branches of the business in Vienna (Salomon), London (Nathan), Naples (Karl) and Paris (James, or Jacob). Amschel Mayer, the eldest son, looked after the family's interests in Frankfurt.

The Hasidic movement

For many Jews of the 18th century, especially in eastern Europe, the oppressive nature of society was not alleviated by traditional forms of Judaism, with their emphasis on rabbinical learning. The Hasidic ("Pious") movement, founded by Israel ben Eliezer (c.1700–60), a Jew from Podolia in Poland, came about as a reaction to this situation. This man's simple piety and joy in God's creation led him to emphasize the place in religion of feeling and emotion, as opposed to book learning and intellectualism, and to add the dimension of dance and song. For him, worship was joyful.

Eliezer's approach was warmly embraced by many Jews, especially uneducated peasants, to whom he became known as the Baal Shem Tov ("the good Master of the Name"), a term applied to miracle workers who used the name of God. He gained many followers throughout eastern Europe, and they became known as the Hasidim. So popular did the movement become that it began to threaten traditionalists. In particular, Elijah ben Solomon (1720–97) of Vilna in Lithuania organized a countermovement, whose followers were known as the Mitnagdim ("Opponents").

In time, the simple piety of the Hasidim degenerated as it evolved into a more formal movement. Some Hasidic leaders, known as Zaddikim, revered by their disciples for their alleged spiritual gifts, often misused their power. They held court, surrounded by credulous followers, and their positions of power became hereditary. Hasidic influence faded during the 19th century, but many Hasidic groups remain to this day, notably New York's Lubavich Hasidim, named for the town in Russia from which they originally came.

Hasidic women dance together during a wedding celebration. Hasidic communities stressed the joy of religious faith, particularly in dance and song. They have also maintained traditional costumes and customs – such as people of the same sex dancing with each other at weddings – which remain stricter than much of contemporary Orthodoxy.

In Europe during the late 17th and 18th centuries, the importance given to the powers of reason and the rights of the individual produced what scholars have termed the Age of Enlightenment. This new emphasis gave Jews a greater freedom to participate in society at large, but in exposing them to a secular, rationalist culture, it cut at the heart of Judaism.

The Enlightenment in France culminated in the revolution in 1789 and, soon after, the Declaration of the Rights of Man. In 1791, France granted its Jewish citizens full rights, the first European country to do so. In 1798, Holland followed suit. Even in Russia and Poland, which still had medieval attitudes, Jews challenged the establishment, striving for a western, secular culture and philosophy, and demanding full political rights.

In Germany, much of the initiative and impetus for change within Jewish life came from the great thinker and scholar Moses Mendelssohn (1729–86) and his circle in Berlin. But there were others who helped to change the prevailing attitude toward the Jews. For example, Christian Wilhelm von Dohm (1751–1820), adviser to Frederick II of Prussia, demanded civil rights for Jews as a way of improving society in general. And the German philosopher and dramatist G.E. Lessing (1729–81) pictured his friend Moses Mendelssohn in his play *Nathan the Wise* pleading for equality in religious life.

But despite some progress, full citizenship rights came slowly. Even those that resulted from the European conquests of Napoleon Bonaparte (1769–1821) were partially rescinded by the Congress of Vienna in 1814/15, which wanted to return to the conservative past. Those Jews who wished to participate fully in the new intellectual climate of western Europe often had to convert to Christianity to further their ambitions. Some of the greatest minds chose this way, including Heinrich Heine (1797–1856), Germany's greatest lyric poet, and F.J. Stahl (1802–61), founder of the German Conservative Party. As Jews gradually entered mainstream European intellectual and cultural life, they

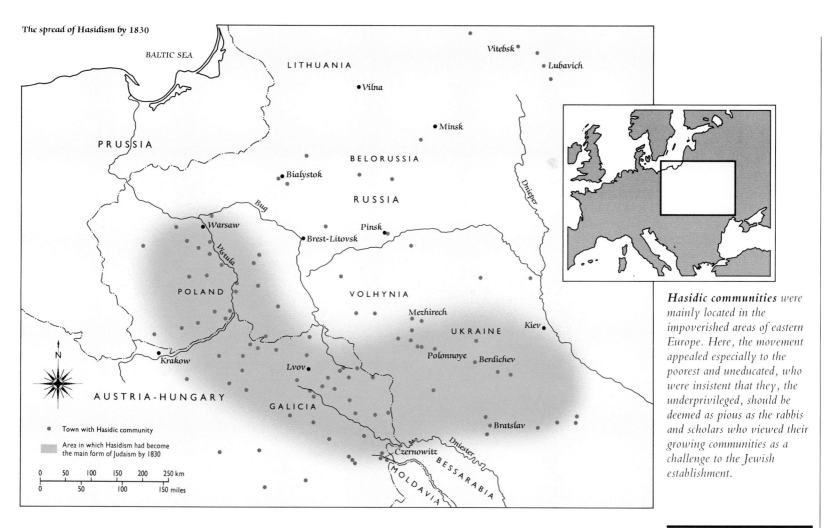

The spread of Hasidism by 1830

BALTIC SEA

LITHUANIA

PRUSSIA

• Vilna

• Vitebsk
• Lubavich

• Minsk

BELORUSSIA

• Bialystok

RUSSIA

Bug

• Warsaw

Pinsk
• Brest-Litovsk

Vistula

POLAND

VOLHYNIA

• Mezhirech

Kiev •

UKRAINE

N

• Krakow

Lvov •

• Polonnoye   Berdichev

AUSTRIA-HUNGARY

GALICIA

• Bratslav

• Town with Hasidic community

Area in which Hasidism had become
the main form of Judaism by 1830

Dniester
Czernowitz

BESSARABIA

0   50   100   150   200   250 km
0   50   100   150 miles

Dnieper

MOLDAVIA

*Hasidic communities were
mainly located in the
impoverished areas of eastern
Europe. Here, the movement
appealed especially to the
poorest and uneducated, who
were insistent that they, the
underprivileged, should be
deemed as pious as the rabbis
and scholars who viewed their
growing communities as a
challenge to the Jewish
establishment.*

also made an important contribution to the commercial world as bankers, for example the Rothschilds (*opposite*), traders and merchants.

Greater access to European culture presented a new challenge to Judaism. Jews who wanted to remain Jews but also to participate in the modern world created a new movement – Reform Judaism, which was rational and humanistic and presented an alternative to total assimilation, partly by making the religion more relevant to the new world. The movement began in Germany at the start of the 19th century and its leading early proponent was Abraham Geiger (1810–74) of Frankfurt. Synagogue practices were modified: organ music was introduced; the liturgy was shortened and the vernacular used; and men and women sat together. Also, dietary laws were modified or discarded.

The Reform movement spread. By the mid-19th century it was established in Britain and the United States. It posed a challenge to traditional Jews who felt it had strayed from traditional Judaism. The most vigorous reply came from Samson Raphael Hirsch (1808–88), also from Frankfurt, who started a movement known as neo-Orthodoxy. This upheld strict traditional Jewish practices based on rabbinic interpretations, but recognized the need to participate in society.

After the many social upheavals in Europe in 1848 and the failure of the liberal-inspired, anti-monarchist revolutions, many Reform rabbis left Germany for the United States, where a free climate and the absence of rabbinic authority had already created a progressive Judaism. This was then fashioned into a dominant movement by Isaac M. Wise (1819–1900), who had arrived in 1846, David Einhorn (1809–79) and others.

In the later 19th century, a movement that became known as Conservative Judaism became established in the United States. Developed by a scholar named Solomon Schechter (1847–1915), the Conservative movement offered a middle way between Orthodox and Reform Judaism, retaining the rabbinic tradition, but modifying worship practices.

According to the rabbis the righteous of all nations have a share in the world to come. MOSES MENDELSSOHN

Moses Mendelssohn (FAR LEFT), *through his teachings, helped to bring Jews out of their ghetto lives during the Enlightenment. He stressed religious freedom in society, rationalist thinking and the need for traditional ritual as part of divine revelation. Moses' grandson Felix (LEFT) was able to enter the modern world fully as one of the great German composers.*

The Rise of Zionism

For Jews in Europe, the 19th century had begun with the relatively open atmosphere of the Enlightenment (pp.34–35). But this faded quickly, and the Jews soon found themselves persecuted again. In Germany in 1819, for example, during the Hep Hep riots (a Latin acronym for "Jerusalem is lost") mobs attacked Jews, who again felt themselves outsiders.

Renewed oppression and the fear of a loss of identity made numbers of Jews turn to the ancient longing, expressed in prayers since the destruction of the Temple in 70 C.E., that Jerusalem would be rebuilt and that they would return to Israel. Many more Jews opposed this

idea. In the United States, the slogan "America is our Israel; Washington is our Jerusalem" was coined. But the Jews suffering in eastern Europe, and those moving to the west, kept the vision of Jerusalem in their hearts.

Gradually, the longing for a return to Zion, the ancient name for Israel, developed into an ideology. It also became a political movement through an Austrian journalist named Theodor Herzl (1860–1904), whose hope for full Jewish participation in European life was shattered by the infamous Dreyfus affair in France. In 1894, Captain Alfred Dreyfus (1859–1935), a Jewish army officer, was found guilty, on false evidence, of spying and was imprisoned for life. Then, in 1898, after a long battle, he was proved innocent, the victim of anti-Semitism.

The case led Herzl to believe that Jews would continue as second-class citizens until they had a homeland of their own. Thus he founded the Zionist movement to create a Jewish state in Palestine. In 1897, the First Zionist Congress took place in Basel, Switzerland, and declared: "Zionism aims at establishing for the Jewish people a publicly and legally assured home in Palestine ... [for] the promotion of the settlements of Jewish agriculturists, artisans and tradesmen...." Herzl then travelled throughout the western world to rally Jews to this cause.

Herzl was seen as a semi-messianic figure, attractive to Jews throughout Europe. At the same time, Zionism began as a minority-backed movement. Many Reform Jews, for example, felt that the Diaspora, not a homeland, was the way for Jews to carry out their role as purveyors of God's truth to the world. In the United States, a Reform conference in Pittsburgh in 1885 totally rejected Zionism, a position that was not reversed until 1935. And immediately after the Basel conference, the combined assembly of German rabbis, with only two exceptions, protested against the proposed settlement.

After Herzl's death in 1904, the Zionist movement continued to grow. Then, on November 2, 1917, the British government, influenced by the British scientist and Jewish leader Chaim Weizmann (1874–1952), issued its momentous Balfour Declaration, expressing the British government's support for the "establishment in Palestine of a national home for the Jewish people". And in 1919, U.S. President Woodrow Wilson confirmed the Balfour Declaration in a letter to the leading German-American rabbi, Stephen Wise.

In increasing numbers, Jews began to emigrate to Palestine and settle there. In 1939 almost half a million Jews arrived in what Herzl had called the "old-new land". And, after World War II, the grim story of the Holocaust (*opposite*) ended much of the opposition to a Jewish homeland. The remnants of European Jewry needed a place for a new life. World Jewry needed Israel as the expression of a Jewish national life which could be linked with the Jewish Diaspora. On November 29, 1947, the United Nations voted to partition Palestine into an Arab and a Jewish state. Finally, on May 14, 1948, the state of Israel was formally established.

Foreign Office,
November 2nd, 1917.

Dear Lord Rothschild,

I have much pleasure in conveying to you, on behalf of His Majesty's Government, the following declaration of sympathy with Jewish Zionist aspirations which has been submitted to, and approved by, the Cabinet

"His Majesty's Government view with favour the establishment in Palestine of a national home for the Jewish people, and will use their best endeavours to facilitate the achievement of this object, it being clearly understood that nothing shall be done which may prejudice the civil and religious rights of existing non-Jewish communities in Palestine, or the rights and political status enjoyed by Jews in any other country".

I should be grateful if you would bring this declaration to the knowledge of the Zionist Federation.

Theodor Herzl (ABOVE) *urged the creation of a Jewish homeland in Palestine. After his death, the Balfour Declaration* (LEFT) *gave support to his dream. It became a reality in 1948 when the state of Israel was declared* (TOP) *by David Ben-Gurion in Tel Aviv.*

The Holocaust

The 20th century has been no stranger to brutality and genocide, the killing of ethnic groups in great numbers. Yet the murder of six million Jews by the Nazi government in Germany, an event which came to be known as the Holocaust, was unique in its criminality and perversion of thought. The mere fact of Jewish ancestry was enough to cause a person to be condemned, irrespective of age or gender.

From a spurious doctrine of Aryan superiority, the Nazis included Slavs, Poles, homosexuals and the mentally ill in the group to be exterminated. The German government became a machine of death, with its bureaucrats selecting victims from their files. The SS and SA (Nazi stormtroops), the agents of this organized terror, stood above the law. German children were indoctrinated against Jews through youth groups, and adults were frightened into compliance. Those who protested were also sent to concentration and death camps.

The road from *Kristallnacht* ("Crystal Night", the burning of synagogues and looting of German Jews' stores and homes one night in November 1938) to the final days of death camps such as Auschwitz and Bergen-Belsen is often not done full justice by modern historians. Yet the American psychiatrist Robert Lifton has pointed out that much of the world "tries to dismiss Hiroshima and Auschwitz from human consciousness. To attempt to do so is to deprive us of our own history, of what we are."

In theology, Christians and Jews have tried to reshape their religious thinking in the dark light of the Holocaust. In psychiatry, survivors of the camps, such as Victor Frankl, Eugene Heimler and Bruno Bettelheim, have created new disciplines which owe much to their perception of how camp inmates fought to resist evil and overcome their suffering. And Elie Wiesel added a new dimension in literature. All Jews take pride in the heroic resistance against the Nazis in the Warsaw ghetto in 1943, in camps like Treblinka, and in the moral resistance shown by leaders such as Rabbi Leo Baeck (p.38), who managed to survive the traumas of the camps and gave hope in the darkness and in the days after deliverance.

Nazi concentration and death camps

- Germany in 1937
- Lands annexed to Germany
- –·–·– International borders in 1937
- ——— German-Soviet border in 1940
- △ Nazi concentration camps
- ▢ Nazi death camps

NORWAY · Oslo
SWEDEN · Stockholm
FINLAND · Leningrad (St. Petersburg)
NORTH SEA
IRELAND · Dublin
GREAT BRITAIN · London
Copenhagen
BALTIC SEA
ESTONIA
LATVIA · Riga
LITHUANIA · Vilnius
Minsk
PONARY
MALY TROSTINETS
WESTERBORK
Amsterdam
NETHERLANDS
Hamburg
NEUENGAMME
Danzig (Gdansk)
STUTTHOF
BERGEN-BELSEN
RAVENSBRÜCK
SACHSENHAUSEN
NIEDERHAGEN
DORA
Berlin
GERMANY
CHELMNO
TREBLINKA
Warsaw
Brest
Pinsk
SOVIET UNION
MALLOES
VUGHT
Brussels
BELGIUM
BUCHENWALD
POLAND
SOBIBOR
MAJDANEK
BELZEC
Kiev
BABI YAR
DRANCY
Paris
LUXEMBOURG
THERESIENSTADT
Prague
AUSCHWITZ
Krakow
Lvov
PITHIVIERS
NATZWEILER
FLOSSENBURG
CZECHOSLOVAKIA
Strasbourg
Rhine
Danube
FRANCE
DACHAU
MAUTHAUSEN
Vienna
Czernowitz
Vichy
SWITZERLAND
AUSTRIA
HUNGARY
Budapest
ROMANIA
Odessa
Milan
ITALY
JASENOVAC
SAJMISTE
Belgrade
Bucharest
BLACK SEA
GURS
AIX-EN-PROVENCE
RIVESALTES
SPAIN
MEDITERRANEAN SEA
YUGOSLAVIA
Rhône

0 100 200 300 400 500 km
0 100 200 300 miles

During the dark years of the Holocaust, one of the great heroic actions involving Jews occurred with the uprising of the Warsaw ghetto in Poland in 1943. Expecting to clear the ghetto in three days, heavily armed German forces came up against fierce resistance from Jewish men and women, such as those above. It took almost a month before the Germans succeeded in their objective.

The systematic murder of Jews in Europe took many forms, but most died in Nazi camps. Concentration camps used slave labour and physical abuse to kill inmates, while death camps murdered Jews, gypsies, homosexuals, communists and others mainly in gas chambers and crematories. The most notorious death camps were Auschwitz, Sobibor, Majdanek, Bergen-Belsen and Belzec. Among the worst concentration camps were Buchenwald, Mauthausen and Gross Rosen.

The State of Israel

The biggest threat to the new state of Israel, founded in 1948, was aggression from its Arab neighbours. The seeds of tension and hostility had been sown by the Balfour Declaration in 1917, which was ambiguous about Jewish and Arab rights, and by the arrival of increasing numbers of Jewish immigrants to Palestine between the two world wars. This had led to extreme resentment among the Palestinian Arabs and to outbreaks of violence in 1921, 1929 and from 1936 to 1939.

Immediately after Israel's foundation, Arab armies invaded Palestine, intent on destroying what they considered to be an upstart nation. But by March 1949, the Arabs had been defeated. Israel was left with more land, but with many problems. A large number of Arabs either left or were forced out of Palestine, and these refugees became the nucleus of what was soon to be known as the Palestinian problem. Housed in United Nations refugee camps, they soon numbered more than a million people. Their children grew up with the conviction they had to repossess Palestine. The Arab resolve to retake their homeland resulted in wars, local uprisings, Russian influence and international tension in the region which has continued to the present.

Israel became an armed camp, with most of its national budget allocated to defence. In 1952, financial support came from German reparations over the Holocaust (p.36) and through annual fund-raising from Jews of the Diaspora. Nevertheless, Israeli culture flourished and influenced Jewish life throughout the world. Hebrew, the language of the land, once again became a spoken language, Hebrew University in Jerusalem became one of the great educational centres of the world, and the arts blossomed.

Collective settlements, known as *kibbutzim*, built with socialist principles, blended immigrants from different nations with success. Sephardi and Ashkenazi Jews mixed freely, even though there were cultural clashes, with many Sephardis, particularly from Yemen, finding themselves discriminated against. Many of the newcomers had lived through the Holocaust and this filled them with a determination that their new land would not be destroyed. Symbolic of this was Yad Va-Shem, the memorial institute for the study of the Holocaust, established in 1957 in Jerusalem.

Able leaders guided the new state through difficult situations, notably David Ben-Gurion (1886–1973) and Golda Meir (1898–1978). And the country was blessed with gifted generals, such as Moshe Dayan (1915–81) and Yitzhak Rabin (1922–), who was also prime minister from 1974 to 1977 and was re-elected in 1992.

In 1967, Israel faced perhaps its greatest challenge in the modern era: the Six Day War. Israel struck out against mounting aggression from Egypt and a dramatic victory resulted in the conquest of the West Bank, the Gaza Strip, the Sinai peninsula and the Golan Heights on the border with Syria. These territories were held as protection against new aggression.

Then, in 1973, the Yom Kippur War, started by the Arabs on the Jewish Day of Atonement, was a much sterner test of Jewish defences. But again the Arabs were beaten back. Since then, Arab aggression has been more in the nature of civil uprisings (*intifada*) in Israel. There have been sporadic attempts at peace talks, but the only real success recorded was the peace pact concluded at Camp David between Israel and Egypt by their presidents Menachem Begin and Anwar Sadat in March 1979, which earned both of them the Nobel Peace Prize.

During the 1980s and early 1990s, the political alliance between traditionalist Jews and Israeli conservatives called into doubt the possibility of a realistic peace treaty based on Israel giving land to the Palestinians in return for guarantees of peace. However, the plight of the Palestinians and the pressures on Israel's economy and psyche make an accommodation between Arabs and Jews a necessary precondition for peace in the area and for the assurance of Israel's future.

Four modern thinkers

In the 20th century, four of the most influential Jewish thinkers and theologians have been the German Jew Hermann Cohen (1842–1918) and his disciples Franz Rosenzweig (1886–1929), Martin Buber (1878–1965) and Leo Baeck (1873–1956). Each made unique contributions to philosophy and theology in the Jewish tradition.

Hermann Cohen is famous as a neo-Kantian philosopher, developing the work of the great German philosopher Immanuel Kant (1724–1804). Cohen taught that Judaism was a religion in accord with reason and that Jews had a mission to teach righteousness wherever they lived. He believed that this mission would be obstructed rather than helped by the establishment of a Jewish state.

Franz Rosenzweig collaborated with Martin Buber on a new German translation of the Bible. His own great work *The Star of Redemption* was composed on postcards that he wrote to his mother daily from the German trenches during World War I. Although the book drew on philosophy, it concludes that the wisdom of thought is inferior to the living experience of divine revelation.

Martin Buber was a theologian, philosopher, biblical scholar and cultural Zionist. He believed in the foundation of the state of Israel through cooperation and brotherhood. Steeped in the Hasidic tradition (p.34), Buber's most famous contribution to modern thought is his notion of the "I-Thou" relationship, which places the relationship between people ("I-Thou") and between people and God ("I-Eternal Thou") at the heart of reality.

Leo Baeck, the leader of German Jewry during the Nazi era, was a rabbi who was both a great scholar and an inspiring leader. His *Essence of Judaism* (1905) upheld Cohen's view of Judaism as a religion of duty and reason, and remains a classic text. Despite offers to escape from the camps, Baeck was taken to the Theresienstadt camp, where he was an inspiration to those around him. He survived to teach the post-Holocaust generation through his works, including *This People Israel: the Meaning of Jewish Existence*, partly written in Theresienstadt.

Leo Baeck (TOP) *and Martin Buber* (ABOVE) *were two of the great Jewish thinkers of the 20th century. Baeck taught about the mystery of the divine and the need for ethical action to underpin faith. In Buber's notion of "I-Thou", people "encounter" each other and enter into relationships through which they acquire knowledge. People can treat each other as things ("I-it") or as partners in dialogue ("I-Thou").*

Jewish soldiers pray at the Western Wall, Jerusalem, after victory in the Six Day War of 1967. The wall is the last remnant of the Temple, destroyed by the Romans in 70 C.E., and the Israeli triumph enabled a new generation of Jews to feel themselves reunited with their ancestors of biblical times.

Jewish life in the modern world is caught up between the polarities of the Diaspora and the homeland. The changing boundaries of Israel (RIGHT) reflect the pressures of a nation caught up in a political struggle since its foundation in 1948. Yet Israel remains at the very heart of Jewish life, even for those Jews scattered throughout the world, from Chile to the Commonwealth of Independent States.

Israeli territory in 1949, 1967, 1973

- Israel in 1949
- Israeli conquests in 1967
- Egyptian reoccupation in 1973
- Israeli conquests in 1973

World distribution of Jews

Jewish population

- Over 5 million
- 1 million to 5 million
- 100,000 to 1 million
- 5,000 to 100,000

39

An Easter festival in the Philippines re-creates the tragic last hours of Jesus' life. The cross and the crown of thorns are central symbols in Christianity. The cross is often shown without Jesus' body, emphasizing the belief that Jesus rose from the dead.

In most Christian traditions, the Lord's Supper (also called the Eucharist, meaning "Thanksgiving", Holy Communion or Mass) is the central act of worship, in which Jesus' life, symbolized by bread or a wafer and wine, is shared with his people. During the failed coup in Moscow in 1991, an impromptu Communion service (RIGHT) was held to boost the morale of Boris Yeltsin's supporters.

In Poland, the Solidarity movement and its leader, Lech Walesa, shown (OPPOSITE) receiving the wafer during Mass, were fortified in their struggle against the communist authorities by the Catholic Church.

CHRISTIANITY

The Way of the Cross

ABOUT 2,000 YEARS AGO IN JUDEA, A provincial backwater of the mighty Roman Empire, an itinerant Jewish teacher and healer named Jesus of Nazareth preached a set of dynamic spiritual truths that became among the most influential words ever uttered. Jesus was considered by his disciples to be the Christ, the "Anointed One", or Messiah, who would usher in the period of God's reign on earth. After Jesus' death, his followers, called Christians, proclaimed his miraculous resurrection. They steadily multiplied in number, and in the fourth century C.E., the religion they professed was adopted by the emperors of Rome.

Two thousand years after it was founded, Christianity now has more followers than any other religion and is established all over the world. As a result, it has had to adapt to a wide range of social conditions. These have ranged from persecution during the Cultural Revolution (1966–76) in China to the active support of countries such as England, where bishops sit in parliament, and Germany and Sweden, where the church is financed by the state.

The relationship between church and state can change quickly over time. In Russia, before the 1917 revolution, the Russian Orthodox Church was popularly seen as a close ally of the tsarist regime, an association that was given credibility by the close relationship that existed between the family of the last tsar, Nicholas II, and the influential monk known as Rasputin. However, the first Russian communist leaders, Lenin and Stalin, in response to Karl Marx's condemnation of religion as "the opium of the people", were bitterly hostile to the church.

Despite being persecuted, harassed and undermined by a degree of collaboration between members of the clergy and the state, the Russian Orthodox Church survived the communist regime. It became first a symbol of spiritual resistance to the corrupt materialism of the Russian Communist Party, gradually attracting more young people in rebellion against prevailing communist orthodoxy. And, in the 1980s, it served as a rallying point for the nascent nationalism of various republics, especially the Baltics, Ukraine, and the Russian Federation.

In the United States, Christianity, in many forms and guises, is part of mainstream culture. One way in which the Christian message is communicated is through the use of the electronic media, especially television. Small sects, usually fundamentalist Christians, run their own television stations, transmitting live services presented by charismatic "televangelists". Their size, technical sophistication and influence are formidable.

By 1977, the Christian Broadcasting Network, presided over by Pat Robertson, was the second largest cable television network in the United States. Its syndicated programmes were broadcast in 60 countries. However, a number of scandals in the 1980s revealed some of the most popular televangelists to be both financially and morally corrupt, severely undermining their credibility.

The increase in numbers of Christians in Africa, one of the fastest growing parts of Christendom, has centred on "churches" that have sprung up around certain charismatic individuals. These include Simon Kimbangu, in what was the Belgian Congo, and William Harris in the Ivory Coast. These prophet-based movements are sometimes referred to as the African Independent churches (p.74) – since they owe no allegiance to, and indeed have sometimes been persecuted by, mainstream historic churches.

Most impressive of these new churches is perhaps the Kimbanguist Church (p.203), which now sends missionaries to a number of other African countries and even to Europe. Also important are the Aladura ("praying people") churches (p.202) which, since 1918, have spread outward from western Nigeria.

In Latin America, the Roman Catholic Church has been dominant ever since the coming of the Spanish conquistadors in the 16th century, who were accompanied on their voyages of discovery and conquest by Roman Catholic missionaries. Recently, however, Protestant fundamentalist sects, most notably the Assemblies of God (p.82), have begun proselytizing vigorously throughout the continent, often supported from the United States. In many urban areas, members of these sects now outnumber those of the Catholic Church, especially among the poor and artisan classes.

The Way of the Cross

Two skulls and three hourglasses add a sinister resonance to the gravestone of an 18th-century British couple. The symbols echo the book Job (14:2), where life is described as a flower that blossoms and withers, fleeting as a shadow.

Life after death

The traditional Christian view of death is encapsulated by John 3:16: "For this is how God loved the world: he gave his only Son, so that everyone who believes in him may not perish but may have eternal life." And this view is substantiated by Jesus' death and resurrection (pp.46–47) – events central to Christianity.

Most Christians believe that every person has an immortal soul, which, after death, undergoes judgment in the afterlife. Those who can claim deliverance by faith in Jesus Christ, whose death is seen as propitiation for people's sins, enter heaven; but those who have denied Christ are consigned to hell. Christians interpret heaven and hell in different ways. Some contrast the fulfilment of union with God with the emptiness of alienation from him. Others emphasize the social, corporate nature of heaven, with souls "in communion" with each other and, through prayer and worship, with the church on earth.

Around this core of traditional belief, there are many areas of disagreement. What happens to the person who leads a good life but has never heard of Christ? Is he or she given a second chance in the afterlife? It was partly to deal with such questions that medieval theologians developed the idea of limbo, where, for example, unbaptized infants were sent.

Modern debates centre on "universalism" versus "judgmentalism". The first emphasizes the absolute love of God and holds that none is finally damned; the second stresses the moral absoluteness of God and holds that the wicked (and/or the faithless) will be eternally punished.

Although the style and doctrines of Christian churches vary greatly both within and between countries, there are four features of Christianity that are nearly universal: initiation, worship, ministry, and "good works". In addition, the churches share as their sacred scriptures the New Testament (pp.50–51), which includes the four Gospels and the letters of St. Paul.

Almost all Christian churches or sects have a place for an initiation ritual involving the use of water. Usually called baptism, the ritual draws its symbolism from two biblical stories: Moses leading the Israelites out of their slavery in Egypt and the miraculous crossing of the Red (or "Reed") Sea dryshod; and the baptism of Jesus in the Jordan River by his kinsman, John the Baptist, or Baptizer.

From its linkage with the freeing of the Israelites, baptism is thus associated with liberation from oppression. This may be viewed as political oppression – a theme emphasized today by the liberation theology movement in Latin America and Southeast Asia which sees justice for the poor as the church's main priority. But it is more usually interpreted as the oppression of sin that separates people from God. By undergoing baptism, people are incorporated into the body of Jesus Christ, namely the church. Their sins are washed away and they are welcomed into the community of believers.

Nearly all Christian churches view worship as central. Christian worship classically contains four elements: praise or adoration; confession of past sins; thanksgiving; and intercession. Some of the formulations used come from Judaism – for example, the recital of

Barbara Harris's consecration as the first woman bishop in the Episcopal Church in Boston in 1989 was seen as a major breakthrough by proponents of the ordination of women into the Christian priesthood.

Baptism in some Christian churches involves total immersion; the picture shows an adult initiate being baptized in a river in Virginia. Other churches prefer water to be sprinkled on the head.

the Psalms – and some date from the church's earliest days. Equally, ancient liturgies are being modernized and new ones written.

The most central act of worship performed by the Christian churches – although it is ignored by Quakers (p.71), some fundamentalist sects, and other traditions – is the celebration of the Lord's Supper. Also known as Holy Communion, Eucharist or Mass, it is the re-presentation of the last supper Jesus ate with his disciples before his death, and which he commanded them to repeat "in memory of me". Since St. Paul's first letter to the Corinthians – a document older than the Gospels – includes this command, most traditions set it at the heart of their worship. The forms of this act, however, can vary from the simplest sharing of bread and wine to the colourful ecclesiastical drama of the Catholic Church, with the idea, more or less explicit, that the bread and wine are actually changed, or transubstantiated, into Jesus Christ's body and blood.

Most churches have some formalized pattern of ministry – the authorized performing of religious functions. This is usually based on Gospel accounts of Jesus giving authority to his disciples to act in his name, especially over the absolution of sinners. More explicit forms of ministry are found in the Epistles (pp.50–51), in which mention is made of bishops, presbyters (or priests) and deacons.

Partly because of the ambiguities in the Gospels and partly because of different political traditions, patterns of ministry vary from church to church. They range from the highly hierarchical, as in most "historic" churches such as the Roman Catholic and Orthodox churches, to the informal or democratic, as in some churches founded since the Reformation (pp.60–61), such as the Presbyterian Church. Women's participation as ordained ministers is accepted in many younger churches – such as the Lutheran and Methodist churches – but is still restricted by most older churches.

Although the style of operation varies, nearly all churches emphasize "good works" – running basic social services such as schools, hospitals, hospices and shelters for the homeless. Some Christians see their obedience to the Gospel as involving them in political action. However, there are widely different viewpoints as to what ideological form that action should take – from the position of the rightist Roman Catholic Opus Dei movement, with bases worldwide, to that of the Marxist-leaning Sandinistas in Nicaragua.

Jesus as Messiah

Jesus was born in about 6 B.C.E. in the small village of Bethlehem in the kingdom of Judea, which was effectively under Roman control. It was a humble beginning for one who would become one of the world's great spiritual leaders. The Gospel accounts differ over the details of Jesus' birth. Luke implies it took place in a stable, since the infant was laid in a manger, and Matthew's account describes the presence of the three Magi, possibly astrologers from the east, who had been guided to the birthplace by a star. Most important is the traditional view that Jesus' mother, Mary, was a virgin at the time of his birth.

The little information that exists about Jesus' childhood comes from the Gospel of Luke. It suggests that he led a conventional life with his family in the town of Nazareth in the northern province of Galilee; and that he immersed himself in the Jewish scriptures and the teaching of the leading religious figures.

Jesus' public ministry began when he was in his thirties. It has three main strands: calling his fellow Jews to repentance; proclaiming the approaching reign of God on earth; and performing miraculous "signs" of the imminence of that reign, such as healing the sick, feeding the hungry, curing the blind and raising the dead.

As well as performing these activities, Jesus flouted the social and religious conventions of the time and had some acrid disputes with the religious establishment. For example, he associated with less respectable elements of society, such as collaborators and prostitutes, and ridiculed what he viewed as the religious exclusiveness of some sects in contemporary Judaism. He gathered around him a group of 12 men, mostly from the lower reaches of society, who became his disciples.

Jesus' principal opponents were the religious leaders who were scandalized by his behaviour and teaching, and worried that he would trigger a confrontation with the Roman regime. Judea had the reputation of being a troublesome colony, and Pontius Pilate, the Roman governor, was expected by his Roman superiors to show no mercy in putting down any resistance.

And such resistance was gathering, especially around a secret society that came to be known as the Zealots. Jesus was known to be in touch with the Zealots, and they may have tried to use him as a figurehead for their

> *I am the light of the world; anyone who follows me will not be walking in the dark but will have the light of life.*
>
> JOHN 8:12

Jesus in Jewish eyes

The province of Judea in the time of Jesus was a seething cauldron of discontent. Deeply divided in religious matters and resentful of Roman occupation, it was a society that spawned a number of religious and quasi-religious "prophets", who gathered followers about them and walked from town to town proclaiming their particular message. Some of these were cranks, some crooks, and a few were genuine – even inspired – religious figures who ardently desired the restoration of Israel's political and religious integrity.

In the eyes of the Jewish religious leaders of the time, Jesus must have seemed an incautious and even misguided example of these prophets. They would probably have acknowledged that Jesus was a successful healer and a good moral teacher, but condemned his attacks on contemporary religious practice and teaching as being exaggerated. These religious leaders would also have argued that Jesus brought about his own downfall as a result of his insensitive approach to the delicate relationship that they had to maintain with the Roman authorities; and, finally, that tales of his miraculous resurrection from the dead were simply fabricated by his followers in an attempt to keep his movement alive.

While his tormentors look on, Jesus is cruelly scourged in this 16th-century Hungarian painting. The theme of Jesus' suffering in Christian art is connected with the motif of Jesus as the Suffering Servant of God, an idea found in the Old Testament and which probably applied originally to the people of Israel as a whole. It was taken over by the church, which quickly came to claim Jesus' Passion as being redemptive for the whole of humanity.

revolt. The Romans thus apparently had reason to be suspicious of Jesus' true intentions. However, those suspicions were not justified: Jesus was engaged in a religious transformation, not a political revolution.

How Jesus saw himself in spiritual terms is much debated. It would not have been in character for him to claim directly to be the Son of God in a way that would alienate ordinary right-living Jews. His preferred title for himself was Son of Man, an ambiguous phrase that many modern scholars think means simply "person", or "fellow". Significantly, it is the fourth – and much the latest – Gospel, that of John, which most heavily invests Jesus with claims of deity; and this Gospel is often considered as much as a theological treatise as a precise historical record.

Like the other Gospels, John's was written in the light of Jesus' resurrection – the event that underpins the claims of Jesus to be unique, to be "the Christ". The liberation that Christianity proclaims is not – or not only – the liberation from political oppression; but from all that distorts or destroys, supremely death itself.

The origins of that message were too subtle and too threatening for the religious and political leaders of the time. Jesus was betrayed by one of his chosen band of 12 and was questioned by priests. He was then brought before Pontius Pilate, who was notorious for his contempt for the Jews. Although Pilate saw that Jesus was not guilty of treason, he condemned him to the cruellest death Roman justice offered: crucifixion.

Was Jesus a pacifist?

Jesus was close to the Zealots, the Jewish sect that was planning an armed rising against the Romans. Yet he refused to join them, and it is evident from his life and his teaching that he preferred non-violent resistance. For instance, he forbade his disciples to resist the posse that arrested him; and he sidestepped questions planted by agents provocateurs to encourage him to preach violence against the state.

Two examples of Jesus' teaching also point toward pacific resistance. His instruction to his disciples to "go two miles" instead of one (Matthew 5:41) is a strategy to humiliate any Roman soldier who was taking advantage of the law that allowed him to force a civilian to carry his pack one mile. Soldiers who abused that law by making a civilian carry it a second mile were harshly disciplined. So by suggesting that Jews carry the pack the second mile, Jesus was effectively telling them to put soldiers in a position where they had to plead for the return of their pack.

Similarly, Jesus' teaching that people should give to anyone who takes their cloak their undergarments as well (Luke 6:29) can be interpreted as a classic device of nonviolent resistance. This is to make the oppressor look ridiculous by appearing naked before him.

Jesus Christ sits in majesty in this illumination from an 11th-century manuscript. Balancing the idea of Jesus as the Suffering Servant is the notion of Christ the Victor, as portrayed by his triumphal pose here. Jesus' victory is over death and human sinfulness, and he is often shown "on the right hand of the Father" – that is, in the position of authority and special favour.

The idea of his victory is often accompanied by the expectation that he will come again "in glory" as judge to reward the good and to punish the evil.

Crucifixion and Resurrection

To die to live

Jesus' example of a sacrificial death unmarred by hatred, and his promise of "eternal" life to those who follow it have produced a steady stream of Christian martyrs. The first was Stephen, who was seen as a threat by the Jewish authorities and stoned to death for blasphemy (Acts 6:8—7:60). And until the Roman emperors converted to Christianity in the early fourth century, thousands of Christians were executed for their faith.

Some 2,000 years later, far from Palestine, Christians are still asked to pay for their religion. In El Salvador, for example, in 1989, six Jesuit priests, their cook and her daughter were dragged from their house on the campus of the Catholic University of Central America in San Salvador and shot dead. They were all identified with the Roman Catholic Church's opposition to the right-wing government and with the longing of ordinary people for peace, land reform and enough to eat. There is no evidence that they were in touch with the antigovernment forces which were in control of one of the provinces, although it is probable that they were sympathetic to their aims.

Jesus is crucified with a crown of thorns pressed into his head in this painting by the Italian artist Guido Reni (1575–1642). The Passion of Jesus began with his arrest in the garden of Gethsemane, which lay just outside the city walls to the east. From here he was taken to the house of the high priest Caiaphas – the location of which (OPPOSITE) is still debated by scholars.

After being condemned to death by Pontius Pilate, Jesus was taken to the hill of Calvary, or Golgotha – the "place of the skull" – where he was crucified. According to the Gospels, two bandits were crucified with him, and he was mocked by jeering bystanders. At his death, there was an earthquake, and the curtain, or veil, in the Temple was torn from top to bottom.

Jesus is unique among founders of world religions in being executed in the manner of a common criminal. But his death on the cross and, three days later, his resurrection from the dead, formed the bedrock on which the church was built.

As two of the Gospels relate, the events immediately preceding Jesus' death begin with his being condemned for blasphemy at a night hearing presided over by the high priest. The usual penalty for what was a religious crime was death by stoning, a fate that later befell Stephen, the first Christian martyr. But the Jewish authorities wanted Jesus to be executed under Roman law – perhaps to safeguard their popularity among the sections of the populace who supported him.

Pontius Pilate, the Roman governor, was unable to charge Jesus with a *civil* offence. He did his best to find a solution, offering to release Jesus as the prisoner customarily freed at the Passover festival and, according to Luke's Gospel, sending him to be tried by a native princeling, Herod Antipas. Neither device worked: Jewish leaders demanded the Roman death penalty, and even brought into question Pilate's loyalty to Rome when he continued to prevaricate.

The Gospels say that Jesus made no attempt to save himself. For most of his trials, he said nothing: when he did speak, he was little short of offensive to those who had his life in their hands. Jesus' behaviour might be due to the fact that by this time he was identifying himself with the mysterious figure of the Suffering Servant who appears in the book of the prophet Isaiah and is glimpsed in some of the Psalms – scriptures that were dear to Jesus' heart. If that were the case, he would have seen his death both as inevitable and as bringing deliverance to his people.

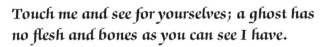

Touch me and see for yourselves; a ghost has no flesh and bones as you can see I have.

LUKE 24:39

The method of Jesus' death was standard Roman practice. He was flogged with a many-threaded whip and mocked and humiliated by his guards. Hearing that he claimed to be a king (which was almost certainly untrue, at least in the sense they took it), they burlesqued his royalty by draping him with a red or purple robe, pressing a crown of thorns hard on to his head, and giving him a bulrush as a sceptre.

Crucified with two criminals (thieves or Zealot revolutionaries), Jesus died quickly, without apparent anger or resentment, although, in Matthew and Mark, he was distraught at feeling he had been abandoned by God. His mother and some women friends watched him die from a distance: only one disciple was at the scene. The rest had fled in fear of their lives.

Jesus' route from his place of trial to Calvary is disputed. Some scholars think he was condemned to death at Herod's Upper Palace, others that he was taken from the fortress of Antonia. It is along the latter route that the traditional 14 Stations of the Cross which commemorate events in Jesus' last journey to Calvary are located.

The stations are as follows:
1 *Jesus is condemned to death.*
2 *He receives the cross.* **3** *He falls down.* **4** *He meets his mother.* **5** *Simon of Cyrene is ordered to carry Jesus' cross.*
6 *Jesus' face is wiped by a woman named Veronica.*
7 *Jesus falls again.* **8** *He comforts a group of weeping women.* **9** *He falls a third time.* **10–13** *He is stripped, nailed to the cross, dies and is taken down from the cross.*
14 *He is laid to rest in a sepulchre.*

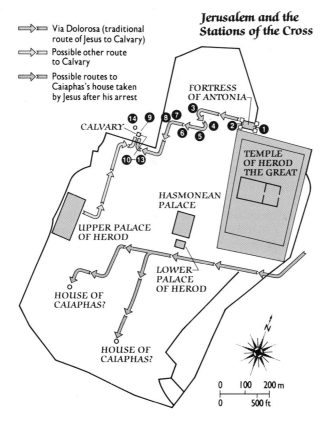

Jerusalem and the Stations of the Cross

Via Dolorosa (traditional route of Jesus to Calvary)

Possible other route to Calvary

Possible routes to Caiaphas's house taken by Jesus after his arrest

FORTRESS OF ANTONIA

CALVARY

TEMPLE OF HEROD THE GREAT

HASMONEAN PALACE

UPPER PALACE OF HEROD

LOWER PALACE OF HEROD

HOUSE OF CAIAPHAS?

HOUSE OF CAIAPHAS?

0   100   200 m
0   500 ft

N

One of the first witnesses of the resurrection was Mary Magdalene, one of Jesus' closest friends, who had stayed at the scene of the crucifixion while his disciples ran away. According to the Gospel of John (20:11–18), Mary was standing outside Jesus' empty tomb weeping, when there appeared someone she at first supposed to be a gardener.

When this person turned out to be the risen Jesus, she made as if to embrace him, as depicted in this illustration from the Ingeburg Psalter, an early 13th-century French manuscript. However, Jesus said to her "Do not cling to me, because I have not yet ascended to the Father."

Jesus' reaction has been variously interpreted. For example, some scholars think that John wished to emphasize the fact that after his resurrection Jesus belonged to the whole world and not just his closest friends.

According to the scriptures, Jesus' resurrection took place on the third day after he was crucified; in fact, he died on Friday and rose on Sunday. On the intervening Jewish Sabbath, the law forbade any kind of work, which would include preparing a tomb for proper burial. As a result, Joseph of Arimathea, a wealthy friend of Jesus, had hurriedly wrapped his body in a shroud and placed it in a new tomb. The Gospels differ in the details of the resurrection. One (John 20:11–18) says that Jesus' first appearance after his death was to Mary Magdalene. When she met Jesus in the garden, she recognized him only when he spoke to her.

Another account (Luke 24:1–12) describes a group of women led by Mary Magdalene, Joanna, and Mary the mother of James, going to the tomb on the Sunday and finding the tomb empty. They see "two men in brilliant clothes" who explain the significance of Jesus' death. But when the women tell this to the (male) disciples, they are told they are talking nonsense.

Matthew and Mark describe the women meeting a single young man in white – whom Matthew calls an angel – who sends them to tell Jesus' disciples to go to Galilee and meet him there. The words of the angel, "He is not here, for he has risen," (Matthew 28:6) became the triumphant cry of Christians in later centuries as they celebrate the day of Jesus' resurrection each year.

The Mission of St. Paul

After his crucifixion, Jesus' early disciples asserted that he had been raised from the dead and had ascended to heaven (Acts 1:9). This faith kept a band of 120 of them united in prayer in Jerusalem, but as yet they lacked a clear vision of their future. Some continued to hope that Jesus would restore the royal glories of Israel (Acts 1:6), and none seems to have envisioned separation from the faith of their fathers.

The central event that changed these first Christians into a daring, missionary church was the gift of the Holy Spirit at the feast of Pentecost. According to Acts 2, they were gathered in an upper room when they heard the sound of rushing wind and saw tongues of fire on each other. They began to "speak in tongues" and were filled with joy.

That event began the long and conflict-ridden process by which the Christian church detached itself from Judaism. In this process, the role of Paul was central. A Jew born in Tarsus, in southeastern Asia Minor, Paul was a Pharisee as well as a Roman citizen. He probably spoke an inelegant Greek and had a quick temper. After his dramatic conversion on the road to Damascus (Acts 9:1–30), he gained a faith in Jesus Christ that revolutionized his life and the course of Christianity.

Paul's conviction that the Christian Gospel was meant by God for all humanity brought him into bitter conflict with those Christians who insisted that the priority of Judaism and its law must be maintained. They insisted that non-Jewish male believers should first become Jews – by being circumcised – before being allowed to join what they saw as the Christian sect of Judaism. For Paul, this was to deny the universal significance of Jesus' death on the cross. He had the vision of a new community, no longer dominated by the law of Moses, but centred on the memorial Jesus had left his disciples: his own body and blood as re-presented in the sharing of the wine and bread in the Eucharist (pp.42–43).

Paul went on four journeys in the pursuit of that vision. In foreign cities, he was sometimes welcomed by the Jewish communities; more often he was rejected by them. Nonetheless, he managed to establish a number of Christian churches in Asia Minor before crossing the Aegean and taking the Christian mission to Europe.

Paul was not universally popular. For example, he had enemies in Corinth; and he continued to be at odds with the church in Jerusalem. This accounts for the emphasis he put on the collection he raised from the new churches for the relief of the poor of the Jerusalem church. For Paul this was more than an act of charity: it was proof of the love which must unite the new humanity of the church.

Paul's greatest achievement was his use of Greek (as opposed to the Aramaic or Hebrew) language to express theological ideas. His development of the doctrine that a person is justified – freed from the guilt and penalty of sin – through faith in Christ alone owed much to the language of Graeco-Roman law. And this doctrine has remained at the heart of Christian thought.

The journeys of Paul

> Everyone is to obey the governing authorities, because there is no authority except from God and so whatever authorities exist have been appointed by God. So anyone who disobeys an authority is rebelling against God's ordinance; and rebels must expect to receive the condemnation they deserve. Magistrates bring fear not to those who do good, but to those who do evil . . .
>
> PAUL'S EPISTLE TO THE ROMANS 13:1-3

ITALY

• Rome

• Puteoli

SICILY

MALTA

> Though I command languages both human and angelic – if I speak without love, I am no more than a gong booming or a cymbal clashing. And though I have the power of prophecy, to penetrate all mysteries and knowledge, and though I have all the faith necessary to move mountains – if I am without love, I am nothing.
>
> PAUL'S FIRST EPISTLE TO THE CORINTHIANS 13:1-2

> My chains in Christ have become well known not only to all the Praetorium, but to everybody else, and so most of the brothers in the Lord have gained confidence from my chains and are getting more and more daring in announcing the Message without any fear.
>
> PAUL'S EPISTLE TO THE PHILIPPIANS 1:13–14

Paul made four long, arduous and dangerous journeys, shown on this map, during which he proclaimed the Christian Gospel. He followed major trade routes, utilizing for his progress overland the network of well-constructed Roman roads, an example of which is shown (OPPOSITE), with the paving stones clearly grooved by cart wheels.

0	200	400	600	800 km		
0	100	200	300	400	500 miles	

— · — · Roman Empire
— — — Paul's first missionary journey (46–48 C.E.)
— — — Paul's second missionary journey (49–52 C.E.)
——— Paul's third missionary journey (53–57 C.E.)
——— Paul's journey to Rome (59–62 C.E.)

> Make sure that no one captivates you with the empty lure of a ''philosophy'' of the kind that human beings hand on, based on the principles of this world and not on Christ.
>
> PAUL'S EPISTLE TO THE COLOSSIANS 2:8

Paul stayed in some of the main centres of Asia Minor and Greece, such as Ephesus and Philippi, gradually building up Christian communities, which he subsequently nourished by correspondence. Extracts from his letters to Christians at Rome, Philippi, Corinth and Colossae are given here.

One community that gave Paul particular trouble was that at Corinth, whose ruins are shown here (BELOW LEFT). A port notorious for its moral laxity, Corinth – visited by Paul in 50/51 and again in 55/56 – was also a centre of Greek culture. It may have been Corinthian Christians still attached to late Hellenistic philosophy who were so critical of Paul. According to an early second-century document, these Corinthians had been "corrupted by false prophets" as well as by philosophy and "sects of the Jewish Law". It is possible – although now usually discounted – that these "sects" refer to the Judaizing Christians led by Peter and based in Jerusalem.

BLACK SEA

Danube

MACEDONIA
Philippi
Thessalonica
Beroea
Troas
AEGEAN SEA
ASIA   MINOR
GALATIA
Antioch
Iconium
Derbe
Athens
Colossae
Lystra
Corinth
Ephesus
Miletus
Perga
Tarsus
SYRIA
Antioch
CRETE
RHODES
CYPRUS
Salamis
Paphos
Damascus
Sidon
Tyre
MEDITERRANEAN SEA
Caesarea
JUDEA
Cyrene
Jerusalem
Alexandria
EGYPT
Nile
RED SEA

The Making of the New Testament

To achieve its missionary aims, the Christian church needed a literature. For how else could the Gospel ("Good News") about the life, death and resurrection of Jesus be carried across ever greater distances to mutually alien cultures in a standardized form? In the event, it was the missionary work of St. Paul that resulted in the earliest Christian writings – which predate the four Gospels.

In his letters to the churches he had established at Corinth, Ephesus, Thessalonica, Galatia, Philippi and Colossae, Paul was uninterested in recording the facts of Jesus' life and death. Instead, he teased out their inner significance, which he commended to the weak and divided Christian communities he had founded.

The first Gospel to be written, that of Mark, did not appear – at least in a form that corresponds to that found in the Bible today – much before 65 C.E. Some scholars think an earlier version, perhaps a few copies in some of the larger churches in Asia Minor, might have existed as early as 46, and that this was then re-edited and issued from Rome 20 years later.

To what extent the other Gospel writers (Matthew, Luke and John) knew of Mark's account; how they treated it if they did know of it; how far Matthew and Luke used another lost Gospel (known as "Q", from the German *Quelle*, "source"); whether Q was one source or many – all of these are matters that are much debated by scholars. What is clear, however, is that John's Gospel is much later than the synoptic Gospels – those of

Matthew, Mark and Luke – so called because they correspond to one another. John's Gospel could be as late as 140 C.E. and no earlier than 90. Most scholars date it at around 110.

The "pastoral" Epistles – 1 and 2 Timothy and Titus – present their own problems. Conventionally ascribed to Paul, they contain much he would have endorsed. However, modern linguistic analysis shows such a different range of vocabulary that most modern scholars ascribe them to some unknown church leader of great

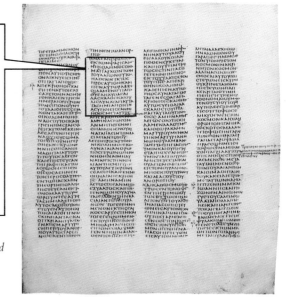

"There was one of the Pharisees called Nicodemus, a leader of the Jews, who came to Jesus by night and said, Rabbi, we know that you have come from God as a teacher; for no one could perform the signs that you do unless God were with him."

JOHN 3:1–2

The Codex Sinaiticus, part of which is shown (RIGHT) with a quotation translated from the Greek, is a fourth-century biblical manuscript and one of the earliest written in Greek on vellum.

The Second Coming

One of the assumptions most New Testament writers made was that Jesus Christ would shortly return in power and glory to re-establish the reign of God on earth. This belief in the imminent arrival of a messianic figure was common among contemporary Jews and certainly coloured the way they reacted to Jesus – and perhaps even the way Jesus conceived of his own ministry.

The failure of the Jewish uprising against Rome and the fall of Jerusalem to the legions of Vespasian and Titus in 70 C.E. profoundly affected both Jewish and Christian hopes for the Second Coming and the end of historical time. In the book that deals most with these themes, the Revelation to John, the need for Christians to persevere is given almost agonizing expression with injunctions such as: "Do not be

afraid of the sufferings that are coming to you. . . . Even if you have to die, keep faithful, . . ." (2:10). And for good reason. The book was almost certainly written during the terrible persecution of Christians that broke out in 91 during the reign of the Emperor Domitian. Christians must have been hoping most earnestly that the long-awaited return of Christ would happen – soon.

Jesus as the Lamb of God is worshipped on an altar in a painting by the 15th-century Flemish artist Jan Van Eyck. The image of Jesus as the Lamb in the Revelation to John stems from the sacrificial lamb killed by Jews at Passover. Christians also view Jesus' death as sacrificial and as leading them into a spiritual liberation.

authority, perhaps a close associate of Paul, writing to new churches in Ephesus and Crete around 120.

Much earlier – perhaps as early as 88 – is the Epistle to the Hebrews. It is not so much a letter as a sermon, possibly composed for Pentecost and rich in its use of Old Testament sources. The church has always been puzzled about its authorship. Clement of Alexandria in 180 thought Luke had a hand in it. Martin Luther (pp.60–61) favoured Apollos of Alexandria. Origen (185–254 C.E.), also from Alexandria and one of the great

---

**In the beginning was the Word:
the Word was with God
and the Word was God.**   JOHN 1:1

---

early biblical scholars, formally accepted that it was written by Paul, but knew the style was not right ("God only knows who really wrote it," he admitted).

By the time the 27 books of the present New Testament had been compiled, there were other texts – letters, accounts of Jesus' life, sermons – circulating in the churches of Asia Minor. Some were at odds with the faith of the church. Others held orthodox views, but came from sources whose authority was limited. The church was guided by three factors in its selection of these texts: the contemporary popularity of oral tradition; the threat posed by the Gnostics, a sect that relied on "secret" knowledge as a way to salvation; and the challenge of the heretic Marcion who, rejecting the Old Testament entirely, propagated a partial version of much of what is now the New Testament, having first removed from it all references to the Old Testament.

Selecting the New Testament canon (literally "rule" or "level") was difficult. But two criteria were essential: linkage to an apostle or a close disciple (which implies that the Epistle to the Hebrews was fortunate to be included) and conformity to the received faith of the church – which excluded the Gnostic scriptures.

The four Gospels, although coming first in the printed order of the New Testament, were written much later than the earliest Epistles. This diagram shows the order in which the books of the New Testament are believed to have been written, as well as their sources. There is particular controversy about the date for James's Epistle, which many scholars believe to have been written later than its traditional date of 46.

The first Gospel, Mark's, does not appear until at least 35 years after the events it records, equivalent to writing from memory the history of a World War II campaign in 1980. Christian scholars defend the accuracy of the Gospels by observing that they draw on oral traditions, which, in preliterate societies, are remarkably precise.

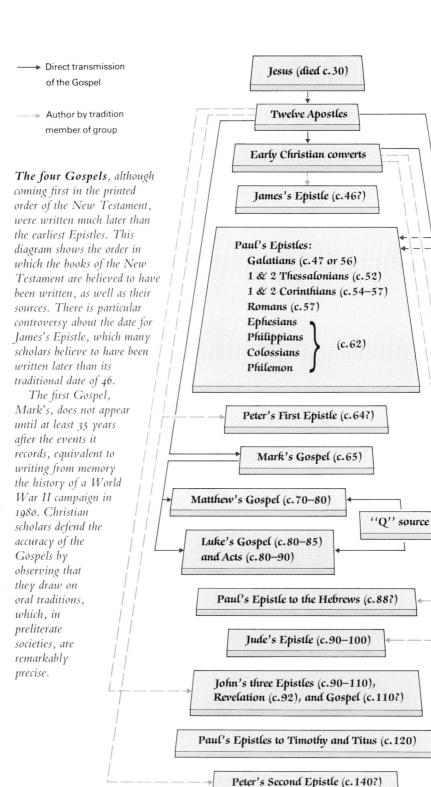

→ Direct transmission of the Gospel

⇢ Author by tradition member of group

Jesus (died c.30)

Twelve Apostles

Early Christian converts

James's Epistle (c.46?)

Paul's Epistles:
Galatians (c.47 or 56)
1 & 2 Thessalonians (c.52)
1 & 2 Corinthians (c.54–57)
Romans (c.57)
Ephesians
Philippians
Colossians
Philemon } (c.62)

Peter's First Epistle (c.64?)

Mark's Gospel (c.65)

Matthew's Gospel (c.70–80)

"Q" source

Luke's Gospel (c.80–85) and Acts (c.80–90)

Paul's Epistle to the Hebrews (c.88?)

Jude's Epistle (c.90–100)

John's three Epistles (c.90–110), Revelation (c.92), and Gospel (c.110?)

Paul's Epistles to Timothy and Titus (c.120)

Peter's Second Epistle (c.140?)

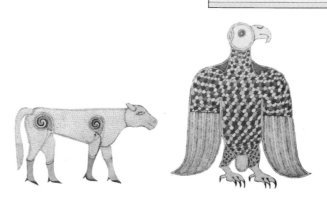

Mark, Matthew, Luke and John, the four Gospel writers, are traditionally ascribed with four symbols. These are respectively, from left to right, a lion, a man, an ox and an eagle. The symbols are taken from a mid-seventh century illuminated Celtic manuscript known as the Book of Durrow.

Christianizing Europe

For about 250 years under the Roman Empire, Christianity was a despised and persecuted sect. But when the religion was embraced by Emperor Constantine (mainly because he believed the Christian God had helped him to win a crucial battle for the imperial throne in 312 C.E.), its future became inseparable from that of the Roman state that had adopted it.

Such a close liaison brought benefits and costs to both sides. From the state, Christians gained protection, respectability and, eventually, significant political power. Conversely, the church gave the state a degree of political and spiritual legitimacy – while also involving it in the frequent disputes over doctrine that racked Christianity from the second century through the so-called Dark Ages (c.500–1000).

One of the hardest-fought disputes was sparked by Arius (c.250-c.336), an Alexandrian priest who had a reputation, among his enemies, for being a demagogue. In simple terms, he argued that Jesus was inferior to God the Father, since Jesus had suffered, while God was "beyond" suffering. To Arius's supporters, this seemed like a welcome return to the literal monotheism of Judaism. By making Jesus no more than a good man (a surprisingly modern view), Arianism made him a more approachable figure.

To other Christians, it seemed a surrender of one of the most basic elements of Christianity – the divine status, or deity, of Jesus Christ. Arguments between the two sides turned to warfare, and tens of thousands were killed in fighting in Egypt and elsewhere. Constantine called the Council of Nicaea in 325 to try to settle the dispute. It found against Arius. But the controversy rumbled on until 381, when the Council of Constantinople again condemned Arianism, effectively ending its influence within the empire.

About the time of the Council of Nicaea, Constantine found himself at the centre of another fierce dispute. Donatus of Carthage (d. c.355) was deeply critical of the new close relationship between church and state: he favoured total separation and a return to severe asceticism. Having split the African church doctrinally, Donatus tried to divide it administratively. He and his followers, however, were finally weakened in the early fifth century by Augustine of Hippo (354–430), who countered Donatism by arguing that the church was holy because its purposes, not its members, were holy.

These and other disputes played their part both in dividing Christendom between east (based in Constantinople) and west (based in Rome) and in weakening the Roman Empire. When Rome fell to the Visigoths under Alaric in 410, it seemed to western Christians, including Augustine, that the apocalyptic events heralded by the scriptures had arrived. The reconstruction of empire and church seemed an impossible dream.

However, the western church received a shaft of light when the influential King Clovis of the Franks, a German tribe that had migrated to what is now modern France, converted to Christianity in 496. But with no central administration and continued political and military confusion, the Christians in the west were hard-pressed to maintain their intellectual and spiritual life. To Gregory of Tours, writing in the sixth century, the

St. Benedict's *Rule*

Monasticism began to develop in the fourth century C.E., when Christian hermits gathered into communities in the Egyptian desert to perfect the spiritual life. In time, it spread to the west, where its development owed much to the great Italian monk Benedict of Nursia (c.480–547).

Given the political and doctrinal turmoil in Europe, many Christians longed for order and stability. Benedict's *Rule*, which he wrote at the age of 60, provided exactly that. By emphasizing a life balanced between prayer, study and manual work, and the spiritual significance of remaining in one place rather than constantly searching for new teachers or fresh inspiration, Benedict provided a spiritual discipline that was at once humane and penetrating. No less significant was his suggestion for a style of government in religious communities that gave the abbot adequate authority to deal with problems of discipline.

By 800, most religious houses in Europe followed the *Rule*. It is perhaps unsurprising that the spirituality of Benedict now rivals only that of Ignatius of Loyola (pp.62–63) in popularity in western Christendom. Nor does it apply solely to monks: there are also orders of Benedictine nuns, such as those (LEFT) at Stanbrook Abbey Convent in Britain, who draw upon Benedict's tradition.

contrast between past order and present chaos held nothing but horror for the future.

Despite these difficulties, missionary expansion did not wholly cease. Pope Gregory the Great (590–604) organized missions to central France and in 596 commissioned a monk, Augustine, to go to England. But only when Charlemagne, grandson of the Frankish leader Charles Martel, was crowned Holy Roman Emperor in 800 was the old Roman Empire in Europe re-established and the church's expansion assured.

The island of Iona (LEFT), *off the coast of Scotland, was one of the great centres of Celtic Christianity. In 635, Oswald, a product of Iona, became king of Northumbria in northern England and encouraged the monastery of Lindisfarne on the northeast coast to develop as a centre of learning and missionary activity throughout the northern British Isles.*

But the tribal and poetic style of the Celtic church did not easily mix with the more sophisticated and rigid Roman Christianity which had been brought to England by Augustine of Canterbury in 597. To heal the conflict, the Synod of Whitby was convened in 664, at which a compromise was fashioned. However, from this time onward the British church tended to look more and more to Rome rather than Ireland.

The Trinity: one God, three persons

No Christian doctrine has caused more intellectual debate than that of the Trinity (that God the Father, the Son and the Holy Spirit are unified in one godhead). The problem is: how can the monotheism that is central to the Old Testament be preserved in Christianity if Jesus Christ is the Son of God? For example, to say that Jesus was not divine (as the Arians did), or that he only *seemed* divine, or was divine but less divine than the Father, did not do justice to the conviction that Jesus was the *unique* Son of the Father.

The Council of Nicaea tried to resolve the issue in part in 325 by stating that Father and Son were "of one substance". That seemed to some Christians, especially in the east, to fail to differentiate between them adequately. The formula was revised at the Council of Constantinople in 381 and gave the western church, at least, a degree of peace.

For the eastern church, the question: how can Christ be both God and man? became an issue in the fifth century. The Council of Chalcedon (451) managed a semantic compromise based on the notion of "one person, but two natures", but failed to convince many Christians. Its formulae became definitive but did not prevent doctrinal disunity raging for over 200 years.

The Christian church spread throughout Europe (RIGHT) from the fourth century. In 800, it benefited from the crowning of Charlemagne – whose reliquary bust is shown above – as Holy Roman Emperor. He treated the senior ranks of the church as his civil service, rewarding them with lands, protection and the right to consecrate the emperor.

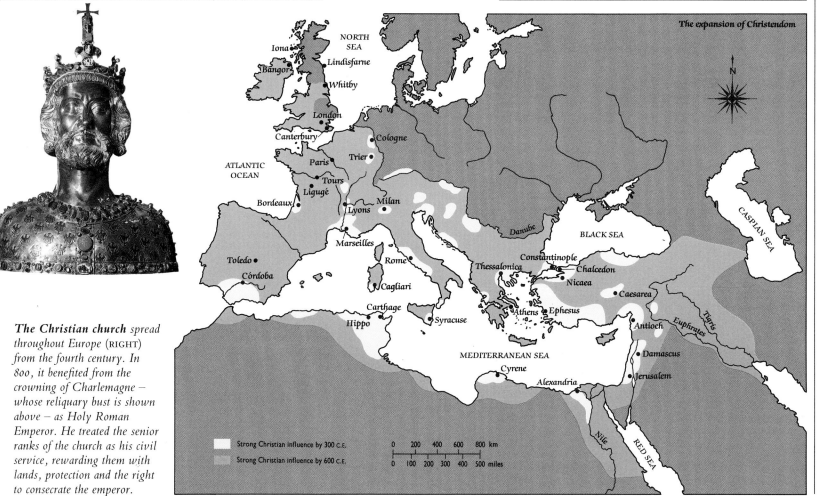

The expansion of Christendom

NORTH SEA
Iona
Lindisfarne
Bangor
Whitby
London
Canterbury
Cologne
Paris
Trier
ATLANTIC OCEAN
Tours
Ligugé
Bordeaux
Lyons
Milan
Danube
BLACK SEA
Marseilles
Toledo
Rome
Constantinople
Chalcedon
Thessalonica
Nicaea
Córdoba
Cagliari
Caesarea
Carthage
Athens
Ephesus
Hippo
Syracuse
Antioch
Euphrates
Tigris
CASPIAN SEA
MEDITERRANEAN SEA
Damascus
Cyrene
Jerusalem
Alexandria
Nile
RED SEA

Strong Christian influence by 300 C.E.
Strong Christian influence by 600 C.E.

0   200   400   600   800 km
0   100   200   300   400   500 miles

Schism

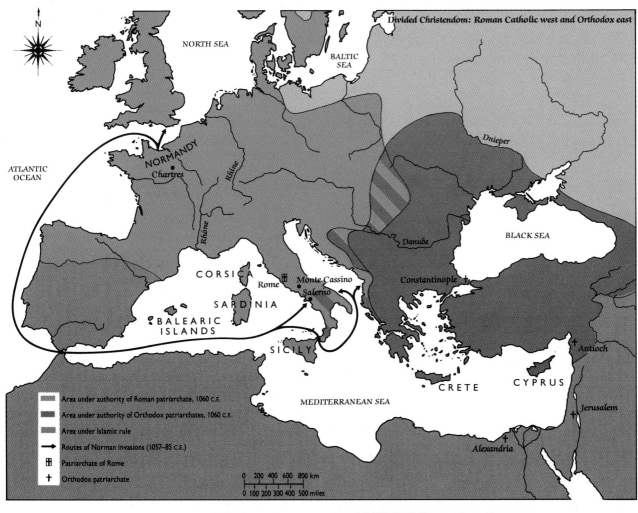

Divided Christendom: Roman Catholic west and Orthodox east

The final break between the Roman Catholic and the Orthodox churches reflected political divisions that can be traced back to when the Roman Empire was divided into western and eastern halves. The religious and cultural differences between the two churches resurfaced in the early 1990s during the civil war in former Yugoslavia. This was primarily between Catholic Croatia and Orthodox Serbia, whose boundaries roughly corresponded to the west-east split of the Roman Empire.

Area under authority of Roman patriarchate, 1060 C.E.

Area under authority of Orthodox patriarchates, 1060 C.E.

Area under Islamic rule

Routes of Norman invasions (1057–85 C.E.)

Patriarchate of Rome

Orthodox patriarchate

With the Roman and Orthodox traditions to choose from, Russia took the latter path, a decision reflected in the Orthodox-style icons and chandeliers typical of Russian churches (ABOVE).

A bullet-riddled Croatian church (LEFT) testifies to the tragic conflict in, and breakup of, Yugoslavia in the early 1990s.

In 1054, the church was rent asunder by a division that still has profound repercussions today. For it marked the beginnings – as distinct entities – of the Roman Catholic and Orthodox churches. This division did not happen out of the blue but was the culmination of differences in the cultural, linguistic, spiritual and political traditions that had grown between the western and eastern halves of Christendom.

From early on, Christianity in Asia Minor and Greece, with the city of Constantinople at its centre, was subtly but significantly different from that of Rome and its northern dependencies. The strain of producing doctrines that would satisfy Christians in the west as well as in the east almost inevitably fractured Christendom along these stress lines.

For the key debates about Jesus' divinity (pp.52–53) had already revealed theological and political differences. Although these disagreements did not correspond directly to east–west geographical divisions, they demonstrated the near impossibility of holding Christendom together. Further strain followed; again the origin was largely cultural and involved the status of religious images, or icons.

In the east, the tradition of representing, in stylized form, biblical figures and early saints had evolved into seeing these icons as a means of receiving God's grace, that is, increasing the effectiveness of prayer. For some Christians, it was then a short step to believing that an icon had spiritual power. And that, to western minds, was – and is – idolatry: the worship of images.

The dispute over icons shook the church to its foundations and lasted from 726 to 843, with a pause of semipeace from 787 to 814. After the Byzantine emperor Leo III's command in 726 that all icons be destroyed, persecution of those who owned or "worshipped" them broke out. Further proclamations in 753, 775 and 814 demonstrated both the determination of those in favour of icons and the ease with which theological dispute could turn to violence.

However, the final breach between west and east was more political than theological. Essentially, the issue turned on the supremacy of Rome and whether the pope, the patriarch of Rome, was pre-eminent or one among equals. Since the ninth century, the eastern patriarchs had favoured rule by the five patriarchs of Rome, Alexandria, Antioch, Constantinople and Jerusalem – with the implication that all were equal. Rome, however, was less than happy with this formulation, pointing out, for example, that Constantinople, unlike the others, did not have a direct connection with the holy apostles.

Even when mutually threatened by the rising power in the west of the Normans in the 11th century, Rome and Constantinople found it impossible to unite. The patriarch of Constantinople, Michael Cerularius (c.1000–59), began to ban Latin rites in areas under his control; Cardinal Humbert (c.1000–61), representing Pope Leo IX, retaliated by charging the eastern, or Greek, church with more than 90 heresies. Meanwhile, the Normans had landed in southern Italy. In 1053, the pope advanced south with an army to bring them to heel. He was defeated and captured.

A year later, the Norman crisis brought the two sides of Christendom together. The Byzantine emperor Constantine IX organized a peace-seeking meeting at his court in Constantinople. It ended in disaster, with the papal delegates leaving a bull of excommunication against Michael Cerularius and his allies on the altar of the great church of Hagia Sophia. The patriarch retaliated by issuing anathemas (formal curses) against the delegates. The two churches went their separate ways, and their mutual excommunication officially ended only in 1965. But the schism is still technically in effect.

> So I now say to you: You are Peter and on this rock I will build my community. . . .
>
> MATTHEW 16:18

The Norman conquerors

The warlike men of Normandy – the Normans – formed one of the great military and administrative powers of their age. Between 1050 and 1100, they conquered England, southern Italy and Sicily, and fought in Wales, Scotland and Spain. They helped to extend the power of the papacy, not least by their crucial role in the First Crusade (pp.56–57). As a result, they established the Norman principality of Antioch in Syria.

Situated in the northwest of present-day France, Normandy had been a Roman and then a Carolingian province, noted by the beginning of the ninth century for its monasteries and the vitality of the life of the church. This situation changed dramatically when the Norwegian Rolf or Rollo (c.860–931) attacked the province after a long career of plundering Ireland and the Western Isles of Scotland. Eventually defeated at Chartres in 911, Rolf was baptized and granted extensive lands in Normandy. His incursion was followed by invasions of other Norsemen from Scandinavia, and chroniclers bewail the destruction they wrought.

But the Normans were not simply warriors. The benefactions of Robert Guiscard (1015–85), conqueror of southern Italy, to the great Italian monastery of Monte Cassino made it one of the greatest centres of learning and of production of illuminated manuscripts in its day. Likewise, his basilica at Salerno in Sicily combined elements of Byzantine craftsmanship, Greek mosaics and Norman architecture.

The explosion of Norman power and creativity was as short-lived as it was impressive. Yet the massive buildings the Normans left, such as the magnificent cathedral at Cefalù (BELOW), on Sicily, still speak of one of Europe's most astonishing peoples.

The two towers of the Norman cathedral dominate the town of Cefalù, in northern Sicily. Situated at the foot of a promontory on the shores of the Tyrrhenian Sea, the cathedral was begun in 1131. The finishing touches of Byzantine-style mosaics, completed in 1148, are among the finest in Sicily.

The Crusades

> So stand your
> ground, with truth a
> belt round your
> waist, and
> uprightness a
> breastplate, . . .
>
> EPHESIANS 6:14

Between the late 11th and 13th centuries, Christian Europe conducted a series of campaigns that were among the most remarkable – but arguably the most misguided – military undertakings in Christian history. The aim of these Crusades was the retaking of the Holy Land from the Muslims and the settlement there of a large enough population to maintain a Christian enclave in the heart of Islam.

Conflict between Christianity and Islam was not new when Pope Urban II preached the First Crusade at the Council of Clermont in 1095. For example, in Spain and especially Asia Minor, where the Islamic kingdom of the Seljuk Turks (pp.100–101) was expanding westward, militant Islam had come face to face with an increasingly aggressive Christianity.

It was the Seljuks who, from 1079, controlled access to Jerusalem, a city that had been under Islamic control since 638. Islamic rulers had been tolerant of the growing numbers of Christian pilgrims to the Holy Land, even permitting the establishment of hospices in and around Jerusalem for them. Under the Seljuks, however, the pilgrimages became almost impossible.

The Crusades were inspired – or driven – by a number of factors. The first was a genuine piety. Jerusalem had a mystique, compounded of history, apocalyptic faith, romance and symbolism, and its liberation from the infidel was worth the desperate privation of a military campaign and the risk of a violent death. Also, Urban II's promise of full remission of sins to all who participated spurred soldiers on with the belief that death brought with it a guarantee of paradise. Second, the Crusades developed their own mystique. In an age of chivalry and romance, which created the ideal of the Christian knight, the means came to be as significant as the end – to go on a crusade was proof of a knight's courtly graces.

Third, and in stark contrast, the Crusades meant land, power and money. They meant land to the commanders who could win and keep tracts of territory formerly occupied by Muslims. The Seljuks were driven out of western Asia Minor and, following the First Crusade and the taking of Jerusalem in 1099, Christian states were established along the coast of Palestine. The Crusades brought power, especially to the papacy; and they brought money to the mercenaries, merchants, financiers and traders. It is no coincidence that in 1204 the Fourth (and least successful) Crusade was financed largely by Venetian merchants and subverted into a disorganized assault on Constantinople, Venice's main trading rival, more than 600 miles from Jerusalem.

In popular literature, the Crusades are associated with knights on horseback and chivalrous champions, such as Richard I, the Lionheart, king of England. Less well known are the ordinary foot soldiers, many of whom were pressed into service for the sake of God, pope and manorial lord and had little commitment to the high ideals of Christian geopolitics. They were there because, as serfs, they had no choice but to accompany their feudal masters. They died in their thousands of starvation, dysentery and cholera – before they ever crossed swords with a Muslim. Four out of every five died, even in the successful First Crusade.

After the Fourth – and last significant – Crusade, there were a number of further, unsuccessful expeditions. But with the final fall of the Crusader states to the Muslims in 1291, the crusading spirit petered out, and the Holy Land was lost to Islam.

White-turbaned Muslims fight Christian knights in this illumination from the 14th-century Chronicles of Godfrey of Bouillon, *a town in present-day Belgium. Godfrey, a leader of the First Crusade, established the Kingdom of Jerusalem after the city's capture in 1099. The kingdom endured until Jerusalem's recapture by Saladin in 1187.*

*One of the many noblemen killed in the Crusades was the English Knight Sir John Holcombe, whose tomb and effigy are shown here (*RIGHT*). Sir John died of wounds after a battle in the Second Crusade.*

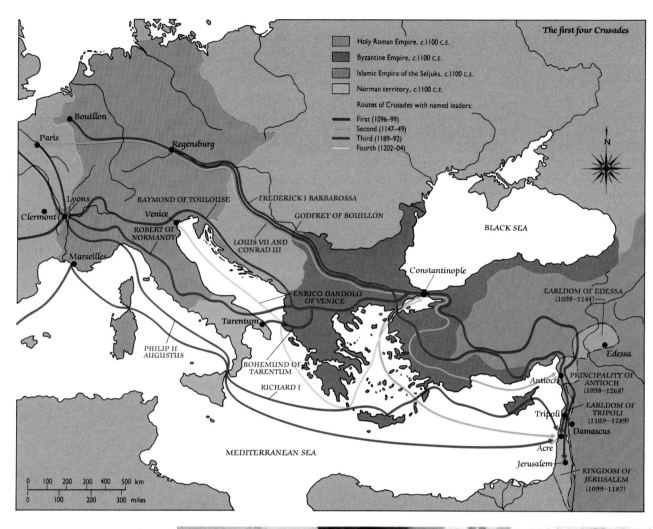

The first four Crusades

Holy Roman Empire, c.1100 C.E.
Byzantine Empire, c.1100 C.E.
Islamic Empire of the Seljuks, c.1100 C.E.
Norman territory, c.1100 C.E.
Routes of Crusades with named leaders:
First (1096–99)
Second (1147–49)
Third (1189–92)
Fourth (1202–04)

Bouillon
Paris
Regensburg
Lyons
Clermont
RAYMOND OF TOULOUSE
Venice
ROBERT OF NORMANDY
Marseilles
LOUIS VII AND CONRAD III
FREDERICK I BARBAROSSA
GODFREY OF BOUILLON
BLACK SEA
ENRICO DANDOLO OF VENICE
Constantinople
EARLDOM OF EDESSA (1098–1144)
Tarentum
PHILIP II AUGUSTUS
BOHEMUND OF TARENTUM
RICHARD I
Edessa
Antioch
PRINCIPALITY OF ANTIOCH (1098–1268)
Tripoli
EARLDOM OF TRIPOLI (1109–1289)
Damascus
Acre
MEDITERRANEAN SEA
Jerusalem
KINGDOM OF JERUSALEM (1099–1187)

0 100 200 300 400 500 km
0 100 200 300 miles

European Christian powers launched a number of Crusades to free the Holy Land from Muslim control between 1095 and the late 13th century. The most important were the first four, whose routes are shown here along with the principal leaders.

The First Crusade (1096–99) led to the capture of Jerusalem and, later, the founding of the crusader states: the Earldom of Edessa, Principality of Antioch, Earldom of Tripoli and Kingdom of Jerusalem. The Second (1147–49), launched to liberate Edessa, retaken by the Muslims, failed. And the Third (1189–92) resulted in a fragile truce worked out by Richard I of England and the Muslim leader Saladin.

The Fourth (1202–04), aimed at invading Egypt, was diverted to Constantinople, where, with the backing of Venice, the largely French and Flemish Crusaders sacked the city and founded the Latin Empire of Constantinople that lasted for over 60 years.

Easter worshippers (RIGHT) of the Orthodox tradition celebrate Jesus' resurrection at the Church of the Holy Sepulchre in Jerusalem. The church, traditionally the site of the crucifixion and the final resting place of Jesus, was the goal of every Crusader.

It became customary for the small proportion of Crusaders who reached it to carve a cross on the portal as a token of thanksgiving. The crosses can still be seen today, and the church remains a central focus for Christian pilgrims.

The Middle Ages

The Angelic Doctor

The most important theologian of the Middle Ages, Thomas Aquinas (1225–74) – known as the Angelic Doctor – is famous for applying the philosophy of Aristotle to Christian theology, set out in his two encyclopedic works, *Summa Theologiae* and *Summa Contra Gentiles*. Aristotle's philosophy came to western Christendom via the Muslims of Spain. At first, deeming it tainted, the church sought to ban its publication, and the University of Paris proscribed Aristotle in 1210. Yet proscription was soon followed by study and finally the brilliant synthesis achieved by Aquinas and his teacher Albert the Great (1206–80).

Instead of seeing Aristotle's thinking and Christian doctrine as mutually exclusive, these two Dominicans – teaching in Paris and other European cities – showed that Aristotle's emphasis on human reason was consistent with the revelation of divine truth and that reason and faith can exist harmoniously. Thus in his *Summa Theologiae* (never completed), Aquinas showed that philosophy could be used to elucidate the principles of the natural sciences. Over and beyond philosophy and science there is the revealed knowledge of God, which can be interpreted by theology.

Aquinas had his critics, notably Duns Scotus (the Scot) and William of Occam, who both challenged the feasibility of the neat synthesis of faith and reason at the heart of his thinking. In many ways, that debate still continues: perhaps the fact that in the course of their training most Roman Catholic clergy in the west are still expected to spend three years studying Aquinas's philosophy suggests that his influence far exceeds that of his critics.

Thomas Aquinas, shown here in the Apotheosis of St. Thomas by the 17th-century Spanish painter Francisco de Zurbarán, based his influential philosophy on the thought of Aristotle. He was canonized in 1323.

Lasting from about 1100 to 1500, the Middle Ages were a crucial, formative time for the church. This medieval period saw the rise of new monastic orders, the building of great cathedrals, the brilliance of mystics and scholars, and the development of the relationship between the papacy and the Holy Roman Emperor.

A continuing theme in western Christendom was the relationship between the church and the state. Which was supreme over the other? From Charlemagne (c.742–814) almost to the end of the 11th century, the leaders of the church had been more or less content to be the junior partners of the Holy Roman Emperor.

By the end of the 11th century, Hildebrand (Pope Gregory VII, 1073–85) had tried to stand that arrangement on its head. In an attempt to protect papal power over nominating bishops, Hildebrand excommunicated the emperor (Henry IV). And he only revoked the excommunication after Henry had been kept waiting for days in deep Alpine snow and then been obliged to kiss the pope's stirrup – a ritual act of feudal obeisance.

The conflict did not end there. Although the Concordat of Worms of 1122 produced a fudged compromise in power sharing between pope and emperor, each side continued to look for an opportunity to gain the upper hand. The papacy was, however, weakened less by conflict with the state than by the internal divisions of the church. From 1378 to 1417, there were two rival popes because the election of Urban VI was declared void when he was found to be wanting, but he refused to step down and acknowledge the newly elected Clement VII. When the schism was finally ended by the Council of Constance (1414–18), there were many who looked

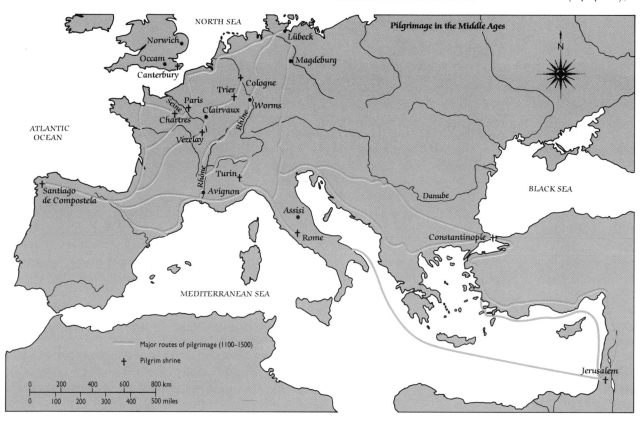

Pilgrimage in the Middle Ages

Major routes of pilgrimage (1100–1500)

✝ *Pilgrim shrine*

```
0    200   400   600   800 km
0   100  200  300  400  500 miles
```

Pilgrimages were popular during the Middle Ages and focused on the healing power of holy relics and the spiritual energy associated with particular places or buildings.

Some of the more important shrines and their relics were: Canterbury, bones of Thomas à Becket; Chartres, Holy Tunic of the Virgin Mary; Cologne, bones of the Three Wise Men; Constantinople, hand of St. James; Jerusalem, the Church of the Holy Sepulchre and other holy sites; Paris, Crown of Thorns; Rome, bones of St. Peter and St. Paul, the True Cross and Jesus' crib; Trier, St. Andrew's sandal; Turin, Holy Shroud of Jesus; and Vézelay, bones of Mary Magdalene.

to a re-emergence of conciliar authority to fill the vacuum left by a divided papacy.

The Italian prince-bishops – the wealthy and powerful Medici and Borgia families – who aspired to the papacy put an end to such hopes. Although their patronage produced some fine achievements – for example, works by Raphael and Michelangelo, the Vatican Library and St. Peter's Basilica – they could not disguise the spiritual impotence of the church's leadership. This showed in the twin institutions of local religious life – the parish and the religious house. Many of the clergy were illiterate, poverty-stricken, unsupervised – or absent. Many were "mass priests", saying endless masses for the dead, rather than nourishing the living. Many conformed to their secular environments; few had the capacity to transform them.

Although the Middle Ages saw a rich flowering of monastic orders (below), the blooms rose from a bed of muck. In France, Spain and Italy, for example, many religious houses had become renowned locally for their laxity, drunkenness and promiscuity.

Yet, paradoxically, this period saw an abundance of scholars and mystics – including a number of women, such as Julian of Norwich, Mecktild of Magdeburg and the Rhineland mystics. Thomas à Kempis's *Imitation of Christ* (1418) is a classic that encapsulates late medieval spirituality, with its emphasis on repentance, the transitoriness of life and the solace of the sacraments. It is too easy for modern scholars, with hindsight, to condemn the late medieval period with the same ferocity as its Reformation critics (pp.60–61) in the 16th century. It had its woes; but it also had its lasting achievements.

Orders of reforming monks

Cistercians: Popularized by St. Bernard of Clairvaux (1090–1153), the order was founded on a strict interpretation of the *Rule* of St. Benedict (p.52) and rapidly spread across Europe.

Augustinians: Originally groups of hermits in northern Italy and southern France, they were united by Pope Alexander IV in 1256 and followed the rule of St. Augustine of Hippo (354–430).

Franciscans: Founded by St. Francis of Assisi (c.1181–1226), they were friars who lived a life of poverty. They gradually abandoned their itinerant life and eventually their poverty, too. Many women sought to follow Francis, so he asked Clare of Assisi to organize them in settled houses. The *Poor Clares* were dedicated to a life of prayer and penance.

Dominicans: St. Dominic (1170–1221), who was born in Spain but active in France, chose the Augustinian Rule for his Order of Preachers in 1216 because the pope had banned new orders. Although Dominic's original intention was to convert heretics, his order played a major role in raising the intellectual life of the European church.

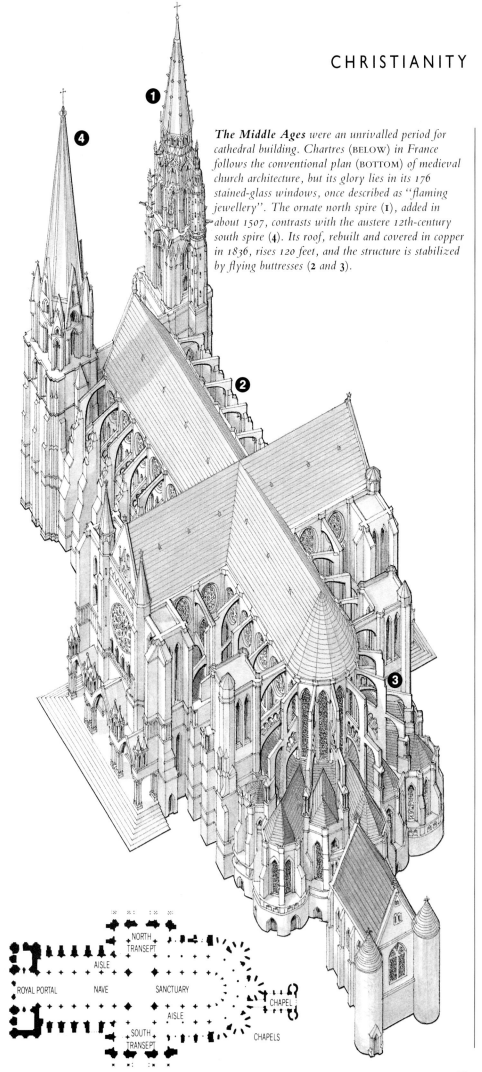

The Middle Ages were an unrivalled period for cathedral building. Chartres (BELOW) in France follows the conventional plan (BOTTOM) of medieval church architecture, but its glory lies in its 176 stained-glass windows, once described as "flaming jewellery". The ornate north spire (1), added in about 1507, contrasts with the austere 12th-century south spire (4). Its roof, rebuilt and covered in copper in 1836, rises 120 feet, and the structure is stabilized by flying buttresses (2 and 3).

NORTH TRANSEPT
AISLE
ROYAL PORTAL   NAVE   SANCTUARY
CHAPEL
AISLE
SOUTH TRANSEPT   CHAPELS

The Reformation

Prophet of the Peasants' Revolt

The early preaching of Thomas Münzer (1490–1525) was directed against the church and especially the clergy. Although influenced by Luther's ideas, this German priest went much further, and he came to see himself as a kind of Old Testament prophet, calling down the vengeance of God on those who did not accept his ideas. Commentators have debated whether Münzer was a political radical, dying a martyr's death in the wake of the collapse of the Peasants' Revolt in 1525; or whether he was a harbinger of the religious fanaticism that cares little for the human cost of religious truth.

Having broken with Luther, Münzer sought to persuade some of the German princes to use their military power to enforce his religious ideas. Later, he despaired even of sympathetic princes, declaring: "The great do all in their power to keep the common people from perceiving the truth." From there, it was a short step to denunciation of private property and the preaching of revolution.

In 1524, German peasants, aggrieved at their social conditions, staged a number of uprisings. Münzer added his influential voice to the revolt and, in 1525, led 6,000 poorly equipped peasants against the heavily armed troops of Duke George of Saxony, convinced that this was the Last Battle, in which God would grant him victory. But Münzer was soon captured and, having recanted his "errors", was beheaded at Muelhausen on May 27.

A Christian man is free from all things; he needs no work in order to be justified and saved, but receives these gifts in abundance from his faith alone.

MARTIN LUTHER

During the 16th century, Europe was rocked by a number of reforming movements that challenged the Catholic Church, which had become worldly and lost much of its authority. These movements, collectively known as the Reformation, altered the face of Christianity. They initiated a new set of relationships between people and God, and religious authorities and people. And they gave birth to new churches known as Protestant, because of their "protest" against the Roman Catholic Church.

The most important reforming movement was begun by Martin Luther (1483–1546), a German Augustinian monk of humble origins who rose to become a professor of biblical theology at Wittenberg University. Luther was appalled at the laxity of the Roman Catholic Church – and especially at the church's sale of "indulgences", by means of which people could buy salvation and escape the punishment of purgatory. At the same time, he was racked with guilt at his own sense of sin and inability to earn God's forgiveness.

As a result of his study of Paul's epistles (pp.48–49), on which he also lectured, Luther became convinced of the great theological truth that "justification is by faith alone". Dismissing the Epistle of James, with its emphasis on good works, as "an epistle of straw", he insisted that God's forgiveness could only be received as a divine gift through faith in Jesus Christ.

To many poor people who could not afford to buy indulgences, Luther's claim offered deliverance from the ever-present threat of purgatory. And it revolutionized their image of God: an angry, implacable judge became

The English Reformation

Few countries better illustrate the opportunism with which secular rulers used the Reformation to their own advantage than England. Initially, Henry VIII was opposed to the ideas of the Reformers and in 1521 was given by the pope the title of Defender of the Faith for attacking them in print. Although some Cambridge University professors espoused Luther's ideas, England looked firmly locked in the Roman camp, until the king wished to divorce his barren wife, Catherine of Aragon. But she was the aunt of the Holy Roman Emperor, Charles V, who had recently captured the pope, Clement VII, the only person who could permit Henry to divorce.

In 1534, Henry made himself the supreme head of the Church in England and divorced his wife. In the same year, he suppressed the monasteries, including Rievaulx Abbey in Yorkshire (LEFT), and distributed their lands to political supporters. But the doctrinal ideas of this English Reformation were slow to take root. Some men of honour resisted them and paid with their lives, including Sir Thomas More. It was not until the accession of Edward VI in 1547 that the new prayer books of 1549 and 1552 finally established a pattern of worship that was recognizably reformed.

a loving father. At the same time, however, it threatened the power and wealth of the clergy, friars and ecclesiastical lawyers – and they were not ready to let either go without a fight.

Yet, despite his bruising attacks on the papacy, Luther was deep down a traditionalist. He wanted to preserve key elements of Roman Catholic teaching on the Mass and preached angrily against the Peasants' Revolt and its main "prophet" Thomas Münzer (*opposite*). He thus could not be reconciled with the two great Protestant reformers who developed his ideas more systematically than he did himself, the Swiss Huldreich Zwingli (1485–1531) and the French-born John Calvin (1509–64).

In Zurich, Zwingli set about applying Luther's scripture-based reasoning more thoroughly. If a doctrine or practice failed this test, it was jettisoned. As a result, out went the Mass, fasting, church music, clerical celibacy, even the notion of priests as mediators between laypeople and God.

In Geneva, Calvin tried to re-create the city of God that Augustine of Hippo (354–430) had despaired of ever seeing on earth. His *Institutes of the Christian Religion* developed the new theological thinking. It showed how government, instructed by church ministers, could order a righteous political state in which religion and the civic virtues reinforced each other. Although this came to have its ugly side – Calvin encouraged the government to hunt down and execute heretics – it was a more constructive approach to the contemporary political turbulence than that of Luther and some of his more enthusiastic associates.

These reforming movements not only split the church but they also caused social upheaval and new political alliances. In Germany, Protestant princes formed the Schmalkaldic League in 1531 and, in the name of the "new truths" of the Reformation, fought against Catholic forces under the Emperor Charles V, seeking to defend the religious status quo. The final outcome was neither glorious nor profound. The Peace of Augsburg in 1555 decreed that each state would adopt the faith of its ruler. Whatever its shortcomings, that compromise is still detectable, more than 400 years later, in the religious geography of Europe.

John Calvin was a quiet, determined intellectual who developed Luther's ideas into his own system of thought. This contemporary caricature may be satirizing Calvin's taste for high living: the baby chicken, drumstick, fish and lustrous fur collar draw a contrast between the way Calvin lived and his puritanical teachings, symbolized by his books.

Wielding a giant quill, Martin Luther writes his theses against the sale of indulgences on the door of the church at Wittenberg as part of the dream sequence of Frederick the Wise, Elector of Saxony, lying in bed on the right of the painting. Frederick twice protected Luther from the wrath of Rome, on the second occasion hiding him in Wartburg Castle for a year.

The devil pipes a melody through the ear of Martin Luther, using his head as the windbag of a 16th-century bagpipe in this contemporary cartoon. Thus Luther is attacked as being full of the devil's hot air and producing tunes for demonic dances.

The Counter-Reformation

Reacting to the gauntlet thrown down by the reformers in Germany and the north, the Roman Catholic Church counterattacked in two ways. The first was a drive to win back souls, territory and influence lost to the Protestants; the second was the removal of the abuses and unsound teaching criticized by Martin Luther and other reformers. This determined response became known as the Counter-Reformation, or the Catholic Reformation, according to Catholics.

The Roman Church in Europe was, however, divided as to diagnosis, strategy and political allegiance. Some Catholics believed the real questions were about discipline and order within the church, while others recognized that the reformers had identified areas of doctrine that demanded reformulation. And there were those – especially in Spanish and French territories – who acknowledged the need for change, but wanted to control it in their own way – without undue influence from Rome.

Teach us, good Lord, to serve you as you deserve; to give and not to count the cost; to fight and not to heed the wounds; to toil and not to seek for rest; to labour and not to ask for any reward . . .   IGNATIUS OF LOYOLA

The depth and bitterness of the internal disputes are illustrated by the fact that the Council of Trent in the Italian Alps, called by Pope Paul III to redefine doctrine and reform discipline, lasted – albeit with one 10-year break and other shorter interruptions – from 1545 to 1563. Politics and theology were interwoven between the different factions; and the prelates divided into hardliners and compromisers. In the end, the hardliners triumphed. Traditional doctrines on the celebration of the Mass, the existence of purgatory and the sale of indulgences were reaffirmed, making any rapprochement with even the most broad-minded of the reformers inconceivable.

The disciplinary decrees of Trent did help, however, to raise the educational level of the clergy, the religious orders and even laypeople. They also emphasized the pyramidal shape of authority within the church, with the pope over the bishops, the bishops over the clergy, and the clergy over the laity. While this effectively improved church administration, it also made church authority rigid and centralized – and therefore more likely to cross swords with secular governments.

In fact, one of the most important parts of the Counter-Reformation had already begun long before the Council of Trent. This occurred with the founding in 1534 of the Society of Jesus (the Jesuits) – paradoxically at a time when religious orders were under suspicion in the Roman Catholic Church and were constantly denigrated by the reformers. The society provided the church with a formidable combat force against not only the Protestants but also, in the society's view, all forms of heresy, vice and ignorance.

The Jesuits were founded by Ignatius of Loyola (c.1491–1556), a Spanish ex-soldier, and were renowned for their intellectual rigour and the long, arduous training they had to undergo. Neither an enclosed nor a mendicant, or begging, order, they wore no special habit and were available for service anywhere. Also, they owed their allegiance solely to the pope and their own head, who was known as the general. And they grew in numbers at an astonishing rate – an eloquent statement of the attractive ideals they projected in a Christendom that was sickened by the tawdriness of a corrupted church. By the time of his death, over a thousand men had joined Ignatius; within the next century, that number increased 15-fold.

The two notorious instruments of the Counter-Reformation were the Index of Prohibited Books and the Inquisition, which was designed to root out moral and heretical offences within the church. Both have attracted far more notoriety, particularly among Protestant propagandists, than their effectiveness deserves. The recovery of the Catholic Church in northern Europe and its revival in Italy, France and Spain owed much more to firm ecclesiastical government, the reaffirmation of Catholic doctrine at the Council of Trent, and the formation of a professional clergy.

***Ignatius of Loyola**, one of the great figures of the Counter-Reformation, was a former soldier who founded the Jesuit order. He wrote* The Spiritual Exercises, *which form the basis of a four-week retreat of meditation and instruction.*

Ignatius's military training had a lasting impact on him. One of his spiritual exercises, "a meditation on two standards", still in use today, draws on military imagery: ". . . see a great plain, comprising the whole region about Jerusalem, where the sovereign Commander-in-Chief of all the good is Christ our Lord; and another plain about the region of Babylon, where the chief of the enemy is Lucifer . . ." In the exercise, it is necessary to choose between the two standards, just as a mercenary soldier in the 16th century had to decide on whose side he would fight.

S. IGNATY. DE LOYOLA

The Council of Trent, shown here during its final meeting in 1563, was one of the most important councils in the history of the Catholic Church, shaping its response to the challenge of the Protestant Reformation. The soldiers in the foreground emphasize how potentially volatile the proceedings were.

Particular heat was generated in a debate – lasting two years – about the requirement that bishops should live in their dioceses, the areas under their jurisdiction. But beneath the issue lay fundamental questions about the pope's commitment to reform.

It was only when Cardinal Morone became the senior papal legate that headway was made and bishops and cardinals were required to take residence. This was seen as an assault on one of the worst abuses, the accumulation by senior prelates of church appointments.

The basic religious geography of Europe had begun to emerge by the end of the 16th century, after the dust of both the Reformation and Counter-Reformation had settled. France, Spain, southern Germany and Italy were firmly in the Catholic camp with generally small Protestant minorities. In France, many of the small group of Protestants known as Huguenots fled in 1685 to avoid persecution under the Catholic king Louis XIV.

In Scandinavia, northern Germany and Britain – but not Ireland – Catholics were in a minority. The frontier between Catholics and Muslims cut across what was Yugoslavia through Bosnia-Herzegovina, an area where both Christians and Muslims were involved in civil war during the early 1990s.

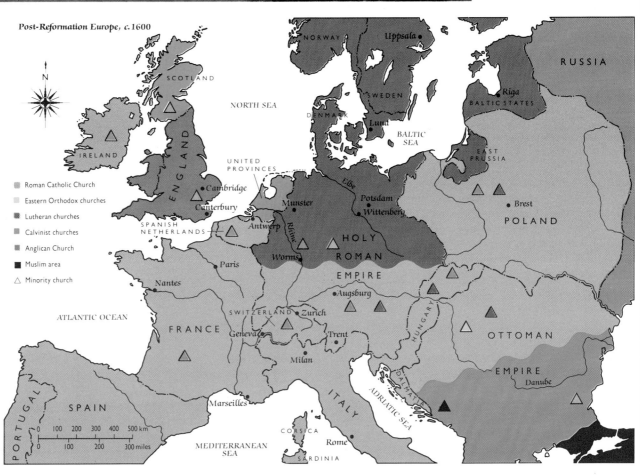

Post-Reformation Europe, c.1600

- Roman Catholic Church
- Eastern Orthodox churches
- Lutheran churches
- Calvinist churches
- Anglican Church
- Muslim area
- △ Minority church

The Path of Spirituality

The history of the church is largely a record of its external affairs – its missionary journeys, doctrinal disputes, wars against heretics and the infidel, the Reformation and Counter-Reformation. Less well known – but no less important – is the church's mystic tradition, in which the inner life takes precedence.

Mysticism may take various forms, both in Christianity and other religions. In general, the aim of Christian mystics is to know or be united with God through a direct interior, often ecstatic, experience – sometimes called the *unio sancta*, or holy union – rather than through the intellect. Thus they put less emphasis on ritual or the Christian community and pursue their vocation through meditation, contemplation or reflection.

Mysticism in Christianity can be traced back to the early fathers of the church, especially desert fathers like St. Antony of Egypt (*c*.251–356), who chose the route of asceticism to personal holiness. Some embraced a "wild and solitary life, without shelter, clothes, food cooked or even cultivated", and most had disciples whom they instructed in the prayer, contemplation and silence that would lead them to the heart of God.

For Gregory of Nyssa (*c*.335–*c*.394) the spiritual life was not one of static perfection but rather one of continuous progress. In his mystical work *Life of Moses*, the Exodus of the Hebrews from Egypt is used as a metaphor to describe the passage of the soul through worldly temptation to a vision of God.

Teresa of Avila, the great Spanish mystic, falls into ecstasy in this sculpture by the 17th-century Italian artist Bernini. Teresa once wrote that she had experienced an ecstasy in which an angel had plunged a fire-tipped spear into her heart, leaving her aflame with a love for God.

Born in 1515, Teresa entered the Carmelite Convent of the Incarnation in Avila when she was 21. At the age of 40, she had a profound religious experience that led her to adopt a more rigorous lifestyle and to leave the convent and found her own in the same town.

Her disciplined life of prayer and fasting led to a series of mystical experiences in which she had direct conversation with Christ. These are described in her four major prose works, of which The Way of Perfection and Interior Mansions are the two best known, as well as her numerous poems and letters.

Christian mysticism has its roots in the isolated and ascetic lifestyle of the Desert Fathers. Antony of Egypt, shown in the painting (OPPOSITE) by the Flemish artist David Teniers (1610–90), was one of the most significant of the Fathers. During his 20-year sojourn in the Egyptian desert, he was beset by a number of temptations that took the form of devilish creatures.

In time, mystical traditions developed within both the western and eastern churches, the latter contributing the important Jesus Prayer – a short prayer addressed to Jesus Christ which is repeated, slowly, meditatively, for long periods. Today the Jesus Prayer is still used, not only in the Orthodox tradition, but also in Roman Catholic and Protestant spirituality worldwide.

The western church in medieval times produced a number of mystics of different hues, including Hildegard of Bingen (1098–1179) in Germany. Also known as the Sibyl of the Rhine, she had the gift of prophecy and recorded her visions in *Scivias*. Continuing the vigorous tradition of feminine spirituality was Julian of Norwich (1342–1416) in England. Her *Revelations of Divine Love* is one of the most remarkable documents of medieval religious experience.

The Counter-Reformation (pp.62–63) brought its own mystical flowering. The partnership between the Spanish Carmelites Teresa of Avila (1515–82) and the poet-mystic John of the Cross (1542–91) was a notable example. Each complemented the other: John was a learned, analytical writer and a poet, while the well-born Teresa, through her friendship with a wide range of people from all walks of life, was able to develop her insight into human nature. Working together in Avila from 1572 to 1577, the two taught the essential unity of human beings – "we aren't angels, we've got bodies", wrote Teresa – and yet the crucial necessity for detachment from worldly activities.

While Spain produced mystics such as Teresa and John, France, too, contributed a steady stream. They include François de Sales (1567–1622), with his special care for the spirituality of "the soldiers' camp, the manual workers' workshop", Blaise Pascal (1623–62), whose *Pensées* have become a religious classic, and, in modern times, Charles de Foucauld (1858–1916).

De Foucauld was an ex-soldier who ended his life as an ascetic in the Algerian desert. To this day, his Little Brothers practise his style of meditation, usually living among the poorest and most neglected of peoples.

Thomas Merton: monk and man of action

The contemplative life continues to enrich the life of the church. One of the most significant figures in this tradition in recent years was Thomas Merton (1915–68). Born in France and educated in England and the United States, Merton shares with the French mystic Charles de Foucauld an early life of comfort and ease, a deep conversion experience, and a restlessness that in Merton's case was satisfied only when he became a Trappist priest in 1949 at an abbey in Louisville, Kentucky. However, it was only when he became a hermit, living largely alone in the forest, that he grew into his deepest spirituality.

Merton found that the nearer he got to the heart of God, the deeper he became involved in the world around him. His writings on prayer and contemplation commanded a huge audience, but by the early 1960s, his writing revealed an increasingly critical attitude to many aspects of American culture, including the Vietnam War. This made him a controversial figure.

Later in life, Merton entered into dialogue with practitioners of the deepest mysticisms in other faiths. While he was at a convention in Bangkok in Thailand to meet such fellow pilgrims, he was accidentally electrocuted and died.

The Scientific Revolution

Caring for the sick

Hospitals originally offered "hospitality" to the sick in body and mind; and the first hospitals in the west were religious foundations, since provision of care for the sick was regarded as a voluntary activity. Today, many Roman Catholic orders have nursing or medical work as their prime function.

Christian hospitals can be traced back to about 370 C.E., when St. Basil of Caesarea, in present-day Turkey, founded a religious institution that also took in the sick, elderly and feeble. St. Basil's example helped to spawn other hospitals in the eastern Roman Empire. In the west, provision for the sick was a major priority at the monastery of Monte Cassino in Italy, founded in the early sixth century; and hospitals were opened at Lyons and Paris in France in 542 and 660, respectively.

In the Middle Ages, hospitals increased in number during the Crusades, when more soldiers died of disease than from the swords of their enemies. In the 11th century, a military order known as the Knights Hospitallers of the Order of St. John was founded which opened up hostels for the sick along some of the pilgrim routes to the Holy Land. The Knights – the ancestors of the present-day St. John Ambulance Corps in Britain – ran a hospital in Jerusalem that housed some 2,000 patients.

Today, the sick in the west are mostly cared for by state-run or private hospitals. But despite the progress of technology in health care, there is still a need for an emphasis on healing that affects both body and soul, and a recognition that a positive mental attitude and a faith in God are elements as important in recovery as peace of mind and personal dignity are to the terminally ill.

Christians derive from Judaism the belief that God created the universe. Although there have been sects that have distrusted or disliked the material world, mainstream Christians have always held in honour the physical universe and living things. However, from the 16th century onward, the progress of science in the west has seriously challenged the Christian view of the origins and nature of the universe and human life.

The first serious scientific tremor to shake the medieval Christian conception of a universe with the earth at its centre came in 1543. In this year, the Polish astronomer Copernicus published a work that argued that it was mathematically more tenable to believe the earth and the other planets revolved around the sun – a proposal that appeared to belittle the earth's status in God's creation. This radical hypothesis was taken up by the Italian astronomer Galileo Galilei (1564–1642), whose book, published in 1632, provoked the wrath of the Inquisition (pp.62–63). Threatened with torture, Galileo recanted and was imprisoned.

Meanwhile, a British contemporary of Galileo named William Harvey (1578–1657) was pioneering research into the human body which showed that it operated on mechanical principles – like the universe – thereby seeming to distance it from God. In 1628, Harvey's discovery of the circulation of the blood, pumped by the heart, made the body seem more like an elaborate piece of machinery than a "living temple" of the soul.

This called into question the relationship between the body and the soul, a matter that still vexes many Christians today. Indeed, whether the body is simply a machine, and how it is connected with a person's identity, is relevant to current debates about abortion, *in vitro* fertilization, artificial insemination by donor, transplant surgery and genetic engineering.

Holding placards aloft, pro- and anti-abortion protesters demonstrate in Miami in 1989. Abortion is one of the issues that deeply divides Christians today. There are those who argue that a foetus is a person, with a soul, from the moment of conception and therefore has a right to live. Others, however, maintain that a foetus becomes a person only in the later stages of pregnancy and that women have a right to choose what to do with their own bodies.

> ## I am here to obey and I have not held this opinion.
>
> GALILEO, RECANTING HIS VIEWS UNDER THREAT OF TORTURE

Perhaps the greatest scientific challenge to Christianity came in the 19th century with the epoch-making book *The Origin of Species* by the British naturalist Charles Darwin (1809–82). Published in 1859, the book proposed a theory of evolution based on natural selection, or survival of the fittest. Many Victorian churchmen found its startling suggestion that humans were descended from apes – not Adam and Eve – deeply offensive to the Creator. Some stoutly defended the literal truth of the creation stories in the Book of Genesis. Others accepted the concept of evolution, but wished to exclude humankind from its process.

It was only when modern biblical scholars (pp.78–79) emphasized the theological rather than the historical

intent of many of the Bible stories that most Christians accepted that whatever its scientific merits, Darwin's theory did not affect the central concerns of the Bible: that humanity is ultimately dependent on God, but constantly seeks to claim independence from him. Although Darwin has proved influential – and his ideas are still being revised – there are many fundamentalist Christians, often called creationists, who still defend the literal truth of the Genesis accounts of creation.

Despite the challenge of science, however, many Christians are far from being antiscientific. While they are concerned about the possible misuse of science, most Christian theologians see science as the use of God-given intelligence to learn more about the wonder of creation. Even highly abstract and complex mathematics can excite theological interest.

A recent example was "chaos theory", one application of which is to show that small changes in one part of the world lead to substantial changes elsewhere. The theory's implied interdependence of all things repeats a theme much emphasized by medieval Christian mystics.

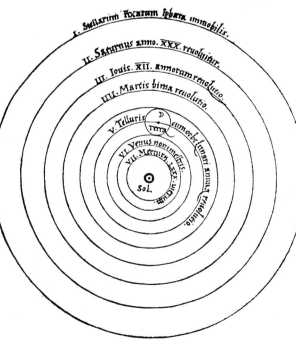

Galileo is tried by the Inquisition in 1633 in this contemporary painting by an unknown Italian artist (ABOVE). *Galileo is seated in the centre facing a rank of judges, with a scribe behind him. He was forced to recant his opinion that the sun was the centre of the universe, an idea first put forward by the Polish astronomer Copernicus.*

The illustration (LEFT) from Copernicus's book, On the Revolutions of the Heavenly Spheres, *shows the sun (Sol) at the centre of the universe, with the planets, including earth, or Terra, orbiting around it. The book was placed on the church's Index of Prohibited Books in the year of Galileo's trial.*

Revival

The primacy given to science and human reason in the west during the period known as the Enlightenment in the 18th century posed an intellectual challenge to the church. Many Christians, especially the Deists whose belief in God was based on reason, denied the irrational aspects of religion such as mysticism, miracles and prophecy. They preferred a cool, "reasonable" Christianity that appealed to the mind rather than to the heart. This trend provoked a reaction in the form of evangelical revival movements, particularly Methodism, that sought to breathe new life into the souls of the believers.

The earliest of these movements was the Moravian Brethren, founded in 1722 by Count Nicholas von Zinzendorf at Herrnhut in eastern Germany. Based on the Bible, prayers and good works, the Moravian approach to personal holiness gained support in Prussia and Saxony, and beyond. By the mid-18th century,

John Wesley preaches in the open air in this detail from an 18th-century painting. Filled with the conviction that people must hear the good news of salvation, Wesley became an itinerant evangelist and made Christianity accessible to all.

As the Anglican Church's opposition to his enthusiasm grew, Wesley was not allowed to preach in churches and he began ordaining his own ministers. The outcome was that Methodism, which had begun as a society within the Anglican Church, became a separate church in 1795.

George Whitefield, one of the most accomplished Methodist preachers, displays his power to move people with words in this 18th-century painting. Even his bearing commanded respect and his plain, often fiery, language added greatly to the fervour of his message.

Wesley in Georgia

In 1735, John Wesley, the founder of Methodism, went to Georgia on a two-year missionary journey, which proved to be unsuccessful. But it did prepare him for the conversion experience he had a year after he returned home in 1737.

Wesley arrived in the colony with his brother Charles and two companions. He became a chaplain in Savannah, from where he hoped to evangelize the local Choctaw and Creek tribes. Soon after his arrival, he and his friends, arrayed in their full Oxford University gowns and regalia, met Tomo-Chichi, the chief of the Lower Creeks. The occasion was not a happy one. Whatever the chief made of these strange white men, Wesley made little of the Creeks. And, despite repeated attempts to launch a grand mission, his contact with the Indians remained superficial and unavailing.

In the meantime, Wesley was having trouble with the colonists. He fell in love with Sophia Hopkey, the local magistrate's daughter, who refused Wesley's two roundabout proposals of marriage. In a fit of pique he renewed his determination to convert the Native Americans, and she quickly married another man. Wesley retaliated by refusing her Holy Communion, whereupon her parents and parents-in-law had Wesley tried on a number of charges and spread the rumour that he had tried to make Sophia his mistress.

Wesley defended himself vigorously, and when the court postponed its findings but suspended him from his duties, he decided to escape. Although prohibited from leaving the colony, he walked through swamp and forest to Charlestown and, on December 2, 1737, boarded the *Samuel* and sailed for England. "What have I learned?" he wrote in his journal. "Why, what I least suspected, that I who went to America to convert others, was never myself converted to God."

there were evangelizing Moravian communities in South Africa, the United States and the Caribbean.

The revival movement that came to have the most influence was Methodism, established in Britain by the Anglican John Wesley (1703–91). It was named for the "methodical" study and prayer practised by members of the Holy Club, founded by Wesley at Oxford University in 1729. With this club, Wesley's aim was to bring together like-minded Anglicans. They all emphasized the necessity of personal conversion, attended by a heightened emotion, and the hope of personal salvation. Among Wesley's fellow founders were his brother Charles, who became famous for his hymn writing, and the talented orator George Whitefield (1714–70).

In 1738, Wesley himself underwent a profound emotional conversion experience, during which he felt a sense of God's forgiveness of his sins. Three years later, he and his colleagues began an extensive missionary campaign all over Britain and Ireland. Travelling up to 8,000 miles a year on horseback, they preached Methodism to thousands of people, mainly in working communities. At a time of increased industrialization with its attendant urban slums, Methodism provided a ray of hope of salvation to the poor.

Methodism spread to the United States through the efforts of George Whitefield, whose visits began in 1739. By 1770, Methodism had become well established east of the Mississippi and, through the energies of the British preacher Francis Ashbury (1745–1816), it spread to the Midwest.

The revivalist message that Whitefield preached – namely that personal salvation comes only through' God's grace and faith in Jesus Christ – was echoed in the preaching of the New England minister Jonathan Edwards (1703–58). Both men were associated with the series of revivals in different regions of the United States known as the Great Awakening, which lasted from about 1728 to 1750 and reached its peak in the 1740s.

The American revivalist tradition was carried into the 19th century by, among others, Charles Finney (1792–1875), an upstate New York Presbyterian, and Dwight L. Moody (1837–99). Moody, who brought revivalism to urban areas, was backed by his colleague and song-leader, Ira D. Sankey. In the 20th century, the revivalist banner has been firmly grasped by, among others, Billy Graham (1918–), whose preaching has stirred large audiences throughout the world.

The evangelical revival, however, went beyond its emphasis on personal salvation to include social involvement. At the end of the 18th and throughout the 19th centuries, there were many evangelicals on both sides of the Atlantic who worked to improve prisons, care for the mentally ill, reform prostitutes, and provide for the blind and deaf. In Britain, notable evangelicals included William Wilberforce (1759–1833), whose efforts to abolish slavery there culminated in government legislation in 1833; and Lord Shaftesbury (1801–85), who in 1874 helped to pass a law that improved the conditions of factory workers.

> *I fear, wherever riches have increased, the essence of religion has decreased in the same proportion.*
>
> JOHN WESLEY

Great revivals have usually owed their momentum and popularity to the charismatic gifts of one or two figureheads, such as Dwight Moody and Ira Sankey in 19th-century America. With their histrionic gifts and catchy tunes, these two men attracted huge audiences such as this one in Brooklyn (LEFT).

Billy Graham, his face projected on a screen (ABOVE) the better to project his message at a meeting in 1989, has his roots in the same tradition as Moody and Sankey. But during his long ministry, spanning 40 years, he has moved closer to the mainstream churches than they ever were.

Into Africa

The spread of Christianity in "Darkest Africa" has been a relatively recent phenomenon compared with the church's efforts in the Americas and other parts of the world (pp.68–69). By the middle of the 18th century, except for the ancient churches of Egypt and Ethiopia, there were only a few isolated trading settlements or military garrisons where Christianity could be found in sub-Saharan Africa.

African missions first began at the end of the 18th century at the Cape of Good Hope at the southern tip of Africa, where a more or less settled and sophisticated European colony had been established since the mid-17th century. Missionaries often faced extreme hostility from settlers, who resented their attentions toward the native Africans, whom the settlers regarded as both beyond the bounds of civilization and competitors for land. Elsewhere in Africa, missionary activity was slow, patchy, largely ineffective, and inhibited by disease, poor communications and a failure to adapt the faith to Africa's cultural environment.

During the course of the next century, three things changed this situation. The first was a renewed confidence in their own effectiveness on the part of the churches of the west which related to their mainly successful efforts in the struggle to end the slave trade. The second was the association of evangelism with the expansion of trade, a link that was especially attractive to the rapidly industrializing countries of Germany and Britain. The third was the scramble for African colonies that gripped the major European powers in the late 19th

African Independent churches

One of the most rapidly growing parts of Christendom today is that represented by the African Independent churches, which became established during the early part of the 20th century. Within these churches, there is a wide diversity of Christian practice; perhaps the only feature they all share is independence – and usually a certain amount of suspicion – of the mainline mission churches.

Many African Independent churches are limited to one gathered congregation; and some depend crucially upon a charismatic leader – for instance, William Harris and Simon Kimbangu, founders of the Harris Church in Ivory Coast and the Kimbanguist Church in Zaire (p.203). These figures are venerated – critics would say worshipped – along with the traditional Christian saints or even Jesus himself. Other congregations depend less on one founder's memory, but still tend to be dominated by one or two charismatic individuals.

The effectiveness of these churches lies in the ease with which they combine some Christian teaching with traditional African concerns and spirituality. For example, they emphasize healing, dance and song, story and re-enactment, hierarchy and defined status, thus giving a sense of security and identity to members of societies often under intense social and economic stress.

The grand Presbyterian cathedral of St. Michael and All Angels in Blantyre, Malawi, with its imposing Victorian architecture, would look more at home in one of the Scottish cities of the missionaries who built it in the late 19th century. To Africans at this time, this awesome building would have spoken of an alien God – a powerful, impressive and demanding God who needed such a grand residence.

Even today, in the modern industrial city that Blantyre has become, the cathedral looks strange and overly imposing against its African backdrop.

century. This subsequently led to the imposition of European administration on virtually the whole of Africa and made the missionary almost indistinguishable, in African eyes, from the colonial official.

The first period of concerted missionary activity occurred between 1830 and 1870, during which time the great British explorer David Livingstone (1813–73) made epic journeys through eastern and central Africa. These journeys epitomized the new missionary vigour and the connection between, in his words, "commerce and Christianity". The direct results of his work were the founding of the successful Scottish Presbyterian mission in what was then Nyasaland (modern Malawi) and the launching of the Anglican Universities' Mission to central Africa.

> ## I go back to Africa to try to make an open path for commerce and Christianity.
>
> DAVID LIVINGSTONE

Livingstone's legacy was perhaps even more important in giving to African missions in many countries of the west a romance and an urgency that no other mission field has ever enjoyed. The result was intense rivalry between different denominations at the end of the 19th and beginning of the 20th centuries. This competition became so fierce that colonial administrators allocated regions to different religious groups, and then restricted them to their allotted territory. It gave the national churches of the colonial powers – Anglican in British colonies, Roman Catholic in French and Belgian – a natural advantage over, for example, the Methodist and Baptist missions.

Despite interdenominational rivalry, however, the influence of the African missions of this period was considerable. Schools and hospitals were built and staffed, new crops were introduced, and agriculture was improved. Skills were transferred to an emerging African middle class, and some of the crueller edges of colonialism were softened with settlers sometimes being called to account. As a result, the number of converts grew and grew.

However, whether western Christianity ever really entered the lifeblood of Africa is still debated. Certainly with the ending of the colonial era, mainly in the 1950s and '60s, the newly independent states treated the mission churches with polite indifference. As their social role in the community was taken over – often less than successfully – by the state and they were challenged by the African Independent churches (*opposite*), the major churches were forced increasingly on to the defensive. Perhaps it will take another generation of genuinely African leadership to find a style and voice that will match the historic traditions of the faith to those of African spirituality.

A sketch map of Africa drawn by the British colonial administrator, Sir Harry Johnston, in 1886 and headed "How Africa Should be Divided" sums up the European attitude toward Africa as a land to be colonized at this time. In fact, it is a remarkably accurate representation of how Africa was parcelled out among the European powers at the end of the 19th century with little regard for the Africans.

Britain and France contested supremacy in western Africa; Britain and Portugal in the south. The Belgian king claimed the Congo basin as his own personal estate. But when his administration was revealed as being excessively corrupt, the Belgian government took over the territory as a colony, acquiring an area of land 80 times greater than its own country.

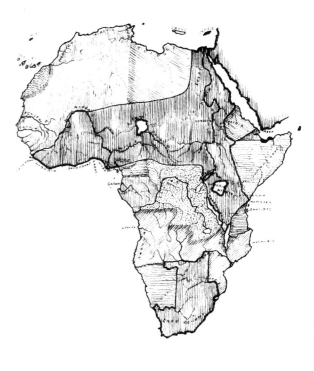

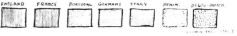

David Livingstone's travels in Africa, his denunciations of the slave trade, and the aura of romance surrounding his name aroused enthusiasm for the missionizing of central Africa. His extensive journeys (BELOW) covered more than six countries in a modern atlas; they included his walk from the west coast to the east coast of Africa on his first journey and his expedition along the Zambezi, or "God's highway to the interior". So vast was the area he covered, it was beyond the resources of Christendom to missionize it effectively for another 50 years.

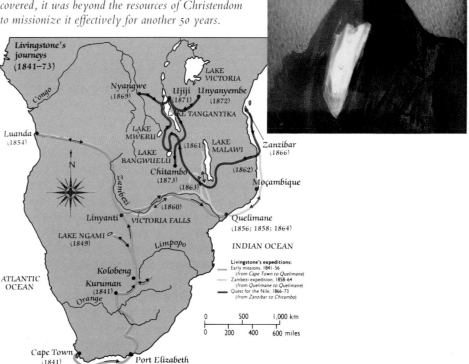

The Orthodox Tradition

Dominant symbol of the Russian Orthodox Church, the cathedral of St. Basil the Blessed, with its multicoloured onion domes, dominates the southern end of Red Square, Moscow. Built between 1554 and 1560 to commemorate the defeat of the Mongols by Ivan the Terrible, the cathedral was originally dedicated to the Virgin Mary. Legend has it that the architect was blinded after completing the work so that he could never create anything like it again.

After the formal split between the western (Roman) and eastern (Byzantine) churches of Christendom in 1054 (pp.54–55), the eastern, or Orthodox, Church followed its own path. Based on the patriarchate of Constantinople, it continued its Greek-oriented tradition with its own liturgy, hymns, lines of authority and emphasis on icons. Over the following centuries, different shoots developed from the main Orthodox root, including the national churches of Greece, Russia, Bulgaria, Romania and Serbia.

The most influential Orthodox branch over the last 500 years has been the Russian Church. It was first founded by Grand Prince Vladimir of Kiev (956–1015) with the mass baptism of largely illiterate and puzzled Kiev citizens in 989, a year after the prince himself had been baptized into the faith by Greek missionaries. Vladimir's motive, at least in part, was to gain entry into the league of Christian nations and expand trade with the west. But the Grand Prince was faced with the dilemma of deciding to which part of the divided church he should attach himself: Rome or Constantinople. Subtly, he hedged his bets, establishing an independent church with Roman organization, but with Orthodox Byzantine ritual.

This divided loyalty was short-lived, however. Vladimir's successor threw in his lot with the Orthodox Church, and in turn his successors maintained relations with the patriarchs of Constantinople, even after Russia was overrun by the Mongol Tartars in three campaigns between 1237 and 1241. In fact, the Mongols, whose dominance of Russia lasted until 1480, proved remarkably tolerant of the Russian Church, in stark contrast to the Turks after they sacked Constantinople.

To some Orthodox Christians, both in Russia and in Greece, the fate of Constantinople was richly deserved because of the compromise of recognizing Roman authority made by the Byzantine emperor and the patriarch of Constantinople at the Council of Florence in 1439. Although this compromise was born out of political necessity, that is, to enlist western help against the continuing Turkish threat, members of the Russian Church, like many of the Greek Church, refused to take it any further.

The fall of Constantinople had more serious repercussions for the Greek Church than for the Russian. Churches fell into disrepair. Clergy were not trained. Bishoprics were sold to the highest bidder. Young males of any physical or intellectual merit were routinely taken into slavery. The Greek Church was in crisis.

Thus, the Russian Church inevitably became the most influential, and numerically the largest, Orthodox Church, especially after the liberation of Russia from the Mongol Tartars in 1480. Little more than a century later, the creation of the patriarchate in Moscow in 1589 made the city a major religious centre, as a result of which it claimed the title Third Rome.

It was not until the 18th century that the Russian and Greek Orthodox churches came closely into contact again. Under Catherine the Great (1762–96), the Russian Empire extended southward to include the Black Sea and abut the empire of the Ottoman Turks. After a period of confrontation with the Turks, the Russians won the right to protect the Orthodox living under Ottoman rule.

Such an offer is in itself symptomatic of the close relationship between the Russian Orthodox Church and the Russian state. These ties continued more or less unchallenged until the Russian Revolution in 1917. However, the Russian Orthodox Church was to pay dear for the alliance during the next 70 years under communist rule. Since the breakup of the Soviet Union in the early 1990s, the resulting new political order has created new opportunities for the Russian Church to emerge from its dark age and confront the religious, social and political challenges of the late 20th century.

Mount Athos, monks and mysticism

On the rocky Chalcidice peninsula in northern Greece, Mount Athos is the principal centre of Orthodox monasticism in the world. The entire peninsula is given over to monastic life and, in its heyday at the end of the 14th century, 40,000 monks are thought to have lived here. The number has since dwindled to about 1,500.

The first monastery was founded in 963 by a monk who became known as St. Athanasius the Athonite. There are now 20 monasteries, including St. Dionysius (RIGHT) on the western coast. Some are tied to national churches, such as those of Greece, Russia and Bulgaria; many contain manuscripts and treasures of Orthodox art. There are three distinct ways of living for monks on Athos: in a community; as ascetics attached to and under the direction of a monastery; and as isolated hermits, many of whom live on inaccessible rocky promontories and receive their food delivered via a basket on a rope.

It was on Mount Athos that the Orthodox mystical tradition known as Hesychasm ("Peace") became established in about the 13th century; it is still much practised there. It consists of the constant recitation of a prayer, which is designed to bring the soul to a tranquil state of repose in communion with God.

Hesychasm gained fresh popularity with the publication in 1782 of the *Philocalia* ("love of what is beautiful"), an anthology of mystical writings drawn from 38 Fathers of the church from the 4th to the 15th centuries. The book was translated into Slavonic and Russian and helped to produce a spiritual revival in 19th-century Russia.

The slow, carefully orchestrated style of Orthodox worship, as shown in this cathedral in Ukraine, serves to remind worshippers that they are in a different realm, where the normal pace and structure of communication give way to something more profound. This is enhanced by the sanctified atmosphere created by chandeliers and candles, whose points of light glint off the traditional Orthodox icons and other surfaces.

Although there is little participation by the congregation, there is much repetition in the liturgy and this, combined with the slow-moving grandeur of the service, can have an almost hypnotic effect on worshippers.

Reading the Bible

Until the 18th century, the authority of the Bible remained more or less unchallenged by Christians. However, the development of biblical criticism, particularly in the 19th and 20th centuries, has led many Christians to the conclusion that the Bible can be read at many levels and from different perspectives. The exceptions are fundamentalist Christians, who hold that the scriptures are unerring.

During the 19th century, textual critics continued the process begun by the 16th-century Protestant reformers of examining biblical manuscripts to assess which gave the truest reading of contested passages. And historical-literary, or "higher", critics looked at the scriptures to discover the literary methods used by biblical authors and the cultural context in which they lived. Anomalies were highlighted, such as the two different accounts of the creation of the world in Genesis; and some books, such as Isaiah, were shown to have been written by more than one person. The effect of this was to undermine the absolute and literal authority of the Bible.

In fact, interpretation of the Bible is almost as old as Christianity itself. The New Testament writers were themselves interpreting both the Old Testament, to show how Christianity could broadly be seen as its "fulfilment", and the events of Jesus' life, to make good the early Christian claim that Jesus was "the Son of God". The early Christian Fathers, such as Augustine of Hippo (354–430), developed their own methods of interpretation, often using allegory. For example, Abraham's sons Ishmael and Isaac could be construed to represent and prefigure Judaism and the new church of Christ, respectively.

Allegory was a favourite interpretative device throughout the Middle Ages. To a degree, the Protestant reformers (pp.60–61) reacted against this trend, tending to revert to a more literal interpretation of the Bible in an attempt to recover the "pure" text.

Protestants have tended to be in the forefront of modern biblical scholarship, perhaps because of the emphasis that they place on the responsibility of the

David Strauss (1808–74) (LEFT), the controversial German theologian, broke new ground in 19th-century biblical interpretation. He was roundly condemned for describing the Gospels as historical myth in The Life of Jesus Critically Examined and was expelled from his university teaching job as a result. Today, however, his ideas and theories are respected by biblical critics.

individual to bring critical but open attention to bear on the word of God. It was German Protestants, for example, who led the way in textual and higher criticism during the 19th century and they who developed "form" criticism at the start of the 20th century.

Form criticism, pioneered by the theologian Martin Dibelius (1883–1947), analyses styles of speech and writing to detect patterns of writing which point to the context in which the passages were conceived and/or used. In the Gospels, form critics have distinguished a writing form they call a "paradigm", by which a saying of Jesus is reinforced by a story to illustrate its point. For example, the story of the landowner who hired labourers at different hours of the day (Matthew 20:1–16) is used to illustrate the saying: "Thus the last will be first, and the first, last."

Form criticism has been supplemented since the 1950s and '60s by the "tradition and criticism" school, which analyses the way in which oral traditions have been incorporated into a text or have influenced its structure.

And from the 1970s to the present, biblical scholars have been joined by scholars in literary criticism who read the scriptures as a literary artefact, studying its dramatic or lyrical qualities as they would a Shakespeare play or a poem by Robert Frost.

We have to learn to let God show us what he wants us to see.

GERMAN THEOLOGIAN KARL BARTH (1886–1968)

Since the 1960s, some Christians have brought a particular perspective to their reading of the Bible. Blacks may read it as the story of liberation; women may find too much of it rooted in an oppressively patriarchal society; and those working with the poor in the third world may give precedence to the Gospel theme of the priority of the poor.

Spreading the word

Christians have constantly experimented with popular ways to communicate the Gospel. In the Middle Ages, mystery plays combined serious teaching about Jesus' life with often bawdy entertainment and comments on current events. However, the Passion play at Oberammergau in Germany, which has been performed every decade for more than 350 years, is simple, direct and usually restrained. Interspersed with the scenes of the play are living "tableaux", often based on famous paintings, of biblical events, such as Jesus' Last Supper (LEFT). That Christians are ever alert to fresh ways of presenting the Gospel is shown by this 1950s British comic strip (BELOW), which also depicts the Last Supper, albeit in a more popular form.

From medieval times to the present, the Christian Gospel has been proclaimed in a variety of literary forms and media, including dramatic productions, poetry, prose, song lyrics and even comic strips. In the Middle Ages, mystery plays were a popular genre that brought to the common people parts of the Gospel, especially the Passion, that is, the suffering of Jesus during the last moments of his life and his death on the cross. And the Passion is also the subject of the famous play performed every 10 years by the people of Oberammergau in Upper Bavaria, Germany,

as an expression of thanks to God for delivering them from the plague in 1633.

The 1970s musicals *Jesus Christ Superstar* and *Godspell* brought, as the mystery plays did in their time, the Christian message in an entertaining form to 20th-century audiences. The message has also been carried by singers in the folk and popular traditions, such as Bob Dylan and Cliff Richard.

Poetry is ideally suited to conveying religious truths because its often imagistic language allows it to express the abstract and ineffable better than prose. Christianity has inspired poets in many languages, giving rise to some of the most famous western literature. This includes the great epic poems the *Divine Comedy* of Dante (1265–1321), with its vision of hell, purgatory and heaven in the afterworld; *Paradise Lost* by John Milton (1608–74), which describes the Fall of Man and its consequences; and *Ash Wednesday* by the American-born poet T.S. Eliot (1888–1965), which explores the poet's own crisis of faith.

In general, hymns, an important medium of Christian instruction, especially in preliterate societies, fail to produce great poetry, perhaps because they are too concerned with doctrinal propositions. For example, the great hymn writers of the evangelical revival (pp.72–73), such as John and Charles Wesley and Isaac Watts, were not seeking to raise questions about the meaning of life. They were encapsulating key Christian dogmas in easily remembered lines that uneducated people could make their own.

In an upstairs room in Jerusalem, on Thursday evening . . .

THIS IS MY LAST SUPPER WITH YOU.

WHAT DO YOU MEAN?

ONE OF YOU IS GOING TO BETRAY ME . . .

BETRAY YOU? ONE OF US?

The Shattered World

The 20th century has witnessed an unprecedented scale of violence, principally in the form of two world wars. For Christians, these and other conflicts have raised profound ethical dilemmas. In particular, they called into question the concept of a "just war", that is, one whose cause can be justified in Christian terms.

The two world wars (1914–18 and 1939–45) provoked a critical self-appraisal within the Christian churches. For the antagonists were in the main Christian countries, with the notable exception of Japan. How could God be on both sides at once? In addition, Christians on either side of the conflicts were split between those who saw their countries' cause as just, and therefore godly, and those who saw the Christian call to nonviolence as prior.

The dilemma for Christians was perhaps reflected most poignantly in Nazi Germany itself, before and during World War II. In the 1930s, the Lutheran Church had generally been supportive of Hitler, appreciating his attempt to overcome the country's economic and social chaos, re-establish a sense of dignity, and clean up the excesses of moral permissiveness. They were further flattered by Hitler's offer of a deal whereby the church would legitimize his regime in exchange for a role in the moral purification of the German people.

The minority view, that of the so-called Confessing Church, emerged only with the formation of a group of Christians who drafted their beliefs and standpoint in the Barmen Declaration in 1934. Led by Martin Niemöller (1892–1984) and Dietrich Bonhoeffer (1906–45), this group spearheaded the Christian resistance to Hitler, which ultimately led to Bonhoeffer's arrest in 1943 and his execution two years later.

After the war, the healing of the divisions between those Christians who had been loyal to Hitler and held senior rank in the Nazi movement and those who had opposed him was long, slow and painful. It was made more difficult by the full realization in the final months of the war of the genocide of Jews, usually known as the Holocaust (p.37).

While Christian churches have been guilty of anti-Semitism throughout their history, the scale and horror of the Holocaust shocked Christians all over the world, leading to a reassessment of Christian-Jewish relations. One result of this was the declaration of the Second Vatican Council (1962–65) that "the Jews should not be represented as repudiated or cursed by God, as if such views followed from the Holy Scriptures".

Another moral question that tested Christians and divided their ranks was the use of nuclear bombs against the Japanese. The Christian view of the just war, more persuasive in Roman Catholic than Protestant circles, condemns the killing of civilians. The death or injury of more than 100,000 Japanese at Hiroshima convinced many Christians that the ends of nuclear warfare could not justify the means. This argument was used not only against the actual use of nuclear weapons but also against their threatened use, and thus cut at the root of western defence strategy from 1945 to the present.

Christian churches since 1945 have also found themselves deeply divided on such issues as armed resistance to racist or oppressive states, for example in South Africa, Nicaragua and El Salvador, and conscription (in South Africa and former communist Poland). This has led some Christians to suggest the intriguing possibility of a "new ecumenism"; that is, a new alignment of Christians that cuts through denominational lines and groups politically left-of-centre Christians from all mainstream churches into one community of faith, and right-of-centre Christians into another.

> **It is infinitely easier to suffer physical death than to endure spiritual suffering.**
>
> DIETRICH BONHOEFFER

A British Royal Air Force chaplain addresses servicemen during World War I, adopting as his pulpit the nose of a biplane. The band on the left stands by to lend rousing musical accompaniment. Despite the invaluable role fulfilled by priests in the armed forces, many modern Christians are uneasy about the church appearing to "bless" military activity.

Dietrich Bonhoeffer was a considerable theological scholar, and his work on the nature of the Christian community is still widely appreciated. He is best known for his Letters and Papers from Prison, *composed while he was awaiting execution by the Nazis.*

Creation from destruction

After World War II, Christians in Europe were faced with the task of rebuilding a huge number of churches throughout the continent. This was especially true in Germany, where carpet bombing of cities such as Dresden and the final offensive by the Allies on the German heartland had destroyed churches on a scale unprecedented in the bloodsoaked history of Europe.

Many churches were rebuilt to their original design and, where possible, to their original specification. Others were so seriously damaged that the only course was to start again in a new idiom. For example, the Kaiser Wilhelm I Memorial Church (LEFT) in Berlin was built next to the ruins of its 19th-century predecessor, which was destroyed during the war. And the pilgrimage church of Notre-Dame-du-Haut in the Saône Valley, France, designed by the modernist architect Le Corbusier (1887–1965), was built to replace a chapel also ruined during the war.

It was not only architects and builders who were involved in the re-creation and continuation of the Christian heritage after the war. Churches and cathedrals have always been embellished externally and internally by specialist craftspeople and artists, including stonemasons, carpenters, silversmiths, stained-glass workers, painters, embroiderers and metalworkers.

This tradition has continued to thrive. At Chichester Cathedral in southern England, for example, the Anglo-German Tapestry (BELOW), finished in 1985, was handwoven in both England and Germany. At Coventry Cathedral in central Britain, consecrated in 1962, a galaxy of internationally renowned artists, such as the painter John Piper (1903–92) and the sculptor Sir Jacob Epstein (1880–1959), was gathered to beautify a structure that stands next to the preserved ruins of the old cathedral, bombed in 1940.

The old and the new buildings of the Kaiser Wilhelm I Memorial Church in Berlin stand side by side, creating a striking and cohesive unit. Most of the medieval building, except for the bell tower, was destroyed in a World War II bombing raid. After the war, the ruin was cleverly combined by the architect Egon Eiermann with the dramatically simple modern church alongside it, and the whole has become a symbol of postwar Berlin.

Symbol of unity and peace, the Anglo-German Tapestry, worked by weavers in both England and Germany, adorns Chichester Cathedral, England. It was dedicated to St. Richard and George Bell, bishop of Chichester from 1929 to 1958. Bell supported the Confessing Church in its opposition to Hitler and also criticized the indiscriminate bombing of German cities by the Allies. With its abstract design in bold, vibrant colours, the tapestry forms a dramatic backdrop in keeping with the modern lines of the altar.

The 20th-Century Challenge

The Archbishop of Canterbury, George Carey, attired in full regalia, talks to Orthodox priests in London, England, symbolizing the growing dialogue between denominations. As spiritual head of the Anglican Communion, Carey is a pivotal figure in the ecumenical movement, since the Anglican Church has long seen itself as a link between Catholics, Orthodox and Protestants. However, in the early 1990s, many Christians doubt whether ecumenism can prosper, especially with the Orthodox and Roman Catholic churches in conflict in many eastern European countries.

In common with other world religions, Christianity has had to come to terms with more technical and social change in the last 100 years than in the rest of its history. Inevitably, severe tensions have developed between those Christians who wish to preserve the tradition of the church and those who wish to respond creatively to the new challenges thrown up by rapidly changing societies. This tension has been highlighted in different ways. Three of the most important conflicts are in the realms of ecumenism – the drawing together of different churches – liturgy and ethics.

In modern times, the ecumenical movement began in the early years of the 20th century, initially as a response to the need of Protestant missionaries in Africa to present a united front to the native peoples. Over the years, other factors that have drawn different churches together include the perceived threat of the prevailing materialism of advanced societies; the rise of a vigorous, proseletyzing Islam, especially in Africa; and, not least, theological scholarship, which tends to emphasize the cultural relativity of much doctrine.

Formally, the ecumenical movement has been led by the World Council of Churches (constituted in 1948) – a slightly misleading title since the Roman Catholic Church has never joined the council, despite a brief flirtation in the 1970s. By the middle of the 1980s, however, the World Council was running out of steam, partly because, having cleared away centuries' worth of suspicion and misunderstanding, churches seemed content to remain in a friendly but still divided relationship. And in 1992, the decision by the General Synod of the Anglican Church to allow the ordination of women priests was widely seen as a barrier to closer ties with the Catholic and Orthodox churches.

There are, however, some striking cases of Protestant denominations actually merging. In Canada, Methodists, Presbyterians and Congregationalists merged in 1925, and in India, the Church of South India was formed in 1947 out of a combination of Anglican, Methodist and other church traditions. But they are exceptions, and the difficulty experienced in becoming united perhaps serves more as a warning than as an encouragement to others.

Tension between tradition and the modern world has also manifested itself in worship. In this area, the major conflicts have been within the Roman Catholic Church itself, in which a watershed was reached with the modernization of the liturgy by the Second Vatican Council (1962–65). This was done by, for example, dropping the universal language of Latin, encouraging greater participation of laypeople, simplifying church ritual, and reducing the emphasis on the priest as a mediator between people and God.

There can be little doubt that for some Catholics these reforms have transformed their understanding not only of worship but of the whole of their faith, making it seem more accessible and relevant. Equally, however, there are others who think that in this process a sense of

Pentecostalists and Charismatics

Since World War II, one of the fastest-growing parts of the church has been the Pentecostal movement. Its adherents believe they can have the same experience that the first Christians had on the day of the Pentecost (Acts 2:1–4), when they received the gift of "speaking in tongues" from the Holy Spirit. Since the 1960s, the movement has become part of mainstream churches – including Roman Catholicism – where it is known as the Charismatic Renewal.

Speaking in tongues, or glossolalia, is usually understood to mean speaking a strange language – an "ecstatic utterance" – unknown to the speaker, which can be grasped only by those who have the gift of interpretation. Sometimes it is associated with healing or with the "giving of a word", which may be a word of encouragement, warning or instruction.

Pentecostalists whose worship (BELOW) is marked by uninhibited exuberance and joy also claim other gifts of the Spirit, including prophecy, healing and exorcism.

Pentecostal groups tend to be conservative or even fundamentalist. Some, such as the Assemblies of God, expect their converts to speak in tongues as a matter of course. The Assemblies of God is a particularly successful movement in Latin America (where in some regions members now outnumber Roman Catholics) and in South Korea.

Many who do speak in tongues, however, often overlook the relatively low status accorded to it by St. Paul. He told the church in Corinth in his first letter to the Corinthians that he would much rather they had the gift of prophecy than that of tongues (14:5).

religious awe, of mystery, of contact with the ultimates of the human spirit has been lost.

The most celebrated challenge to the Vatican reforms came from Archbishop Lefebvre (1905–91) of France who sought to establish a counter-church that would protect the "true faith". He died before his plans were fully implemented, and although the style of thinking he articulated lives on, especially in Latin countries, there is now little danger that the modernist issue will split the Roman Catholic Church.

Social changes and the advance of technology have raised new ethical questions and polarized those who wish to maintain the traditional position of the church and those who do not. From the role of women in society to abortion, from transplant surgery to genetic engineering, from the right of resistance to the state to sexual morality in and out of marriage, Christians have debated – and continue to debate – the issues vigorously and generally inconclusively.

It seems to hold true that the firmer the official teaching of the church, the more passionate has been the debate. Classic examples are the Right to Life/Pro Choice campaigns in the United States; and the issue of Catholic opposition to artificial contraception. This was reaffirmed in the 1980s and early 1990s by Pope John Paul II and is a contentious matter in a world whose population is fast outstripping its resources.

> **Brothers, I urge you, in the name of our Lord Jesus Christ, not to have factions among yourselves . . .**
>
> I CORINTHIANS 1:10

John Paul II, pope since 1978, is renowned for his firm stand on traditional Catholic values and his energetic world tours. Here he blesses one of his flock in Nigeria.

A world map of Christianity at the end of the 20th century charts missionary endeavour over the last 400 years. Asia remains largely untouched, except for the Philippines and South Korea. Latin America was an almost exclusive preserve of the Roman Catholic Church, but Protestant sects are now challenging its dominance.

World distribution of Christians

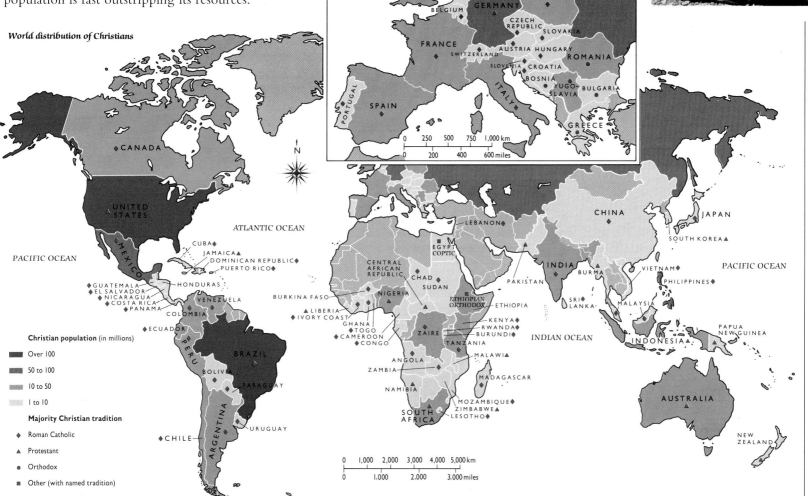

Christian population (in millions)
- Over 100
- 50 to 100
- 10 to 50
- 1 to 10

Majority Christian tradition
- ◆ Roman Catholic
- ▲ Protestant
- ● Orthodox
- ■ Other (with named tradition)

Armed with an automatic weapon, *an Iranian woman parades in the streets of Tehran in support of the revolutionary Shiite Muslim government that came to power in 1979, after the fall of the shah. In theory, Muslim men and women have equal rights and obligations. In practice, however, a woman's duties are generally in the home, although this does not prevent her from having an occupation as a teacher, a nurse or in the police. Moreover, according* to Muslim tradition, or hadith, *women participated in war in the Prophet Muhammad's time.*

Rows of Muslims bow down to pray in the Juma Mosque in Delhi, India. Mosque attendance for prayer (salat) is only mandatory at noon on Fridays, when traditionally a sermon, or khutbah, is delivered. However, Friday is not comparable to the Jewish Sabbath or the Christian Sunday. There is no day-long suspension of everyday work and activity; life goes on in the market and elsewhere except for an interval at noon, when everyone gathers for congregational prayers at the central mosque.

ISLAM

Submission to God

ARABIA IN THE EARLY SEVENTH CENTURY C.E. was a land torn by feuding nomadic Bedouin tribes, living under the shadow of the Christian Byzantine and the Zoroastrian Persian empires. All this changed, however, with a man named Muhammad, a trader from Mecca in what is now Saudi Arabia. Muhammad received divine revelations (pp.88–89) that were to transform not only the region but much of the known world. These revelations – later collected into scriptures known as the Qur'an (Koran) – form the basis of the religion called Islam ("submission [to God]") – a faith that regulates all aspects of people's lives, from eating habits and dress to education and economics.

Within 30 years of Islam being founded, Muslims – those who submit to the will of God, or Allah – exploded out of their Arabian heartland to establish a powerful Islamic empire. Now there are an estimated 860 million Muslims in the world. They form nearly total majorities in countries of the Middle East, northern Africa, central Asia and Indonesia, and also substantial minorities in the west and many other parts of the world.

Early Islam's success inevitably brought it into conflict with Christianity, initially with parts of the Byzantine Empire and later, in the Middle Ages, with the Crusader armies of western Europe (pp.56–57). Now, a thousand years later, God-centred Islam, more vigorous than ever, is challenging the west and its modern traditions of democracy and capitalism, as well as its liberal social values.

Modern western apprehension of Islam began after World War II with the rise of Egypt's Gamel Abdul Nasser as the leader of the Arab world in 1952 and his nationalization of the Suez Canal in 1956, in defiance of the wishes of Britain and France. Another sign of Islam's reassertion occurred 17 years later with the massive increase in oil prices by the Islam-dominated OPEC (Organization of Petroleum Exporting Countries) states in 1973. This not only led to worldwide recession but also made the west aware of the economic muscle of the Muslim Middle Eastern states.

However, any hope Muslims might have had of building a united Arab and/or Islamic front on this stronger economic foundation capsized in 1979 with the Camp David peace treaty between Egypt and Israel – the "old enemy". This was both startling and unwelcome, particularly to the moderate Saudis, who believed it would radicalize Arab politics.

In 1979 came another impetus to Arab radicalism when the shah of Iran was overthrown and replaced by a militant Islamic leadership under the Ayatollah Khomeini. For the west, Khomeini's rule

Submission to God

(1979–89) epitomized an ideology that emphasized living by Islamic law, and condemned western influence and its godlessness. It saw an unprecedented rise in numbers of Muslim fundamentalist movements, especially in the Middle East. Among them was Hizbollah (p.205), one of the principal groups responsible for taking a number of westerners hostage in the Lebanon in the 1980s.

In late 1991 and 1992, the emergence from the ashes of the Soviet Union of mainly Muslim republics, such as Kazakhstan and Uzbekistan, in possession of nuclear weapons was also alarming to the west. Although the newly formed Commonwealth of Independent States agreed that all nuclear weapons would be moved to Russia, this did not alleviate the west's anxiety that former Soviet scientists might be induced to assist potentially hostile Muslim leaders to develop a nuclear capability.

Just as significant as the rise of militant Islam has been the growth of peaceful, and for the most part politically passive, Islam elsewhere in the world. For example, in sub-Saharan Africa its expansion has been much faster in this century – largely due to modern communications – than at any other time since it took root there in the 11th century. Moreover, since the mid-1960s Islam has become an important presence in western society, from the United States to England, France and Germany. No major western European power can any longer afford to ignore the opinion of its own Muslim citizens in its dealings with the Muslim world.

Belief in one God, Allah, is the cornerstone of Islam. Indeed, Islam's purpose from the outset has been to uphold the oneness of God. Muslims regard their holy book, the Qur'an (pp.92–93), as the final, unchanging word of God. However, they also believe that the Jewish Torah (pp.28–29) and Psalms and the Christian Gospels (pp.50–51) are important too, being God's revealed word.

Muslims, therefore, believe in 18 Old Testament Jewish prophets and in John the Baptist and Jesus, and honour them as genuine messengers of God (Arabic *rusul*). They do not, however, follow Christians in believing that Jesus is the Son of God. There is also a belief in various classes of angels, who rank below the prophets and above humankind. Their duties include guarding the gates of hell and recording the thoughts and actions of every individual while on earth. There are also fallen angels, the chief of whom is Satan, called Shaitan or Iblis. While Islam insists that God is the creator of everything, individuals are nonetheless free and will be judged according to their deeds.

For Muslims, there are five main observances, known as the pillars of Islam. The first is a profession of faith (*shahada*) in the oneness of God (Allah): "There is no god but God and Muhammad is his messenger." Muslims are to perform the second pillar, compulsory prayer (*salat*), five times a day, facing toward the holy city of Mecca: at dawn, noon, mid-afternoon, evening and night. Muslims attend communal prayer at the mosque on Fridays, which is preceded by ablutions (*wudu*) to ensure bodily purity.

The third pillar, giving alms or charity to the poor, is also regarded as an act of worship. It is of two kinds: legal (*zakat*), whereby the alms are assessed at one-fortieth of a person's income; and voluntary (*sadaqa*). Fasting (*sawm*), the fourth pillar, is intended to foster obedience to God and unity among Muslims. During Ramadan, the ninth month of the Islamic year, all adult Muslims in good health, excluding pregnant women, fast from dawn until sunset, for 29 or 30 days, depending on the length of the lunar month. The Qur'an is recited daily and one night, the Night of Power (Lailat ul-Qadr), is especially important, for it is believed that on this night the Qur'an was revealed to Muhammad.

Ramadan ends with Eid ul-Fitr, the festival of the breaking of the fast, on the first of Shawwal, the 10th month of the Muslim year. It is a joyful occasion: presents are given, family and friends are visited, and special prayers are said at the mosque. The final pillar of Islam is the pilgrimage, or *hajj* (pp.88–89), to Mecca, which all Muslims are expected to make once in a lifetime.

In addition to the pillars, there is *jihad*, or "striving in the path of God". This is not simply or even primarily holy war against infidels – as it is often perceived in the west. It can take many forms including learning, good works and self control. *Jihad* as holy war is not a pillar, because it is a duty imposed on the community as a whole, not on every individual.

A Muslim Hummumat nomad of Mauritania in west Africa kneels down in the desert to pray. All Muslims pray facing Mecca, and in mosques the direction is indicated by a niche known as the mihrab.

In desert places, other pointers must suffice. For example, the nomadic Tuareg, who are found throughout the Sahel regions of Africa, will dismount from their camels, draw the outline of a mosque-like structure in the sand and, using the sun as their guide, will "enter" the mosque image and perform salat *facing the holy city of Islam.*

Death, judgment and reward

Muslims who are about to die repeat to themselves the *shahada*, the profession of faith: "There is no god but God and Muhammad is his messenger." After death, the body is taken to a Muslim morgue where it is washed and wrapped in a winding cloth, three layers for a man and five for a woman. The burial takes place as soon as possible. The funeral rites involve throwing earth over the body as those present recite the following passage from the Qur'an with its implication of resurrection of the dead: "We created you from it and deposit you into it and from it will take you out once more."

Only God knows when the resurrection of the dead will occur. On the Last Day, the angel Israfil will sound the trumpet and all will rise up from the grave. Except for martyrs, who go directly to their eternal reward, all are interrogated by the angels Munkar and Nakir. They place a book containing the results of their judgment into the right hands of the righteous, for whom every kind of material and spiritual bliss awaits in paradise, which is guarded by the angel Ridwan.

For the damned, the same book will be placed in their left hands. They will then be condemned to the torments of hell, in the charge of the angel Malik. The damned even suffer fire "in their hearts" – the experience of hell, like that of paradise, being both spiritual and physical.

After the judgment, Death is summoned and slain by God. And the prospect of no more death will bring joy to those in heaven and anguish to those in hell.

Coffin bearers carry the deceased during a funeral in Peshawar in Pakistan. Muslim burial customs can vary according to the region; however, cremation is universally forbidden on the grounds that the dead body must be respected and in no way harmed. Also, the head of the dead person is always positioned in the grave facing in the direction of Mecca.

Muhammad, Seal of the Prophets

The Prophet of Islam, Muhammad ibn Abdullah, was born into an aristocratic family declining in wealth, in about 570 C.E. His childhood must have been a difficult time, for he was born just after the death of his father, Abdullah; and his mother, Aminah, died when he was six. His grandfather, Abd al-Muttalib, who had been looking after him, died soon afterward, leaving him in the care of his uncle Abu Talib, head of the Hashimite branch of the Quraish clan.

The Quraish had responsibility for the Ka'aba, a Meccan shrine and place of pilgrimage in pre-Muslim Arabia. Going on pilgrimage and offering sacrifices were two of the main religious practices in pre-Islamic Arabia, where people worshipped natural phenomena, such as trees and rocks, and numerous gods. Among the latter were al-Uzza, the Mighty One, and al'Lat, the great Mother Goddess. Muhammad was familiar not only with indigenous beliefs and practices but also with those of the Jewish and Christian settlers in Arabia.

According to tradition, Muhammad received no formal education and could neither read nor write. However, he found work in commerce in Mecca, managing the caravans of a business lady, Khadija, whom he married at the age of 25. Disturbed by the materialism, intertribal warfare, and polytheism around him, Muhammad began to frequent the caves of Mount Hira, near Mecca, for reflection and meditation.

It is said that while visiting a cave in 610, when he was 40, he had a vision of a majestic being, later identified as the angel Gabriel, and heard a voice. Overwhelmed, he fell prostrate on the ground, only to hear the voice command: "Recite." On asking what to recite, he was told: "Recite: In the Name of thy Lord who created, created Man of a blood-clot." (Qur'an: 96:1–3).

He "was a prophet when Adam was still between water and clay". Then he was born in his created form as the seal of the prophets.

IBN AL-ARABI (d.1240)
QUOTING A TRADITION

The pilgrimage to Mecca

The fifth and final pillar of Islam is the pilgrimage or *hajj* to the holy city of Mecca and its sacred, cube-shaped shrine, the Ka'aba. The pilgrimage takes place during the 12th month, Dhu'hijja, of the Muslim year. All Muslims, and only Muslims, who are physically and financially capable of performing the pilgrimage must do so at least once in a lifetime. More than two million Muslims from around the world and from all walks of life flock to Mecca to make the pilgrimage each year.

Certain traditions state that Adam laid the foundations of the Ka'aba, Abraham restored it, and hundreds of prophets are buried around it. The Ka'aba was a polytheistic shrine housing in its sanctuary innumerable statues of gods, including Hubal, the god of Mecca, until it was cleansed by the Prophet Muhammad in 632. Male pilgrims put on two sheets of seamless white cloth to symbolize the equality of all before God, while women wear their ordinary clothes and are covered from head to ankles.

A central part of the pilgrimage to Mecca is walking anticlockwise around the Ka'aba (RIGHT) seven times. The pilgrims proceed to Mina and then Mount Mercy on the plain of Arafat (ABOVE). Here, they erect tents for protection against the burning sun and perform the essential ritual of standing before God in meditation from noon until sunset. They then return to Mecca via Muzdalifa and Mina.

Until his death in 632 C.E., Muhammad received further revelations which he believed came directly from God. But the Meccans were mostly hostile to his message, which attacked vices common in the city, such as pride and reliance on money, not God. So Muhammad sent his followers to the nearby town of Yathrib (later called Medina, city of the Prophet) to meet a group who had previously heard Muhammad preach and were sympathetic to him.

Muhammad himself left Mecca to join them in September 622 and his journey or *hijra* ("emigration") marks the beginning of the Muslim calendar or year 1 A.H. (*anno hijra*). Muhammad consolidated his community in Medina through diplomacy and combat, winning an important military victory over the Meccans at Badr in 624. But not everyone accepted his message or submitted to his authority. In 627, the

Medinan Jewish community was virtually destroyed for assisting the Meccan leader Abu Sufyan in his bid to take control of Medina.

Muhammad and his opponents in Mecca signed a truce in the Treaty of Hudaybiyyah in 628. But the treaty soon collapsed and, in 630, Muhammad and his forces re-entered Mecca, this time meeting with little resistance. Muhammad destroyed many of the idols at the Ka'aba and other shrines, reorganized its administration, and put down opposition. Returning to Medina, he promulgated a constitution which, among other things, regulated relationships between Muslim communities in the region. Soon he had extended his control over much of Arabia by treaty and by force.

Muhammad made his last pilgrimage to Mecca in March 632 and died in Medina in June without having appointed a successor. A leadership struggle ensued.

At the time of Muhammad, the Middle East was dominated by two regional superpowers: the Christian Byzantine and the Zoroastrian Persian Sasanian empires. Arabia itself was crisscrossed with trade routes and formed a trading link between the Mediterranean world and India and the Far East. Mecca, situated near the Red Sea, held a prime position for travelling caravans and became the greatest trade centre in the peninsula.

The pilgrimage begins on the first day at Mecca when the pilgrim walks seven times around the Ka'aba (**1**). Next, the pilgrim runs seven times between two small hills, al-Safa and al-Marwa, now enclosed and joined by a walkway (**2**). It was close to here that Abraham was ordered by God to leave his wife Hagar and his son Ishmael and where, in her desperate search for water, Hagar ran furiously up and down the hills until she discovered the well of Zamzam nearby.

The next two stages are the five-mile walk (**3**) to Mina, followed by a 10-mile journey (**4**) to the plain of Arafat. Here, the day is spent in meditation and part of the evening in a search for 49 small stones for the next stage of the pilgrimage, the five-mile hike (**5**) to Muzdalifa and the return (**6**) to Mina. The pilgrims then throw the stones they have collected at three pillars that mark the place where the devil (Shaitan) was stoned by Ishmael as he tempted him to disobey Abraham.

The last stage (**7**) takes the pilgrim back to Mecca. The *hajj* ends with the festival of the sacrifice (Eid ul-Adha) when a sheep, goat, cow or camel is sacrificed in remembrance of Abraham's faith and obedience when he was told by God first to sacrifice his son – who, according to Muslims, was Ishmael, not Isaac – and later to substitute for his son a sheep. A final walk around the Ka'aba completes the pilgrimage.

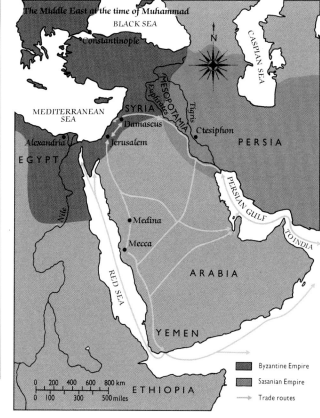

The Middle East at the time of Muhammad

■	Byzantine Empire
■	Sasanian Empire
→	Trade routes

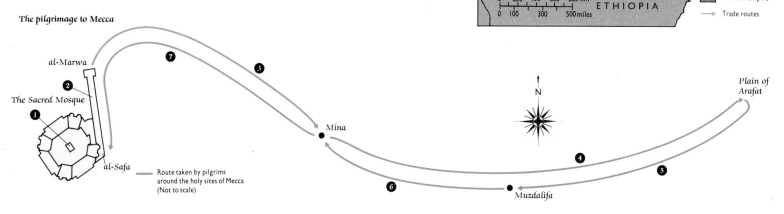

The pilgrimage to Mecca

al-Marwa
The Sacred Mosque
al-Safa
Route taken by pilgrims around the holy sites of Mecca (Not to scale)
Mina
Muzdalifa
Plain of Arafat

The Umayyads

The caliphs of the Umayyad dynasty (661–750) ushered in a dynamic period of Muslim history. During their reign, they extended the borders of the empire westward to Spain and eastward to India, and presided over an artistic and architectural revival that included, for example, the building of the magnificent Dome of the Rock in Jerusalem.

Between 634 and 650, before the dynasty was established, Umayyad forces paved the way for their success by routing armies of both the powerful Persian and Byzantine empires and by taking control of Libya, Egypt, Palestine, Syria, Iraq and most of Persia. The statesmanship of Caliph Mu'awiya (661–80), his important administrative and legal reforms, and his suppression of internal revolts laid the foundations for even more Islamic conquests, including the annexation of Morocco and Spain between 690 and 720.

The Dome of the Rock in Jerusalem is one of Islam's most ancient and holiest shrines. Built in 691 during the reign of the Umayyad caliph Abd al-Malik (685–705), the Dome encloses an outcrop of rock which is sacred to Jews and Christians as well as Muslims, who revere it principally as the Prophet Muhammad's starting point for his ascension to heaven (Qur'an 53:8–18).

Islamic expansion eastward was just as spectacular. Muslim troops marched across the Caucasus, beyond the Iranian plateau, and through the vast territories of central Asia to India and the borders of China.

In less than a hundred years after the death of Muhammad, Islam had spread like wildfire over much of the known world. One major stumbling block, however, was the route to eastern Europe, which was barred by the Byzantine emperor. (The Byzantine capital of Constantinople managed to survive Muslim assaults in 673 and 717, but finally fell to the Ottoman Turks in 1453.)

The Muslim armies that achieved this astonishingly successful expansion were composed mainly of Arabs until about 700. Then Persian, Berber and Turkish converts to Islam were used in greater numbers. This, however, did not solve the shortage of military manpower that occurred after the Frankish king Charles Martel defeated the Muslims at Poitiers in southern France in 732, halting their expansion in the west.

Although the Umayyads resorted to every means to sustain themselves in power, they found it impossible to legitimize their authority among Shiites (pp.90–91), who regarded them as usurpers, and other rebellious groups. Lacking the necessary legitimacy in the heartlands of Islam, they were unable to impose their will on subject territories.

It is not surprising, therefore, that the Umayyads – and none more so than Hisham (724–43) – were preoccupied with creating unity and cohesion out of an ethically, politically and religiously diverse empire. One way of achieving this might have been to islamize the conquered territories. However, the Umayyads made little attempt at converting, and Jews and Christians were allowed to practise their own faith, subject to the payment of the *jizya*, or poll tax.

Despite being plagued by social, political and religious unrest, the Umayyads sponsored a revival of the arts, especially poetry, and architecture. It was not, however, a question of art for art's sake. For the Umayyads realized that splendid public architecture could help to prop up their authority, which had little other than military might to rest on.

The propagandist potential of poetry was also perceived, which helps to explain why eulogy was a major genre of the period. And it is poetry – typically self-indulgent and escapist in flavour compared with the ascetic tone of early puritanical Islam – that reveals the *zeitgeist*, or spirit of the age. For much of the anxiety and restlessness of this time rises to the surface in the lines of love poetry and satirical verse. In the end, however, the discontent expressed in literature was actually resolved in 750 by force of arms.

Later Muslim commentators and historians often contrasted the Umayyad caliphs' worldly dissolute ways with those of their "upright" successors, the Abbasids, but their misgivings were exaggerated, since many Umayyads led virtuous and devout lives.

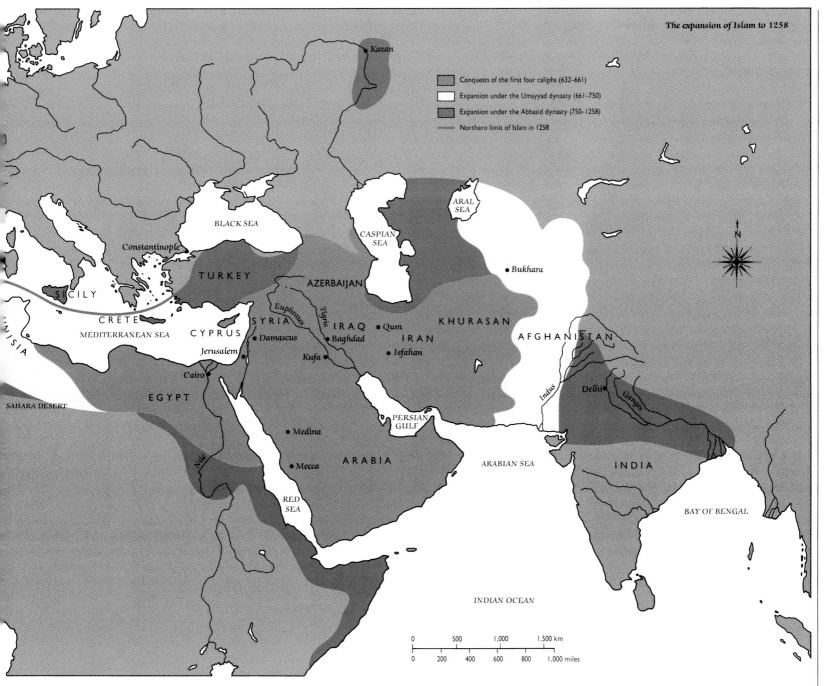

The expansion of Islam to 1258

- Conquests of the first four caliphs (632–661)
- Expansion under the Umayyad dynasty (661–750)
- Expansion under the Abbasid dynasty (750–1258)
- Northern limit of Islam in 1258

KAZAN

BLACK SEA

CONSTANTINOPLE

ARAL SEA

CASPIAN SEA

TURKEY

AZERBAIJAN

Bukhara

SICILY

CRETE

CYPRUS

SYRIA

Euphrates

Tigris

IRAQ

Qum

KHURASAN

AFGHANISTAN

MEDITERRANEAN SEA

Damascus

Baghdad

IRAN

Jerusalem

Kufa

Isfahan

Delhi

Ganges

Cairo

Indus

EGYPT

SAHARA DESERT

PERSIAN GULF

TUNISIA

Nile

Medina

ARABIA

ARABIAN SEA

INDIA

Mecca

RED SEA

BAY OF BENGAL

INDIAN OCEAN

| 0 | 500 | 1,000 | 1,500 km |
| 0 | 200 | 400 | 600 | 800 | 1,000 miles |

Built in 876 during the Abbasid era, the magnificent Ibn Tulun Mosque in what is now Cairo consists of a mosque surrounded by three outer courtyards, or ziyadahs. In this courtyard (LEFT), the domed structure covers the mosque's fountain; the minaret towers in the background.

The mosque is named for its builder, Ahmad ibn Tulun, who had been a slave in the service of the Abbasid caliphate. He later served under the Abbasid governor of Egypt and went on to found the Tulunid dynasty (868–905). This was the first local dynasty of Egypt and Syria to rule independently of the Abbasid government in Baghdad.

In its long and varied history, the mosque has been restored several times and used as a belt factory and as shops. Since its classification as an historic monument in 1890, it has been fully restored.

Independent Kingdoms

Although the rule of the Abbasid caliphs limped on until 1258, their power had effectively ended in the 10th century. During this complex 300-year period, a number of independent Muslim kingdoms came to power in different parts of the empire. Several were Shiite of various kinds (pp.90–91) and included the Imamite sect (p.109), also known as Twelvers.

One of the most revolutionary challenges to the Abbasids came from the Fatimid dynasty (909–1171), which took its name from Fatimah, the Prophet's daughter, from whom they claimed descent. The Fatimids belonged to a branch of Shiism known as Ismaili, or Sevener, founded in 765 to support the claims of a certain Ismail over another claimant to be the seventh imam – the religious head of the Shiites.

Under their leader Ubadayyah al-Mahdi, the Fatimids established a rival caliphate to that of the Abbasids, first in Tunisia and later in Egypt, where they founded the city of Cairo. In Tunisia, they replaced the Aglabid dynasty (800–909) which had ruled the country while recognizing overall Abbasid sovereignty. The Fatimids, on the other hand, broke tradition by claiming to be the sole rightful heirs to the caliphate. Until then, all Muslim princes had held their lands – at least nominally – in fief from the Abbasid caliph.

The Fatimids showed deep commitment to Islamic culture and learning. In 970, they founded the University of al-Azhar in Cairo, still the most prestigious in the Muslim world. But their attempt to establish an Ismaili caliphate was undermined by discontent and civil strife caused by famine and dynastic rivalry.

In 1094, an internal struggle for the Fatimid caliphate occurred between two brothers, al-Mustali and al-Nizar, and their supporters. Al-Mustali was the victor

The place of prostration

Muslims congregate to worship God in a mosque (Arabic *masjid*), which literally means a place of prostration. The act of prostration is the sign of submission to God and the essence of Islam.

Mosques can vary greatly in shape and size, from magnificent edifices, such as the Mosque of the Shah at Isfahan in Iran and the Omar ali Saifuddin Mosque in Brunei, to the plainest, most basic of buildings. Indeed, the very first mosque, which was built by Muhammad and his companions in Medina, was a simple structure made of tree trunks with palm fronds covering the roof.

Although mosques may differ in detail, they share a number of fundamental features. These include an enclosed hall, where Muslims perform their prayer; an interior niche (*mihrab*) in the *qibla* wall that indicates the direction of Mecca, which worshippers must face when praying; a pulpit (*minbar*), from which the sermon is spoken; and, except in Indonesia, a minaret or tower, situated outside the mosque, from which the call to prayer is issued to the faithful.

Some mosques also have a courtyard with a pool of clear water in the centre. This is symbolic of the fact that the worshipper must be ritually pure before approaching God. But in most mosques, the place of ablutions is found outside the walls.

The mosque's absence of statues and representational art is an eloquent statement of Muslim belief both in God's oneness and in God as Maker of all things, and therefore not to be imitated by human beings. Decoration is optional, and if it is in evidence, its purpose is purely aesthetic instead of being designed to teach. When decoration is intended to convey a message, it takes the form of flowing calligraphic inscriptions of verses from the holy book of the Qur'an.

The mosque was the first Islamic architectural form, and although some features are common, the design can vary. A 17th-century Turkish mosque (ABOVE) in Rethymnon, Crete, shows a classic simplicity, with its dome topping a square-shaped structure. By contrast, the green minarets of a 1970s mosque (LEFT) in London, England, lend an exotic note to a suburban street. And in Islamabad, Pakistan, the Shah Faisal Mosque (LEFT ABOVE), built in 1988, combines the traditional, symmetrical shape of a Bedouin tent with the stark lines of modernist building styles.

and continued Fatimid rule, which lasted another 77 years until the great Saladin, famous for his part in the Crusades (pp.56–57), established his Ayyubid dynasty (1171–1250) in Egypt.

Meanwhile, the Nizaris broke away and developed into a sect known as the Assassins, a name derived from "hashish", which they reputedly smoked to induce ecstasy before going into battle. From their hill fortresses in Syria, the Assassins acted independently of the Fatimid caliphs and fought against the Crusaders, who made their name known in Europe. The Assassins' downfall eventually came in the 13th century, largely as a result of incursions by Mongol invaders.

Elsewhere in the Muslim Empire, other dynasties rose and fell during this turbulent period. These included the Shiite Carmarthians (c.894–c.1100) of eastern and central Arabia; the Turkish-led Ghaznavids (977–1186), who extended Islamic rule over Khurasan, Afghanistan and northern India; the Almoravids (1056–1147), who forged Berber kingdoms out of nomads from the steppes of the Sahara; the Almohads (1130–1269), who replaced the Almoravids in Morocco; and the Umayyad dynasty of Spain.

In Morocco, the Almoravid dynasty founded Marrakesh as their capital in 1062 and expanded from there. In 1085, they crossed the strait to enter Spain, ostensibly to shore up Umayyad rule, which was gradually being eroded by Spanish Christian rulers. However, because of regional differences, the Almoravids presided over a gradually shrinking Muslim kingdom until their own demise in 1147. Shortly afterward, the Almohads took on responsibility for Spain and kept the Christian kingdoms at bay until internal dynastic disputes in the 1220s forced their withdrawal.

> **From whatsoever place thou issuest, turn thy face toward the Holy Mosque.**
>
> QUR'AN 2:145

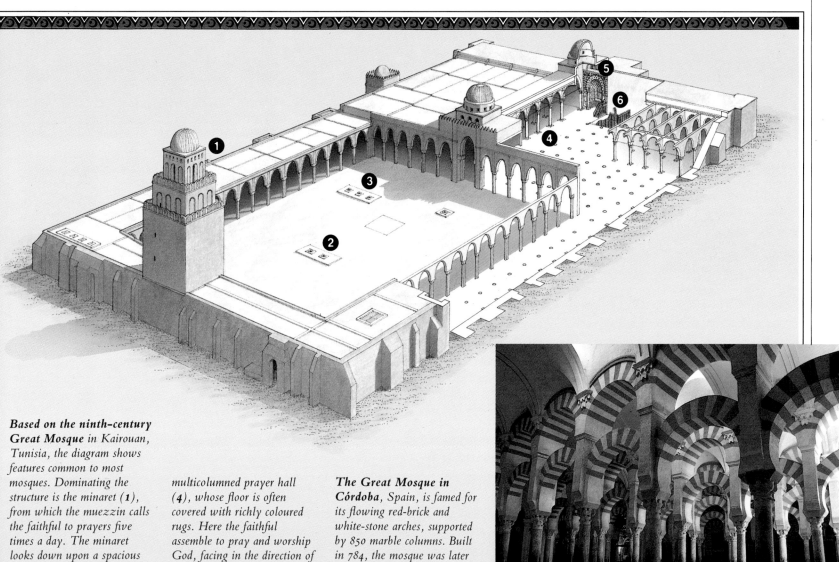

*Based on the ninth-century **Great Mosque** in Kairouan, Tunisia, the diagram shows features common to most mosques. Dominating the structure is the minaret (**1**), from which the muezzin calls the faithful to prayers five times a day. The minaret looks down upon a spacious courtyard, in which there are fountains (**2** and **3**) whose waters symbolize purity.*

*Surrounding the courtyard are shady arcades and the multicolumned prayer hall (**4**), whose floor is often covered with richly coloured rugs. Here the faithful assemble to pray and worship God, facing in the direction of Mecca, which is indicated by a niche, or* mihrab (**5**). *Beside it is the staired* minbar *and an ornate wooden screen, or* maqsura (**6**).

***The Great Mosque in Córdoba**, Spain, is famed for its flowing red-brick and white-stone arches, supported by 850 marble columns. Built in 784, the mosque was later extended to become one of Islam's largest sacred structures.*

The Way of the Sufi

The "proof of Islam"

For Muslims, the great synthesizer of Islamic philosophy, theology, law and mysticism was Muhammad al-Ghazali (1058–1111). His reputation is such that Muslims refer to him as the "proof of Islam". Born in Tus in Persia, al-Ghazali received his early education there and later studied law, philosophy and theology at various other institutions, including one at Jorjan on the Black Sea. He so impressed the vizier that he was appointed chief professor at the Nizamiyya madrasa, or college, in Baghdad, and spent time as a theologian and jurist at the court of the Seljuk rulers.

Dissatisfied with the rationalistic thought of his contemporaries, al-Ghazali wrote *The Inconsistency of the Philosophers*, a devastating critique of the writings of philosophers such as Ibn Sina, better known in the west as Avicenna (p.101). In 1095, disturbed by his colleagues' worldly values and a spiritual crisis, al-Ghazali turned to Sufism with all the zeal of the convert, disposing of his

wealth – after providing for his family – and becoming a wandering dervish, or holy man.

From then on, al-Ghazali insisted that pure philosophy – which he called "simply thinking" – and theology were no basis for belief: personal experience rather than intellect was the best path to spiritual understanding. He was also critical of jurists and despised their over-subtle arguments and reasoning. However, although he realized the limitations of philosophy and theology, he stressed in his great work *The Revival of the Religious Sciences* that they were needed as safeguards for true belief and practice.

Paradoxically, many believe that, despite his passion for Sufism, al-Ghazali's greatest achievement was his use of Greek philosophy, which he learned from Avicenna, to defend orthodox Sunni theology. Toward the end of his life, he returned to his birthplace, where he lived among his Sufi disciples until his death.

With their robes billowing out around them, whirling dervishes of the Turkish Sufi Mawlawiyya, or Mevlevi, order perform a dance around their master, simulating the rotation of the planets around the sun.

Although orthodox Islam frowns upon musical accompaniment to religious rituals, Sufi orders developed their own distinctive ritual observance, or dhikr, involving singing, drums and dancing. In the case of the Mawlawiyya, founded by the Persian mystic Jalal al-Din Rumi, the dance takes the form of a rhythmic, all-engrossing movement of the body to induce a trance and thereby gain union with God.

> O God! Whatever share of this world you have allotted to me, bestow it on your enemies; and whatever share of the next world you have allotted to me, bestow it on your friends. You are enough for me.
>
> RABI'A AL-ADAWIYYA

In the 12th century, a number of Sufi orders or brotherhoods (tariqas) arose, some of the more important of which are shown here. The golden age of Sufism in the 13th century saw the spread of Islam to India, central Asia, Turkey and sub-Saharan Africa, through the disciples of various Sufi brotherhoods.

The mystic tradition in Islam is known as Sufism (from *suf*, the simple woollen garment which Sufis wore). Like mystics of other religions, Sufis desire union with God, a goal achieved through certain practices, such as renunciation of the world, abstinence, poverty and meditation. Broadly, there have been two complementary periods in the history of Sufism, the first covering its initial development from the 7th to 10th centuries; the second spanning the 11th to 13th centuries, during which time Sufis began to organize themselves into formal brotherhoods.

The origins of Sufism have been the subject of debate. Some scholars believe it was practised by the Prophet Muhammad and is therefore as old as Islam itself. They point to the mystical strain found in some verses of the Qur'an, which describe the presence and nearness of God, who brings life to barren soil with water; the transience of the world; the pleasures of paradise; and the beauty of virtue. Others, however, believe that Sufism began as an attempt to restore to Islam a religious purity which had been neglected during the Umayyad dynasty (pp.92–93).

Whatever its beginnings, the first Sufis were influenced by the ascetic practices of Christian monks in Syria, and probably by Zoroastrians (pp.120–23) of Persia, and Hindu Vedanta philosophy (pp.132–33). During its first three centuries, Sufism grew from its roots in asceticism and a contempt for the world.

Chief among the Sufis of this early period was Hasan al-Basri (642–728), the "father of Muslim mysticism". Although he did not found a movement, al-Basri's disciples formed a monastic-style community in Abbadan near Basra in Iraq. It included among its members one of history's most famous female mystics, the former slave girl Rabi'a al-Adawiyya (721–801), who is said to have spent her life in search of God.

Other schools of mystics existed at Baghdad and Kufa, but the spirit of Sufism at this time is perhaps encapsulated by the influential al-Muhasibi (781–857) of Baghdad. He taught that people should despise the world and search for inner perfection by submitting to God's will as a slave submits to a master.

Sufi notions of union with God often frightened orthodox Muslim theologians. In 922, for example, the Persian Sufi al-Hallaj was executed in Baghdad for his alleged heretical ideas and his utterance: "I am God." Taken literally, these words would have violated the most fundamental tenet of Islam expressed in the profession of faith: "There is no god but God." However, al-Hallaj may merely have been expressing his union with God – the ultimate aim of the Sufi – and not challenging God's uniqueness. But the example of al-Hallaj and others like him made Sufism suspect to the orthodox.

In the second broad period of Sufism from the 11th to the 13th centuries, a number of Sufi brotherhoods arose, whose members lived in communities and practised a monkish lifestyle, which involved prescribed rituals, communal services and music. This was also the time of the greatest of Muslim thinkers, the Persian scholar and mystic al-Ghazali (*opposite*), who tried to reconcile Sufism with theology.

The deep concern of the Sufis of the 12th and 13th centuries was to discover the nature of the true self and its purpose. This tendency is shown to brilliant effect within the *Mathnavi*, the great poetic work of the Persian mystic Jalal al-Din Rumi (1207–73). The "Qur'an of the Persian language", the *Mathnavi* consists of six long books and is a storehouse of mystical lore expounded in stories and lyric poetry. Its dominant theme is the exploration of the relationship between the self and the One God.

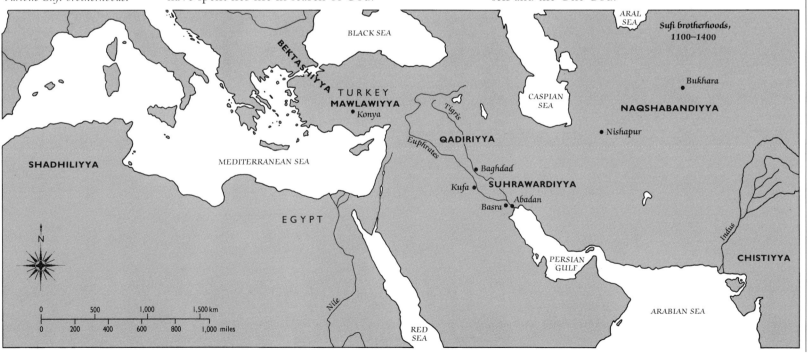

The Clash with Christendom

The Moorish genius for ornate decoration is evident in these intricately carved pillars in the Alhambra Palace in Granada, Spain. The stark exterior of this fortress palace, built chiefly by the Nasrid dynasty (1238–1492) in the 14th century, gives no clue to the delicacy of the interior, with its graceful arches and shady courtyards and fountains.

Since Islam largely forbade representational art, the Moors embellished their plasterwork with abstract designs and often incorporated flowing Islamic script from the Qur'an.

At the start of the 11th century, the politically impotent Abbasid caliphate in Baghdad experienced an injection of new blood. The new power-brokers were the Seljuks, a branch of the nomadic Turks who had previously entered military service under the Abbasid caliphs. By seizing Baghdad, the Seljuks released the Abbasids from the tutelage of the Buyid dynasty (945–1055), and they established an Islamic state that lasted from 1038 to 1194.

Unlike the Fatimids, who claimed to be the sole rightful heirs to the dynasty (pp.96–97), the Seljuks did not claim absolute authority, but ruled in the name of the Abbasids. The Seljuk sultan, their political head, was invested by the caliph with the authority to protect the Muslim community and defend Islam by *jihad*, or holy war, against the infidel. Thus the division between the religious and secular arms of government was established, a situation similar to the one a century before when the Buyids had stripped the Abbasids of all but moral and spiritual power.

The truly novel element in the Seljuk state was twofold. First, it was founded on a partnership of "men of the sword", mostly of Turkish origin, and bureaucrats and jurists of mainly Persian and Arab blood; and, second, there arose an alliance between the merchants and the landowning classes.

Unlike other parts of the Muslim Empire at this time, the Seljuk states were relatively stable and prosperous. They included Iraq, Persia and, after 1071, when Byzantine forces were defeated at Manzikert in present-day Armenia, parts of Anatolia. Seljuk rulers maintained order by imposing a common law, and they brought increased wealth through trade along the sea routes of the Mediterranean, Black Sea and Indian Ocean and the land routes of Asia.

Seljuk success, however, led to a titanic clash with Christian Europe when the Byzantine emperor appealed to the pope and the Latin west for help. The outcome was a series of Crusades, beginning in 1096 and continuing for almost two centuries (pp.56–57). Although the Muslims suffered defeats and surrendered territory, they ultimately regained almost all the lands they lost during these wars. Also, the arts continued to flourish, and Islam spread into new parts of central Asia and as far southeast as Indonesia (pp.110–11).

Seljuk power began to weaken in the second half of the 12th century as the Mongol advance threatened it (pp.102–3). Islam also started to encounter serious difficulties elsewhere, particularly in Spain, where the *Reconquista* – the Christian reconquest – gained momentum as the withdrawal of the Almohads (pp.96–97) to northern Africa got underway in 1225. The Almohad departure allowed the Christian armies to subjugate rapidly the remaining Muslim kingdoms, with the exception of Granada in the southeast.

With the union of the kingdoms of Aragon and Castile through the marriage in 1469 of Ferdinand II of Aragon to Isabella of Castile, Spain was united. As a result, Granada's continued existence became uncertain and, in 1492, the year Christopher Columbus discovered the New World, this last Muslim bastion fell to the Spanish Christian armies.

However, the Muslim presence in Spain was not completely eradicated. Many Muslims, known to the Spanish as *mudejars*, remained in the country only to experience a variety of forms of discrimination until their final expulsion by edict in 1614. It was the end of an Islamic Spain that had produced great thinkers contributing much to western civilization. This was especially so of the jurist and philosopher Averroës (*opposite*), who spent much of his life as a judge in Seville and Córdoba, and the historian Ibn Khaldun (1332–1406), whose *An Introduction to World History*, containing as it does brilliant and incisive observations on economics, politics and education, ranks among the finest histories that have ever been written.

Moorish chess players ponder their moves, attended by a musician and serving women, in this detail from a book made for Philip II (1527–98) of Spain for the library at El Escorial outside Madrid. Chess, which originated in India, was brought to Europe by Muslims in the 10th century.

Their hands clasped in prayer, Ferdinand of Aragon and Isabella of Castile are depicted in this 15th-century painted carved wood panel. Spain was united by their marriage, paving the way for Spanish Christian armies to conquer Granada and thus banish the last Moors from Spain.

Avicenna and Averroës

Although the last three centuries of Abbasid rule (10th to 13th centuries) were racked with political confusion, they were also a period of great learning. The dominant intellectual challenge of the time was to reconcile Greek philosophy and science with religious belief. Among those who set about tackling this problem were the remarkable thinkers Ibn Sina (980–1037) and Ibn Rushd (1126–98), better known in the west as Avicenna and Averroës.

Educated in Bukhara in central Asia, Avicenna was reputed to be brilliant in law, philosophy and medicine by the age of 17. He was influenced by the Greek philosophers Plato and Aristotle, and much of his thought is contained in two works, the *Shifa* and the *Najat*, which state that there is no inevitable conflict between Greek philosophy and science and Islamic doctrines.

In a similar vein, Averroës argued that if religion and philosophy are both true, then they cannot contradict each other. But he also held that religious truth, founded as it is on revelation, is superior to philosophical truth, which is based on pure reason. Averroës was convinced that theology could benefit from Aristotle's thought, and criticized al-Ghazali (p.98) for his attack on it.

Yet Averroës was far less influential than al-Ghazali in the Islamic world. Conversely, his influence on the west has been enormous. His commentaries on Aristotle provided western Europe with its first main introduction to Aristotle. This in turn contributed to the development of medieval thought, typified by that of Thomas Aquinas (p.58).

Central Asia

Mighty ruler and brilliant commander, Genghis Khan holds court in his sumptuous tent in this Persian miniature (RIGHT). Genghis and his Mongol descendants conquered huge territories, including parts of the eastern Islamic empire.

The empires of the Il-Khanid ruler Mahmud Ghazan and, later, Tamerlane covered vast stretches of central Asia and the Middle East (RIGHT). In the early 1990s, centuries after the deaths of these potentates, Islam still remains strong in the region.

In the Commonwealth of Independent States six Islamic republics (INSET) have emerged from the communist era and have attracted diplomatic overtures from both Iran and Turkey. The states' possession of nuclear weapons has been a matter of concern to the west, anxious that weapons of mass destruction should not fall into the hands of hostile governments.

During the 13th and 14th centuries, the Islamic empire in the east came under ferocious attack. The assailants were the Mongols, nomadic peoples from the Siberian forests and steppes and the deserts of central Asia, who were united and led by their brilliant and ruthless ruler Genghis Khan (c.1162–1227). From his descendants arose the Il-Khanid dynasty (1256–1353), which controlled vast territories in Persia, Iraq and Anatolia (modern Turkey) and whose later rulers converted to Islam.

The collapse of Seljuk rule (pp.100–101) and the effects of the Crusades (pp.56–57) disturbed the balance of Muslim power in the Middle East and left the eastern part of the empire vulnerable to attack. In 1243, a Mongol army forced the Seljuk chieftain in Syria to become its vassal, and in 1258 a Mongol force under Hulagu Khan, grandson of Genghis, sacked Baghdad and finally put an end to Abbasid rule (pp.94–95) in Iraq. But in 1260, at the Battle of Ain Jalut some 50 miles north of Jerusalem, the Mongols were stopped from expanding farther in the region by the Mamluks of Syria. The Mamluk sultans (1250–1517) were in control of Egypt and had invited the Abbasids to establish the caliphate in Cairo.

Nevertheless, Hulagu ruled the region of Persia, Iraq, the Caucasus and Anatolia, and assumed the title of Il-Khan, "subordinate of the Great Khan", for which the Il-Khanid dynasty was named. Hulagu's great-grandson Mahmud Ghazan (1295–1304) was the first Il-Khan to convert to Islam. Under him, the Il-Khanid kingdom entered a golden age, marked by financial and agricultural reforms and the building of bridges, caravanserais and whole towns.

Not all the Mongol khans, however, were in favour of Islam. For example, east of the Caspian Sea, parts of the region known as Transoxiana, ruled by the descendants of Chaghatay (1227–41), one of Genghis's four sons, were farther removed from the major centres of Islam than Il-Khanid Persia and so less influenced by the religion. Indeed, the Chaghatayid ruler Duwa (1291–1306) and his descendants and their nomadic subjects were extremely hostile to Islam.

The survival of the Il-Khanid kingdom in Persia

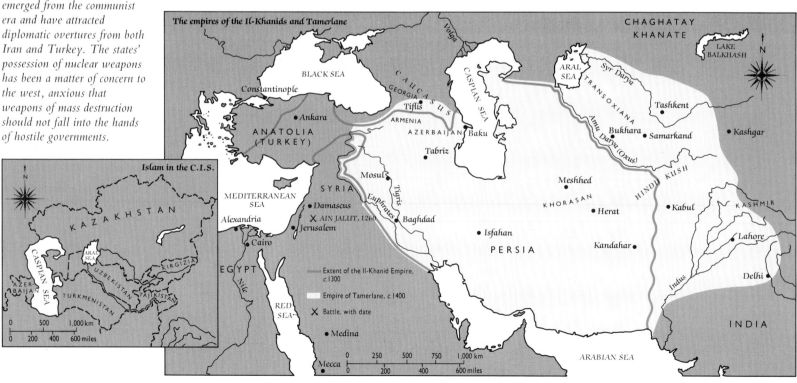

was assured for a time by Timur Lenk, or Tamerlane (1336–1405), a Muslim Turkoman prince from Samarkand in Transoxiana, who built an empire over vast tracts of Asia and beyond. More Turkish than Mongol, and a product of a sophisticated Muslim, settled society, Tamerlane made Samarkand the capital of this empire, adorning it with splendid buildings. From here he conquered a huge area stretching from southern Russia northeast to Mongolia and south to India, Persia and Mesopotamia.

Islam's presence in central Asia and the former Soviet Union long predates the arrival of Tamerlane and the Mongols, although exactly when it became established is uncertain. However, when the Moroccan traveller Ibn Battutah (1304–68) passed through central Asia in the 14th century in the course of his extensive journeys, he noted that the people lived in Muslim states, spoke Turkish as their main language, and belonged to the Hanafi school of Islamic law (p.94).

Hundreds of years later, Islam can still be found in central Asia. Often subject to persecution both before and during the Soviet communist era in the 20th century, Islam managed to survive the Soviet regime. Now, in the early 1990s, a number of predominantly Muslim independent states – Uzbekistan, Kazakhstan, Tajikistan, Kirgizia, Turkmenistan and Azerbaijan – exercise an important political and military influence in the region as part of the new Commonwealth of Independent States (C.I.S.).

The ribbed turquoise dome of the Bibi Khanum Mosque is a reminder of the splendours of Tamerlane's capital of Samarkand. An ancient city situated on a trade route linking the Middle East with China, Samarkand was sacked by Genghis Khan in 1220. It revived under Tamerlane, who built an array of mosques, palaces and formal gardens.

With the death of Tamerlane in 1405, his empire began to collapse. Nevertheless, during the first half of the 15th century, his successors, the Timurids, were great sponsors of the arts, with architecture, painting and Turkish and Persian literature flourishing under their patronage. During this period, Samarkand remained a splendid capital enriched with elegant structures, including Tamerlane's mausoleum, a detail of which is shown (RIGHT), and an observatory built by his grandson Ulugh Beg.

A Muslim wedding in Turkmenistan, one of the Islamic republics of the Commonwealth of Independent States, is an occasion for celebration and an assertion of Islamic culture. Turkmenistan formally became a Soviet republic in 1925. Its people, mostly Turkic-speaking Turkomans, who are Sunni Muslims, managed to survive under the communist regime until the early 1990s, when they became part of the C.I.S.

Islam in India

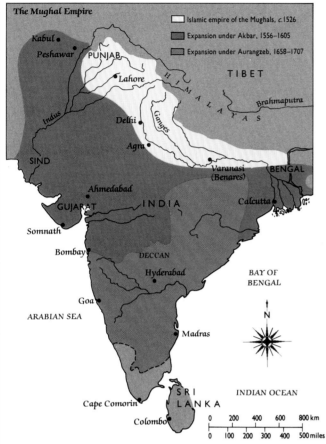

Mughal forces under Babur had, by about 1526, carved out a substantial empire in northern India. Under Emperor Akbar, the limits of the empire extended south to the Deccan plateau, while Aurangzeb pushed the boundary to its farthest extent, almost to the southern tip of the subcontinent.

"A soaring bubble of marble", as Mark Twain called it, the Taj Mahal is the most famous mausoleum in the world. It was built in Agra by Shah Jahan for his wife Mumtaz Mahal, who died in childbirth in 1631. The building's surfaces are inlaid with intertwining floral and arabesque motifs. The entrance to the complex is via a massive gateway inscribed with verses from chapter 89 of the Qur'an, which concludes with an invitation to the soul to enter paradise.

For about the first thousand years C.E., India was dominated by two major faiths – Hinduism and Buddhism. After this time, a series of Muslim dynasties, including the Ghaznavids (977–1168), the Delhi sultanate (1206–1398) and the Mughals (1526–1857), began to control large areas of the subcontinent, spreading Islamic culture and religion. Islam remained influential in the country after the Mughal era ended and during the subsequent British rule, which lasted until 1947 when India gained its independence and the new Muslim state of Pakistan was created. Today there is still an influential, if small, Muslim presence in India itself.

Islam was first implanted in India as early as the Umayyad period (661–750), largely through Muslim traders from the Near East settling in Gujarat, Bombay and the Deccan. But Islam's arrival was not solely through peaceful means: in 711, for example, an expedition by an Umayyad army captured the region of Sind. However, the effects of this first Muslim presence were negligible. The strength of Hindu life, built around the caste system (pp.128–29), prevailed, and as a result Islam was almost totally submerged.

During the early centuries of the Abbasid caliphate (750–1258), cultural contacts between India and Baghdad, now the centre of the caliphate, increased as numerous Indian scholars were invited to the caliph's palace. However, an important change in the peaceful relations between the Islamic world and India occurred

Shah Jahan sits on the Peacock Throne, symbol of Mughal power, in this Indian miniature. Like his Mughal forebears, Shah Jahan was both a man of action and a cultured patron of the arts. In 1658, his son Aurangzeb took over the throne and imprisoned him in the fort at Agra until Shah Jahan's death in 1666.

with the rise of the Turkish Ghaznavid dynasty in Afghanistan. Ghaznavid aggression resulted in Muslim political authority being established in northwestern India by force as well as by the annexation of the cities of Multan and Lahore, in present-day Pakistan.

Northwestern India was badly plundered during the Ghaznavid era, and its people deeply resented the looting of its temples and the assault on its culture and way of life. At the same time, the incursions brought Muslim holy men and scholars to India, and they became the focus of new Muslim communities.

From the 13th to the early 16th centuries, northern India was dominated by a number of Afghan-Turkish dynasties which ruled from Delhi. The last of these, the Lodis (1451–1526), was swept away by the forces of Zahid al-Din Babur (1483–1530), the Turkish ruler of Kabul (the capital of present-day Afghanistan). Babur ("Tiger") claimed descent from both Genghis Khan and Tamerlane (pp.102–3), an awesome pedigree for any conqueror; and it was he who founded the Mughal (derived from "Mongol") dynasty.

The Mughal era witnessed a great burgeoning of culture in India, including the building of masterpieces such as the Red Fort at Delhi and the pearly domed Taj Mahal, a mausoleum built for his wife by Shah Jahan (1628–58). There was also a general liberalization of many areas of life, especially during the long reign of Akbar (*below*), who encouraged intermarriage between Hindus and Muslims. Akbar also extended his empire to cover the whole of northern and central India and integrated into his army and administration the martial Hindu clans known as the Rajputs, who had previously been hostile to Islam.

The opposite of the tolerant Akbar was Aurangzeb

(1658–1707), whose attempts to revive religious orthodoxy, like those of his two immediate predecessors Jahangir (1605–27) and Shah Jahan, alienated a large proportion of the Hindu population. Aurangzeb's intolerant policies, by which Hindu temples were destroyed and punitive taxes imposed on the Hindu population, sowed social discord and were one of the main reasons for the decline of Mughal power in the 1700s.

Aurangzeb's criticism of Akbar's tolerance toward Hindus was later taken up by a number of Muslim mystics and scholars. Notable were Shaykh Ahmad Sirhindi (1564–1624) and Shah Wali Allah (1702–62), who both urged Muslims to return to a strict, traditional way of Islamic life.

O soul at peace, return unto thy Lord . . . Enter thou My Paradise   QUR'AN 89:28–30

Built by Shah Jahan, the Red Fort in Delhi, named for its sandstone walls, was the seat of the Mughal administration from 1638. Overlooking the River Jumna, a tributary of the Ganges, the fort housed the imperial palace and the Pearl Mosque, whose domes are shown here, built by Aurangzeb in 1659.

Akbar, the tolerant emperor

The third Mughal emperor and a contemporary of Elizabeth I of England, Akbar (1556–1605) was highly controversial in matters of religion. He practised Islam and took theology seriously; so much so, in fact, that by a decree of 1579 he asserted his authority over the scholars, or *ulama*, in this area of study.

However, he clearly also spoke and acted in ways that caused offence to the orthodox Muslim community. He encouraged intermarriage between Muslims and Hindus and he himself married a Hindu princess, who continued to practise her faith. He abolished anti-Hindu taxes, appointed Hindus as civil servants and discouraged the building of mosques and the study of Islamic law and Arabic.

Akbar seems to have genuinely desired to foster better Muslim-Hindu relations. And his invitation to Jesuit missionaries to discuss with

him their faith suggests he was strongly committed to religious tolerance and harmony at a time when a number of new religious movements, including Sikhism (pp.172–75), were appearing in India. He is even thought to have formulated his own religion, known as the Divine Truth, which seems to have been a personal cult and may have involved worship of the sun. However, his attempts to promulgate this religion failed.

Akbar presides over a lively debate between scholars of different religions in this Indian miniature. The group includes two Jesuit missionaries, sitting at the far left of the picture wearing dark, fezlike hats.

The Ottomans

For about 450 years, from 1453 to 1924, the Ottoman Turks presided over one of the great empires of world history. At its peak, during the reign of Suleiman the Magnificent (1520–66), the Ottomans controlled most of the Near East, northern Africa, western Asia, the Balkans and Hungary. The army was well trained and well equipped. And the arts flourished, particularly architecture, with mosques, schools, hospitals, aqueducts and public baths enriching Ottoman towns. This was especially true of Constantinople, the old capital of the Byzantine Empire, which the Ottomans captured in 1453 and renamed Istanbul.

The Ottomans were named for Osman (Othman), the son of their founder Ertugrul, a 13th-century Turkish chieftain. From their rise until 1453, they expanded haphazardly without a central government. However, after Sultan Mehmed (1451–81) conquered Constantinople, the way lay open for Ottoman expansion both by land and by sea. In the west, territories such as the Balkan regions and what is now Herzegovina and much of Bosnia, in former Yugoslavia, were occupied; while in the east, the khanate of the Crimea became a vassal state in 1475, making Hungary the only regional rival to Ottoman dominance.

The pace of expansion slackened during the reign of Bayazid II (1481–1512), which saw the rise of the powerful Safavid dynasty in Persia (pp.108–9). The Safavid threat to Ottoman power did not prevent the Ottomans defeating the Mamluks in Iraq, Syria and Egypt. The effect of these conquests was to invest in the sultan supreme spiritual and political power and to place him in charge of the holy places not only of the Muslim world but also of Christendom.

By the time of the death of Sultan Selim I in 1520, the Ottoman Empire stretched from the Red Sea to the Crimea. But its greatest period was yet to come, under Suleiman the Magnificent, who brought unity to the Muslim world. During his reign, more of Serbia, including Belgrade, and Rhodes, Hungary, and large parts of present-day Iraq and Iran were added to the empire, and his formidable navy dominated the Mediterranean. Suleiman was also a great patron of the arts and a champion of the *shari'a*, or Islamic holy law.

Suleiman interpreted his success as a divine reward for the promotion of Islam, and he encouraged all things Islamic: the widespread use of Arabic script in Turkey itself; the emergence of Turkish artists who excelled in Arabic calligraphy and textiles such as carpets and prayer rugs; the introduction of the Qur'an as the basis of education; and the building of magnificent mosques.

Ottoman rule was generally tolerant. Muslims constituted less than half the total population of the empire and were subject to direct rule. They also had to perform military service (which non-Muslims did not). On the other hand, non-Muslims had to make a financial contribution toward the army and pay the *jizya*, or poll tax; but they were given considerable autonomy under a form of indirect rule known as the millet system.

This left them free to administer their own spiritual affairs as well as their educational and judicial ones.

With the death of Suleiman I in 1566, the Ottoman Empire began a long, slow decline. Nepotism, corruption and the inability to adapt to change and compete with European states such as Spain, Portugal and England undermined the administration and the main fighting force, the Janissaries. Known as the Sick Man of Europe during the 19th century, the empire was formally dismantled after World War I (1914–18).

Janissaries: the heart of the Ottoman army

The Ottoman state has been described as an army that made itself into an empire. The chief role of the early sultans was that of supreme military commander, and the army had an important place in the empire. At the heart of the army was the formidable fighting force known as the Janissaries, whose members were *yenicheri* ("new troops") – young men conscripted from the non-Muslim subject populations. The youths were then converted to Islam and formed into professional regular soldiers.

Reliable, effective and widely feared, the Janissaries in time were granted many privileges, such as positions for their sons in the imperial civil service. However, nepotism, corruption and indiscipline gradually destroyed their effectiveness; and from the time of Selim III (1789–1807), attempts were made by sultans to disband them.

Selim's reforms known as the *Nizam i-Jedid* ("new order") included the introduction in 1792 of a new volunteer military force modelled on western armies at the time. Military and naval schools were set up with French officers providing technical training. Threatened by these reforms, the Janissaries staged a revolt in 1807 and forced the abolition of the new volunteer army.

But in 1826, determined to succeed where Selim had failed, Sultan Mahmud II surrounded the Janissaries' barracks in Constantinople with loyal troops and annihilated them. This action, which became known as the Auspicious Incident, laid the foundations for the modernization of the Turkish army.

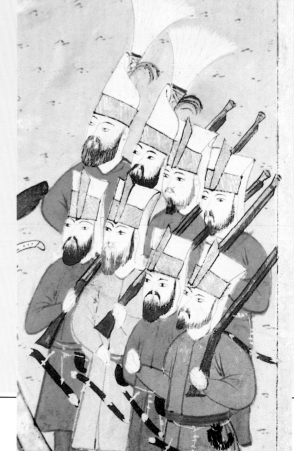

The Janissaries, shown here in this illustration from a Turkish manuscript, formed the regular infantry of the Ottoman Turks from the first half of the 14th century for about 500 years. The troops were mainly Christian boys from the Balkans who had been converted to Islam. From 1581, membership of this elite force tended to be hereditary. A feature of their dress uniform was a predominantly white felt hat, with a piece of white cloth at the back. Each regiment had its own emblem on its flag and barracks doors; it was sometimes tattooed on to the soldiers' limbs.

Suleiman the Magnificent
was a brilliant soldier and
statesman under whose guiding
hands the Ottoman Empire
reached its peak. He conducted
several successful campaigns,
including the annexation of
Hungary, and was famed for
his legal reforms and
enthusiastic patronage of the
arts. During his reign, Sinan,
the greatest Ottoman architect,
built many splendid mosques,
including the Sulemaniye in
Istanbul, as well as palaces,
hospitals, bridges and other
structures.

The harem, which refers both to the caliph's wives
and their secluded quarters, was for a time influential
in the affairs of state after the death of Suleiman in
1566. Here, the interior of the Ottoman-period harem
in Hamah, Syria, shows the style and luxury to
which the women were accustomed.

This 16th-century Ottoman plate shows the
skill with which the famed potters of the town of
Iznik achieved a sense of fluidity and movement in
their art. The ship motif is also a reminder of
Ottoman naval prowess, which was unmatched in the
Mediterranean until the Battle of Lepanto in 1571,
when the Ottomans were defeated by a Christian
fleet under the command of Don John of Austria.

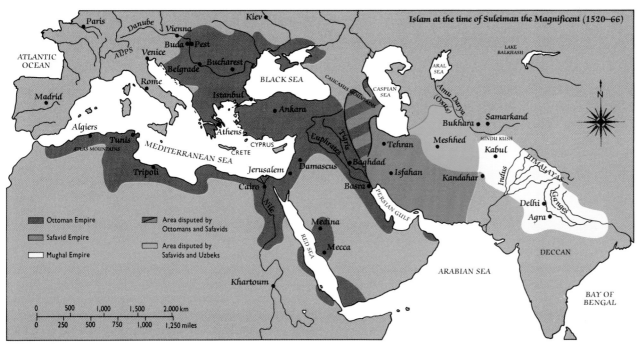

Islam at the time of Suleiman the Magnificent (1520–66)

Ottoman Empire

Safavid Empire

Mughal Empire

Area disputed by
Ottomans and Safavids

Area disputed by
Safavids and Uzbeks

During the course of
Suleiman's reign, the Islamic
world was dominated by three
major powers: the Ottomans,
the Safavids and the Mughals.
The area west of the Caspian
Sea, which covered parts of
what is now Azerbaijan,
Armenia, Iran and Turkey,
was frequently disputed by the
Ottomans and the Safavids.
During the 16th century, the
Ottomans had the upper hand
in the region, but in the early
17th century, they were ousted
by the Safavid emperor, Shah
Abbas I.

The Safavids

In the 16th century, the Ottoman Empire (pp.106–7) reached its zenith. This period also saw the rise of two other powerful Muslim dynasties: the Mughals in India (pp.104–5) and the Safavids (1501–1732) in Persia. By about 1550, these three dynasties either occupied or controlled territories stretching from Morocco in the northwest of Africa to the foothills of the Himalayas and the Bay of Bengal in the east.

While the Ottomans and the Mughals were Sunni Muslims, the Safavids were Shiites (pp.90–91) and had originated from a Sufi mystical brotherhood in Azerbaijan in central Asia founded by Shaykh Ishaq Safi al-Din (1252–1334). Originally Sunni, the order had become Shiite by the 15th century.

The first Safavid ruler, Ismail (1501–24), seized control of Azerbaijan in 1501 and by 1510 had subdued most of Iran. The type of Shiism that is known as

The Safavid era produced many fine illustrated manuscripts. This page comes from an edition of the Shahnameh, an epic poem by Firdawsi (940–1020). The scene shows the vizier Buzurjmihr inventing the game of backgammon. He and the surrounding figures wear the distinctive Safavid turban with a slim baton, normally coloured red, rising from the middle.

Perhaps the greatest patron of manuscript painting was Shah Tahmasp (1524–76), who studied the art and befriended the leading painters of the time. The royal library at Tabriz combined book learning with book production, including paper making, calligraphy, illustrating and binding.

The Royal Mosque, or Masjid-i-Shah, whose courtyard is shown here, was built by Shah Abbas I in Isfahan in the early 17th century. Its multicoloured light-reflecting tilework creates a dazzling effect, enhanced by the pool of water.

Shah Abbas made Isfahan, which lies on the central Iranian plateau surrounded by mountains, his capital and turned it into one of the most beautiful cities in the world. Its one million inhabitants could stroll along elegant, tree-lined avenues or in parks, or escape the fiery heat in one of the numerous public baths or mosques. The city was also an important industrial centre, with metalwork, textiles, pottery and carpets all major products.

Twelver (*below*) was imposed as the state religion. This was the single most important political and religious act of the Safavid rulers because it turned Shiism from a sectarian movement into a national religion and gave Persia a new sense of cohesion which has survived, with a few interruptions, into modern times.

The imposition of Twelver Shiism incensed the Sunni Ottomans, however, and they then attacked this "heretical" kingdom with unrelenting hostility. But despite frequent Ottoman invasions, loss of territory and the enforced removal of the capital from Tabriz to Qazvin and then to Isfahan, the Safavids enjoyed much military, political and cultural success.

This was particularly so during the reign of Shah Abbas I (1588–1629), during which the Ottomans were removed from Azerbaijan, and Persia's control over the eastern Caucasus and the Persian Gulf was extended. In the cultural sphere, the mosques built in Isfahan, with their brilliant peacock colours, epitomize the style and delicacy of Safavid art.

At the same time, the increasingly powerful Shiite clerics began a vigorous campaign to suppress both Sunnism and popular Sufism. The influence of the clerics was also shown by the way they questioned the religious pretensions of the Safavid kings, whose lax conduct contradicted many of the explicit tenets of Twelver Shiism. The result was tension and strife between the royal regime and the religious purists – a situation similar to that in the modern era when Ayatollah Khomeini condemned the shah of Iran for his rejection of Islam (pp.118–19).

The decline of the Safavid dynasty became obvious from the death of Shah Abbas II in 1666. Not only was clerical opposition to the monarchy difficult to quell, but anti-Shiite forces in regions such as Zandahar in Afghanistan also proved too strong. By the beginning of the 18th century, the dynasty was incapable of preventing the breakup of its empire as Mir Way, the Safavid governor of Afghanistan, declared himself independent. This secession was followed by the invasion and control of much of Persia by Mir Way's son, Mahmud, in 1722. Mahmud's action resulted in the devastation of cities, the ruin of the economy, a revival of tribalism, and the effective end of Safavid rule.

Twelvers and the Hidden Imam

The largest branch of Shiite Islam is the Twelver, or Imami, group, which is also known as Ithna'ashariyya. Most Iranians are Twelvers and there are smaller Twelver communities in southern Iraq, Syria, Lebanon, Saudi Arabia, the Gulf states, Azerbaijan, Pakistan, India, the United States and western Europe.

Twelvers recognize twelve imams, or religious heads, in the line of descent from Ali, the Prophet Muhammad's cousin and son-in-law who was caliph from 656 until his assassination in 661 (pp.90–91). Twelvers maintain that the Prophet appointed Ali as his successor but that the first four caliphs usurped his position. Shiites stress the sacredness of the families of Muhammad and Ali. They also hold that only those who are direct descendants of Ali and his wife Fatimah, daughter of the Prophet, are true imams and, as such, infallible in religious matters.

The most distinctive Twelver belief is that of the return of the Hidden Imam. For Twelvers hold that in 874, the last of the twelve imams, Imam al-Mahdi, disappeared and went into hiding in accordance with God's plan. They also believe that he is still alive and will one day return to guarantee the triumph of his followers, an event that will usher in the Last Judgment.

No one knows when the Hidden Imam will return. There was speculation among some Muslims in Iran that the Imam had come in the person of the Ayatollah Khomeini, who displaced the shah of Iran in the Islamic Revolution in 1979. Meanwhile, the *majlis*, or parliament, of Iran has been established under the protection of the Hidden Imam who, according to Shiites, is the chief interpreter of the Imami school of law (p.94). However, in his absence, interpretation of legal matters is conducted by qualified jurists known as *mujtahids*.

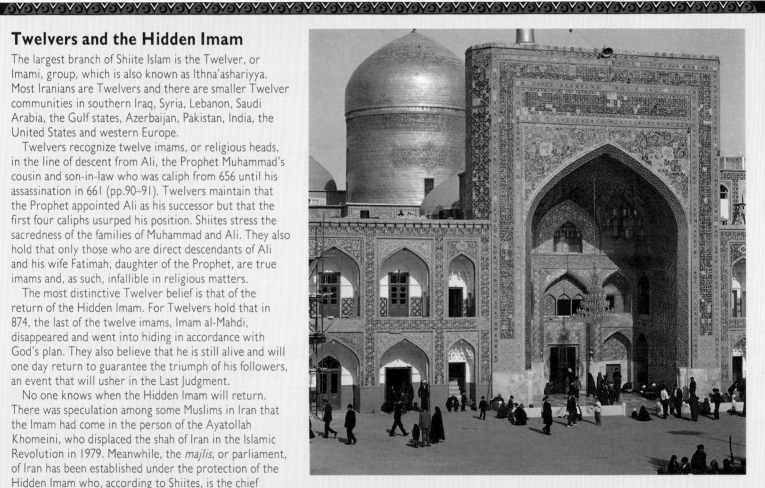

The town of Meshhed with its shrine of Ali al-Rida (c.768–818), eighth imam of *Twelver Shiism, is the most important place of pilgrimage for Iranian Shiites. It is also a major centre for legal and theological studies.*

The Far East

For many in the west, Islam is almost exclusively identified with the Middle East and Arab-speaking peoples. However, for more than a thousand years, there have been substantial Muslim communities in the Far East, especially China, Malaysia and Indonesia, which have combined Islam with native culture.

The first Muslim settlers in China were Arab and Persian traders, who, arriving in the eighth century via the sea routes around India, soon found the commerce rewarding enough to remain in Chinese coastal cities. At first, Muslims lived apart and retained their own language and customs. Gradually, through marriage, they became integrated into the Chinese way of life.

In the 13th century, Muslim influence in China grew when the borders of central Asia were prised open by the Mongols (pp.102–3). As a result, Muslims travelled along well-established trade routes to settle in China's northwestern and southwestern provinces, in what is now Yunnan and Gansu. Moreover, during the Yuan (Mongol) dynasty (1279–1368), Muslims worked as government officials throughout the country.

During the second half of the 14th century, China became isolated following assaults by Mongol tribes. Cut off from Muslim peoples to the west, the Muslims in China turned inward and immersed themselves in Chinese culture: they spoke Chinese, adopted Chinese names, wore Chinese dress, ate Chinese food and in all outward appearances were identical to other Chinese.

Chinese Muslims enjoyed a settled pattern of life until the 19th century, when Muslim insurrections occurred, fuelled by discontent over Qing rule (1664–1911) and inspired by the fundamentalist stance of the Naqshaban-diyya, a central Asian Sufi brotherhood (pp.98–99). These revolts created turmoil in the northwest and southwest of China before they were quelled. During the 20th century, Muslims have been treated with varying degrees of tolerance by the communist government, and the desire of Chinese Muslims to be distinct and separate remains.

In the Indonesian islands, the first solid evidence for Islam suggests that it arrived with traders from India in the 11th century. Conversion to Islam in Indonesia and the Malay peninsula proceeded gradually, through trade and, occasionally, coercion by pro-Islamic rulers. When the Venetian traveller Marco Polo (c.1254–1324) visited the northern part of the island of Sumatra in 1292, only one of its major cities, Ferlec (Perlak), was Muslim.

In Java, the first Islamic state – Demak, on the northern coast – did not emerge until the 15th century. In the course of the next century, many cities on the island of Borneo, east of Java, also adopted Islam. In the early 1600s, the southern part of the island of Sulawesi (Celebes) was converted, and by 1750 the communities of Java's eastern coast had turned to Islam. Indonesia continued to become Islamic during the 19th century, and, by the late 20th century, some 90 percent of the 130

Festive lights and decorations proclaim the Muslim New Year in Singapore, an island off the southern tip of the Malay peninsula. Singapore was part of the Muslim state of Johore, on the peninsula, until 1819, when the British arrived and soon effectively took it over. The island gained independence in 1965. In the early 1990s, there were nearly half a million Muslims on the island – about 17 percent of the total population – and some 1,500 mosques.

Chinese Muslims in Gansu province hold banners aloft at the head of a procession. Islam has been present in the country since the eighth century, when it arrived with Muslim merchants. By the 15th century, Chinese Muslims were similar in appearance to other Chinese people. And today, Muslim communities still maintain their own religious and cultural traditions.

million population was Muslim, the largest Muslim nation in the world.

But Indonesia's indigenous way of life has by no means been eradicated. For example, unlike in other Muslim countries, Islamic law has been confined almost exclusively to family law, and the mosque is seldom used as a centre for Islamic higher education. Also Indonesian in style is the architecture of the mosque, with its high, layered roof and the absence of a minaret (the call to prayer is made by the beating of a heavy drum).

In short, Islam in Indonesia has a distinctive local character, varying in degree and content from region to region. In central Java, where Hinduism and Buddhism have had a profound influence, Islam, although firmly embedded, can appear to the casual observer like a thin veneer when compared with the Hulu Sungai area northeast of Banjarmasin in southern Borneo, where there is little trace of any local pre-Islamic culture.

Traditional Javanese puppets, or wayang, *such as these, are used to relate tales from the island's mythical past in shows performed in cities and villages on festive occasions. Since the 16th century, this essentially Hindu-Javanese art form has been influenced by Islam – the figure first on the left in the back row is, for example, a Muslim character. Indeed, an entire Muslim play cycle, featuring the exploits of Amir Hamzeh, an uncle of the Prophet, has been introduced into the puppeteers' repertoire.*

The Spread into sub-Saharan Africa

This grand fortresslike mosque is in Jenne, Mali, in west Africa. Dating from the 14th century, the building is made of pisé, or rammed clay, and timbers whose ends protrude from the walls – an architectural style typical of the region. By the 14th century, this part of sub-Saharan Africa was recognized as an important centre of Islam by places as far away as Cairo and Damascus to the northeast.

Although Islam has dominated northern Africa for more than a thousand years, its establishment in regions south of the Sahara Desert is not so well known. Yet as many as 140 million Muslims, about one-sixth of the total world Muslim population, live in sub-Saharan Africa, with about one-third of that number living in Nigeria. The people of the former French west African colonies – Mauritania, Senegal, Mali and Niger – are mainly Muslim, and there are substantial Muslim populations in the Sudan, Ethiopia and Tanzania. Djibouti and Somalia in the Horn of Africa in the east are exclusively Muslim.

Sub-Saharan Africa's contacts with Islam go back 12 centuries, when seafaring merchants from southern Arabia and the Persian Gulf started to trade along the eastern coast of the continent. Evidence for this includes the remains of a mosque at Lamu in present-day Kenya, which date back to the eighth century. In eastern Africa, Islam remained a largely coastal phenomenon with a distinctive and pronounced Arab character until the 19th century and the opening up of the interior by European colonial powers.

From the Muslim settlements on the eastern coast, Islam did not begin the progression inland, to Nubia in northern Sudan, until the Mamluk dynasty came to power in Egypt in 1250. From this time, marriages between Mamluk Arabs and Nubian royal women, plus military pressure, brought about Muslim rule in Dongola, the capital of the Nubian state of Maqurra, in the early 14th century. Two centuries later, the foundation of Funj state, with its capital at Sennar on the Nile, did much to foster the growth of Islam in the Sudan until the second half of the 18th century. From then on, a decline set in which continued under Ottoman rule of the region (1821–85).

East of the Sudan, a trade route from Tripoli, capital of present-day Libya, running south across the Sahara to Lake Chad was in use as early as the eighth century. By the 11th century, the ruler of the kingdom of Kanem on Lake Chad was a Muslim. And it was largely through trade that Islam came to other parts of west Africa in the 11th century. Muslim merchants from the north, seeking to exchange salt for west African gold and slaves, influenced local rulers. They in time converted to Islam,

doubtless impressed by the literacy and numeracy of the Muslim traders as well as by the commercial advantages of knowing Arabic.

By the last quarter of the 12th century, the west African kingdom of Ancient Ghana had a Muslim ruler; and before long, west African rulers were making the pilgrimage to Mecca. According to the Arab historian Ibn Khaldun (1332–1406), when Mansa Musa, the ruler of the empire of Mali which replaced Ancient Ghana as the regional power in the 13th century, made the pilgrimage to Mecca in 1324, he took with him several thousand followers and much gold.

In his account of a visit to Mali in 1352, the Arab traveller Ibn Battutah (1304–68) recorded that despite

> **If the king is a Muslim, his land is Muslim; if he is an unbeliever, his land is a land of unbelievers.**
> SHAYKH USUMAN DAN FODIO

the presence of some traditional pre-Islamic customs and practices, he was impressed by the observance of the five daily prayers, the congregational prayers on Friday, and the importance attached to learning the Qur'an by heart. He also noted that some traditional indigenous practices had become mixed in with Islamic ones.

This assimilation occurred elsewhere in west Africa and was one of the prime factors behind Muslim reform movements in the late 17th century that sought to "purify" Islam. Some of these movements resulted in the establishment of Muslim states, of which the Sokoto caliphate (*below*) in northern Nigeria was one of the largest and most durable.

Muslims attend a service in a mosque in Senegal in west Africa. Islam has been present here since the 11th century, making it one of the oldest sub-Saharan Muslim countries. Today, more than 90 percent of Senegal's four million inhabitants are Muslims.

The Sokoto caliphate

Founded in 1809 in Hausaland in northern Nigeria, the Sokoto caliphate – named for the town in which it was based – was one of the most thoroughgoing Muslim states ever to be established in the history of Islam in Africa. Its founder was the Muslim scholar and mystic Shaykh Usuman dan Fodio (1752–1817).

In 1804, Usuman launched a *jihad*, or holy war, against contemporary Muslim rulers who mixed Islamic practices with indigenous ones, such as the veneration of trees and the offering of sacrifices to spirits that were believed to inhabit wells, streams and rivers. He also condemned them for imposing harsh and unjust taxes and for their failure to establish an Islamic system of government.

Usuman's *jihad* was fought across an extensive area roughly corresponding to present-day northern Nigeria and western Chad. Success came rapidly. By 1808, the *jihad* was effectively over and a period of consolidation began. A year later, a central government

was established at Sokoto under a caliph and a prime minister, or vizier. The *shari'a*, or Islamic law, was introduced, and the provision of Qur'anic education – in which many women played an important role – was extended throughout the caliphate. Literacy in Arabic increased; and this in turn helped to improve literacy in local languages, especially Hausa, through the use of Arabic characters.

When Usuman died in 1817, his son Muhammad Bello succeeded him as *sarkin musulmi*, or commander of the faithful, and became the first sultan of Sokoto. In the course of the 19th century, the caliphate gradually declined in both power and prestige. In the early 20th century, the British began their conquest of northern Nigeria and encountered resistance from the caliphate. However, under colonial rule, the caliphate regained much of its vitality and continues to influence Nigeria's Muslim population.

Crisis and Reform

Throughout the 18th and 19th centuries, the Ottoman Empire, which had become overstretched, economically weak and resistant to change, increasingly fell prey to the confident, expansionist powers of Europe. The Ottomans' resistance to "infidel learning", which delayed the printing of works in Turkish until 1727, is but one example of their failure to adapt and compete with Europe.

Ottoman supremacy was dealt a further blow by the decline of the Janissaries (pp.106–7) – the backbone of the Ottoman army – into an undisciplined rabble. Moreover, in time, the Ottoman sultans came to see the Janissaries and the Sufis, Islamic mystics, as equally subversive and dangerous. In 1826, Sultan Mahmud II wiped out the Janissaries in their barracks, then moved to suppress their long-time ally, the Bektashiyya Sufi brotherhood. In the following year, the Ottoman navy suffered a severe setback when Britain, France and Russia defeated the Ottoman fleet in Navarino Bay off southwestern Greece.

France and Britain were also competitors for Ottoman territory in northern Africa and the Middle East. France took control of Algeria in 1847 and Tunisia in 1881; and Britain occupied Egypt in 1882 and, a decade later, created a joint Anglo-Egyptian rule of the Sudan. Russia also became an important imperial power in the 19th century and extended its control over parts of Muslim central Asia, including much of Azerbaijan in 1828 and Bukhara in 1868. Meanwhile, in the Far East, the Dutch tightened their grip over Indonesia.

In all these Muslim lands, there were a variety of responses to colonialism. Some took up arms, others offered passive resistance. Radical Muslim fundamentalists, who, in India and Arabia, had attacked lax Muslim practices before the advent of colonialism, became more active. At the same time, progressive Islamic thinkers tried to reconcile Islam with the modern world. In Turkey, for example, a coterie of intellectuals known as the Young Turks, who came to power in 1908, believed that religion and politics should be kept separate. They began to secularize the country by increasing the power of secular courts and modernizing education, a policy continued by Kemal Atatürk (pp.116–17).

In Egypt, reform was largely inspired by Muhammad Abduh (1849–1905), the principal of al-Azhar University in Cairo, who believed that faith, reason and western learning could be compatible. His teachings influenced the emergence of a modern secular outlook not only in Egypt but also in the Middle East and Indonesia, which separated religion from the state. On the other hand, one of Abduh's pupils, Rashid Rida (1865–1935), was the inspiration behind a fundamentalist movement which rejected all authority other than the Qur'an and the *Sunna*, or practice of the Prophet Muhammad.

These modernist and fundamentalist tendencies still dominate the Muslim world today. For Muslim modernists one of the biggest obstacles is to convince their coreligionists that science and technology are not the sole preserve of the west and that adaptation is necessary. For traditionalists, the task is to resist encroaching secularization and affirm the place of God at the centre of people's lives.

Warships of Britain, France and Russia destroy the Turkish-Egyptian fleet in Navarino Bay, southwestern Greece, in 1827. The allies put out of action 57 enemy vessels in the short engagement, which contributed to the liberation of Greece from the Ottoman Empire.

The Suez Canal, seen here with its northern end in the foreground of this 19th-century panorama, was planned by the French engineer Ferdinand de Lesseps. It was opened in 1869, with Britain and France its main shareholders, showing that rival colonial powers could cooperate with each other.

The beginnings of the decline of the Ottoman Empire date back to the failed siege of Vienna in 1683. Soon after, the empire came under threat in different regions, with Hungary, for example, being reconquered by Austro-Hungarian forces in 1699.

During the 19th century, the empire, known as the Sick Man of Europe, gradually fell apart, with large territories either breaking away or coming under the control of European powers. Nevertheless, a series of sultans retained control, at least nominally, over a still sizable empire until the early 1920s. In 1924, Atatürk, the leader of Turkey, abolished the caliphate and set his country on the road to becoming a western-style republic.

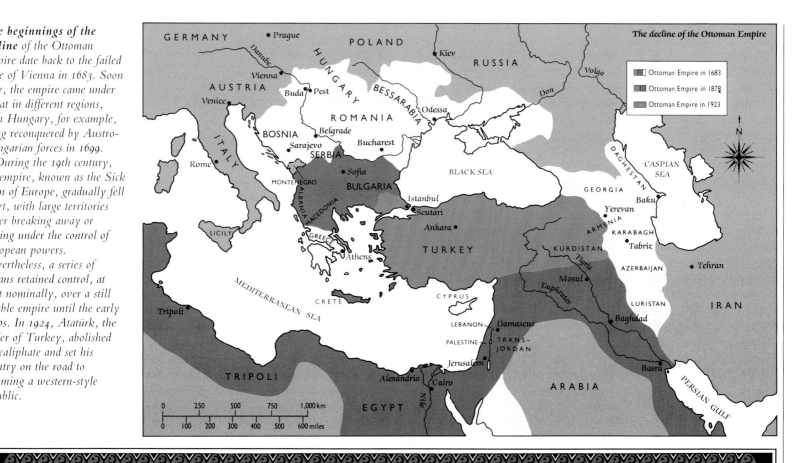

The decline of the Ottoman Empire

- Ottoman Empire in 1683
- Ottoman Empire in 1878
- Ottoman Empire in 1923

The Mahdi of the Sudan

From the early centuries of Islam, it was believed that the Mahdi would introduce an era of justice and righteousness and guarantee the final triumph of Islam. This would soon be followed by the Judgment Day. In the 19th century, there was great expectation throughout the Muslim world – and nowhere more so than in tropical Africa – that the Mahdi, the "God-guided one", and final reformer of Islam, would appear.

A number of political leaders have claimed to be the Mahdi. One of the most famous was Muhammad Ahmad ibn Abd Allah (1844–85), known as the Mahdi of the Sudan. Muhammad was aware of the various signs, regarding family background, place of birth, age and appearance, that distinguished a true claimant from a false one. In a letter to Sayyid al-Nahdi al-Sanussi, a prominent Muslim mystic in Libya, Muhammad wrote of the signs (one of which was a mole on his right cheek) that he believed made him the awaited Mahdi.

Muhammad claimed absolute authority over all Muslims and declared *jihad*, or holy war, against the Turks and their vassals the Egyptians, whom he accused of corruption, loose living, arbitrary justice and exploitation. This uprising, which broke out in the Sudan in 1883, involved Britain, which had occupied Egypt the year before.

The battle for the Sudan was fierce. This vast land was reconquered by the British only with great loss of life, including that of Major General Charles Gordon (1833–85) (BELOW), who was killed defending the town of Khartoum against attack from the mahdist forces. The Mahdi himself also died that year, in Omdurman, the capital of his theocratic state, which eventually fell to the British General Kitchener's forces in 1898. Although it was finally defeated, the mahdist movement did lay the foundations of Sudanese nationalism.

The tomb of the Mahdi of Sudan, in Khartoum, is a revered pilgrimage site for his Sudanese followers, who are known as Ansars.

Islam and Nationhood

Mustapha Kemal, known as Atatürk, or Father of the Turkish Nation, is shown here dancing with his adopted daughter. An astute politician as well as a brilliant soldier, Atatürk was first elected president of Turkey in 1923 and remained in this position until his death in 1938.

His energetic programme of westernization included the introduction of the Roman alphabet to replace Arabic characters, the banning of the fez, and the emancipation of women. Although he abolished the caliphate in 1924, people were still permitted to practise Islam; however, it was placed under the control of a government office.

Nasser and the Suez crisis

In the 1950s and '60s, the Egyptian soldier and statesman Gamal Abdel Nasser (1918–70) (RIGHT BELOW) became the inspiration for nationalist movements both in the Arab world and the third world. As a start, he played a crucial role in the army coup that overthrew King Farouk of Egypt in 1952. In 1954, he became Egypt's prime minister and, two years later, its president for life.

At first, he actively pursued a policy referred to as Islamic socialism, which was based on Islamic principles. He received support from all shades of Muslim opinion, including the fundamentalist Muslim Brotherhood (pp.205–6). But the Brotherhood soon became dubious of Nasser's commitment to Islam and, in 1954, they tried to assassinate him. Nasser reacted by banning the movement and executing its leader, Hadaibi, along with many of its prominent members.

Nasser's first international crisis came when he nationalized the strategically and economically important Suez Canal. Because the British government and French investors were the majority shareholders in the canal company, the result was military intervention by these two countries along with Israel. But the United States strongly disapproved of the action, and it was halted by the United Nations. Thus, having stood up successfully to the west, Nasser became a folk hero and assumed the moral leadership of the Arab world.

During the second half of the 19th century, the Ottoman Empire continued its decline. Waiting in the wings to take control of Ottoman territory were the powers of Europe. Accordingly, vast areas in northern Africa came under French and British control, and the Balkan provinces either gained autonomy or were colonized by the Austro-Hungarian Empire.

After the Ottoman defeat in World War I (1914–18), the remains of its empire in the Middle East were placed under British and French control by a League of Nations mandate. Britain, which already governed Muslim lands in eastern and southern Arabia, Iran, Afghanistan, India (including present-day Pakistan and Bangladesh), the Malay states, Egypt and the Sudan, was given responsibility for Iraq, Palestine and Transjordan. France added Syria and Lebanon to its Muslim territories in northern and western Africa.

The end of Ottoman rule in its homeland of Turkey came in 1924, when the Turkish leader Mustapha Kemal (1881–1938), or Atatürk, abandoned all claims to sovereignty or leadership of the Muslim world and created a new Turkish state. The Ottoman sultanate was over. In its stead was a constitutional republic based on secular, not Islamic, law.

But despite the apparent dominance of the European colonial powers over Islamic lands, their grip was not secure. Muslim nationalist movements had appeared before World War I, for example in Egypt, India and Indonesia, and the trend continued after the war. By 1921, Afghanistan had thrown off British rule and, four years later, Iran followed suit. In 1932, Saudi Arabia, a British protectorate since 1915, was formally established as an independent kingdom by Ibn Saud (c.1880–1953), and the same year, Iraq secured formal independence.

World War II (1939–45) stretched the colonial powers to their limits and left them dependent for manpower and raw materials, such as rubber and tin, on their colonies, some of which made independence a condition of cooperation. After the war, the greater part of Palestine became the state of Israel in 1948, and the Palestinian Arabs were forced to take refuge mainly in Jordan, the Lebanon and Syria. Elsewhere, Indonesia broke free of the Dutch in 1949, and Malaya did the same with the British in 1957. By 1962, after a fierce war against France, Algeria had also won its independence.

But in many countries, colonialism was replaced by neocolonialism as the old powers deepened their economic interest in their former territories, particularly the major oil-producing ones, such as Saudi Arabia, Iran and the Gulf states. For example, British and American influence in post-independence Iran led to the overthrow of prime minister Muhammad Musadeqq after his decision to nationalize Iranian oil in 1951.

After their independence, many Muslim countries experimented with European-style governments. However, most of them quickly became one-party states or military dictatorships, often claiming that a strong, central government would protect the country from its enemies, create a sense of national unity, and speed up the pace of modernization.

However, the drive to modernize led to what many Muslims regarded as excessive westernization and the rejection of traditional religious values. The result was the growth of radical fundamentalist Islamic opposition groups such as Hasan al-Banna's Muslim Brotherhood in Egypt, which condemned Islamic leaders who led western lifestyles and paid only lip service to their religious duties. The fundamentalists' demand was simple: a radical transformation of the theory and practice of government policy and social mores along Islamic lines.

Algerian women take a military salute during the civil war against France which ended with Algeria's independence in July 1962. In 1991, the Islamic Salvation Front party, committed to Islamic government, won a moral victory in the national elections, but was thwarted from taking power by a military takeover.

A convoy of Kurdish refugees makes its way from Iraq to the Turkish border in September 1988. The Kurds are Sunni Muslims and live mainly in the mountains where Turkey, Iraq and Iran meet. They have been in conflict with these countries on and off since the 1920s and, in Iraq, as recently as 1992, a year after the Gulf War.

Revolution and Reform

God is the Light of the heavens and the earth. QUR'AN 24:35

Islamic countries have increasingly had to confront a fundamental dilemma during the second half of the 20th century. Should they impose a total Islamic way of life on their population and in their dealings with other countries? Or should they attempt to come to terms with the developed, western world and its ideals of democracy and liberalism, and a culture that is pervaded by secular values?

The problem has provoked a variety of responses. Some countries, such as Iran and Libya, have generally taken a fundamentalist anti-western stance. Others, such as Turkey and Tunisia, have separated religion from politics and are strongly influenced by western culture. Still others, such as Saudi Arabia and the Gulf states, have preserved Islamic institutions but have also accommodated alliances with western nations. And the decision whether to embrace or reject western culture has also divided minority Muslim communities living in the west, particularly in the United States, France, Germany and Britain.

During the 1980s, there were a number of signs pointing toward a rapprochement between Islam and western states. For example, in 1981, the peace treaty between Egypt and Israel, supported by the west, was a considerable triumph, given that it came soon after the Arab-Israeli wars of 1967 and 1973; and, during the Gulf War in 1991, Muslim and western states joined together to counter Iraq's invasion of Kuwait. Also, the vigorous resistance by Muslims in Afghanistan, first to Soviet-imposed government in 1973 and then to the Soviet invasion in 1978, gained popular approval and material support from the west.

On the other hand, Muslim nations moderate in their dealings with the west have been balanced by those to whom the west embodies a decadent, irreligious force.

The takeover in Iran by Ayatollah Khomeini in 1979 sent shock waves reverberating throughout the west as it saw a fundamentalist Islamic regime hold sway and unleash highly charged rhetoric against those who had tried to prop up the dictatorial rule of the deposed shah, Muhammad Reza.

The west's allegedly moral, legal and military impotence was graphically shown when members of the American Embassy in Tehran, the capital of Iran, were taken hostage and held from 1979 to 1980. This was followed by a decade of hostage-taking in the Lebanon by militant Muslim groups backed by Iran. And in 1989, Ayatollah Khomeini pronounced a death sentence on the British novelist Salman Rushdie, whose book *The Satanic Verses* was held to be blasphemous.

To many, moderation had become a concept alien to the Muslim world. Where moderate Muslim leaders did emerge, they risked assassination by hardliners, as was the case with the Egyptian leader President Anwar Sadat (1918–81), who was killed by members of the al-Jihad Islamic group. One of the principal reasons for the killing was the Sadat-Begin Camp David peace treaty between Egypt and Israel, which the fundamentalists deemed to favour Israel at the expense of the Palestinians and the Muslim cause generally.

What the Muslim opposition in Egypt wanted to achieve was an Islamic policy of nonalignment. This was, and is, also the position of most of the Muslim world, including post-Khomeini Iran; the Islamic Salvation Front in Algeria, which won a moral victory in the elections in 1991 but was prevented from taking power by a military coup; and the various Afghan *mujahedin* guerrilla movements, which waged continuous war for 14 years (1978–92) against Soviet-backed regimes in Afghanistan.

The rise of more radical fundamentalist groups and regimes has also had its effect on Muslims living in the west. During the 1960s, Islam became more noticeable in Europe largely through increased Muslim emigration from India and Pakistan to Britain, from northern Africa to France, and from Turkey to what was West Germany. As a result of this influx, France's Muslim population in the early 1990s stood at around 2.5 million, Germany's at over 1.5 million and Britain's at just under 1 million. In the United States, landmark changes in the immigration law of 1965 meant that unprecedented numbers of Muslims were admitted into the country. In 1989, there were about six million Muslims in the United States, many of whom have settled in Chicago, which has some 25 mosques or Friday prayer centres.

Although they are influenced by the customs and values of their homelands, Muslims in the west are constructing an Islam which they believe is true to the Qur'an but shorn of much of the cultural baggage that accompanied it from the Muslim countries from which they originally came. To this extent, for the first time in history, a western form of Islam is in the making.

A Muslim woman in Malaysia studies her computer screen while a colleague looks on. One of the dilemmas Islam has had to face in the 20th century is whether or not to embrace the technological advances of the west and thereby risk the threat that they bring to traditional culture.

British Muslims *protest outside the Houses of Parliament in London against the publication of* The Satanic Verses *by the novelist Salman Rushdie. The book and the angry reaction to it by Muslims around the world has raised the question of how successfully conservative Islam can coexist in relatively liberal western societies.*

The simple but imposing colonnade *of Petrol University in Saudi Arabia speaks eloquently of the wealth generated by oil revenues in this and other Muslim countries of the Middle East since the 1920s. Income from oil has brought dramatic political, economic and educational change to the region and has made Saudi Arabia – the largest Middle Eastern oil producer – a growing influence in both regional and international affairs.*

World distribution of Muslims

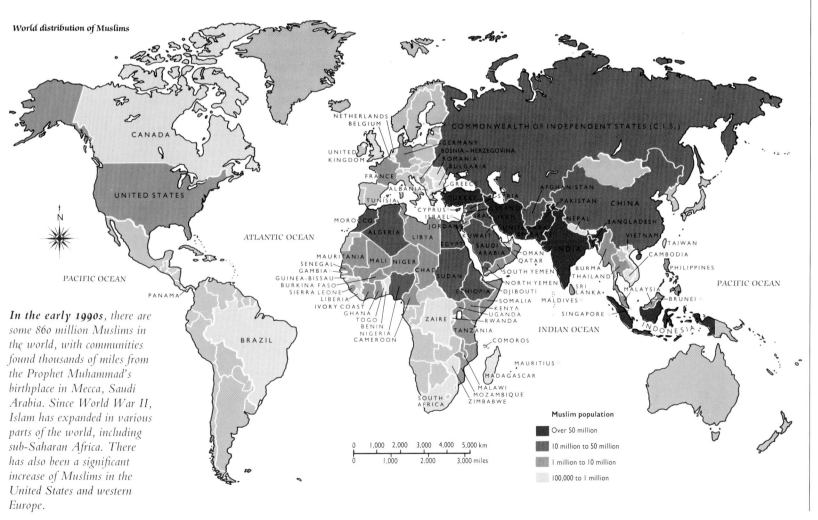

In the early 1990s, *there are some 860 million Muslims in the world, with communities found thousands of miles from the Prophet Muhammad's birthplace in Mecca, Saudi Arabia. Since World War II, Islam has expanded in various parts of the world, including sub-Saharan Africa. There has also been a significant increase of Muslims in the United States and western Europe.*

Muslim population

- Over 50 million
- 10 million to 50 million
- 1 million to 10 million
- 100,000 to 1 million

The sacred fire, *the central symbol of Zoroastrianism, provides a focal point as Zoroastrian priests officiate at a ceremony of blessing, or jashan. Such services may be connected with seasonal festivals, historical events in Iran (the religion's homeland) and honouring the dead, or simply acts of worship made, for example, in thanksgiving.*

The ceremony is performed by two or more priests for the well-being of both the spiritual and physical worlds. At the end of the ceremony, those present partake of the consecrated fruits and other special foods that may be included, such as darun, consecrated bread, and malido, a sweetened wheat-flour pudding.

Keepers of the Fire

ALTHOUGH THERE ARE LITTLE MORE THAN 100,000 Zoroastrians living in the world today, their faith, which has its roots in ancient Iran, has had an influence out of all proportion to their current numbers. Zoroastrianism was founded more than 3,000 years ago by an Iranian prophet named Zarathushtra (Greek Zoroaster), who has been called the first monotheist.

His teachings included the concept of one God (Ahura Mazda), heaven and hell, the coming of a saviour figure, the resurrection of the dead and a last judgment – ideas many scholars believe have permeated Judaism, Christianity and Islam.

Today, the Zoroastrian faith is practised mainly by the Parsis (pp.122–23), who fled from Iran to northwestern India at the end of the ninth century C.E. to escape persecution from their Muslim oppressors. Parsis (''Persians'') constitute roughly four-fifths of the Zoroastrians in the world today. They are mainly found in Bombay in western India, although there are small communities in Britain, Canada, the United States and Australia.

Zoroastrianism's founder, the prophet Zarathushtra, is thought to have lived in a region around the southern steppes of what is now the Commonwealth of Independent States. Although there is a tradition that he lived in about 600 B.C.E., most modern scholars now place him between about 1400 and 1200 B.C.E., a time of great social upheaval, when the Stone Age culture of the region was giving way to that of the Bronze Age. Zarathushtra evidently experienced the destructive effects of encroaching warlike tribes who brought violence and disorder to what had been essentially a peaceful, pastoral society for thousands of years.

At some point in his life, Zarathushtra, following a divine revelation, began to teach his vision of God, the universe and the world. His teachings reflect the society in which he lived, with their allusions to cattle-herding, law, justice, kinship and hospitality. And a sense of injustice born from the disruption of the society in which he lived led him to preach a novel faith. At the heart of this was a radical dualistic creed whose central doctrine was based on the origins and nature of good and evil. He taught that there was one God, Ahura Mazda, eternal and uncreated, who made this world in order to bring about the destruction of his adversary, the Evil Spirit Angra Mainyu. Also uncreated, the Evil Spirit will ultimately perish and the forces of evil will cease to exist.

God brought into being six lesser divinities, the Amesha Spentas (pp.122–23), who, together with God's Holy Spirit, formed the Divine Heptad, or group of seven. Once God's creation had been accomplished, Angra Mainyu attacked it. Zoroastrian doctrine says that the Evil Spirit slew the uniquely created bull and the first man, and caused the first plant to perish. He ruptured the sky of stone and made the earth into a desert. He made pure water salty and, finally, defiled the seventh creation, fire, by making it smoke.

The Amesha Spentas reacted in turn by creating life from death, thus beginning the cycle of regeneration. Humans differ from the other creations in that they may choose between good and evil. Through good thoughts, words and deeds they can contribute to the salvation of the world.

One of Zarathushtra's early converts was a tribal prince named Vishtaspa (Greek Hystaspes) and through his influence the prophet's teachings spread. Over the following centuries, the Iranian people, among whom Zoroastrianism had become established, migrated south to the land that came to bear their name, spreading throughout the eastern reaches of the country.

During the first millennium B.C.E., Zoroastrianism reached the western part of Iran, later becoming the state religion of three great empires in the region: the Achaemenians (559–330 B.C.E.), a dynasty that united the Persian and Median peoples; the Parthians (c.247 B.C.E.–224 C.E.); and the Sasanians (224–651 C.E.). In Achaemenian times, the religion entered recorded history through Persian inscriptions and the works of the fifth-century historian Herodotus, one of several Greek writers who refer to Zoroastrian beliefs and practices.

Crossing the bridge

Zoroastrians believe in an afterlife and in the judgment of the soul. Zarathushtra taught that every person is judged at death according to his or her merits. If the good deeds outweigh the bad, the soul passes over a broad bridge and ascends into heaven. But if bad deeds outweigh the good, the bridge becomes as narrow as a blade-edge and the soul falls into hell. At the end of time, a great battle will take place between the divine beings and the demons, and the good will triumph. A world saviour, born of the seed of the prophet and a virgin mother, will bring about the resurrection of the dead and the Last Judgment. Thereafter, the wicked will perish and hell will be purged. God's kingdom will come on earth and the world will return to a state of perfection.

Zoroastrians do not cremate or bury their dead, or immerse them in water, because fire, earth and water must be kept pure. Consequently, since ancient times Zoroastrians have exposed their dead to birds of prey. In both Iran and India, circular stone structures known as *dakhmas*, or towers of silence, were specially built for this purpose.

Keepers of the Fire

After the Muslim Arab invasion of Iran in the seventh century C.E., the Zoroastrian faith was gradually supplanted by Islam. Eventually, to escape persecution, a small group of Zoroastrian Iranians set sail from their country at the end of the ninth century and finally landed on the west coast of India in 936 C.E. The Indians knew them as Parsis, or Persians, and allowed them to practise their religion and establish a sacred fire, the symbol of their faith.

The Parsis prospered as farmers and small traders and, in time, other settlements were founded along the coast. Centuries later, with the arrival in India of European merchants in the 17th century, the rural Parsi community rapidly became urbanized, and the development of a wealthy and well-educated Parsi middle class contributed significantly to the economic growth of Bombay. Down the centuries, the Parsis maintained contact with the Zoroastrians of Iran, asking them about ritual and observance, the answers to which were recorded in a series of letters known as the Persian *Rivayats*.

One of the most essential Parsi observances is the cult of the ever-burning hearth fire, which is thought to go back to ancient times. Before Zarathushtra, the nomadic Iranian peoples needed a portable form of worship, since it was not practicable to set up fixed structures of worship such as a temple, altar or statue. Religious observances made by laypeople therefore involved offerings to fire and water, and to the gods, and these rites also formed part of the priests' act of worship. Zarathushtra's great innovation was the idea that fire was the representative of truth and righteousness, *Asha*; thus, praying before the hearth fire, the sun or the moon helped to focus on this concept.

During a 24-hour period, Zoroastrians pray five times facing a source of light. As they do so, they untie and retie the symbolic sacred cord, or *kusti*, which is passed three times around the waist over a sacred shirt. In modern times, worshippers may pray before a lamp, which is kept constantly alight in the home in place of a hearth fire, or before the sacred fire in the fire temple – the Zoroastrian place of worship.

Zoroastrianism stresses the need to avoid pollution of any kind, although its demanding purity laws are now rarely kept by city dwellers. Zoroastrians perform ritual ablutions before saying their prayers and before any religious ceremony, such as a wedding. Among orthodox families, women are still segregated during menstruation and for 40 days after the birth of a child. The "inner" rituals of the faith, such as the *yasna*, or act of worship, which includes the reciting of texts such as the *Gathas*, are performed by priests, usually in an enclosure adjoining the fire temple. Before they are qualified to perform such rituals, priests must undergo a purification rite, followed by a retreat of nine days. The "outer" rituals, such as a *jashan*, or ceremony of blessing (p.120), may be performed in any clean place.

Rituals and observances

In Zoroastrianism, there are six benevolent divine beings, known as the Amesha Spentas, which, with God's Holy Spirit, Spenta Mainyu, are linked with God's creation, certain priestly rituals, observances by laypeople and the seven holy days of obligation. These are set out in the chart below. The holy days are probably the legacy of ancient seasonal festivals refounded in honour of Ahura Mazda and the divinities created by him. The Amesha Spentas are believed to dwell within each of their creations while at the same time remaining aspects of God's nature.

AMESHA SPENTA (with English equivalent)	CREATION	REPRESENTATION IN PRIESTLY ACT OF WORSHIP	SEVEN HOLY DAYS OF OBLIGATION	OBSERVANCE IN EVERYDAY LIFE
Khshathra Vairya (Power, Dominion, Kingdom of God)	Sky (at first thought of as stone and later as metal)	The stone pestle and mortar, flint knife (later, metal implements)	Midspring	Exercising proper authority; being honest, thrifty, charitable
Haurvatat (Wholeness, Health)	Water	Consecrated water used in libations	Midsummer	Keeping water unpolluted; being temperate, self-disciplined
Armaiti (Piety, Devotion)	Earth	The ground of the ritual enclosure	Bringing in grain	Tilling and enriching the soil; being patient, enduring, productive
Ameretat (Long life, Immortality)	Plants	Plants, such as haoma; wheaten cakes; symbolic bundle of twigs (now metal rods) held by priest	Homecoming (of herds)	Nurturing plants and trees; being temperate, self-disciplined
Vohu Manah (Good Purpose, Good Thought)	Cattle	The sacrificial beast, or its products, such as milk and butter	Midwinter	Caring for animals; having good intentions
Spenta Mainyu (Holy Spirit)	The just man	The priest	All Souls	Looking after one's own physical and moral being
Asha Vahishta (Right, Truth, Order)	Fire	The ritual fire	New Year's Day	Keeping fire unpolluted; being just and righteous in thoughts, words, actions

There are many holy days in Zoroastrianism besides the seven obligatory ones. For example, there is one for the waters, when people pray and make offerings by the seashore or any natural water, and one for fire, when offerings of sandalwood are made to the temple fire.

Many of the problems facing Zoroastrian communities today, such as whether or not to accept converts from other religions and intermarriage between Zoroastrians and non-Zoroastrians, date back to when the Parsis settled in India, where, as a minority group, they wished to preserve their Iranian heritage. In the area of doctrine, problems arose in the 19th century, when European scholars began to translate and interpret Zoroastrian texts, challenging the traditional view of them. As a result, various reform movements were founded in Bombay, and still remain at variance with one another. Nevertheless, the various Zoroastrian groups share as a basis Zarathushtra's fundamental teaching that the ultimate aim of living a good life is to bring about the salvation of this world.

Zoroastrian scriptures

For many centuries, Zarathushtra's teachings were passed down by word of mouth since they were considered too sacred to be committed to writing. It was not until Sasanian times (224–651 C.E.) that they were finally written down in an alphabet especially invented for the purpose. The Avestan language in which they had been composed had by then ceased to be understood by all except the priesthood and was otherwise unrecorded. The Sasanian *Avesta*, as the scriptures were called, consisted of a total of 21 books, all of which were destroyed during the conquest of Iran by the Arabs and, later, by Mongol and Turkish invaders.

However, a substantial secondary religious literature survives, written in Middle Persian, or Pahlavi, the language of the Sasanians. There are also translations and summaries of the lost Avestan books. With the exception of the *Gathas*, 17 hymns attributed to the prophet himself, the Avestan texts and most of the Pahlavi literature are anonymous, the composite works of priestly poets and scholars.

The *Gathas* are short texts that take the form of inspired utterances, mainly addressed by Zarathushtra to Ahura Mazda, expressing what he felt were divinely inspired truths as well as expressions of philosophic enquiry.

The winged disc, here from the Achaemenian city of Persepolis, shows a figure holding the "ring of divinity". The disc may represent the king's guardian spirit, Ahura Mazda, or divine grace.

A Parsi woman weaves a kusti – the sacred cord worn as a girdle by Zoroastrians. Children are invested with the cord at the age of seven.

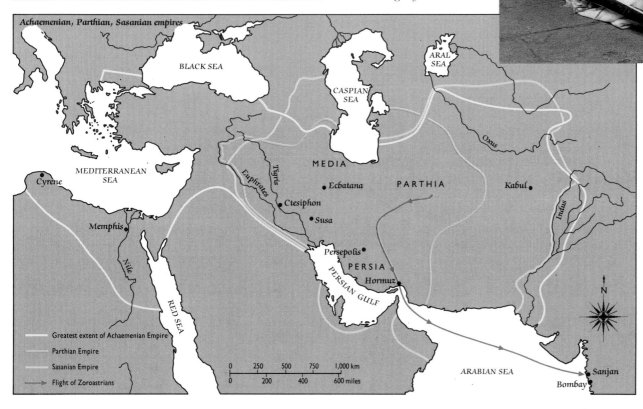

Zoroastrianism was the religion of the first Persian Empire founded by the Achaemenian king Cyrus the Great. The conquest of the empire by Alexander the Great (356–323 B.C.E.) was followed by the rise of the Parthians, a people from northeastern Iran, who also made Zoroastrianism their state religion.

The Parthians were succeeded by the Sasanians, through whom the religion as an imperial faith is best known. Toward the end of the ninth century, a group of Zoroastrians fled Iran and finally settled on the west coast of India.

Achaemenian, Parthian, Sasanian empires

BLACK SEA

ARAL SEA

CASPIAN SEA

MEDITERRANEAN SEA

Cyrene

MEDIA

Ecbatana

PARTHIA

Oxus

Kabul

Euphrates

Tigris

Ctesiphon

Susa

Memphis

Nile

Persepolis

PERSIA

Hormuz

PERSIAN GULF

Indus

RED SEA

— Greatest extent of Achaemenian Empire
— Parthian Empire
— Sasanian Empire
→ Flight of Zoroastrians

0 250 500 750 1,000 km
0 200 400 600 miles

ARABIAN SEA

Sanjan

Bombay

Many Paths, One Goal

FOR WESTERNERS, THE HINDU RELIGION can conjure up a wide variety of images, from cross-legged ascetics and richly carved temple-towers to the cremation fires by the side of the Ganges and animal-headed gods. Hinduism is as difficult to grasp as a snake. It has no founder, no single scripture or creed. There are many gods – Vishnu and Shiva among the most prominent – but there is only one ultimate reality. It resists neat definitions and rejoices in diversity. Perhaps the only way of describing it is the aggregate of practices and beliefs of some 1,400 million Hindus living in the Indian subcontinent and other parts of the world today.

The term Hindu comes from the word coined by ancient Persians to describe those who lived opposite them on the other side of the Indus River. Modern Hindus prefer the phrase *sanatana dharma* to describe their religion. This can be translated as "the eternal way of conduct" – eternal because it is divine in origin, and way of conduct because it covers every aspect of life.

Some Hindus believe that their sacred law, or *dharma*, can be practised only in India; if they crossed the *kala pani*, "the black ocean", it would render them impure and unable to live as Hindus. Others do not share this view; and, during the last 100 years, many Hindus, most of them economic migrants, have moved to other parts of the world. Today, these migrants are to be found especially in Britain and countries of the British Commonwealth, for example the Caribbean, Canada and eastern Africa, as well as in the United States and Europe.

The cultural impact of Hinduism in the west in the modern era can be dated precisely to 1893, when the World Parliament of Religions in Chicago was attended by a Hindu ascetic named Vivekananda (pp.142–43). He so impressed the gathering with his spirituality and view of Hinduism as a great universal faith that afterward there were many westerners who questioned the wisdom of continuing to send Christian missionaries to India.

Encouraged by the interest Vivekananda had stimulated and perhaps by the enthusiasm for things Indian that Queen Victoria demonstrated (she even learned Hindustani, but could not visit the "jewel" in her crown for health reasons), prominent Hindus and Hindu-inspired organizations went to the west from that time onward. In recent times, one of the most visible groups with its roots in Hinduism has been the Hare Krishna movement (p.206). Founded in the United States in 1966, the movement gained much publicity from its association with the British pop star George Harrison, formerly of the Beatles.

But the trend has not been in one direction only. Some Hindus, including Mahatma Gandhi (p.142), were influenced by the 19th-century western thinkers John Ruskin and Leo Tolstoy, as well as by the teachings of Jesus. Also, in 1893, Annie Besant, an Irish woman by birth, went to India and established the Central Hindu College at Varanasi (Benares), which eventually became a university. She worked energetically for the education of Hindu women, as well as

The Kumbha Mela festival, held every 12 years in turn at Hardwar, Nasik, Ujjain and Prayag (LEFT), *near Allahabad, attracts Hindus literally in their millions.*

Devotees of the Hare Krishna movement, shown (RIGHT) *in Amsterdam, Holland, belong to the Hindu tradition and are often seen in the streets of western cities.*

Many Paths, One Goal

for the promotion of theosophy, an esoteric religious system, which was heavily influenced by Hindu ideas.

In the late 1950s, Bede Griffiths, a British Benedictine monk, established a religious centre, or ashram, based on Indian lines in southern India. His teaching and meditation techniques combine aspects of both Hindu and Christian spirituality. Indeed, as travel and communications continue to shrink the distances between the world's continents, the interaction between Hinduism and Christianity – and many other faiths – is likely to increase.

Although there is a great diversity within their religion, most Hindus share a body of beliefs and acknowledge traditional paths to follow toward the realization of ultimate reality. They would also all emphasize the importance of striving to attain purity and avoiding pollution, and the regular practice of worship, or *puja*, both in the home and in the temple.

Most Hindus accept the authority of the ancient scriptures known as the Vedas (pp.130–31); the fourfold social division (*varna*) divinely sanctioned in the *Rig Veda* scripture; and the occupational groups – castes or *jatis* – which developed later. They believe their lives are governed by *samsara*, a cycle of birth, death and rebirth, and that the soul (*atman*) is reincarnated until it gains release (*moksha*).

The concept of *Rita* – the power giving the universe order and rhythm, controlling birth, growth, decay and renewal – described in the Vedas, becomes in later scriptures *Brahman*. This is the universal spirit and ultimate reality, and is more akin to the Christian idea of an impersonal godhead than a personal God.

The Hindu's ultimate goal is to attain *moksha*, that is, personal liberation from the cycle of *samsara*. This can be achieved through *dharma*, best described in this context as following a sacred code of conduct that entails performing certain rituals (prayers, worship) and behaving in a moral way to oneself, one's family and society. In addition, Hindus recognize a number of specific traditional paths that lead to liberation. These are principally three: the paths of devotion, action and knowledge.

The path of devotion (*bhakti*) requires no specialist help from a priest or guru (a spiritual teacher) and is the simplest way of experiencing the union that exists between the individual soul (*atman*) and the universal spirit (*Brahman*). It entails believing in and completely surrendering to a personal god or goddess, as well as putting an unquestioning faith in *Brahman*. The final goal is to break the cycle of *samsara* and be in God's presence eternally by merging the *atman* into *Brahman*.

Death and the continuance of life

Hindus believe that at death only the body dies, while the spirit or soul (*atman*) lives many times in different bodies until *moksha* is achieved – the liberation from the cycle of birth, death and rebirth. A dying person is ideally given water from the sacred River Ganges and encouraged to utter God's name, usually "Ram Ram", so that the soul can attain peace.

When a person dies, his or her corpse is bathed and dressed in new clothes. All adult relations now enter a state of ritual pollution for 10 days. The men in the family prepare a stretcher made of bamboo staves and, having placed the corpse on it, they cover the body with a new white cloth and red flowers, and tie it securely. By tradition, the eldest or the youngest son, who carries live coals in an earthen pot, walks before the corpse as it is carried to the funeral ground near a local river.

Hindus cremate their dead, but very young babies and *sannyasins* (those who have renounced the world) are buried. When the pyre has been constructed and the corpse placed on it, the son performs his religious duty of lighting it while the priest chants mantras (sacred verses) to sanctify the fire. Then the son walks around it three, five or seven times, holding a burning torch.

Sometimes, a small hole is drilled in the earthen pot, which is then filled with water. As the son walks around the pyre, dripping water forms a limiting line to prevent the soul from escaping back to earth as a ghost. When the heat of the pyre cracks the skull of the corpse, the mourners bathe in the river and return home, leaving the cremation ground staff to tend the pyre. On the third day after the cremation, the ashes are collected and, on or after the tenth day, they are cast into a holy river.

Just as the spider spins its thread, or as sparks fly out from a fire; just in the same way, from this self all energies, all worlds, all the deities, all beings come forth. That self is called the "truth of truths".

BRIHADARANYAKA UPANISHAD

Smoke billows skyward as the body of a dead person is cremated on a funeral pyre. Traditional Hindus cremate the dead – only babies and wandering holy men known as sannyasins *are buried. Properly performed death rituals are important in releasing the soul (*atman*) so that it may continue its journey toward liberation (*moksha*).*

The path of action (*karma*) requires Hindus to think thoughts and carry out actions selflessly, so that the consequent effects, both good and evil, do not bind the *atman* to successive lives in different bodies. The simplest way of achieving this is to follow an occupation that can benefit both society and the individual.

The path of knowledge (*jñana*) has to be learned from a guru, who can explain from the sacred scriptures the nature of *Brahman*, *atman*, the universe, and people's place in it. A clear understanding of this ancient knowledge results in breaking the bonds of attachment to the material world and the attainment of liberation.

Another way of leading the soul to liberation is through yoga (possibly meaning "yoke"), which broadly refers to a number of physical and mental disciplines used by ascetics and others as aids to spiritual contemplation. Yoga is also well known in the west, particularly Hatha Yoga, which seeks to achieve *samadhi*, a state of superconsciousness, through eight stages of physical exercises, and Raja ("Royal") Yoga, which emphasizes body posture, breath control, concentration and meditation.

On a more mundane level, Hindus attach great importance to purity and pollution – in terms of both physical cleanliness and spiritual well-being. This influences worship in the home and the temple, as well as a Hindu's social position, which depends on his or her occupation and the degree to which it involves pollutants, such as blood and waste matter. It also affects the preparation and eating of food. Vegetarian food is popular among many Hindus because it is free from blood, which is considered to be a pollutant, while the veneration of the cow arises from the same impulse coupled with the animal's economic usefulness.

Cows pass the time of day in the central reservation of a highway in the city of Delhi. The cow retains a special place in Hinduism, and Mahatma Gandhi said that it represents India. Killing or harming these sacred animals is prohibited, and they are allowed to wander freely in cities. They are also valued for their nutritious milk and their dung, which can be used as a fuel and, mixed with water, as a purifying agent.

Private and public worship

For Hindus, worship, or *puja*, of a particular deity can take place either in the home or the temple. In the home, *puja* often occurs in the kitchen, considered to be the purest part of the house. It is led by a senior member of the family, who must bathe beforehand.

This domestic *puja* involves washing and drying images (*murtis*) of deities and offering them red kumkum and yellow turmeric powders, water, rice grains, flowers, food, incense and light. The *arati* ritual is then performed by passing a ghee-lamp (fuelled by clarified butter) before the images, while sacred verses of praise are sung. Food placed before the deities is received back as *prasad*, or "blessed offering".

Temple worship revolves around the consecrated image of the deity, to whom the temple is dedicated. The image is situated in the inner shrine, which is the holiest part of the building. The daily *puja* consists of making various offerings (*upacharas*), normally supervised by male priests.

Any worshippers present at the morning and evening *puja* can obtain a view of the god image (*darshan*) by standing at the door to the shrine. After the *puja*, an elaborate *arati* is performed – the priests bring a tray laden with ghee-lamps and camphor out into the temple hall, and the worshippers receive the *arati* light and the deity's blessing. The priests then bow before the deity, and *prasad* is distributed among the worshippers.

Members of a Hindu family perform morning worship in their home in London, England. Most Hindus have a shrine at home, which may consist simply of a picture.

The System of Caste

Stages of life

For "twice born" Hindus – those belonging to the first three *varnas* – there are traditionally four stages of life. These are known as the four *ashramas* and consist of: *Brahmacharya*, the celibate student stage; *Grihasthya*, the married householder stage; *Vanaprasthya* ("forest dwelling"), the retirement stage; and, finally, *Sannyas*, the stage when worldly concerns are renounced.

Most people pass through the first three stages, performing duties for themselves, for their families and for the community. Very few enter the fourth, optional *ashrama*. This entails becoming a *sannyasin*, a homeless wanderer, depending on others for food, meditating on *Brahman*, the universal spirit, and seeking liberation from the cycle of birth, death and rebirth.

The sacred thread

Hindu scriptures recommend 16 rites of passage in a person's life, but many Hindus experience only the initiation, marriage and cremation rituals. However, boys from the first three *varnas* (Brahmin, Kshatriya and Vaishya) can undergo a ceremony in which they are invested with the "sacred thread", signifying a second birth – hence the first three *varnas* are referred to as "twice born".

The ritual is performed by the boy and his father while a family priest chants mantras (sacred verses). Before the ceremony, the boy has his last "childhood" meal with his mother, both eating from the same plate. Then the boy prays to the sun god, presents offerings of ghee (clarified butter) to the god Agni (Fire), and is invested with the sacred thread, a white cord which is worn over the left shoulder and under the right arm from that day onward.

He also prays to the sun god for intelligence and is taught the Gayatri verse from the *Rig Veda* as a symbolic start to his scriptural study: "We meditate upon the excellent power of the sun god, the sustainer of the earth, the interspace and the heavens. May the sun god stimulate our intellect." The boy has now attained his spiritual adulthood.

A young Hindu boy is here invested with the sacred thread, a ceremony that may be at least 3,000 years old. In the past, this ceremony, or upanayana, *was followed by a period of spiritual education by a guru at his religious centre, or ashram.*

For millions of Hindus worldwide, the system of social division, known in the west as caste, is of the first importance. Caste affects what occupations they follow, their choice of marriage partners, what food they must eat, or avoid, and many other considerations. The word "caste" comes from the Portuguese *casta* ("race", "breed"), but Hindus recognize four major social categories known as *varnas* ("colours"), which are subdivided into countless occupational groups, or *jatis*.

The four *varnas* derive from the culture of the ancient Aryan invaders of India and their Vedic scriptures (pp.130–31). They are, in descending order of superiority: Brahmins, or Brahmans (priests, professionals); Kshatriyas (rulers, administrators, soldiers); Vaishyas (peasant-farmers, merchants); and Shudras (artisans). These categories were originally based on people's natural qualities and functions and they were not the rigid divisions that they later became – and still are.

To this fourfold division was later added – but not included within its structure – a fifth group, probably by about 1000 B.C.E. This group originally consisted of the pre-Aryan inhabitants of India, who were obliged by their Aryan masters to carry out the "unclean" jobs within society. These involved tasks such as tanning leather and removing dead animals from their villages.

Because of the dirty and spiritually polluting nature of their work, these non-Aryans lived in special sections of the villages away from those who did "clean" jobs. Even today, this type of segregation exists. Formerly, this fifth group were termed "untouchables"; in this century, the great Hindu reformer Mahatma Gandhi (p.142) named them *Harijans* ("Children of God"), but now they prefer to call themselves *dalit* ("depressed").

From about 300 B.C.E. onward, occupational groups, or *jatis*, evolved within the *varna* framework. In time, these *jatis* became hereditary and exclusive in nature, giving rise to distinctive customs and strict rules forbidding marriage between, and dining with, members of different castes. Now there are thousands of *jatis*.

In modern India, the administration of caste depends primarily on the question of ritual purity and pollution. Hindus believe they can be polluted by lower castes – by proximity, by eating food cooked by a lower caste member, or by drinking water from the same well. However, low-caste Hindus cannot become more "pure" by associating with those above them.

Because all Hindus are now entitled to an education in India, they can learn skills that depart from those associated with their caste, which has thus become much less important in employment. In the large cities of India, caste barriers in matters of eating together and social mixing have broken down, discrimination on grounds of untouchability has been illegal since 1950, and "reserved" places for education and jobs have given greater opportunities to the *dalits*. But despite official attempts to create a fairer society, caste remains important, especially concerning marriage and in rural areas where discrimination still persists.

In Hindu weddings, both bride and groom, such as this couple from Bombay, are gaily adorned. By tradition, the bride's hands and feet are decorated with jewels (ABOVE) or a henna dye. A patterned stencil of non-absorbent material is placed on the skin and the henna paste is pressed on top and kept in place with a bandage, which is later removed to reveal the intricate design (LEFT).

Breaking the cycle

Although a person's caste status traditionally cannot be altered during his or her lifetime, movement to another caste can occur in a future rebirth. This depends on a person's *karma* – a word that has two meanings: "action" and "the good or evil results of all mental and physical activity". Hindus believe that the effect of a person's actions binds his or her soul (*atman*) to the long, but not endless, cycle of birth, death and rebirth called *samsara*.

A person carries the burden of *karma* over from one existence to the next, and it is increased or decreased by his or her activity in that existence. The *Bhagavad Gita* scripture, a famous and much-loved text that occurs within the *Mahabharata* epic (pp.134–35), declares that the *karma* of selfless and desireless actions does not bind the soul to *samsara*.

In other words, every soul, over a number of lives, can achieve the goal of liberation (*moksha*) by breaking the cycle of *samsara* through performing dutiful, selfless actions. In this way, *karma* can be seen as a positive force, rather than the fatalistic concept it often appears to be.

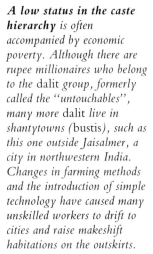

A low status in the caste hierarchy is often accompanied by economic poverty. Although there are rupee millionaires who belong to the dalit *group, formerly called the "untouchables", many more* dalit *live in shantytowns (*bustis*), such as this one outside Jaisalmer, a city in northwestern India. Changes in farming methods and the introduction of simple technology have caused many unskilled workers to drift to cities and raise makeshift habitations on the outskirts.*

The Indus Valley and the Aryans

Hindus today practise a religion which mainly developed during the first thousand years of the common era. Its roots, however, reach back a further 2,500 years to the brilliant Indian civilization that flourished in the Indus Valley from about 2500 to 1700 B.C.E. The Aryan peoples who invaded northwest India in about 1500 B.C.E. incorporated some of the beliefs and practices of the Indus Valley people into their own religion; and this, conveyed through their ancient scriptures, is one of the cornerstones of Hinduism.

In the early 1920s, the archaeologists Sir John Marshall, D.R. Sahni and R.D. Banerji revealed the results of their excavations in the Indus Valley, particularly at Mohenjo-daro and Harappa. They established that a river civilization had existed there from about 2500 B.C.E. for some 1,000 years. The script of the Indus people, which was found on soapstone seals, has not yet been deciphered, so all information about their culture is based on the evidence of their material remains.

Although no place of worship has been unearthed at the Indus sites, depictions on the seals shed some light on the people's religious beliefs. For example, one seal shows a female figure nursing a baby, and perhaps represents a form of the Mother Goddess, a deity found in most ancient cultures. The god Shiva (pp.136–37) may be prefigured on seals that depict a deity surrounded by animals. Some show him with a crescent moon on his head; and one has him in a cross-legged posture, suggesting that yoga meditation was practised.

The final demise of the Indus civilization occurred perhaps as a direct result of the Aryan invasion. However, the Indus cities may have been in a state of terminal decline by the time the Aryans first reached them, possibly as a result of an epidemic or climatic change.

The Aryan, or Indo-European, newcomers were a tall, fair-skinned people believed to have migrated from central Asia in about 2000 B.C.E. One group settled in northern Greece and another in Iran (whose name is derived from "Aryan"); those who eventually entered India probably split off from the Iranian branch. Knowledge of the Aryans is mostly derived from the heritage of their sacred literature, known as the Vedas, especially the *Rig Veda*, a collection of hymns.

Originally hunters and nomads herding cattle, the Aryans became, after they had settled in India, farmers, and worshipped nature deities. They spoke an early form of Sanskrit and organized themselves into tribes, subdivided into interrelated families. The tribe was controlled by a chieftain, and people formed functional and occupational groups (pp.128–29), although not in a rigid system.

The Aryans practised sacrifice and from contact with the Indus people gradually adopted new deities, including the Mother Goddess, and probably the idea of ritual purity. In time, they intermarried with the indigenous inhabitants and gradually extended their settlements toward the Ganges Valley. By 1000 B.C.E., Aryan culture had become predominant in northern India.

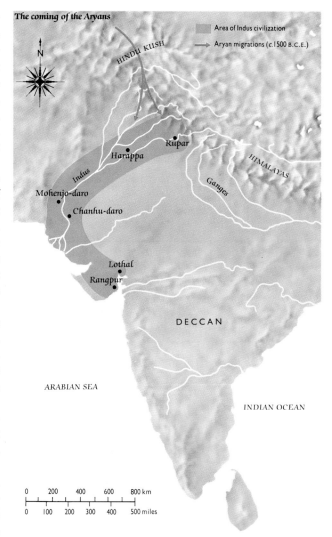

The coming of the Aryans

Area of Indus civilization

Aryan migrations (c.1500 B.C.E.)

HINDU KUSH

Rupar

Harappa

HIMALAYAS

Indus

Mohenjo-daro

Chanhu-daro

Ganges

Lothal

Rangpur

DECCAN

ARABIAN SEA

INDIAN OCEAN

0   200   400   600   800 km

0   100   200   300   400   500 miles

Aryan invaders entered India from the northwest in about 1500 B.C.E. The civilization they encountered, known as the Indus or the Harappan, after one of the principal sites, covered a larger area than either contemporary Egypt or Mesopotamia. Indus towns were carefully laid out, with wide streets and covered sewers. Houses were made of sun-dried bricks and had flat roofs.

The Great Bath at Mohenjo-daro, reconstructed below, was built of brick and consisted of a central bathing area surrounded on all four sides by small rooms. Since there are no written records, the bath's purpose is unknown. However, scholars believe that it was connected with ritual cleanliness and that it may even have prefigured the purificatory tanks still found beside Hindu temples. If that is the case, ritual ablutions in India may have a history of 4,000 years.

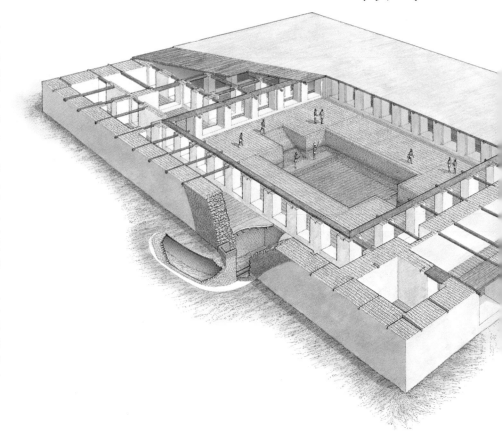

Aryan religion

The beliefs and religious practices of the Aryans – sometime after they had settled in India – are known from their sacred texts, known as the Vedas. (Veda means "knowledge", and its adjectival form "Vedic" is conventionally used to describe the Aryans, their religion, and also the period of Indian history between 1500 and 600 B.C.E.)

The Vedas were compiled over a period of hundreds of years, reaching their final form at about the end of the 10th century B.C.E. They consist of four, early collections of hymns – the *Rig Veda*, *Sama Veda*, *Yajur Veda* and *Atharva Veda*; the *Brahmanas* and *Aranyakas*, which deal with ritual and philosophy; and the Upanishads (pp.132–33).

In the Vedas, the Aryans are shown to be aggressive and probably less civilized than the dark-skinned people they conquered. The hymns of the *Rig Veda* and their praise of natural phenomena such as the sun, ocean, rivers, hills and dawn suggest that early Vedic religion centred on the worship of nature.

There were no fixed places of worship, and the central ritual of sacrifice could be performed anywhere. The gods were invoked through singing and propitiated with offerings in the sacrificial fire so that they might confer material benefits. The priests played a central role in the performance of the rites and rituals, and preserved tribal history and hymns, passing them down orally to the next generation.

Important Vedic deities were **Aditi**, a mother goddess, and her children the **Adityas**; **Indra**, god of conquest; **Agni**, god of fire and sacrifice; the **Ashwins**, the heavenly twins, and **Saranyu**, their mother; **Dyaus**, the sky god; the **Maruts**, gods of storm; **Rudra**, the chief storm deity; **Prajapati**, Lord of Creatures; **Prithivi**, the earth goddess; **Surya**, the sun god; **Varuna**, Lord of the Waters; **Yama**, god of death; and **Soma**, a deity of plants.

Indra, one of the supreme Vedic gods, was the destroyer of demons and the great warrior, as his martial aspect here suggests.

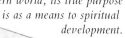

The practice of yoga
(RIGHT) *could well date back to the Indus civilization, as the cross-legged figure on the seal* (INSET) *from Mohenjo-daro suggests. Some scholars have speculated that the yogin in the seal is a forerunner of the later god Shiva, in his aspect of "lord of the animals". Although yoga's physical aspects have received particular attention in the western world, its true purpose is as a means to spiritual development.*

The Vedanta Age

Philosophy and religion are closely intertwined in the Hindu tradition, and Hindu thinkers through the ages have produced the subtlest of speculations on the nature of reality. By about the beginning of the common era, a number of Hindu schools of philosophy had developed, of which six in particular (*opposite*) were considered to be significant. The most important school was known as Vedanta. It took its name as well as its core themes from the Upanishad scriptures, which were seen as the end (*anta*) of the Vedas (pp.130–31).

Written between 800 and 500 B.C.E., the Upanishads – the "Himalayas of the Soul" – are one of the world's great spiritual texts. Their breadth of thought, profound insights and evocative language have attracted mystics, philosophers and poets from the time of their inception to the modern era. The German philosopher Arthur Schopenhauer (1788–1860), for example, said that reading them "has been the consolation of my life, and will be of my death".

The Upanishads traditionally number between 108 and 200, but there are only between 10 and 13 principal ones. They consist of dialogues between teacher and

A teacher reads the holy scriptures to a rapt group of villagers. The oral tradition has always played an important role in India.

At the feet of the guru

Gurus (spiritual teachers) have played a major role throughout the evolution of Hinduism – primarily as oral transmitters of wisdom. Because sages in ancient times were believed to have heard God's revealed words, the Vedic scriptures are called *shruti* ("that which is heard"). The sages composed the Vedic hymns and passed them down orally to the next generation, who preserved the Vedas. These *shruti* texts were not written down for many centuries – for example, the earliest manuscript of the *Rig Veda* dates from about 1400 C.E., more than 2,000 years after its original formulation.

The oral method of teaching was ideal for communicating the scriptures and philosophy to individuals, such as the prince and his servant (LEFT) consulting a guru in this 19th-century Indian miniature; and also to the small groups of Brahmins who came to learn the sacred tradition. Gurus could also discuss their theories with other scholars in open debate. Although gurus such as Shankara, Madhva and Ramanuja, right up to Aurobindo (1872–1950) and Radhakrishnan (1888–1975) in the 20th century, used writing, their debates continued the oral tradition. Shankara, for example, debated his theory of nondualism with *pandits* (scholars) at Varanasi (Benares).

The oral transmission of knowledge has also been indispensable to the spread of the *bhakti* movement (pp.138–39) and in the communication of the great epics of Hindu literature, the *Mahabharata* and *Ramayana* (pp.134–35), which were brought by itinerant gurus to village folk who could not read Sanskrit. Many modern gurus, such as the Maharishi Yogi, founder of the Transcendental Meditation movement (p.207), mainly use the oral method to convey their message to their followers. Since the 1980s, gurus, such as this one addressing a devoted crowd with a microphone (RIGHT), have become "electronic", using modern technology to transmit Hinduism.

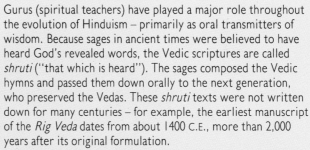

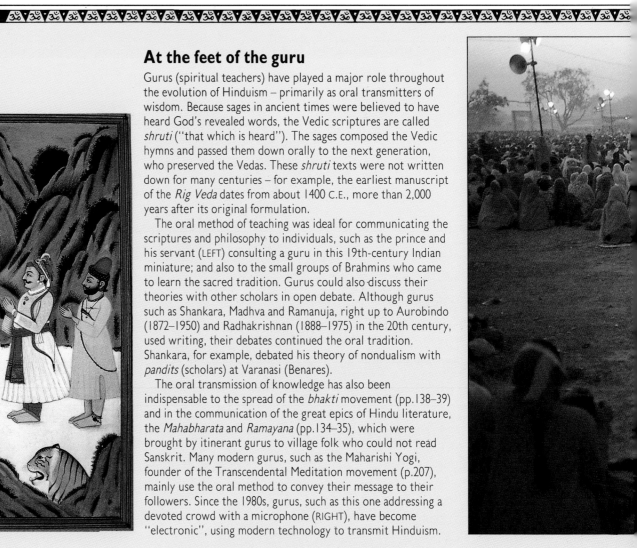

Six systems of philosophy

Of the various schools of philosophy that developed after the time of the Upanishads (*c.*500 B.C.E.), six systems – the Shad-Darshanas – were particularly influential. Although the dates are disputed, the systems were formulated by the beginning of the common era. To varying degrees, they accept the ideas of social division and the four stages of life (pp.128–29), support the belief in transmigration of the soul, and hold *moksha*, personal spiritual liberation, as their final goal. The main texts are composed in abbreviated aphorisms known as sutras. This table sets out in brief the six systems (in bold), the names of their founders (in parentheses) and the key propositions.

Nyaya (Gautama)   Primarily concerned with logic, analysis and the nature of reasoning.

Vaisheshika (Kanada)   Essentially atheistic and dualistic, it teaches that reality is made up of soul and matter, and that matter is composed of atoms.

Samkhya (Kapila)   Like Vaisheshika, a dualistic system differentiating between matter, or nature (*prakriti*), and countless souls (*purusha*); souls must distinguish themselves from matter before they can be liberated from it.

Yoga (Yajñavalkya?; codified by Patañjali)   Emphasizes that *moksha* can be achieved through a set of specific mental and physical disciplines.

Purva Mimamsa (Jaimini)   Interprets the philosophy and rituals of the Vedas; it was later superseded by the Vedanta system.

Vedanta (Badarayana)   The most important of all the systems (see main text).

pupil or between sages, and their main doctrines can be summarized as follows: although the power of *maya* ("illusion") makes the world appear real, *Brahman* is the formless, ultimate reality.

People possess a soul or spirit (*atman*) which is indestructible and identical with *Brahman*, and the created things of the world share a spiritual oneness. The *atman*'s future existence is determined by *karma* (the result of all actions), and the *atman* can achieve liberation (*moksha*) from the long cycle of successive births and deaths (*samsara*).

From the Upanishads derive the ideas of the Vedanta philosophy. These were first set out in a text known as the *Vedanta Sutra*, or *Brahma Sutra*, thought to have been written by a philosopher named Badarayana at about the start of the common era. The Vedanta's central theme is "monism" – namely that there is only one indivisible reality (*Brahman*) and the soul or *atman* is one with it. To understand *Brahman* fully, Badarayana states, intuition, not intellect or logic, is essential.

Vedanta philosophy was later developed by three important schools based on the interpretation of their founders – Shankara, Ramanuja and Madhva. The first of these, Shankara, was a philosopher, mystic and poet, who, according to tradition, was born in 788 C.E. and lived for only 32 years. His saintliness was such that he was regarded as an incarnation of the god Shiva.

Shankara's teachings formed the Advaita, or "non-dualism", school. People believe, he taught, that the everyday world is real only because they are ignorant.

> *Who but the atman is capable of removing the bonds of ignorance, passion and self-interested action?*
>
> SHANKARA

(For example, in poor light, a rope may be mistaken for a snake.) In fact, the world is *maya*, or illusion. The only reality is *Brahman*, which is identical with the *atman*. Liberation from the cycle of *samsara* can only be achieved through knowledge and the merging of the *atman* with *Brahman*.

In contrast to Shankara, Ramanuja (*c.*1017–1137) taught that the everyday world is not an illusion. And the *atman*, although a fragment of *Brahman*, is not identical with it. Liberation, best achieved through *bhakti*, or love of God, occurs when the *atman* is reunited with *Brahman*, yet keeps its individuality. His school is known as Vishisht-Advaita – "qualified nondualism".

Madhva (1197–1280) put forward yet another view. He taught a system of Dvaita – "dualism" – stating that *Brahman* was distinct from *atman*. Both remain separate from each other, not only in the created world but even after the *atman* has achieved liberation, although it does come into close proximity with *Brahman*.

Challenges to the Vedic Tradition

The great epics and the *Gita*

The *Ramayana* and the *Mahabharata*, the two great Sanskrit epics of Indian literature, are poetic renderings of myths and legends and originally had no religious import. However, over a period of two or three centuries preceding and following the start of the common era, the original stories were expanded to include material which illustrated the virtues of Brahminical Hinduism.

The *Ramayana*, the story of Prince Rama, contains 24,000 verses arranged into seven books and tells how Rama married Sita, the daughter of King Janaka, after winning an archery contest. However, the prince's fortunes change when his rightful claim as heir to King Dasharatha's throne is disregarded and he is exiled to a forest with Sita and his brother, Lakshmana.

During the exile, Sita is kidnapped by Ravana, King of Lanka (Sri Lanka). With the help of the king of the monkeys, Sugriva, and his monkey general, Hanuman, Rama crosses the sea with an army of monkeys and attacks Lanka. In a final battle, Ravana is killed, Sita rescued and Rama is later restored to his kingdom. The epic portrays

ideals of human virtues: Rama himself embodies the obedient son, loving husband, dutiful king and affectionate brother. Hanuman is the ideal servant and Sita the ideal faithful wife.

The *Mahabharata* in its present form contains 100,000 verses subdivided into 18 *parvas* (books) and is the longest epic in world literature. The original core of 24,000 verses describes the conflict between royal cousins, the Kauravas and the Pandavas. The epic grew at the hands of later editors, who introduced various episodes to illustrate human virtues and vices, such as parental and brotherly love, wifely faithfulness, stoic acceptance of misfortune, inordinate ambition, uncontrollable jealousy and the evil influence of close relations.

The *Bhagavad Gita*, a short text of 700 verses arranged in 18 chapters, is arguably the most popular and widely revered of all Hindu scriptures. Scholars believe it was added to the sixth book of the *Mahabharata* to promote Brahminical Hinduism and the worship of Krishna. The *Gita* relates how Arjuna, one of the Pandavas, revolts at the idea of having to kill his kinsmen before the final battle between the two warring families. Krishna, Arjuna's charioteer and an incarnation of Vishnu, argues that Arjuna should follow his duty as a noble and fight.

The book goes on to explore the nature of *atman* and *Brahman*, and paths of liberation (*moksha*), and compares the philosophies of the Samkhya and Yoga schools (p.133). It also describes the moral and religious duties of the

four *varnas* (social categories) of Hindu society, and examines the concept of desireless action. Krishna, as an incarnation of Vishnu, is the supreme deity and object of devotion in the *Gita*, and his answers to Arjuna's questions are believed by many Hindus to be the word of God.

*The **Mahabharata** is the longest epic in the world and has been retold for hundreds of years in various media. The archers (ABOVE) come from a 1990 movie of a dramatic production by the British director Peter Brook. The Indian painting (RIGHT) shows Arjuna in a chariot drawn by white horses shooting off the head of his enemy, Karna, with a bow and arrow.*

During the sixth and fifth centuries B.C.E., a number of different movements threatened to undermine the foundations of the Vedic religion (pp.130–31). One group of atheist philosophers, for example, not only denied God's existence, the authority of the Vedic scriptures, and the concept of reincarnation, but also refused to acknowledge the position of the Brahmin priests – the very guardians of sacred teaching, ritual and sacrifice. In addition, the followers of Gautama Buddha (pp.152–53) and of Mahavira, founder of Jainism (pp.146–47), broke away from the Vedic tradition and pursued their own religious paths.

Nevertheless, the Vedic religion, as interpreted by the Brahmins, retained its dominant position up to the founding of India's first great empire by Chandragupta Maurya (c.321–c.297 B.C.E.), based on the state of Magadha in northern India. But when Chandragupta's grandson Ashoka (pp.154–55) converted to Buddhism and threw his authority behind it, the Brahmins suffered a setback from which they took a long time to recover.

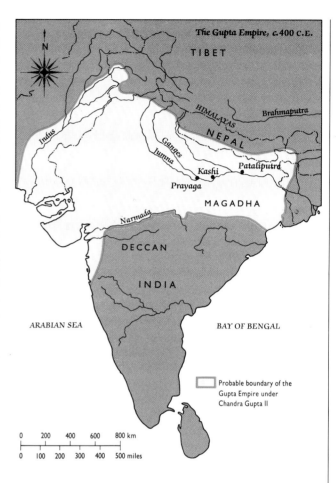

If the light of a thousand suns suddenly arose in the sky, that splendour might be compared to the radiance of the Supreme Spirit. And Arjuna saw in that radiance the whole universe in its variety, standing in a vast unity in the body of the God of gods.

BHAGAVAD GITA 11:12–13

During the fourth century C.E., *the Gupta Empire expanded, reaching its greatest extent during the reign of Chandra Gupta II (c.380–c.415), when it stretched across northern India from the Arabian Sea to the Bay of Bengal.*

Mauryan power declined after Ashoka's death in 238 B.C.E., and by the end of the second century B.C.E., the empire had disintegrated. The new kingdoms of northern India, which rose from the ashes of the empire, followed Ashoka's example and espoused Buddhism. From about this time to the end of the third century C.E., northwestern India suffered many invasions. And during this turbulent period, the Brahmins began to reinterpret and breathe new life into the Vedic religion.

They scaled down ceremonies and stopped animal sacrifice, and developed their own tradition of philosophical speculation (pp.132–33). They also restructured the great Indian epics, the *Ramayana* and the *Mahabharata* (*opposite*) to support their authority. Both epics were given the sacred status of holy scriptures, and their heroes were turned into incarnations of Vishnu. And, from about 100 C.E., Brahminical law was systematically compiled in the *Manu-Smriti* (Laws of Manu). This comprehensive manual, still influential today, pronounced on various subjects, such as forms of marriage, funeral rites, duties of kings, the caste system, the superiority of the Brahmins, the concept of *karma* (p.129) and the nature of the soul.

In the fourth century C.E., political stability returned to north-central India when a dynasty known as the Guptas rose to power in Magadha. Under the rule of Chandra Gupta II (c.380–c.415 C.E.), grandson of the dynasty's founder, ancient India reached its cultural peak, and poets, scientists and philosophers were received at court. The Gupta emperors gave local government more power and ensured land revenue was collected more efficiently. Highways, studded with numerous rest houses, linked up bustling cities, and increased commerce brought more wealth to the empire. Buddhist monasteries flourished, and Hindu priests received imperial patronage.

This age of peace and prosperity continued through the fifth century, when the first inklings of the *bhakti* movement (pp.138–39), whereby people expressed their love and devotion to a particular god, arose in southern India. This movement marked a shift away from the Vedic pantheon of nature deities to the two separate cults of monotheistic worship of two hitherto insignificant Vedic gods: Vishnu and Rudra, who was later known as Shiva (pp.136–37). However, this golden age was not to last: toward the end of the fifth century, the Gupta throne came under threat, as attacks by Asian nomads known as the Hunas, or White Huns, increased.

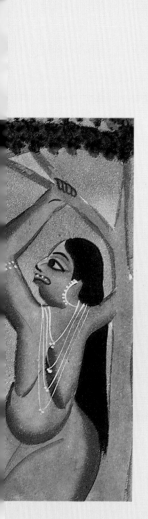

Rama, the hero of the Ramayana, and his brother Lakshmana kill the evil spirit Taraka in this 19th-century Indian miniature. Taraka lived in a forest beside the Ganges and terrorized everyone in the neighbourhood. So the local sage Vishvamitra, depicted bottom left, asked Rama (shown here with green skin) and his brother to kill her. At first, her powers of sorcery rendered futile all attempts to overcome her, but finally she was killed by arrows.

Classical Hinduism

One God, many gods

For Hindus, the concept of *Trimurti*, three gods in one image, illustrates the continuity and change which is an important feature of their religion. Reflecting elements of the Aryan and Indus traditions (pp.130–31), the *Trimurti* consists of three gods – Brahma, the creator, Vishnu, the preserver, and Shiva, the destroyer and regenerator – who are considered to be aspects of *Brahman*, the one God or universal soul described in the Upanishads. In practice, the *Trimurti* has always appealed more to the intellect than to the hearts of the Indian people.

In classical Hinduism, female deities also have important roles. The consorts of Brahma, Vishnu and Shiva are Saraswati, Lakshmi and Parvati, respectively; and the concept of the Mother Goddess, which the Aryans adopted from the Indus people, is fully developed in the worship of Shakti, who is identified with Parvati, also known as Amba, Durga or Kali.

Although *Brahman* is said to be *nirguna* (without attributes) and *nirakara* (without form), it can be made more meaningful to the worshipper through *murtis* or images of deities, such as the one being carried by villagers (BELOW), which represent its various aspects. The *murtis* show the deities with certain emblems that symbolize their powers (RIGHT).

The advancing tide of White Huns into northern India was stemmed for a while by Skanda Gupta (455–67 C.E.), the last important emperor of the Gupta dynasty. But his weak successors failed to provide the cement to hold the empire together. By 500, it had broken into pieces, and the later Guptas ruled over small kingdoms in northern India. Although Gupta kings liberally endowed Buddhist monasteries and had Buddhist advisers at their courts, it was from this time that Brahminical Hinduism, as interpreted by the Brahmins, or priests, emerged in a form recognizable today.

The coming of the Huns had the effect of disrupting the caste system and of creating a number of new sub-castes. Although at this time caste restricted certain occupations to particular groups, in military matters it was for the most part ignored. Hindu armies not only consisted of Kshatriyas – the warrior caste – but also

Brahmins (priests, professionals), Vaishyas (peasant-farmers, merchants) and Shudras (artisans). And, in the seventh century, the kings of Alwar, Rohilkhand and Kanauj, small kingdoms situated in northern India, were Shudras or Vaishyas.

It was in the north, between 300 and 800 C.E., that classical Sanskrit literature flowed from the pens of a number of important writers, especially the fifth-century poet and dramatist Kalidasa, whose play *Shakuntala* was later admired by the great German writer Goethe (1749–1832). And from about 500 to 1000 or later, the important *Puranas* – myths and legends glorifying Brahma, Vishnu and Shiva (*above*) – were composed. Written in verse, the *Puranas* are a treasure-trove of folklore and wisdom, and their topics include the periodic destruction and renewal of the world and the genealogy of Hindu gods and heroes.

Brahma has four faces which represent the four Vedas (pp.130–31), the four epochs of time and the four *varnas* (pp.128–29), while his four arms are the four quarters of the universe. He also has a rosary which controls time, a book containing all knowledge, and a water pot representing the waters of creation.

Saraswati, consort of Brahma, holds a book and a musical instrument, symbolic of her position as goddess of learning and the arts.

Vishnu is often represented as one of his traditional 10 incarnations that took a variety of forms. Pictured around the god in the 18th-century Indian painting (FAR LEFT), they were, left to right, top row: Matsya the fish; Kurma the tortoise; Varaha the boar; second row: Narasimha the man-lion; Vamana the dwarf; third row: Parashurama the Brahmin; Prince Rama; bottom row: Krishna; the Buddha; Kalki, the incarnation yet to come.

Lakshmi, consort of Vishnu, holds a lotus, symbol of beauty, and gives gold coins to her devotees.

Durga, one of the names of Shiva's consort, rides a lion and, in her eight arms, representing the eight directions, she holds weapons to destroy evil and protect her devotees.

Ganesha, the remover of obstacles, has a human body and an elephant's head with one tusk. He keeps his devotees on the path of righteousness with his goad, rewards them with sweetmeats, and blesses them with his right hand. The snare and serpent show his control over death.

Hanuman, the monkey god, holds an Indian club representing physical strength.

Shiva is here the cosmic dancer of creation in a fiery circle (**1**) representing the destruction and re-creation of the world. The drum in his right (**4**) hand keeps the rhythm of creation; the fire in his left (**2**) destroys it. His right foot tramples the demon of ignorance (**3**); his raised left foot and lowered left hand indicate liberation.

However, as the plains of northern India became a hunting ground for successive invaders from the north-west between 550 and 1200, Hindu culture rapidly developed in southern India and the Deccan plateau. The dynasties of the Chalukyas and Rashtrakutas ruled alternately in the Deccan between the 6th and the 10th centuries, and in the south, the Cholas held sway between 906 and 1120. The latter conquered Sri Lanka and, through a naval expedition, occupied parts of Sumatra, Malaya, and Burma for a few decades.

In spite of these political upheavals, the influence of Brahminical Hinduism was taking root, which resulted in a flowering of richly carved temples, dedicated to either Vishnu or Shiva, at Khajuraho, Bhubaneshwar, Kanchipuram and Tanjore. Worship of gods became widespread as the *Puranas* helped to popularize them and explain their mythology.

From the 9th to the 13th centuries, Hindu thinkers helped to persuade local rulers to abandon Buddhism and turn to Hinduism all over India. But in Bihar and Bengal, Buddhism remained strong until the Muslim occupation in the early 1200s. And in southern India, the Upanishads, the *Brahma Sutras* and the *Bhagavad Gita* were interpreted anew through commentaries of Shankara, Ramanuja and Madhva (pp.132–33).

By the 13th century, some Hindu practices, such as *sati* – the immolation of widows on their husbands' funeral pyres – and child marriage had become common (they were condemned by Hindu reformers in the 19th century). As the Muslims (pp.110–11) established their political domination over a large part of India, Hinduism began to look inward. Nevertheless, it still continued to provide a cultural unity for its followers through theology, philosophy and patterns of worship.

The *Bhakti* Movement

From the Middle Ages on, the rise to prominence of the Hindu *bhakti* movement, encouraging people to express devotion to a personal god based on love, coincided with the Muslim period in India (pp.104–5); and it may have been influenced by Sufism – Islamic mysticism (pp.98–99). The *bhakti* attitude of passionate self surrender to a deity emphasized the heart, not the mind, and was an important corrective to Hinduism's more philosophical and ascetic approaches.

This attitude was not a new phenomenon; it can be traced back as far as the *Svetasvatera Upanishad* in about the fifth or fourth century B.C.E.: "His form cannot be glimpsed, none may see him within the eye: whoso should know him with heart and mind as dwelling in the heart becomes immortal" (4:20). And the theme is echoed in the *Bhagavad Gita* (pp.134–35), which states that God's gracious love is available to anyone who comes to him, including outcastes and women.

The Alvars, Vaishnavite (devotees of Vishnu) *bhakti* poets who flourished in southern India during the second half of the first millennium C.E., were also important to the movement. However, it is the *bhakti* saints, or *bhaktas*, Kabir (*below*), Caitanya, Mirabai, Tukaram and Tulsi Das, and others such as Ravidas and Guru Nanak of the Sikh tradition (pp.172–75), that most Hindus think of today in conjunction with the *bhakti* movement. These inspiring individuals are best seen through their intense poetical works which convey a powerful sense of devotion to God.

Born in Bengal into a Brahmin family, Caitanya (1485–1533) was a scholar who became devoted to the god Krishna, an avatar of Vishnu. A hugely influential figure – his own followers came to regard him as an incarnation of Krishna – Caitanya is also the inspiration behind the Hare Krishna movement (p.206). This excerpt from his catechism is in the form of questions and answers: "Which knowledge is highest of all? There is no knowledge but devotion to Krishna. What is counted wealth among human possessions? He is immensely wealthy who has love for Radha-Krishna. What is the heaviest of sorrows? There is no sorrow except separation from Krishna."

Another devotee of Krishna was Mirabai (b.1550?), said to be a Rajput princess who renounced the world and regarded herself as Krishna's bride. She wrote hundreds of songs and poems – still sung today – that express her strong devotion. When her husband died, she refused to follow the custom of *sati* (self-immolation) since she saw herself not so much as the widow of a mortal but the bride of a deity.

Tukaram (1607–49), born into a wealthy family of grain merchants, embraced poverty and expressed his spirituality in his short songs – especially the pain of separation from and the joy of finding God. He also considered pilgrimages and other external religious practices to be ineffectual and enjoyed great popularity among the rich and the poor. A slightly older contemporary of Tukaram was Tulsi Das (*c.*1543–1623). A Brahmin who renounced his wife to devote himself to Rama, Tulsi Das spent most of his life in Varanasi (Benares) in north-central India. Here he composed in Hindi the *Ramacaritmanas* ("Sacred Lake of the Acts of Rama") – a work that has inspired millions of Hindus.

How much, if anything, the *bhaktas* of northern India owed to Sufism is uncertain. What is certain is that they made God available to low-caste and outcaste men and women to the extent that conversion to Islam as the only way of gaining spiritual satisfaction became unnecessary. Nevertheless, many low-caste people did convert, some for religious reasons, others to escape from the caste system. Islam, however, ultimately failed to provide relief from caste, as did conversion to Christianity during the period of British rule which succeeded the Mughal Empire.

Kabir: opposing sectarianism

A low-caste weaver of Varanasi (Benares), Kabir (1440–1518) was greatly influenced by both the Muslim and Hindu traditions and was a committed opponent of religious sectarianism. He came from a clan that had probably converted to Islam sometime before his birth. One legend claims that Kabir's mother was a Brahmin who became miraculously pregnant after visiting a Hindu shrine. Since she was not married, she abandoned the newborn Kabir, and he was found by a Muslim weaver.

Although scholars are sceptical, some traditions affirm that when he grew up, Kabir came under the influence of the famous Hindu ascetic Ramananda (*c.*1400–*c.*1470). Kabir's own teaching shows traces of both Islam and Hinduism: he accepted Hindu notions of reincarnation and *karma*, but rejected caste and image-worship and stressed the idea of one God, the essential belief of Islam. At the same time, Kabir's opposition to all religious sects shows that, for him, God transcends the claims of both Hinduism and Islam: "If God be within the mosque, then to whom does this world belong? If Ram be within the image which you find upon your pilgrimage, then who is there to know what happens without?"

I am longing for you, O my Lord, for the season of the swing has come and you are not beside me. MIRABAI

Temples of the gods

Although some devotees of the *bhakti* movement in the later medieval period declared that only human bodies could truly be temples of God, the stone temples dedicated to Hindu deities are among the most impressive forms of architecture to be found in the world. These great gravity-defying structures, some resembling sculptured mountains whose strata have been revealed, soar into the sky all over India, including at Tanjore, Konarak, Bhubaneshwar and Khajuraho. Providing a focal point for both the spiritual and cultural lives of the locality, the temple is primarily a sacred space where individuals can perform personal acts of worship, or *puja* (p.127).

First and foremost, the temple is the house of a god or goddess, providing a place on earth where people can approach the divine. The sacred image of the deity, in which he or she is believed to reside after various rituals have been performed by priests, is kept in a sanctuary known as the *garbhagriha*, or "womb-chamber", in the temple's very heart. But the entire fabric of the temple, inside and out, is considered to be sacred, giving rise to the plethora of sculptured images of deities and mythological figures that adorn the walls in a sometimes bewildering profusion of intricate detail.

The Lakshmana Temple (BELOW) in Khajuraho in northern India is one of more than 30 temples built on this site during the rule of the Chandella dynasty from the mid-10th to the mid-12th centuries C.E. Elevated on a terrace (**4**) and surrounded at its four corners by smaller shrines (**3** and **5**), the temple is built along an east-west axis and is dominated by the great pyramidal roof (*sikhara*) (**2**). This is surmounted by a finial (**1**) from which a flag is often flown. The entrance porch (*ardhamandapa*) (**6**) leads through a hall to the *garbhagriha*, the innermost part of the sanctuary, which lies beneath the *sikhara*.

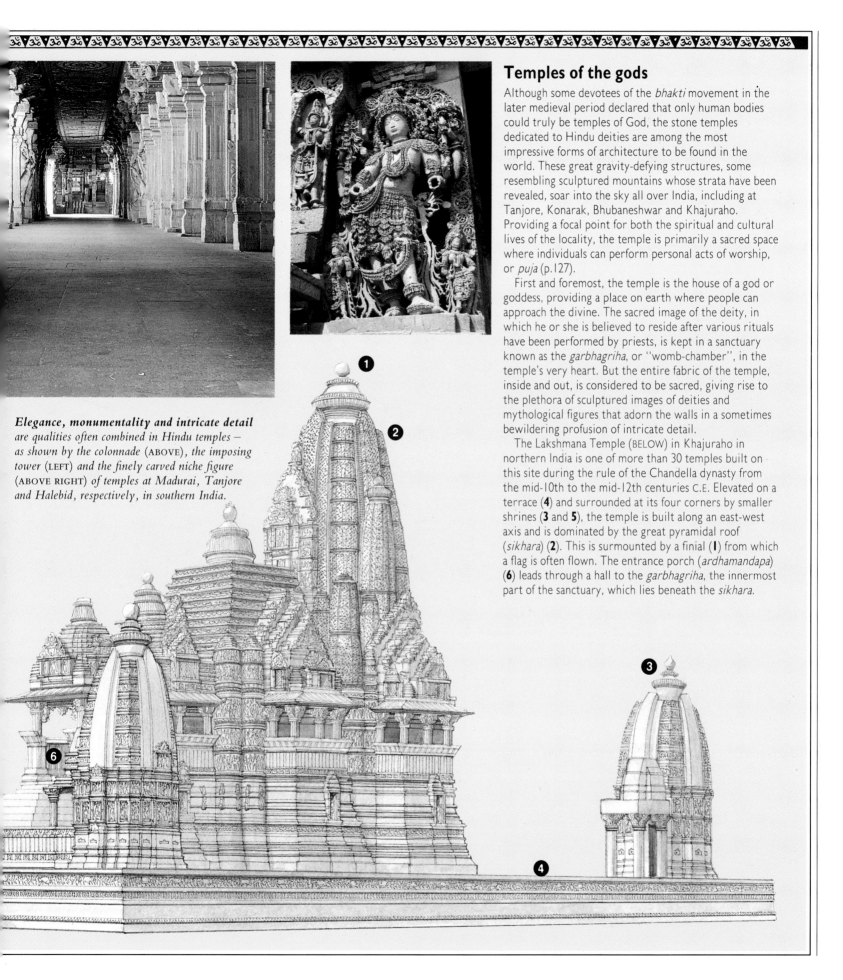

Elegance, monumentality and intricate detail are qualities often combined in Hindu temples — as shown by the colonnade (ABOVE), the imposing tower (LEFT) and the finely carved niche figure (ABOVE RIGHT) of temples at Madurai, Tanjore and Halebid, respectively, in southern India.

Pilgrimage

For Hindus, pilgrimage, or *yatra*, is such an important feature of their practice that almost anywhere in India can be considered holy enough for it to be a focus for pilgrims. Hindus may put the number of pilgrimage places, or *tirthas*, variously at between 58 and 64,000 depending on whether they are counting only major sites such as Varanasi (Benares) and Hardwar, or including local and little-known places as well. For Hindus living abroad, even a visit to India might itself be considered a *yatra*.

Holy places, for Hindus, are usually located on the banks of rivers, coasts, seashores and mountains. Points of convergence between land and water, two rivers or, still better, three frequently assume a sacred significance. And a place might have additional importance because of an historical or legendary association. Thus Varanasi is where the god Shiva manifested himself and lived as an ascetic – although it is also associated with Rama, an incarnation of Vishnu.

At Kurukshetra in the northwest, a place sacred to Vishnu, the great battle described in the *Mahabharata* (pp.134–35) was fought. According to an ancient text, Kurukshetra was originally "the holy lake of Brahma". It was later ploughed by a seer named Kuru, whence it became known as Kurukshetra, or Kuru's field. The text goes on to say that whoever remembers Kurukshetra is purified both inside and out, regardless of whether he or she is clean or unclean.

Special times may attract pilgrims. The date of the great Kumbha Mela festival, held at four different venues, is determined astrologically, and pilgrims who attend it value the auspicious timing of the pilgrimage as much as the place. Also, every year at the time of the Dusserah farming festival in October/November, the story of the *Ramayana* (pp.134–35) is enacted in a cycle lasting 30 days. And visitors to Vrindaban and the surrounding countryside, associated with Krishna, hope to see, especially at the time of his birthday or at the Holi festival connected with the spring equinox, a vision of Krishna disporting with his friends, the *gopis* (cowgirls).

A Hindu pilgrim enjoys a ride on her way to the source of the Ganges, in the foothills of the Himalayas. The holiest river in India, the Ganges is deemed to be none other than Ganga – the "swift-goer" – the goddess whose waters wash away the sins of whosoever bathes in them.

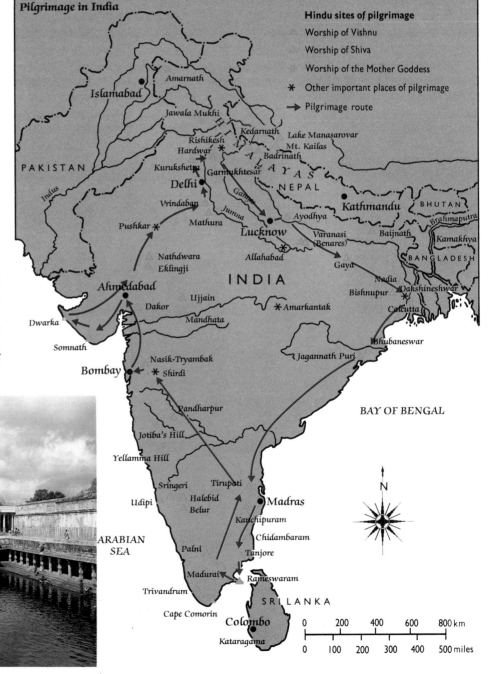

Pilgrimage in India

Hindu sites of pilgrimage
- Worship of Vishnu
- Worship of Shiva
- Worship of the Mother Goddess
- * Other important places of pilgrimage
- → Pilgrimage route

Many Hindus undertake an all-India pilgrimage by train, shown on the map (OPPOSITE). The journey takes about 10 weeks, depending on how long pilgrims stay at any one place. Highlights include the lake at Pushkar (BELOW), meaning "blue lotus flower", where the sole remaining temple to Brahma, the creator, is said to exist; Puri, famous for its temple of Jagannath – the title of Vishnu in his guise as "world lord"; the temple complex of Kanchipuram (BELOW LEFT); and Rameswaram, on the southeastern tip of the country. Here, Rama in the epic poem Ramayana invoked the aid of Shiva against Ravana, who was holding his wife Sita prisoner in Sri Lanka.

There are also modern *tirthas*, for example the place where Mahatma Gandhi (p.142) was cremated near the bank of the Jumna River in Delhi. Visiting heads of state are taken there, and hundreds of Hindus go there daily to lay their garlands of flowers.

Pilgrimage can be a great equalizer. In the Ganges, the pure are made even more pure, and the impure have their pollution removed, if only temporarily. In the

---

As morning dew is taken up by the sun so my evil deeds are taken up by the sight of the Himalayas. TRADITIONAL HINDU PROVERB

---

sacred water, and perhaps anywhere in the holy cities of Varanasi or Hardwar, distinctions of caste are supposed to count for nothing. Hindus may think caste divinely ordained, but it has no eternal significance, and the sincere pilgrim, regardless of caste, is held to enter eternity at least for the time of the pilgrimage.

The value of a pilgrimage in terms of merit depends on the way it is regarded by the devotee. Some Hindus consider merit to be reckoned by the distance travelled, the means of transport (walking is the superior method), the auspiciousness of the timing, the holiness of the place itself, and the purpose of the pilgrimage.

While most Hindus hold pilgrimage in great honour, some question its worth, arguing that true pilgrimage is the inner journey of the soul. Ramprasad Sen, an 18th-century devotee of the goddess Kali, said: "What have I to do with Varanasi? Kali's feet are places of pilgrimage enough for me. Meditating on them deep in the lotus of the heart, I float on the ocean of bliss."

Against this must be set the experience of Hindus who have successfully combined an inner spiritual pilgrimage with a journey to Varanasi. The sacredness of this most holy of Hindu cities is summed up in an ancient scripture called the *Kashi Khanda*: "Are there not many rivers running to the sea? yet which of them is like the river of heaven at Kashi [Varanasi]? Are there not many fields of liberation on earth? Yet not one equals the smallest part of the city never forsaken by Shiva."

Hinduism in the Modern World

On May 20, 1498, the Portuguese explorer Vasco da Gama sailed into the port of Calicut, on the southwestern coast of India, thus opening up a route for European trade with the east that was not dependent upon Muslim countries. From this time on, Europeans began to establish trading posts in India, but it was not until 1757, when the British soldier and statesman Sir Robert Clive defeated the French and their allies, that the prospect of European colonization became a reality. With the Mughal Empire (pp.104–5) in terminal decline, Britain took over the reins of power and ruled India until 1947.

Calcutta, in Bengal in the northeast, became the centre of British power in India, and it was in this region that much interaction between Hinduism and Christianity occurred during the 18th century and after. The encounter with Christianity, and along with it western technology and ideas about society and education, led to a reform within Hinduism, largely inspired by the influence of a number of charismatic individuals. They included Ram Mohan Roy, Dayanandi Sarasvati, Sri Ramakrishna and Rabindranath Tagore.

Ram Mohan Roy (1772–1833), a Bengali Brahmin, was much influenced by Christianity. He campaigned against child-marriage, sati – the immolation of widows on their husbands' funeral pyres – and the use of images, or murtis, in worship. In 1828, he founded the Brahma Samaj (Brahma Society), which stressed a strict monotheism and helped prevent many Indian intellectuals from forsaking their cultural and spiritual heritage.

The next great Hindu reformer was Dayananda Sarasvati (1824–83), a Brahmin from Gujarat, who devoted his life to returning Hinduism to the purity of the Vedas (pp.130–31), which were for him the source of all knowledge. He denounced worship of murtis, the caste system, and the concept of divine incarnation. He also founded the Arya Samaj, a society still active today, which uses missionary methods to take its teachings to villages of all castes.

A contemporary of Sarasvati and better known in the west was Sri Ramakrishna (1836–86), a poor Bengali Brahmin, whose mystic visions convinced him that God can be found through any religion. His most famous disciple was Swami Vivekananda (1863–1902), whose leadership of the Ramakrishna Mission, founded to relieve the suffering of the needy through good works, played a significant part in bringing Hinduism to the attention of the west. Also from Bengal was Rabindranath Tagore (1861–1941), who won the Nobel prize for literature in 1913. His emphasis on divine love and his denunciation of nationalism as "organized selfishness" made him attractive to the liberal intelligentsia

---

The universe, whatever moves in the world, is pervaded by God. When you have renounced it then you may enjoy it; do not covet anyone's wealth.

A FAVOURITE VERSE OF MAHATMA GANDHI FROM THE *ISA UPANISHAD*

---

of the west at the time of the founding of the League of Nations in 1919.

Since World War II and the founding of the Indian republic in 1947, Hinduism has continued to evolve. Although conservative orthodoxy lives on, particularly in the nationalistic Bharatiya Janata political party, new expressions of Hinduism arise, for example, in the cult of Santoshi Mata. The daughter of the elephant-headed god Ganesha, Santoshi Mata was a little-known deity until her portrayal in a movie transformed her into a popular goddess overnight. The respect for Hinduism which Mahatma Gandhi (*left*) and others have created, as well as the rise of Hindu-derived groups, such as the Hare Krishna movement (p.206) and Transcendental Meditation (p.207), have maintained the west's interest in this oldest of living religions.

India's "Great Soul"

Once described as "a saint of action rather than contemplation", Mohandas Karamchand Gandhi, known as Mahatma ("Great Soul"), is revered by Indians both as an astute political leader and a charismatic holy man. His moral authority during the struggle for Indian independence also gained him respect around the world.

Born in Gujarat in 1869, Gandhi studied in London from 1888 to 1891 and, two years later, practised law in South Africa, where he championed the rights of the Indian population. He returned to India in 1914 and began his campaign of nonviolent protest against British rule. Gandhi's efforts toward Indian independence were finally realized in 1947 but, to his dismay and disappointment, he was unable to stop the division with Pakistan. A year later, he was shot dead by a Hindu fanatic.

Gandhi's compassion and beliefs can be summed up in the "Gandhi Talisman" – advice to those who would imitate him (although he did not encourage such adulation): "Recall the face of the poorest and most helpless person whom you may have seen and ask yourself if the step you contemplate is going to be of any use to him, will he be able to gain anything from it? Will it restore him to control over his life and destiny? In other words, will it lead to swaraj [self-rule] for the hungry and also spiritually starved millions of our countrymen? Then you will find your doubts and your self melting away."

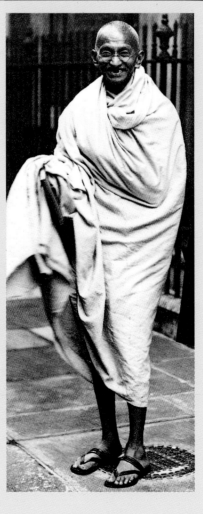

The Hindus of Bali

One of the most important Hindu communities outside India is that on the Indonesian island of Bali. Here, most of the population – nearly three million – are proud of being Hindus. Indonesians first came into contact with Hinduism in the second century C.E. through Indian traders. Eight centuries later, a Hindu king of east Java conquered Bali, and Javanese Hindu priests gradually left their imprint there.

Today, some Balinese traditions differ from Indian ones. For example, although Hindus usually cremate their dead, the Balinese sometimes bury them for years beforehand until they can afford the expense involved in cremation and funeral rites (flamboyant to a degree unknown in India). On the other hand, clear links with India include ancient temples in honour of the gods Brahma, Vishnu and Shiva, images of Ganesha, the widely known Gayatri mantra and other Sanskrit prayers, and the popularity of the great epics, the *Mahabharata* and *Ramayana* (pp.134–35).

The Balinese, like Hindus elsewhere, enjoy colourful festivals. The "monkey dance" (BELOW) illustrates a scene from the Ramayana epic; and statues of the goddess Durga (LEFT) are often the focus of celebrations.

World distribution of Hindus

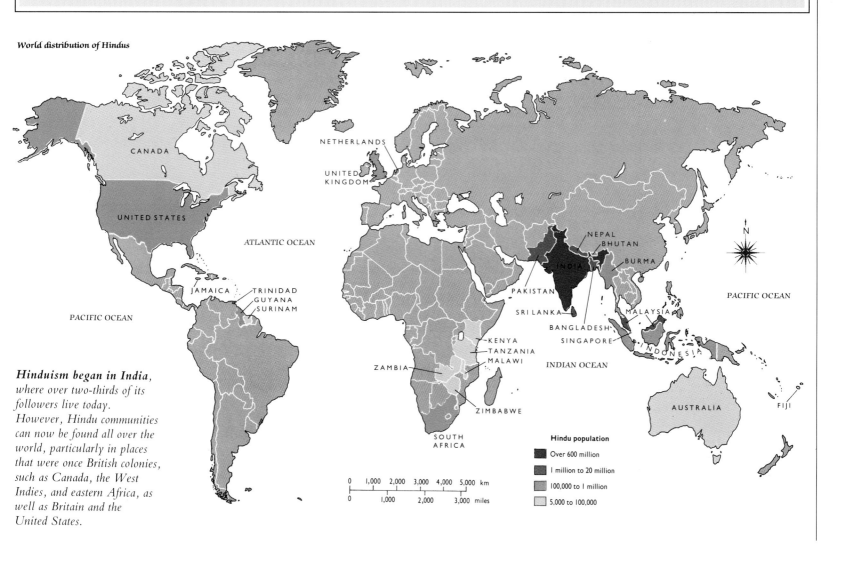

Hinduism began in India, where over two-thirds of its followers live today. However, Hindu communities can now be found all over the world, particularly in places that were once British colonies, such as Canada, the West Indies, and eastern Africa, as well as Britain and the United States.

Hindu population

- Over 600 million
- 1 million to 20 million
- 100,000 to 1 million
- 5,000 to 100,000

The granite statue of the Jain saint Lord Bahubali, erected in 981, dominates the southern Indian town of Shravana Belgola, the oldest and most important Jain pilgrimage centre. At a great festival, every 12 to 14 years, the head of the statue is anointed with thousands of offerings, as shown here.

One of the daily rituals performed by a pious Jain, after bathing, is worship of the Tirthankaras, the 24 spiritual guides of the Jain tradition. The devotee stands in front of the Tirthankara images, some of which are shown here in this Jain temple in Rajasthan, India, and bows before them. Then an offering of the "five nectars" – a water solution of milk, curds, ghee (clarified butter), sugar and flowers – is poured over each image, which is then washed in pure water.

Reverence for Life

JAINISM IS ONE OF THE SMALLEST RELIGIONS in the world, with an estimated following of about 3.5 million, nearly all of whom live in India, Jainism's homeland. However, their strong ethical ideals, especially their stress on non-violence (*ahimsa*), and their austere way of living have been much admired down the centuries. Jains take their name from *Jinas*, or Conquerors, that is, those who have won the victory of enlightenment. In particular, *Jinas* refers to the 24 spiritual guides known as Tirthankaras, or "ford-markers", who Jains believe existed in past times, ending with Vardhamana Mahavira (pp.146–47), who, according to tradition, lived during the sixth century B.C.E.

A Jain's life is based on the three jewels (*triratna*), which consist of right faith, right knowledge and right conduct. For Jain monks, right conduct means strictly keeping five "great" vows. These are not injuring life, speaking the truth, not stealing, abstaining from sexual intercourse and sensuality, and not being attached to worldly possessions or living things. Laypeople view these vows as ideals that they must fulfil if they are ultimately to enjoy spiritual liberation. However, in practice, they take "lesser" vows of non-violence, truthfulness and charity. This has led to lay Jains leading austere, industrious lives, with many becoming successful businessmen.

Jains do not believe in a personal, creator God. Instead they venerate the 24 Tirthankaras, who act as inspiring examples of how to live in the world. Images, or *murtis*, of these teachers are found in Jain temples, and monks regard them as being helpful to laypeople by providing them with a focus for worship. Jain monks themselves do not participate in worship, or *puja*. Instead, those who officiate in Jain temples are lay Jains or even Hindu priests, an indication of how Hinduism has influenced the Jain religion.

The Jain community is made up of monks, nuns and laypeople. Monks and nuns should devote themselves to pious living, which involves meditating and studying Jain scriptures. Contact with the outside world is confined to the daily, or sometimes less frequent, alms round and to teaching laypeople. Novices are given a broom to clear the path so that they do not harm any creatures inadvertently; a piece of cloth to wear over their mouths to prevent living creatures in the air being harmed by their breath; a loin cloth; and an alms bowl for food. Jains are vegetarians, and since they believe that plants also possess souls, they are naturally sparing in their diet. And because the alms round necessarily involves injury to small living beings, it is preceded by confession and penitence.

Lay believers are divided into two groups, *shravakas*, or listeners, who listen to monks' discourses, and *upasakas*, or practitioners, who minister to their needs. In addition to keeping the five great vows, they have to fulfil other obligations, such as the cultivation of a right state of mind, meditating, fasting and confession.

Special periods that require fasting and confession include the festival of Paryushan, the most popular of Jain festivals, which brings together monks and laypeople. This lasts for 8 to 10 days and takes place during the rainy season, when monks relinquish their normally solitary life to take residence in buildings near a temple. During the festival period, there is an opportunity to confess past transgressions and be pardoned. The festival ends with an image of a *Jina* being carried in procession, a ritual act that again shows Hindu influence.

Awakening the soul

The Jain view of death is bound up with their notions of soul or life (*jiva*) and *karma*. Jains believe that every living thing possesses life (*jiva*), which is embodied in between one and five senses. Humans, gods, higher animals and demons who inhabit hell all have five senses; below them come lesser beings, down to those which have only one sense.

Jainism is dualistic, drawing a firm distinction between that which is alive (*jiva*) and that which is non-living (*ajiva*). Jains consider *karma* to be *ajiva* because it is matter that literally becomes attached to the soul, weighing it down and

dulling it so that it ceases to be aware of its true blissful and wise nature. Through the example and teachings of Mahavira (pp.146–47), the *jiva* can be awakened to an awareness of its true state. Purification of mind and body can prevent additional *karma* from accruing, and observance of the three jewels, as well as the monastic vows, eventually leads to the removal of *karma* and to liberation from rebirth. The *jiva* can then rise to a realm of the universe where liberated souls are held to dwell.

Consequent upon the Jain world view that everything has life, as well as on their strong

ideal of non-violence to living things, is the belief that the best death for a monk – following the example of Mahavira – is by prolonged meditation, during which the basic human needs, such as eating, are set aside and liberation is attained. The emphasis is on relinquishing life in a peaceful, positive and voluntary way, in response to a higher ideal. In practice, however, this rarely happens. For Jains, disposal of the dead, usually by cremation, is merely a necessary activity. Post mortem rituals are not usually required, although they may occur if, for example, a family is influenced by Hinduism.

Reverence for Life

The Jain universe

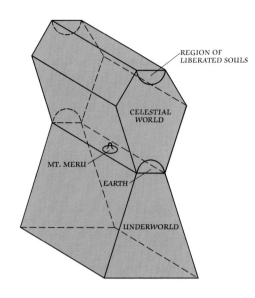

REGION OF LIBERATED SOULS

CELESTIAL WORLD

MT. MERU

EARTH

UNDERWORLD

The Jain concept of the universe is based on an ancient teaching that there are three worlds – the underworld, the earth and the celestial world. Beyond the celestial world is the pure region of liberated souls. The centre, or navel, of the earth is the site of the mythical Mount Meru, or Mandara, which, in Hindu teaching, was the abode of the gods Indra and Brahma.

The historical roots of Jainism date back to a time in India during the middle of the first millennium B.C.E. when the authority of the Hindu priests, the Brahmins, and their scriptures was being challenged by certain groups and individuals. Among the dissenters were the Buddha (pp.152–53) and Vardhamana, the last of the 24 Jain Tirthankaras, who became known as Mahavira ("Great Hero").

According to Jain tradition, Mahavira lived from about 599 to 527 B.C.E. He was born in northeastern India, into the Kshatriya, or warrior, caste (pp.128–29). His parents followed the teachings of a spiritual guide named Parshva, who had lived about 250 years earlier and is regarded as the 23rd Tirthankara. After his parents' death, Vardhamana, then 30 years old, left home and became a monk. He lived a life of extreme austerity for more than 12 years, eating little, keeping long periods of silence to purify his speech, and meditating intensely to cleanse his mind. Eventually he became detached from the *karma* (p.145) accumulated during this life and previous lives and achieved enlightenment. Thus he became a Conqueror, or *Jina*.

Mahavira taught for 30 years, practising self-discipline and austerities which, together with meditation, guaranteed that he acquired no further *karma*, good or bad. Eventually, at the age of 72, he passed away in Pava, a village near modern Patna, after meditating for two

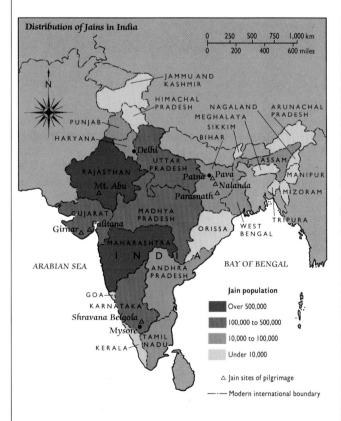

Distribution of Jains in India

Jain population

Over 500,000

100,000 to 500,000

10,000 to 100,000

Under 10,000

△ Jain sites of pilgrimage

‒ ‒ ‒ Modern international boundary

Most of the Jain population of the world lives in India, the Jain homeland, especially in the western states of Maharashtra and Rajasthan. Although recent surveys put the number of Jains at about 3.5 million, some Jains believe the figure could be as high as 10 million.

days. By honouring Mahavira, following his precepts and imitating his example, Jains believe that they, too, may be liberated from bondage to the material world.

Mahavira won many disciples among all ranks of Indian society by teaching the way of asceticism, until then considered the prerogative of the Brahmins alone. After his death, his notable early followers included Emperor Chandragupta Maurya (c.321–c.297 B.C.E.), founder of India's first great empire (pp.134–35).

Patronage by important figures such as Chandragupta contributed to Jainism's spread to various parts of India. Its establishment in Gujarat in the west, where it is still strong, dates from the 12th century, when the local king Kumarapala (c.1142–73) supported it. In Gujarat, as elsewhere, official patronage was underpinned by the merchant classes, whose thrift, an outcome of Mahavira's ascetic principles, made an important contribution to society. In later centuries, certain Mughal emperors (pp.104–5), especially Akbar, looked favourably on Jain teachers.

A formal division in Jain ranks occurred in 79 C.E.; it still exists today. However, its origins go back much earlier to some 200 years after Mahavira's death, when famine forced a group of Jains to move south from the Ganges plain. The monks who remained took to wearing white clothes, contrary to Mahavira's tradition, to afford themselves some protection from the climate, and they became known as Shvetambaras ("white-clothed"). Those who migrated south remained unclad, in accordance with Mahavira's example, and were called Digambaras ("sky-clothed"). But today, Indian law dictates that Digambaras must wear a loin cloth in public.

Doctrinally, the Digambaras believe that the oral teachings passed down from Mahavira have been lost, but that their substance has been preserved, as well as possible, in their writings, most of which have not yet been made public. The Shvetambaras claim that their texts, particularly the 11 *Angams* or *Angas* ("Limbs") are directly based on the original teachings of Mahavira.

In the 15th century C.E., a reform movement within the Shvetambaras led to the emergence of a group, the Sthanakvasis, who do not use images in worship. Instead, they perform their rites in plain meditation halls. Although these movements still maintain their separateness, their differences belong more to the realm of practice than belief. One important difference, however, is that Shvetambaras, unlike Digambaras, admit women and claim the possibility of *moksha*, or spiritual liberation, for them.

Jain nuns (LEFT) *cover their mouths to minimize the risk of harming any living thing and to avoid the impurity that results from causing suffering. This doctrine of non-violence, or* ahimsa, *lies at the heart of the Jain religion.*

One of the many Jain temples on the Shatrunjaya hills south of Palitana in northwestern India shows the consummate skill for which Jain architects and craftsmen are famed. Jains consider it proper to beautify buildings which house sacred images, as a sign of their piety. The beauty of the temple also encourages a spirit of worship in the devotee.

Young saffron-robed Buddhist monks *practise their meditation at a large gathering in Thailand. The type of Buddhism found in Thailand is known as Theravada – the "Way of the Elders" – and is one of the two major divisions in the religion. Meditation is as important to Buddhists as prayer is to, say, Christians or Muslims; it is considered to be a way of freeing the heart from suffering and the mind from ignorance.*

Tenzin Gyatso, the 14th Dalai Lama, *here addressing a group of followers* (RIGHT), *is the spiritual leader of Tibetan Buddhism and an internationally respected figure. He fled from Tibet in 1959, eight years after the country was annexed by the Chinese. The Dalai Lamas are believed to be incarnations of the bodhisattva ("buddha-to-be") known as Avalokiteshvara, the embodiment of compassion.*

The Path to Nirvana

ABOUT 2,500 YEARS AGO, AN INDIAN prince named Siddhartha Gautama, dissatisfied with his spiritually barren life, left his home, his wife and his son and set out to find enlightenment. After a period of six years spent in constant searching, Gautama finally reached enlightenment, or Nirvana, while sitting under a tree in a long, profound state of meditation. Henceforth, he became known as the Buddha – the Enlightened One – and his teachings and the example of his life form the basis of Buddhism.

Taking the universal experience of change and suffering in life as a starting point, the Buddha taught that suffering can be overcome by following a path to Nirvana. This is the unchanging state that is reached by all enlightened beings (buddhas), and Buddhists believe that it constitutes the true nature of reality. Nirvana, which resists verbal definitions and can only be suggested by analogies, is the ultimate state of pure being. For Buddhists, there is no belief in, or worship of, a personal creator God. To reach Nirvana involves the development of morality, meditation and wisdom – the very essence of Buddhism.

After the Buddha's death (pp.152–53), his followers carried his teachings to other parts of India, adapting it to local cultures. Buddhism then spread south and east to what is now Sri Lanka, Burma (Myanmar) and Thailand and north into the Himalayan regions of modern Nepal, Bhutan and Sikkim. From there it was taken along the silk route to China, Mongolia, Korea and Japan. Buddhism has also been transplanted to Vietnam, Laos, Cambodia and Indonesia and, most recently, to the United States (p.168), Europe, Australia and New Zealand.

Over a period of time, Buddhism developed into different schools, which evolved their own traditions. In Sri Lanka, Burma and Thailand, the main tradition is called Theravada – the "Way of the *Theras*", or senior monks or elders (pp. 160–61). Conservative in its approach, Theravada holds that its tradition reflects the earliest and most authentic Buddhist beliefs and practices. Theravada scriptures, written in the ancient Indian language of Pali and known as the Pali Canon, are believed to contain the actual words of Gautama Buddha. Although these scriptures do not contain a continuous life story of Gautama, legend and poetry have been added to the core of historical facts to make a narrative that Buddhists retell as a model for the human quest. This form of Buddhism is sometimes called Pali Buddhism, or Southern Buddhism.

The other main division of Buddhism, Mahayana (pp. 158–59), or "Great Vehicle" or "Great Way", emphasizes the variety of paths it provides. Its scriptures emerged from the first century B.C.E. to the second century C.E., and are written in the Sanskrit language, thus it is also called Sanskrit or Northern Buddhism. The types of Buddhism that Mahayana embraces include Tibetan Buddhism, whose spiritual leader, the Dalai Lama, is a familiar figure in the west; Chan (Japanese, Zen); and Pure Land, which began in China and developed in Japan. There are also new religious movements, such as Rissho Kosei Kai and Soka Gakkai (pp.207–8), which started in Japan and are growing fast in other parts of the world.

During the 20th century, Buddhism – arguably the most pacific of the religions – has had to face up to conflict and violence within various countries. The new Buddhist movements in Japan, for example, have helped the Japanese to live through times of rapid change and turmoil after World War II. The Vietnamese Zen monk Thich Nhat Hanh has voiced the sufferings of his people and founded a Buddhist Peace Fellowship, while in Sri Lanka, Buddhism is part of the national identity of the Sinhalese, who are involved in a

The Path to Nirvana

Death in life

One of the key teachings in Buddhism is that "all is impermanent" and that "decay is inherent in all compound things". Death is only one example of a process that continues throughout people's lives and can be seen as just one more state of transition. As the modern Buddhist scholar Edward Conze wrote: "Death is not to be regarded as a unique catastrophe which happens when one existence comes to an end, but it takes place all the time within that existence. The ideal attitude toward death is based on this awareness and involves acceptance of the process of change."

Buddhists believe that the constant changes people undergo from birth to old age help to teach that there is no unchanging "essence", "soul" or "self". What is ordinarily termed a "person" is in reality a chain of life, a continuity of constant becoming that carries on beyond physical death. It is also believed that the dead are reborn according to their *karma* – the moral law of cause and effect, based on a person's intention behind a deed.

People are reborn in one of the five or six realms of existence – depicted in the Buddhist wheel of life. These include heaven and hell, impermanent realms from which rebirth depends on the progress made there. In the end, all beings will go to the "deathless" realm or state of being that is Nirvana.

The state of mind of a person at the moment of death is important in determining the state of rebirth. Family, friends and monks stay by the bedside of a dying person to recite scriptures and help him or her to meditate. In Tibet, the *Book of the Dead* is used to prepare the person for the journey involved in dying.

Funerals are important for Buddhists. People are usually cremated three days after death, but other forms of disposing of the body are used – for example burial in Japan. During the waiting period before and at the funeral, monks chant passages of scripture and teach about impermanence. After the cremation, there are often ceremonies transferring merit to the deceased, which also take place on anniversaries of the person's death.

On the verge of death, Gautama Buddha reclines with his hand supporting his head in this sculpture from the Wat Pho Temple in Bangkok, Thailand. Buddhist tradition records that the Buddha spent his last moments on earth lying on his right side between two trees. Sculptures such as this one provide Buddhists with an ideal of calm acceptance of death.

struggle with the Tamil minority. And in Tibet, there is a continuing struggle as a vastly reduced number of monks keep alive the Buddhist tradition following the Chinese invasion in 1951.

Buddhists are interested first and foremost in the truth about the way things are, which is a common translation of the word *dharma* – to be differentiated from the Hindu sense of the word (pp.124–25). The *dharma*, which can also mean teaching, or the law of life, is what the Buddha discovered at his enlightenment and what he then taught to others. The different Buddhist paths can be seen as different ways of putting this truth into practice; Buddhists do not usually assert that one path is right and others wrong. This tolerance often extends to other religions, too.

At the root of the Buddhist quest is a sense of the unsatisfactoriness of life and the suffering that it involves. Buddhists use the term *samsara* for the state of constant change and death that characterizes existence. *Samsara* consists of three qualities: suffering (*dukkha*), impermanence (*anitya*) and the absence of any eternal soul or self that survives death (*anatman*). Buddhists do not use the conventional labels "I" or "person" to imply a permanent personality. Instead, they consider a person to be "a flow of being", subject to constant physical and psychological change, which continues through life beyond death.

For Buddhists, the aim is to live selflessly and to understand *samsara*. The latter is often likened to a house burning with the fires of greed, hatred and ignorance. When these three fires die down and are extinguished, there is Nirvana, literally meaning "cessation or extinction [of the fires]".

The way toward Nirvana involves renunciation. This is primarily an inner renunciation of false ideas and of all greed, hatred and ignorance and with this the development of generosity, loving kindness and wisdom. The different Buddhist schools offer various ways to accomplish this, but most schools involve two distinct groups of people, world renouncers (*bhikshu* and *bhikshuni*, monks and nuns) and householders, or laypeople. Together they make the *sangha*, an assembly or community, although sometimes it refers to monks and nuns only.

Monks observe a strict way of life which involves celibacy, having only a few basic possessions, and being completely dependent on laypeople for one daily meal, shelter and clothing. They wear saffron, maroon or black robes which, together with their seven items of basic equipment, constitute the Eight Requisites prescribed by Gautama himself. The other items are an alms bowl, a belt, a razor, a needle, a filter for straining live organisms from water before drinking it, a staff and a toothpick. Monks meditate, study and point to the wise and selfless way of life respected in Buddhist countries. In return for what they receive from laypeople, monks give to them what they consider to be a greater gift – the *dharma*.

Laypeople try to lead a moral life based on five precepts. These consist of not harming living things, not taking anything that is not given, not misusing the bodily senses, refraining from wrong speech, and abstaining from drugs and drink that cloud the mind. Laypeople show respect for monks by enabling them to live "the holy life", and they show respect for the Buddha by placing offerings of flowers, incense and light in front of images of him. Offerings are usually made individually and are encompassed by the Sanskrit term *puja* ("worship"), since they acknowledge the worth of the Buddha, who is said to have set in motion the wheel of the teaching out of compassion for all sentient beings.

However little a monk may receive, if he despises not what he receives, even the gods praise that monk, whose life is pure and full of endeavour.

DHARMAPADA 25:366

The three jewels

In Buddhism, there are three fundamental aspects, known as the three jewels (*triratna*) because of their preciousness – which form a basis for belief and practice. The first jewel is the Buddha, who, after years of searching, found the path to enlightenment and subsequently taught it to others. The second is the *dharma*, the teaching or the truth about the way things are. The last one is the *sangha*, the community of monks, nuns and laypeople who practise and help others to practise the teaching.

Buddhists often assign a medical symbolism to the three jewels. Buddha is the physician; the *dharma* is the remedy; and the *sangha* is the nurse who administers the remedy. Also, the jewels can be portrayed in Buddhist art. For example, one Tibetan *tanka*, a cloth painting, shows a lotus, often used to represent Buddhist teaching, or *dharma*, blossoming above the Buddha. From the lotus there rises the figure of a monk, symbolizing the *sangha*.

The three jewels are also called the three refuges. In order to become a Buddhist, a person "takes refuge" and shows that he or she depends on the jewels for release from the suffering inherent in life. This is done in either a public or private ceremony by repeating this formula three times: "I go to the Buddha for refuge; I go to the *dharma* for refuge; I go to the *sangha* for refuge."

In the early light of morning, Theravada monks carrying alms bowls walk through the countryside near the Thai city of Chiang Mai. They walk in single file in order of seniority, which is determined by the length of time they have been monks. Local householders wait to place food in their bowls. As they present their offerings, they thank the monks for the opportunity this gives them to obtain merit for a better existence in a future rebirth.

Almsgiving emphasizes the close relationship that exists between laypeople and the Buddhist sangha, or community. The monks eat only one meal a day so that they are not a burden on the local people. They take the food back to their monastery and eat it before noon.

A Tibetan Buddhist prostrates himself before the sacred Jokhang Monastery in Lhasa, the capital of Tibet. Full prostration – typical in Tibetan Buddhism – is a way of showing respect in holy places. For Buddhists, it both expresses and develops humility and is performed with the totality of body, speech and mind.

Gautama the Buddha

The path to enlightenment

Two of the most important summaries in the Buddha's teaching, which are basic to all the Buddhist schools, are the Four Noble Truths and the Noble Eightfold Path. These he realized at his enlightenment and taught in his first sermon. The truths are often compared to a doctor's diagnosis of a disease and his remedy for it.

The first truth is that life is all suffering (*dukkha*), in other words that existence in the world is innately unsatisfactory. The second suggests that the origin of *dukkha* is thirst (*tanha*), a synonym for desire and greed. This is one of the three fires and root evils (ignorance and hatred being the others) that underlie the unsatisfactory nature of life. The third truth confidently expresses that there can be an end to or cessation (*nirodha*) of suffering and desire. The fires of greed, hatred and ignorance can be "blown out" and Nirvana attained. According to the fourth truth, there is a path (*marga*) which leads to happiness. This involves eight stages, known as the Noble Eightfold Path. This path to happiness is based on three considerations: ethical conduct (*sila*), mental discipline (*samadhi*) and wisdom (*prajna*). It is possible to begin at any point on the path, since all the parts interact.

Ethical conduct consists of: right speech, which means not only not lying but also not talking in any way that will encourage malice or hatred; right action, as exemplified by the five precepts – avoiding taking life, taking what is not given, inappropriate sexual relations, false speech, and intoxicants; and right livelihood – earning a living in a way that does not cause harm to others.

Mental discipline requires: right effort – to prevent evil arising in the mind and to stimulate good thoughts; right mindfulness, which is a total attentiveness to the activities of the body, speech and mind; and right concentration, which is the training of the mind via the stages of meditation.

Wisdom involves: right understanding of the world as it really is, without delusions; and right thought, that is, the purification of the mind and heart and the growth of thoughts of unselfishness and compassion that will lead to action.

Venturing forth from his palace, the young Siddhartha Gautama – yet to become the Buddha – sees a corpse, pecked by black birds, in this 19th-century Chinese manuscript. The spirit of the dead man is shown watching the scene from above. Gautama's meeting with the corpse was one of the Four Signs that made him determined to set out to find a way of overcoming ignorance and death.

Work out your salvation with diligence.

THE BUDDHA'S LAST WORDS

Gautama Buddha, shown here in a Thai statue, was the historical founder of Buddhism. Although he is not worshipped as a god, images of him abound in the Buddhist world. They serve as reminders of the possibility of enlightenment to Buddhists, who bring to them offerings of flowers, incense and light in the form of burning candles. This statue shows the Buddha's long ear lobes, stretched by princely jewels, and a topknot on his head, symbolizing both wisdom and light.

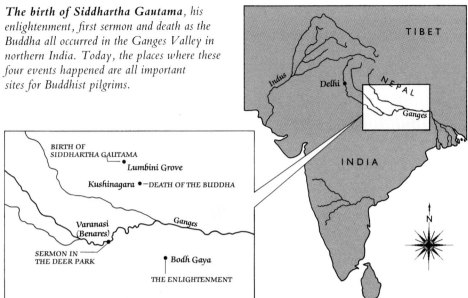

The birth of Siddhartha Gautama, his enlightenment, first sermon and death as the Buddha all occurred in the Ganges Valley in northern India. Today, the places where these four events happened are all important sites for Buddhist pilgrims.

Animals gambol in a Disneylike setting in this illustration from a 19th-century Burmese Jataka tale. Jataka, or birth, stories are a Buddhist genre of literature that describe the previous lives of Gautama Buddha. The tales contain elements of Indian folklore and include stories involving both animal and human characters.

Buddhists believe that all beings are reborn many times before they reach Nirvana. Only enlightened beings, or buddhas, remember their previous lives. Gautama Buddha spoke about his past existence to illustrate the type of life people should lead to make progress toward enlightenment. Thus many Jataka tales emphasize moral qualities, such as generosity, patience and renunciation; the stories are told to Buddhist children to encourage them to lead moral lives.

The title Buddha means "Enlightened One" and usually refers to Gautama Buddha, an Indian prince who traditionally lived in northeastern India from 566 to 486 B.C.E. (Some scholars now argue that his dates could be as late as 448 to 368 B.C.E.) Buddhists also believe there were other buddhas who existed before Gautama and that there is at least one more yet to come.

Gautama is also referred to by other names: Gautama is his family name, and a personal name, Siddhartha, appears in late Buddhist texts. He is also named Shakya-muni, the "sage of the Shakya clan"; and the titles Bodhisattva, meaning "a being on the way to enlighten-ment", and Tathagata, a synonym for Buddha, are also used. Gautama's parents were local rulers in a small kingdom in the Ganges Valley in northeastern India. On the night of his conception, his mother, Queen Maya, saw a white elephant – the sign of an exceptional being – enter her womb.

Gautama was born in Lumbini Grove, in what is now Nepal, and his birth was accompanied by miraculous signs. His mother died soon after his birth and he was brought up by his aunt Prajapati. According to tra-dition, astrologers told Gautama's father Suddhodana that his son would be either a great world ruler or, if he witnessed great suffering, a great religious teacher. Suddhodana, therefore, tried to protect the young Buddha-to-be from encountering suffering.

When he grew older, Gautama married a princess called Yasodhara, by whom he had a son, Rahula. But even though his life was a happy one, Gautama became restless and persuaded his charioteer, Channa, to take him outside the palace grounds against his father's orders. There, on separate occasions, he saw an old man, a sick man, a corpse being carried to the cremation grounds and a wandering holy man. These Four Signs prompted Gautama to think about old age, sickness, death and the importance of searching for a meaning in life. At the age of 29, after an inner struggle, he left

his family, cut off his hair and went to lead a homeless life – an event known as the Great Renunciation.

Gautama went into the forest where he came across two religious sages, who taught him meditation and asked him to join them as teachers. But reckoning that he had not progressed far enough spiritually, Gautama declined and instead decided to fast strictly until he could "feel his backbone through his stomach". This failed to bring the desired enlightenment and was to lead to his teaching that the best spiritual way is a middle path between extremes of self-denial and self-indulgence.

Six years after his renunciation, Gautama came to a sacred tree (later known as the Bodhi or Bo tree) at Bodh Gaya and resolved to meditate there until he had found the answer to his search. During the next night, he sat in the lotus posture with legs crossed and fought an inner battle – described in the scriptures as temptation by Mara, the personification of change, death and evil. Gautama is often pictured touching the earth with his hand, asking it to bear witness to the fact that he was worthy of enlightenment because he had practised virtues such as patience and generosity in previous lives.

Mara was defeated, and Gautama gained enlighten-ment, usually described as a state of great clarity and understanding of the truth about the way things are. According to tradition, a high god of the religion of the time (now called Hinduism) asked him to try to teach people the nature of their existence and help them out of their suffering. Gautama agreed and went to the Deer Park at Sarnath near Varanasi (Benares), where he found five seekers of truth whom he had known before. They saw a new radiance and authority in his manner and listened to his first sermon on the Four Noble Truths and Noble Eightfold Path (*opposite*). They were only the first of many followers who came from all backgrounds. Gautama taught until he was 80 and died peacefully at Kushinagara, lying on his side – his death is called the *parinirvana*, or entry into final Nirvana.

Ashoka

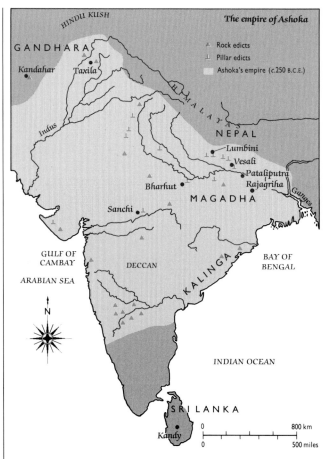

The empire of Ashoka

△ Rock edicts
⊥ Pillar edicts
▨ Ashoka's empire (c.250 B.C.E.)

> I wish the members of all religions to live with honour in my kingdom. ASHOKA

Ashoka, the greatest ruler in Indian history, became a Buddhist after he was filled with remorse at the slaughter of so many people in his campaign against the Kalingas in about 260 B.C.E. He extended the empire established by his father and grandfather until it covered most of the subcontinent – shown by the distribution of the numerous rocks and pillars inscribed with his edicts.

In the third century B.C.E, the great Indian emperor Ashoka ruled over the largest empire India was to see for two millennia. It covered about two-thirds of the subcontinent and was centred on the city of Pataliputra (modern Patna) in the northeast, an area where the Buddha had lived. Ashoka began his reign (c.265–238 B.C.E.) by fighting to consolidate the Mauryan Empire, founded in about 324 by his grandfather Chandragupta Maurya. However, in a successful campaign against the people of Kalinga (in the modern state of Orissa), he was so sickened by the bloodshed and the suffering he caused that he turned to Buddhism and vowed in the future to rule by righteousness.

Ashoka received instruction from members of the Buddhist community, or *sangha*; and he came to embody the ideal ruler, described in the Buddha's teachings, who creates a peaceful and generous society where people can follow the path to enlightenment (p.152). Buddhists continue to view Ashoka both as an ideal ruler and an ideal layperson for his moral integrity and support of the *sangha*.

Ashoka's concept of righteousness clearly echoes the Buddha's teachings about the way people should behave in society. He encouraged tolerance for all religious groups and the support of all world-renouncers. He also discouraged the killing of animals, abolished the death penalty and had trees planted and wells dug along roads for travellers.

Ashoka's inscriptions

One of the lasting remains of Ashoka are his inscriptions, carved on rocks and pillars throughout India. They were set up to teach people righteousness, or *dharma* (pp.150–51), and Ashoka appointed officials to read the texts to villagers and encourage them to live as the words suggested. Since there are no surviving examples of writing in India before the third century B.C.E., the inscriptions are also important as literary texts. The following quotations from the inscriptions give an idea of the moral values that Ashoka espoused:

"Ashoka, the conqueror of the Kalingas, has felt deep sorrow because the conquest of the people involved slaughter, death and captivity."

"Ashoka now teaches you to respect the value and sacredness of life, to abstain from killing animals and from cruelty to living things."

"I desire men of all faiths to know each other's beliefs and acquire sound doctrines themselves. By honouring others, one exalts one's own faith and at the same time performs a service to others."

"No task is more important to me than the well-being of my people. Such work as I accomplish contributes to discharging the debt I owe to all living creatures to make them happy in this world and to help them attain heaven in the next."

Inscribed on one of Ashoka's pillars, this detail is part of an edict that warns against the creation of a division within the Buddhist community. The inscriptions still carry their sometimes inspirational messages – especially those advocating the tolerance of all religions – into the 20th century.

The great Indian statesman Jawaharlal Nehru (1889–1964) once wrote that the "memory of Ashoka lives over the whole continent of Asia, and his edicts still speak to us in a language we can understand and appreciate. And we can still learn much from them."

Knowledge of Ashoka comes from the inscriptions he had made on rocks and pillars (*opposite*) and from the Theravada Buddhist chronicles, which were written down in Sri Lanka at the beginning of the fifth century C.E. from an oral tradition that had been gathered as far back as the third century B.C.E. One inscription states that Ashoka sent messengers to other kings – a reference possibly corroborated by the chronicles, which say that Buddhism was spread by missions to other countries, such as Sri Lanka. The chronicles also say that a senior monk named Tissa Moggaliputta organized nine missions, the most famous being the one to Sri Lanka. Here, Ashoka's son Mahinda, who was a monk, and his daughter Sanghamitta, a nun, established the *sangha* in about 250 B.C.E.

The inscriptions also mention that Ashoka encouraged the monastic community to stay united and recommended that anyone who tried to split it should be forced to revert to lay status. This may tie in with details in the Theravada chronicles which say that laypeople impersonated monks to benefit from the royal support given to the *sangha*, particularly at Pataliputra. When the true monks did not cooperate with these imposters, Ashoka and Tissa Moggaliputta went to find the frauds. The *sangha* was duly purified, and then a Buddhist council was held at Pataliputra. This resulted in the final form of the Pali version of the Buddhist scriptures.

Ashoka is also said to have gone on pilgrimage to various places, such as Lumbini, where the pillar that he set up can still be seen. He built many new stupas, or reliquary mounds (pp.156–57), and renovated old ones all over India. The symbols of Ashoka's reign, the lions and wheels carved on his pillars, have been assumed by the Indian state as national symbols, for example the wheel on the flag. This is an indication of the esteem he is held in by all Indians, Buddhists and non-Buddhists.

This lion-headed capital topped one of the edict pillars of Ashoka. The lions are symbolic of royalty, and the wheel, which represents earthly rule and kingship, has been adopted by the Indian government to embellish the country's flag.

Visual Teaching

During the reign of Ashoka (c.265–238 B.C.E.), the Buddha and his teachings were represented by symbols. This was probably because symbols could convey his spiritual essence more effectively than any human likeness; but there may also have been an influence from the ancient Indian Vedic tradition (pp.130–31) of rendering deities symbolically.

Symbolic images were carved on the gateways to the earliest Buddhist sacred areas and included the wheel, the lotus (below), an empty throne, a stylized Bodhi tree, footprints and small stupas or reliquary mounds. Like all symbols, they embody many layers of meaning, some knowledge of which helps in the appreciation of the resonance of Buddhist iconography.

The wheel is an ancient Indian sign and represents the "wheel of the law" or teaching (dharma chakra). It can have between six and a thousand spokes, the latter giving it a sunlike form associated with kingship. Ashoka used the wheel as a symbol of earthly rule and had it carved on pillars, but it also denotes the Buddha as a spiritual world ruler who "set in motion the wheel of law" at his first sermon after his enlightenment. An eight-spoke wheel symbolizes the Eightfold Path (p.152).

The empty throne echoes the idea of the Buddha as a spiritual ruler and is also a reminder that he was a prince before he renounced the world. He is not shown sitting on the throne in the early centuries because it was thought that there was no adequate way of portraying someone who had entered the state of Nirvana.

The footprint, like the throne, is a reminder of the Buddha's presence in his teaching. And the stupa

(opposite), originally hemispherical in shape, is linked particularly with the Buddha's death. It later became the typical architectural feature of the Buddhist world, developing in style from culture to culture.

Images of the Buddha (rupas) were not made until some time between the first century B.C.E. and the first century C.E. According to one theory, they were first made in Gandhara in northwestern India, an area influenced by Greek culture in which the human image was a popular subject for sculptors. It is also thought that Buddha images began during the same period, or even earlier, at Mathura in the Ganges-Jumna valley.

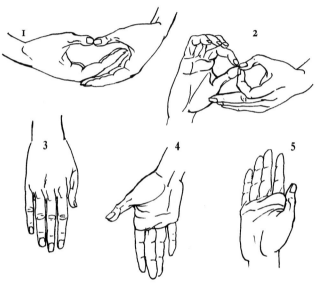

A lay Buddhist chooses a bunch of lotus flowers so that she can offer them at a shrine or temple. Lotuses symbolize the possibility of enlightenment from a state of ignorance.

The blossom of enlightenment

The image of the lotus, which has its roots in mud but blossoms on the surface of still water, is used by Buddhists to show that enlightenment can flower in an unsatisfactory world. The mud in which the lotus takes root can be compared to the universal experience of suffering or ignorance. The task for Buddhists is to nourish the root of potential enlightenment within themselves, so that it can grow and emerge from the darkness of the material world of delusions to the purity of the state of Nirvana.

According to a Buddhist text known as *Questions of King Milinda*, "as the lotus is untarnished by water, so is Nirvana untarnished by any evil disposition. This is the one quality of the lotus inherent in Nirvana." And the beauty of the lotus, in contrast to its unpromising surroundings, is used effectively in this quotation from the *Dharmapada*, one of the oldest Buddhist texts, to distinguish the enlightened soul from the benighted many: "Just as on a heap of rubbish thrown upon the highway grows the lotus sweetly fragrant and delighting the heart, even so among those blinded mortals who are like rubbish the disciple of the truly enlightened Buddha shines with glory by his wisdom."

The wheel and the Bodhi tree (LEFT) are both symbols of the Buddha. The hand gestures – when seen on a Buddha image – show the Buddha to be meditating (1); actively turning the wheel of law (2); touching the earth as a witness to his worthiness for Buddhahood (3); being generous, including teaching (4); and reassuring or protecting an approaching person (5).

Buddha images are reminders of Gautama and his teaching. The various hand and body gestures show the Buddha meditating, teaching, blessing or showing generosity toward the onlooker. His eyes are often half-closed, but his hands are active – as if expressing a desire to help the world. The images depict beauty and spiritual attainment, and show some of the 32 major and 80 minor marks that Buddhists believe are signs of a great person. The Buddha's long ear lobes are both a sign of beauty and a reminder of the heavy ear jewellery he wore before his renunciation of the world. The circle of hair on the forehead is a reminder of his wisdom, as is the turbanlike bump, or *ushnisha*, on his head, which may have begun as a topknot of hair over which an Indian prince's turban was worn. His torso is rounded with the fullness of meditative breath and earthly beauty.

As Buddhism spread to different countries, Buddha images changed in style, making them relevant to people of different cultures. In China and Japan, for example, the faces of the Buddha have oriental features. Likewise, there are experiments in the west to make Buddha images with western faces. The point is not to make a definitive historical Buddha, but to embody in an image a universal teaching of meditative peace.

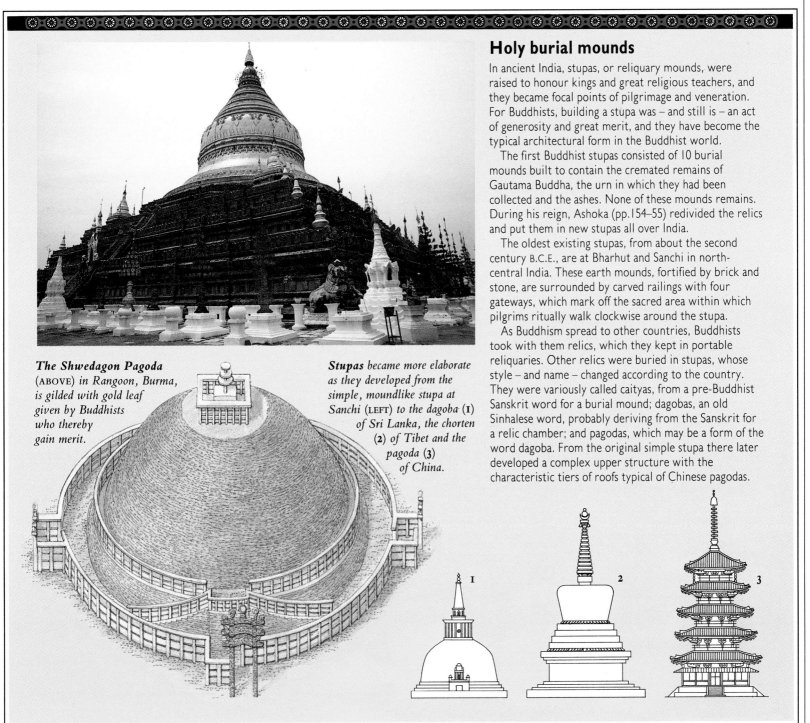

The Shwedagon Pagoda (ABOVE) *in Rangoon, Burma, is gilded with gold leaf given by Buddhists who thereby gain merit.*

Stupas became more elaborate as they developed from the simple, moundlike stupa at Sanchi (LEFT) to the dagoba (1) of Sri Lanka, the chorten (2) of Tibet and the pagoda (3) of China.

Holy burial mounds

In ancient India, stupas, or reliquary mounds, were raised to honour kings and great religious teachers, and they became focal points of pilgrimage and veneration. For Buddhists, building a stupa was – and still is – an act of generosity and great merit, and they have become the typical architectural form in the Buddhist world.

The first Buddhist stupas consisted of 10 burial mounds built to contain the cremated remains of Gautama Buddha, the urn in which they had been collected and the ashes. None of these mounds remains. During his reign, Ashoka (pp.154–55) redivided the relics and put them in new stupas all over India.

The oldest existing stupas, from about the second century B.C.E., are at Bharhut and Sanchi in north-central India. These earth mounds, fortified by brick and stone, are surrounded by carved railings with four gateways, which mark off the sacred area within which pilgrims ritually walk clockwise around the stupa.

As Buddhism spread to other countries, Buddhists took with them relics, which they kept in portable reliquaries. Other relics were buried in stupas, whose style – and name – changed according to the country. They were variously called caityas, from a pre-Buddhist Sanskrit word for a burial mound; dagobas, an old Sinhalese word, probably deriving from the Sanskrit for a relic chamber; and pagodas, which may be a form of the word dagoba. From the original simple stupa there later developed a complex upper structure with the characteristic tiers of roofs typical of Chinese pagodas.

Tradition and Development

After the Buddha's death, his followers fanned out from northeastern India to the west and south, preaching in local dialects the path to enlightenment (p.152). In time, Buddhism spread all over the Indian subcontinent and into Sri Lanka. By the start of the common era, there were two main streams: Theravada, "Doctrine of the Elders", the more conservative and doctrinally rigid tradition; and Mahayana, "Great Way", which embraces many different paths to salvation and stresses the role of the *bodhisattva* (*opposite*). How did these two schools develop?

Buddhist tradition accepts that two councils to decide on doctrine were held within 100 years of the Buddha's death. One was in Rajagriha, attended by 500 monks, while the other happened in Vesali. At these meetings, the pre-eminence of the oral teachings called the *Sutra Pitaka* ("basket of discourses") and the *Vinaya Pitaka* ("basket of disciplinary regulations") was agreed on.

Over a period of time, monastic practice and ideas became more diverse. It seems that only Theravada Buddhists acknowledged the authority of the third council in Pataliputra, convened by the Emperor Ashoka (pp.154–55), and the *Abhidharma Pitaka* ("basket of higher teaching"), the third section of the Tripitaka – which is also known as the Pali Canon.

There is no evidence showing decisive moments in the divergence between Theravada and Mahayana. More likely there was a gradual widening of doctrine and practice, but with a coexistence between the two movements, even in monasteries, for some time. But there are important milestones indicating the course Buddhism took. These include, in the Theravada tradition, the taking of Buddhism to Sri Lanka in the time of Ashoka and the writing down of the Tripitaka, believed to be the actual words of the historical Buddha.

Perhaps the most distinctive aspect of Theravada that developed was the ideal of the *arhat* (*opposite*), the "saint" who had diligently trod the path to enlightenment. This striving for personal salvation was viewed by Mahayanists as essentially selfish and contributed to their calling Theravada the "Lesser Way", or Hinayana.

The formative period of Mahayana, which is better viewed as a spiritual movement than a school or set of schools, began from at least the second century B.C.E. Of central importance to Mahayana are the ideal of the *bodhisattva*; the concept of *shunyata*, meaning emptiness or void, as the best way of describing ultimate reality; the idea of an eternal buddha, who from time to time manifests himself as an earthly buddha – Gautama being one such example; and the related notion of there existing innumerable "buddha-worlds", each presided over by a cosmic buddha.

Mahayana traditions are contained in a body of sutras, or scriptures, which were probably written down between the first century B.C.E. and second century C.E. These are core texts for both doctrine and practice. Among them are the *Prajnaparamita* ("Perfection of Wisdom") sutras, which contain the famous *Heart Sutra*, important in Zen Buddhism (pp.162–63) and which encapsulates the importance of *shunyata* with the words "Form is no other than emptiness; emptiness no other than form." And there is the *Diamond Sutra*, which stresses that everyday reality is an illusion.

There is also the *Lotus Sutra*, which states that the many paths to enlightenment are all "skilful means" that lead people on the one great way; and the *Sukhavati Sutras*, which teach about the realm of Amida Buddha, central to the Pure Land school (pp.162–63). Originally in Sanskrit, these texts have been translated into Tibetan, Chinese and Japanese, and are seen as having the authority of the Buddha without being his exact words.

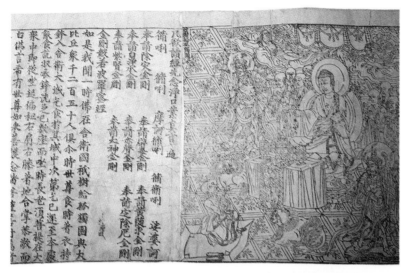

The written word has played a major part in the spread of Buddhism. Monks (MIDDLE) in Ladakh, Kashmir, study their texts – a crucial part of their training. Books are stored in Tibetan-style libraries, such as the one here (BOTTOM), where the manuscripts are wrapped in cloth and placed between two boards and kept in compartments. The *Diamond Sutra* (TOP) is the world's oldest printed book.

Arhats and *bodhisattvas*

Both Theravada and Mahayana Buddhists refer to becoming enlightened or buddhas. Each has its own distinct ideal – for Theravadins this is the *arhat*, "one who is worthy", often translated as "saint"; for Mahayana Buddhists it is the *bodhisattva* – the "enlightenment being".

To become an *arhat* involves the highest spiritual level a person can reach, the state of Nirvana itself. This means that someone who is a buddha can also be called *arhat*, but the latter refers more specifically to someone who has worked out his or her own salvation by following the teaching of a buddha. Buddhas, however, are enlightened by finding the path

for themselves. Unlike buddhas, *arhats* do not initiate a stream of teaching of their own.

Bodhisattva also has both a general and a more specialized usage. Generally, it refers to someone destined for enlightenment – a "buddha-to-be" – because of the merit he or she has made in previous births. In this sense, Gautama is called a *bodhisattva* before his enlightenment under the Bodhi tree (pp.152–53). Mahayanists use the term more specifically for those who are capable of enlightenment and whose intention is to help all sentient beings reach Nirvana, at whatever cost to themselves. Mahayana Buddhists say that this attitude is less

selfish than the *arhat's* personal quest for salvation, but Theravadins reply that the way of the *arhat* involves compassion for all beings.

When they take their vows, *bodhisattvas* follow a path based on six perfections – they should be perfectly generous, virtuous, patient, energetic, meditative and wise – and 10 stages. *Bodhisattvas* are also seen as transcendent beings, who appear in various forms to help others reach enlightenment, and are worshipped by believers. Perhaps the most famous is Avalokiteshvara, whom Tibetan Buddhists believe is incarnated in the Dalai Lama (pp.164–65).

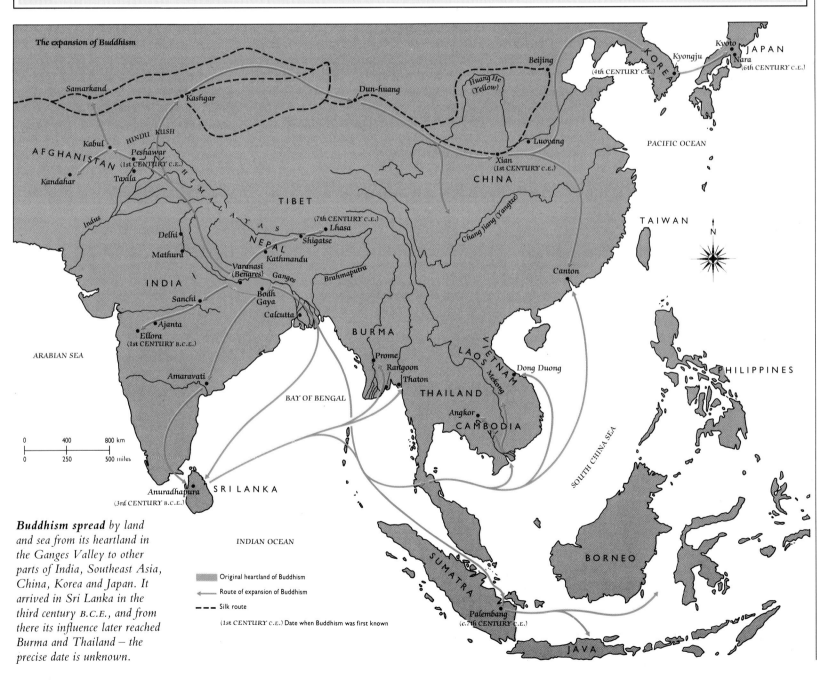

The expansion of Buddhism

Buddhism spread by land and sea from its heartland in the Ganges Valley to other parts of India, Southeast Asia, China, Korea and Japan. It arrived in Sri Lanka in the third century B.C.E., and from there its influence later reached Burma and Thailand – the precise date is unknown.

Original heartland of Buddhism
Route of expansion of Buddhism
Silk route
(1st CENTURY C.E.) Date when Buddhism was first known

The Theravada Tradition

Laypeople place food in the alms bowls of Theravada monks in this typical early morning scene in a Thai city street. The monks do not ask for food and accept anything that is offered to them, provided that any meat included has not been killed especially for them. The householders, who are grateful for the opportunity that almsgiving affords them to make merit for a better rebirth, thank the monks as they make their donations.

The Buddhist world is broadly divided into two main traditions – Theravada and Mahayana. They roughly correspond to two vast areas of the globe: Southeast Asia and northern and eastern Asia (Tibet, China, Korea and Japan), respectively. In Sri Lanka, Thailand and Burma, the way of the *theras*, or senior monks, has been dominant for centuries, influencing the moral, social and political fabric of these countries. In particular, the relationship between the monks and the laypeople has forged a remarkable degree of religious and cultural coherence, as it still does.

In Sri Lanka, it is the majority tradition; in Thailand, it dominates national life and the king still has the right to appoint the most senior monk in the land; and in Burma, there is a proverb that to be Burmese is to be Buddhist. Theravada was also once strong in Laos and Cambodia, but political turmoil since the 1960s – especially the brutal regime of Pol Pot in Cambodia in the 1970s – has destroyed both Buddhist monasteries and culture in these countries.

According to tradition, Buddhism first reached Sri Lanka through the missions of Emperor Ashoka (pp.154–55) in the mid-third century B.C.E. By the fifth century C.E., there were, according to the Chinese monk Fa Xian, who visited the island at this time, about 60,000 Sinhalese monks and numerous monasteries supported

Coming of age

In the Theravada countries of Southeast Asia, many boys and some girls, usually between the ages of 8 and 12, are initiated into adulthood in a ceremony for becoming a novice monk or nun. Families believe they gain merit for organizing the initiations, whose cost is such that many families share the expense. They are also expected to give presents to monks and to provide for feasts on the evening before and early on the day of the ceremony.

The children to be initiated are dressed up as princes and princesses (LEFT), in imitation of Prince Gautama before he became the Buddha, and taken to the local monastery in a colourful procession accompanied by musicians and guests. When they arrive, they take the three jewels (p.151), which entails repeating the formula "I go to the Buddha for refuge; I go to the *dharma* for refuge; I go to the *sangha* for refuge", and the Ten Precepts (*opposite*).

They then have their heads shaved and exchange their royal garb for simple saffron robes – to symbolize their renunciation of the world. Sacred texts are chanted and the senior monk gives an address. Afterward, the boys usually stay with the monks for varying lengths of time – perhaps as little as a night or a week, or, if they want to pursue a monastic education, a few years.

by the king, who had the capacity at his palace to feed 5,000 monks at one sitting.

Thailand and Burma also have legendary links with Ashoka, but there is no historical evidence to support this. Up to the 11th century C.E., both Theravada and Mahayana forms probably existed side by side in these two countries. Then, a resurgence of Buddhism in Sri Lanka brought travelling Sinhalese Theravada monks to their shores. In the middle of the 11th century, King Anawrahta of Burma united his country and made Theravada the dominant religious force. In Thailand, King Rama Khameng (c.1275–1317) made Theravada the official religion, and his grandson later invited monks from Sri Lanka to the country to strengthen the *sangha*, or Buddhist community.

At the heart of Theravada society lies the interdependence between monks and laypeople, or "householders". The latter make offerings of food, clothes and dwellings to the monks and try to live a moral life based on generosity and the first five of the ten precepts (*below*) that form the basis of life for a novice monk. Their motivation is to make merit for a better rebirth, since it is unlikely – although not impossible – for a layperson to attain Nirvana: future rebirth as a monk or a nun will bring them closer to enlightenment.

The diverse needs of Theravada society and the different interests and abilities of the monks have produced different types of monks. Those who live in small groups in villages often do not practise meditation much but are involved in the lives of the villagers as spiritual guides or teachers, officiating at the rites of passage linked with the coming of age and death. Some monks, especially in Sri Lanka, prefer to study and become university scholars of Buddhist texts and history. And there is also the tradition of the "forest"

monks, who emphasize meditation, prefer remote forest regions to cities, and try to live as close as they can to the monastic rule at the time of the Buddha.

In Theravada and other Buddhist countries, Buddhism has gently infiltrated indigenous cultures and religions and tolerated the spirit worship it has encountered. Laypeople often continue to pray and make offerings to local gods and spirits to obtain help with illness, an arranged marriage or a business deal – areas of life they feel are not the concern of Buddhism.

In Theravada monasteries, the patimokkha, *or monastic rules, are read aloud at a fortnightly meeting. Monks, such as the one bowing down here, acknowledge rules they have broken. Serious offences, such as sexual misconduct, result in expulsion, but more minor ones are forgiven by confession.*

In Southeast Asia, remains of temples and pagodas often indicate important Buddhist sites of the past. The remains of numerous pagodas in Pagan, on the River Irrawaddy, are testament to the city's importance as the capital of Burma for about 250 years from the ninth century c.e. Angkor, in Cambodia, shows Hindu and Buddhist influences in its temple architecture in the centuries before becoming a Theravada kingdom in the 1300s.

The Ten Precepts

Buddhist monks make a commitment to the *sangha*, or community, by taking ten vows – the Ten Precepts – which date back to the time of the Buddha. Although ordination of women has died out in Theravada countries, some women live as "nuns", following the Ten Precepts, but they generally have less authority with laypeople than their male counterparts. The precepts take the form of personal undertakings to refrain from:

1 Harming any living thing.
2 Taking what is not given.
3 A misuse of the senses, i.e. unchastity.
4 Wrong speech.
5 Intoxicating drugs or drink.
6 Eating after the midday meal.
7 Dancing, music, singing and unseemly shows.
8 Garlands, perfumes and personal adornments.
9 Using high and luxurious seats (and beds).
10 Accepting gold and silver.

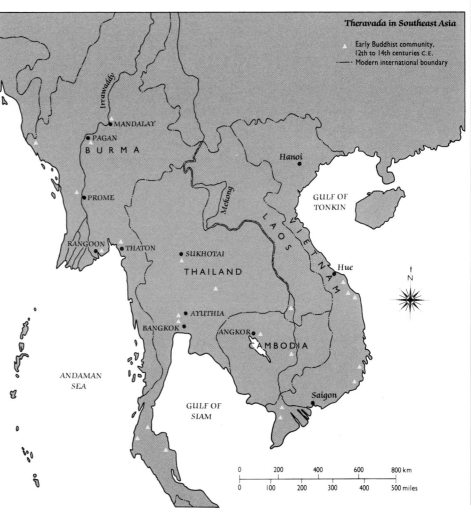

Theravada in Southeast Asia

▲ Early Buddhist community, 12th to 14th centuries C.E.
------ Modern international boundary

The Japanese Inheritance

Buddhism reached Japan in its Mahayana form from China via Korea in about the middle of the sixth century C.E. Different schools developed along the lines of their Chinese prototypes and became part of the religious fabric of Japanese society, coexisting with and influencing the indigenous Japanese religion of Shinto (pp.196–201). Among the movements to become established were Tendai, Shingon, Nichiren and, most important, Pure Land and Zen.

The Tendai school takes its name from the Chinese Buddhist sect Tiantai. Its doctrines were brought to Japan in 805 C.E. by the Japanese priest Saicho (767–822), who had travelled and studied in China the previous year. Saicho's monastery, Enryakuji, established on Mount Hiei near Kyoto became an important training centre for monks, who were required to stay there for some years before leaving to join the world as priests or teachers. The most influential Tendai teaching, common to all Mahayana schools, is that enlightenment, or Buddhahood, is not the sole preserve of monks and is open to everyone.

A younger contemporary of Saicho was the monk Kukai (774–835), who also went to China to deepen his knowledge of Buddhism. On his return to Japan in 807, he founded the esoteric Shingon school (Chinese Chen-yen), centred at his Mount Koya monastery, 50 miles south of Kyoto. Central to Shingon is the figure of

Direct pointing to the mind of man; Seeing into one's own nature.

ZEN MASTER NAN QUAN
DESCRIBING ZEN TEACHING

Buddhism first came to Japan in the sixth century C.E. and since then a number of sacred sites have become established, most of them clustered on the island of Honshu. Shihi, Tsurumi and Toyokawa are especially revered by the Soto Zen school. The other Japanese Zen school, Rinzai, is centred on Kyoto and Kamakura, site also of the famous statue (OPPOSITE, BOTTOM LEFT) of Amida Buddha, venerated by members of the Pure Land sect.

The art of Zen

In many forms of Buddhism, there is an emphasis that everyday actions, such as sweeping leaves, can be used as a means of meditation. This is particularly true of Zen, which encompasses a range of disparate activities, or arts, that helps the doer achieve a state of understanding. These Zen arts, which involve a powerful simplicity, include the tea ceremony (*chado*); flower arranging, with an underlying emphasis on the interpretation of nature, through symbolism (*ikebana*); making a garden; writing (calligraphy); painting and poetry; as well as military arts such as archery and swordsmanship.

In literature, the form of poetry developed by the Zen tradition is the haiku – a poem consisting of 17 Japanese syllables. The haiku pares expression down to its essence and aims to capture a moment of true reality:
"The still pond, ah!
A frog jumps in.
The waters' sound."
This was written by the 17th-century poet Basho, who is said to have realized enlightenment when he heard this sound. Frogs have also been a subject for Zen artists – perhaps because, like meditators, they remain still for hours, alert with total awareness.

Landscape is another important theme in Zen painting. Scenes are reduced to their bare essentials with deft brush strokes typically showing trees, mountains, the sea and human figures against a backdrop of great space, which is considered as real as the individual objects. Thus painters

emphasize the belief that the everyday world and the infinite are both part of the same ultimate reality.

In the *chado* ceremony, performed with precise, formalized actions, the ordinariness of making tea becomes a ritual redolent of peaceful beauty. Every action is done mindfully and with great care, turning a mundane activity into a meditation. Likewise, Zen gardens can be used for meditation, especially in monasteries. Often no more than rocks and raked sand, they capture the rhythms of natural landscape, of mountains, sea and space, which are seen in their essential, most basic, forms.

The way of life in Zen monasteries is based on a simple routine of meditation combined with the work that is required to maintain the monastery and guarantee the smooth running of monastic life. Here, a monk wearing his working clothes tidies a garden of raked sand. A feature of Zen monasteries, these gardens convey the simple lines and proportions of a natural landscape, or even the ocean, and are useful aids to meditation.

Vairocana (Japanese Dainichi), the celestial Buddha of Infinite Light, through whom enlightenment is attained. Shingon also stresses the importance of meditation and mandalas (cosmic diagrams), which are used to help the meditator reach Buddhahood.

The Nichiren sect is named for its founder, who studied Tendai on Mount Hiei from 1242. Nichiren was impressed by Tendai's emphasis on the scripture known as the *Lotus Sutra*, which he made the cornerstone of his school. It is a sutra that stresses that the different paths to enlightenment are "skilful means", but all have the same goal. Nichiren exhibits strong nationalistic tendencies and is now divided into several schools, of which Soka Gakkai (p.208) is an example.

The largest Buddhist tradition in Japan is Pure Land, whose essential belief is that it is possible to be reborn in a paradise, or "pure land", presided over by the celestial Amida Buddha. Sometimes called Amidism, Pure Land developed in Japan during the 12th and 13th centuries through the monks Honen (1133–1212) and Shinran (1173–1263), who founded the Jodo-shu (Pure Land) and Jodo-shin-shu (True Pure Land), respectively.

Adherents of both sects set great store by Amida's compassionate and enlightened mind, which shines out on all beings, activating the Buddha nature within them. Their faith, expressed in the repetition of the name Amida in the mantra *Namu Amida Butsu* ("Veneration to Amida Buddha"), is considered adequate to gain rebirth in Amida's Pure Land, where he will help them in their quest to reach Nirvana.

For westerners, Zen Buddhism is the best known form of Japanese Buddhism and is associated particularly with meditation techniques, the development of intuition and distinctive art forms (*opposite*). Zen (Chinese Chan, "meditation") took root in Japan from China in the 12th century and developed into two schools – Rinzai, founded by Eisai (1141–1214), and Soto, founded by Dogen (1200–53).

The essence of Zen lies in the directness of its teaching, which bypasses intellectual study, and the possibility of a sudden insight into reality (*satori*). This can be achieved by the practice of sitting meditation (*zazen*), as well as by the use of paradoxical questions, or *koans*, such as: "What is the sound of one hand clapping?" and "What did your face look like before you were born?" *Koans* aim to break down or bypass the habitual intellectual processes of the mind and elicit a sudden insight like a flash of lightning. Rinzai and Soto, still active today, differ only in the emphasis that they put on either meditation (Soto) or *koans* (Rinzai).

Zen monks often journey to pilgrim sites in Japan, bearing their few possessions on their shoulders. This prospective pilgrim (RIGHT) has a wicker hat to protect him from sun and rain, and wears traditional black robes, wicker sandals and a cloth alms bag around his neck. His shaven head shows he has renounced worldly vanities.

Members of the Tendai sect add fuel to the flames during a fire ceremony (BELOW RIGHT), a practice which they have adopted from the Shingon school. Fire is a universal symbol of purification, and by feeding the fire the officiators aim to cleanse symbolically all worldly defilements.

This massive bronze statue of Amida Buddha, the central figure of the Pure Land school, dominates its surroundings in Kamakura on the island of Honshu, Japan. Cast in several parts in 1252, it was housed until 1495 in a vast wooden temple, which was finally destroyed by floods. The sense of balance and harmony conveyed in the colossal figure, as well as the evocative simplicity of the detail, make it easy to see why the statue is now considered a Japanese national treasure.

Himalayan Paths

The people of Tibet, "the high plateau of the snows", have their own distinctive form of Buddhism. It combines traces of the pre-Buddhist Bon religion, with its shaman priests, sorcery, rituals and nature spirits, and the type of Mahayana Buddhism (pp.158–59) known as Vajrayana – the vehicle of the diamond or thunderbolt, symbol for ultimate reality, the void.

Vajrayana is based on powerful esoteric teachings known as tantras and makes use of *mudras* (sacred hand gestures), mantras (sacred verses) and mandalas (cosmic diagrams) as aids to spiritual life. It once thrived in all the Himalayan regions but has been concentrated in Tibet since the eighth century C.E. Here, the strong guru-disciple relationship in Vajrayana took root, and the Tibetan guru, or lama, came to be viewed as the fourth "jewel" of Buddhism, after the Buddha, the *dharma* (teaching) and the *sangha* (community).

The history of Buddhism in Tibet begins with King Sangtsen Gampo (*c*.608–650 C.E.), whose two wives, one Nepalese, the other Chinese, persuaded him to invite Buddhist teachers from their countries to Tibet. The king also sent Tibetans to India to study Buddhist traditions and bring back scriptures for translation.

The introduction of Buddhism, however, threatened the established priests of the native Bon religion. In the eighth century, when an outbreak of smallpox occurred, they seized their chance and blamed the disease on the people's growing interest in Buddhism, putting pressure on the king to expel Buddhist teachers. However, in the same century, the religious fate of Tibet was settled in favour of Buddhism with the arrival in 765 of a holy man and teacher, known as Padmasambhava, from north-western India. This man's influence on the country was such that he came to be regarded as a second Buddha.

Padmasambhava travelled all over Tibet and succeeded in integrating Bon beliefs and rituals into the Vajrayana Buddhism he practised. He also organized the first monastery, Samye (*c*.775), and helped train the first Tibetan monks. And he is also the traditional founder of the Nyingmapa ("Ancient One") school of Tibetan Buddhism, which allows its lamas to marry and has stayed close to the lives of ordinary people.

The next important period occurred from the 11th to the 15th centuries, a period which saw the rise of a number of sects. The Kargyupa tradition, begun by Marpa (1012–97), famed as a translator, emphasized the oral tradition of passing secret doctrine from teacher to pupil, as well as meditation. His disciple Milarepa (1040–1143) continued the tradition and became Tibet's most renowned poet and a great ascetic. The Sakyapas were founded in 1073 by a member of the Khon clan; a male descendant heads the sect today.

The Gelukpas ("partisans of virtue") became the pre-eminent sect. Also known as the Yellow Hats, they were set up by the scholar Tsong Khapa (1367–1419), who founded the monastery of Gaden – one of the three main centres of Gelukpa authority along with Drepung and Sera. In contrast to what it considered to be laxities among the other sects, including the right to marry, the Gelukpa tradition stressed monastic discipline and celibacy as well as a gradual path to enlightenment.

The head of the Drepung Monastery is the Dalai ("Ocean") Lama. He is believed to be the incarnation of Avalokiteshvara, the celestial *bodhisattva* ("buddha-to-be") held to embody infinite compassion. The 14th Dalai Lama, Tenzin Gyatso (1935–), fled Tibet to escape Chinese repression in 1959 and set up a base at Dharam-sala in northern India, from where he endeavours to preserve Tibet's spiritual and cultural heritage and publicize the plight of his people.

Tibetan prayer wheels (ABOVE) *are inscribed with sacred verses, or mantras, and each turn of the wheel is equivalent to reciting the mantra aloud once. The prayer wheels' cylinders are often attached to water wheels or windmills so that they can be kept in almost perpetual motion.*

A Tibetan lama, *or teacher, engages his pupils in an intense debate on some aspect of Buddhist philosophy. Boys usually begin training to become monks at an early age, following a rigorous programme traditionally involving the interpretation of Buddhist texts as well as the study of natural medicine.*

Set on a rock in the middle of a plain, with the holy city of Lhasa clustered around it, the Potala Palace was the spiritual centre of Tibetan Buddhism for more than 300 years from the 17th century. Tibetans on pilgrimage to Lhasa traditionally walked around the Potala, performing ritual prostrations on the way as a sign of respect.

Most of this magnificent structure, with its 13 storeys and numerous halls and temples, was built by the fifth Dalai Lama between 1645 and 1653. The palace was the residence of the Dalai Lamas until 1959 when the 14th Dalai Lama was forced into exile by the Chinese occupiers of Tibet. Since then, many monasteries have been damaged and pillaged, but the Potala has survived, albeit as a museum.

Mantras and mandalas

Tibetan Buddhists place considerable importance on the role of sacred phrases and diagrams – mantras and mandalas – as spiritual aids to enlightenment. In fact, Buddhism in Tibet is sometimes known as Mantrayana, the way of the mantra.

The word mantra means "tool for [meditative] thinking" or "instrument of mind", and it can be a single sound, such as Aum or Om, a short phrase or part of a sacred text. Each of these is constantly repeated to invoke protection or a blessing, or as an aid to meditation. The great Tibetan mantra is *aum mani padme hum*, which invokes Avalokiteshvara, Tibet's patron *bodhisattva*. This mantra refers to Avalokiteshvara as the jewel (*mani*) in the lotus (*padme*), images widely used in Buddhism to denote what is precious and durable.

Mandala literally means a circle, but now is used to refer to a sacred diagram used as a psychological and spiritual "map" in meditation. Mandalas such as this one (RIGHT) are notable for their symmetry and are usually made up of circles, squares and triangles, and can also contain Buddha figures. In Tibet, they are often painted on scroll-like hangings called *tankas*, but they are also made of coloured sand or as models, or simply visualized by the meditator.

In one use of a mandala, the meditator focuses attention on "doorways" in the outer edges of the diagram and moves through them to the various abstract forms that represent different levels of spiritual understanding. The journey to the centre symbolizes the meditator's inner quest from the multiple patterns of life to a unified state of being.

The Practice of Meditation

This Thai monk and stone statue of the Buddha, both in meditation pose, convey a sense of stability and peace that is central to Buddhism. Both figures sit in the lotus position, with legs crossed and spine straight, which makes the body stable and encourages deep breathing. The purpose of meditation, with the attentive quietness it brings, is to make meditators more alert to what is going on in their hearts and minds and also to the needs of the world around them.

Images of the Buddha show him meditating while standing, sitting, walking or lying down — indicating that it is possible to meditate at any time and in any of these positions.

Practising *metta*

Buddhists consider *metta*, which means "loving kindness" or "friendliness", to be one of the four highest states, along with compassion, sympathetic joy and equanimity. The practice of *metta* is possible at many different levels both for laypeople and for monks and nuns. It attempts to break down barriers between people and to develop kindness, so increasing the capacity for harmonious living.

Buddhists compare the commitment to the cultivation of *metta* to a mother who would protect her only child at the risk of her own life. To nurture *metta*, Buddhist meditators might visualize loving kindness becoming established in their hearts and feeling its warmth. They might then think of a person to whom they feel well disposed and beam out thoughts of loving kindness toward him or her. The next step is to repeat the process with someone who evokes neutral feelings and then one who arouses hostility. Meditators must overcome enmity by reminding themselves that this person, like everyone, wants happiness. Having done this, meditators should be able to send thoughts of loving kindness to all corners of the world without hindrance from hatred.

For Buddhists, meditation is the central religious practice. Many would say that they meditate to understand the truth about the nature of reality, or "the way things are", which is one way of translating the term *dharma*. As they come to understand this truth, they develop harmony with it. They compare people's minds and hearts to pools of water that have been stirred up and clouded with troubling thoughts and feelings. The stillness that meditation brings helps the mud to settle down so that the meditator can see deep down and understand what is there, underneath the activity.

Buddhist meditation techniques are rooted in Indian culture. Gautama Buddha (pp.152–53) learned meditation from Indian teachers before his enlightenment. Afterward, he continued to use body postures, such as the cross-legged lotus position, and breathing techniques that are also used by Hindu yogis. Buddhist schools may use slightly different but related methods and all emphasize the need for a good teacher, that is, one who knows how to help different types of people.

Meditation often begins with simply sitting in a stable, upright position on the floor or on a chair in a quiet place. Mental calmness can then be encouraged by the simple chanting of a mantra, or sacred verse; or by watching the rhythmic ebb and flow of breath and using it as a focal point to which the attention is brought back whenever it wanders. This type of meditation is called *samatha*, "calmness", or "peaceful abiding". Adepts can also go on to the technique called *vipassana*, by which they hope to gain insight, or penetrating vision, into reality. This is achieved by looking inward beneath the surface of consciousness at deep underlying emotions and thoughts and simply being aware of them without interacting with them and creating more activity.

Underlying all meditation is basic mindfulness, which means being totally aware of the present moment. Once this is well established, it can be practised when standing, sitting, walking or lying down, and Gautama Buddha is portrayed being mindful in all of these states. Zen Buddhism (pp.162–63) particularly emphasizes that meditation can be performed while carrying out the most basic activities of life, such as "hewing wood and drawing water". Formal meditation classes are only to develop the capacity for mindfulness that can be applied to all of life.

In the Theravada tradition (pp.160–61) in Southeast Asia, meditation has traditionally been viewed as the "work" largely of monks, particularly those who choose to live isolated and solitary lives in the forest. However, it has recently become more common for laypeople to meditate either with monks or in lay meditation centres.

Through meditation, Buddhists seek to awaken the source of spiritual power or what some call the Buddha-nature within. Meditation differs from prayer in that the aim is to develop an inner spirituality – either silently or by chanting a sacred verse – rather than invoke a suprapersonal agency or reality. However, the distinction between meditation and prayer is sometimes difficult to discern, and the repeated invocation made by members of the Japanese Pure Land school (pp.162–63) to the celestial Amida Buddha outwardly resembles a prayer but is actually designed to realize an inner spiritual state – the Pure Land within.

> *Watchfulness is the path of immortality: unwatchfulness is the path of death. Those who are watchful never die: those who do not watch are already as dead.*
>
> *DHARMAPADA* 2:21

Hanging skeletons, *such as these, are used by Buddhists as a meditation tool to remind them of the inevitability and naturalness of death. In Buddhism, the realization that the world is impermanent is held to be of paramount importance for people to live wisely.*

Skeletons are hung in meditation halls and at the end of walking-meditation paths to reinforce the awareness that men, women and children are subject to suffering, old age, sickness and death. Realization and acceptance of this brings, Buddhists believe, enlightenment and final peace.

Buddhism and the West

Since the dawn of the 19th century, the influence of eastern religions, especially Buddhism, on western societies has increased at a steady pace. This has been especially true of Britain, Germany and the United States (*below*), countries in which a number of Buddhist organizations have been founded during the course of the past two centuries.

The first impact of Buddhism on the west came largely through western scholars who encountered it because of their countries' colonial dominance of the Indian subcontinent and Southeast Asia. Notable among the early scholars was a British civil servant, T.W. Rhys Davids (1843–1922), who learned Pali while he was stationed in Sri Lanka (then called Ceylon). In 1881, he founded the influential Pali Text Society for the translation and publication of Pali Buddhist texts and commentaries. Other scholars included the German Hermann Oldenberg (1854–1920), whose work on early Buddhism, based on primary sources, is still highly regarded today.

Perhaps most significant in drawing western attention to Buddhism were the Russian-born spiritualist Madame Helena Blavatsky (1831–91) and the American Colonel Henry S. Olcott (1832–1907). In 1875, they founded the Theosophical Society (p.210), whose esoteric spirituality drew partly upon Buddhist ideas. Also, their visit to Sri Lanka in 1880 and their affirmation of Buddhism imparted confidence to the island's

Buddhists, who were unaccustomed to their religion being taken up by westerners.

One figure who was impressed by their visit was the Sri Lankan Don David Hewavitarne (1864–1933), who took special Buddhist layman's vows and assumed the name Anagarika Dharmapala. He was a Buddhist representative at the World Parliament of Religions in Chicago in 1893, which brought Buddhism and other oriental religions to the notice of the west. He also founded the important Mahabodhi Society in Colombo in 1891. This aimed to unite Buddhists of all countries and to raise support for the rebuilding of sacred Buddhist sites in India, which had fallen into disrepair.

The sorry state of India's shrines had already been noted and brought to public attention by the British scholar and poet Sir Edwin Arnold (1832–1904). His long poem *The Light of Asia*, about the life and teaching of the Buddha, had had a strong impact both in Britain and the United States after its publication in 1879. As a result of reading it, for example, the Briton Alan Bennett McGregor (1872–1923) converted to Buddhism and, in 1902, became the first European Buddhist monk in Burma.

In Britain, Buddhism first became an institution when the Buddhist Society was founded in 1907, with T.W. Rhys Davids as its president. It was given new direction between 1924 and 1926 by Christmas Humphreys (1901–83), a lawyer who rose to become a judge and

> *It may be . . . that Buddhism can better serve the west by offering, not the ready-made cathedral of a new philosophy, but the cut and well-used stones of Buddhist principles.*
>
> CHRISTMAS HUMPHREYS

Buddhism in the United States

Almost all forms of Buddhism, especially those of the Chinese and Japanese traditions, have taken root in the United States. Well-established university programmes of Buddhist studies and centres focusing on Buddhist-Christian dialogue have been set up and continue to flourish.

Interest in oriental culture, including Buddhism, first became common during the 19th century among intellectual and artistic figures such as Ralph Waldo Emerson (1803–82), Henry Thoreau (1817–62) and Walt Whitman (1819–92). In the latter part of the century, the work of the theosophists Madame Blavatsky and Colonel Olcott and the increase of immigrants from east Asia, especially China, helped to raise Buddhism's profile.

For the last 100 years, Chinese Buddhism has continued to thrive and remains strong, especially as a result of the work of the scholar-translator Master Hsuan Hua. Arriving in 1962 from Hong Kong, Hsuan began to teach in San Francisco's Chinatown. In 1968, he founded the Sino-American Buddhist Association and later established an important monastic community called the City of 1,000 Buddhas just north of the city.

America's historical links with Japan make it natural that Japanese Buddhism, particularly in its Zen form (pp.162–63), has been important throughout this century. Foremost of the Zen teachers was Daisetsu T. Suzuki (1870–1966), whose numerous books on Zen brought it to wide audiences. In the 1960s, Zen became particularly popular with the counterculture movements associated with Jack Kerouac, Gary Snyder and others.

Tibetan Buddhism has also become established in the country, especially after the Chinese suppression of the Tibetan uprising in 1959 and the consequent flight to the west of many Buddhist lamas. One of the best known of these refugees is Chogyam Trungpa Rimpoche (1939–87) (RIGHT), an abbot of a large Tibetan monastery who left his native country in 1963 for the west. He managed to reach Britain, where he set up a meditation centre in Scotland. In 1969, he went to the United States, where he remained until he died. During this time, he helped to promote Tibetan Buddhism in the country and founded a number of Buddhist centres, including the Naropa Institute in Boulder, Colorado.

Christmas Humphreys, shown here in conversation with a Buddhist monk, was a leading figure in the development of Buddhism in Britain. A distinguished lawyer who later in his career became a judge, Humphreys wrote a number of books on Buddhism, including a popular dictionary of religion, as well as poetry. He reached even greater audiences with his broadcasts on radio and television.

who wrote several influential books on Buddhism. The Buddhist Society is now the oldest existing Buddhist organization in Europe and has some 20 affiliated groups. There are also other British Buddhist organizations, most of which are non-denominational, accepting members from a variety of Buddhist schools.

In Germany, Buddhism first came to the notice of the intelligentsia through the philosopher Arthur Schopenhauer (1788–1860). He declared it the best of all religions, noting especially its rejection of the Hindu caste system and its ethical emphasis on being kind to animals. Schopenhauer's writings influenced the young scholar Karl Neumann (1865–1915), who studied Sanskrit and Pali at Leipzig University and subsequently translated many Buddhist texts into German, making them widely available to the educated public.

Germany can also lay claim to the second European monk, a violinist named Anton Gueth (1878–1957), who was received into the Buddhist *sangha*, or community, in 1904. Under the name Nyanatiloka, he lived mainly in Sri Lanka, becoming the abbot of a monastery that he founded there in 1911. The monastery has attracted a number of European monks throughout the 20th century. In Germany itself, in more recent years, the German Buddhist Society was founded in 1955. Three years later, it was renamed the German Buddhist Union and incorporated all of the country's different Buddhist groups.

Buddhist monks receive an offering of food from a family in Sussex, southern England, maintaining the tradition of the alms round more usually associated with Buddhism in, for example, Southeast Asia. In Britain, many Buddhist laypeople live near Buddhist monasteries so that they can invite monks and nuns for a meal or give them food as alms. However, the bulk of a monastery's food is taken there by laypeople at weekends and prepared by helpers each day.

Buddhism and Society

Tibetan monks *march in protest against the Chinese annexation of their country. The destruction of much of Tibetan culture by the* *Chinese has forced many monks to abandon Buddhism's tradition of pacifism and to show their discontent openly.*

The 20th century has brought much upheaval to traditional Buddhist cultures, and the religion has had to adapt to a variety of new social, economic and political pressures. A common trend has been for Buddhists to take a more active interest in the problems of everyday life and to form organizations aimed at alleviating those problems.

The western emphasis on a religion being as much an agent for transforming society as a means for personal salvation has helped to shape the socially engaged side of Buddhism in various parts of the world. There is, for example, a Green Buddhist movement concerned with ecology and reforestation, an animal rights group, a hospice movement, civil rights movements, self-help groups, and a prison-visiting organization that is called Angulimala, after a murderer whom Gautama Buddha is said to have reformed. These, and many other groups, all show the capacity of a religion, founded more than 2,500 years ago, to respond to new pressures and contexts and to adapt its central message of calmness, wisdom and compassion to situations very different from those in which it began.

Buddhist followers of this socially oriented tendency see their roots firmly in the tradition of historical figures such as the Emperor Ashoka (pp.154–55). They also point to the emphasis that Mahayana places on compassion and involvement of laypeople in the world. One of the notable fruits of this social concern has been the Buddhist Peace Fellowship. The organization is international in scope and draws much of its inspiration from the teachings of Thich Nhat Hanh, the contemporary Vietnamese Zen poet and activist.

From its very beginnings, Buddhism has always been culturally adaptable, and as different social and political pressures have occurred in both the east and the west, a variety of emphases, forms and movements has developed within the religion. In Japan, for example, rapid social change has produced a number of religious movements, many of them Buddhist. Among these is the Buddhist Rissho Kosei Kai (p.207), which runs its own schools, old people's homes, hospitals and youth projects. Another important movement is the dynamic Soka Gakkai (p.208), whose members believe that Buddhists should not withdraw from society but should instead be actively involved in transforming it.

In Tibet, the breakdown of Buddhist culture as a result of the Chinese invasion in 1951 and their suppression of an uprising in 1959 has forced countless monks and nuns to flee the country. Many of them have trekked to Dharamsala in northern India, the headquarters in exile of the Dalai Lama, their political and spiritual leader. Those who remain are often involved in civil disobedience as a protest against Chinese rule. For many Buddhists, social and political activism seems contrary to the teaching of the Buddha, with its emphasis on calm acceptance of worldly reality. However, in Tibet, the destruction of so many monasteries and scriptures has prompted a more vocal and active resistance.

Monks have also played prominent political and social roles in Burma and Sri Lanka. In particular they were influential and active campaigners for independence from British colonial rule. In Sri Lanka, the ongoing tension and fighting between the island's Hindu Tamil minority and its Buddhist Sinhalese majority have frequently drawn some monks into the fray, sometimes to the point of violence. In 1959, for example, a Buddhist priest assassinated Prime Minister Bandaranaike for what were perceived as his insufficiently stringent measures against the Tamils.

The social aspect of Sri Lankan Buddhism was influenced by Christian missionary movements earlier in the century when the country was under British rule. This has given rise to a number of groups such as the Young Men's Buddhist Association, modelled on its Christian prototype, and the so-called Buddhist Sunday Schools, as well as Buddhist catechisms – elements that some modern western scholars group under the term Protestant Buddhism.

Ajahn Ponsak, *a Thai monk, has spoken out against the deforestation of parts of northern Thailand. In an attempt to repair the damage, he has organized local* *villagers to replant trees, build dams and irrigate the land. He sees no contradiction between his life as a monk and the practical help he can give to his people.*

World distribution of Buddhists

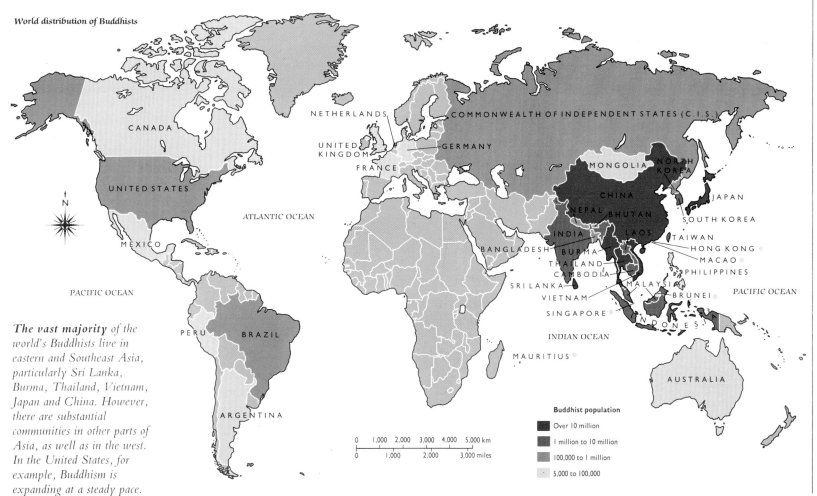

The vast majority of the world's Buddhists live in eastern and Southeast Asia, particularly Sri Lanka, Burma, Thailand, Vietnam, Japan and China. However, there are substantial communities in other parts of Asia, as well as in the west. In the United States, for example, Buddhism is expanding at a steady pace.

Buddhist population

- Over 10 million
- 1 million to 10 million
- 100,000 to 1 million
- 5,000 to 100,000

Devotion to the Guru

THE SIKH RELIGION WAS FOUNDED BY A spiritual teacher named Guru Nanak (1469–1539) in the Punjab in north-western India – where some 12 million of the 16 million Sikhs (meaning "disciples") in the world still live. At a time when this part of India was influenced by both Hinduism and Islam, Guru Nanak (pp.174–75) taught that there was only one God and one humanity and those who sincerely seek God will discover the divinity within themselves. After Guru Nanak's death, his teaching was carried on by nine successive Gurus, ending with Guru Gobind Singh (1666–1708). The teachings that were revealed to the Gurus, contained in the Sikh holy scripture known as the *Guru Granth Sahib*, or *Adi Granth* (p.175), are the cornerstone of Sikhism.

During the last century, and especially since 1945, Sikhism has emerged as a world faith both in distribution and, to some extent, outlook. The modern process of Sikh dispersion dates from the British annexation of the Punjab in 1849. Impressed by the Sikhs' martial prowess and loyalty, the British recruited many into their army. As a result, Sikhs served overseas in British-controlled lands, such as Hong Kong and Singapore, where they frequently settled.

Sikhs can now be found in many countries of the world, particularly Britain, the United States and Canada. However, they still look to the Punjab as their homeland, and Punjabi is the language of worship. In the United States, several thousand Americans have converted to Sikhism as the result of a movement known as the Healthy Happy Holy Organization (pp.206–7).

For Sikhs in India, a major cause for concern is living as minority people in their homeland. Some Sikhs have responded by demanding an independent Sikh state. Many find the prospect of total independence impracticable, but most Sikhs would want the Punjab to have greater autonomy in a new, federal India. Sikhs overseas are more often exercised by religious customs that owe more to Punjab cultural traditions than religious truths. They are particularly concerned with liberation from the caste system (pp.128–29) and sex discrimination, and the preaching of a faith which is accessible to the whole of humanity, not only those of Punjabi origin.

From Sikhism have emerged movements that emphasize different aspects of teaching and practice. Two of the most important are

The Golden Temple at Amritsar in Punjab is one of the holiest sites of Sikhism. Set in the middle of a lake, the temple was built by Guru Arjan (1563–1606) on the site where Guru Nanak, the founder of Sikhism, is said to have meditated.

the Nirankari and Namdhari groups, founded in the 19th century by the Sikh reformers Dayal Das (1783–1853) and Baba Balak Singh (1799–1861), respectively. Dayal Das reemphasized the centrality of the *Guru Granth Sahib* in naming and marriage ceremonies, while Balak Singh, with his successor Baba Ram Singh, recalled Sikhs to the high ideals of the Gurus' teachings against the use of drugs and alcohol, caste, the isolation of widows, and extravagant marriage ceremonies, including dowries. Both movements retain a personal leadership which conflicts with the sole Sikh authority of the *Guru Granth Sahib* and the *Panth* – the Sikh community.

In the past, Sikhs have been mistaken for a Hindu sect, and the Nirankari and Namdhari groups helped to pave the way for a more formal definition of Sikh identity. This finally culminated in the Gurdwaras Act of 1925, passed at the request of Sikhs. Through the act, custody of Sikh places of worship, or *gurdwaras*, which had often passed into the hands of non-Sikh families, was restored to Sikhs. For these purposes it was necessary to define a Sikh. The following declaration was formalized for those claiming to be Sikhs: "I solemnly affirm that I am a Sikh, that I believe in the *Guru Granth Sahib*, the Ten Gurus and that I have no other religion."

The True Guru and freedom from rebirth

Sikhs, in common with Hindus, believe that the soul is reborn after death. By living in a God-centred way, people can attain liberation from rebirth in their present existence through God's grace. Sikhs accept the everyday world as real – not as an illusion as some Hindus do – but they should not be so this-worldly that they lose sight of eternity. This is summed up in the *Guru Granth Sahib*: "Know the real purpose of being here, gather up treasure under the guidance of the True Guru [God]. Make your mind God's home. If God abides with you undisturbed you will not be reborn." What form liberation takes is unclear. Some Sikhs express it in terms of being absorbed into the Absolute; others refer to living eternally in God's presence in a state of bliss (*anand*).

When a Sikh dies, there is no special concern about the disposal of his or her mortal remains. Cremation is usually practised, since Sikhs have always lived in a mainly Hindu culture, but burial is accepted without demur by Sikhs living in Muslim countries, for it is not what happens to the body, but to the soul, that matters. For the benefit of the bereaved rather than of the dead person's soul, which is in God's care, Sikhs read the *Guru Granth Sahib* periodically during 10 days of mourning.

Devotion to the Guru

Guru Nanak sits with the other nine Gurus, who are haloed, in this stylized painting. Also included in the picture are a Hindu named Bala, sitting next to Guru Nanak and holding a peacock feather fan; and a Muslim musician named Mardana, a companion of Guru Nanak.

Guru Nanak, the founder of Sikhism, was born into a Hindu family in the Punjab in 1469. At the age of 30 he believed he was called by God to begin his ministry to Muslims and Hindus of all castes and to untouchables. The spiritual message he taught had three aspects to it: meditation (which now often involves chanting hymns composed by the Gurus); honest toil; and almsgiving. Meditation is considered to be particularly important, through it the spiritually nourished person sees God in the faces of all humanity.

Sikhs believe that Guru Nanak travelled widely beyond the confines of India, preaching his message in a variety of languages. He did not intend to found a movement, far less a religion, but by the time of his death in 1539 he had many disciples who still needed a leader. He therefore appointed a successor.

In all, there were 10 Gurus, from Guru Nanak to Guru Gobind Singh (1666–1708). Some were more significant historically than others, but all preached the same message. Some scholars have pointed out a difference in outlook between the essentially peaceful Guru Nanak and the martial 10th Guru Gobind Singh, who armed his followers to fight against the injustice of the contemporary Mughal emperor Aurangzeb (1658–1707). Sikhs, however, regard this as a false distinction. Guru Nanak was also concerned about social injustice – for example, he condemned the Mughal emperor Babur (1483–1530) for sacking the town of Saidpur – and Guru Gobind Singh was continuing this tradition of social concern in

> **One cannot find the right way without the grace and guidance of the True Guru [God].**
>
> *GURU GRANTH SAHIB*

his doctrine of the just war, *dharam yudh*. This doctrine states that force should always be a defensive last resort, to be used only against assailants, never against noncombatants.

Just before he died after being stabbed, Guru Gobind Singh declared there would be no further human Guru to lead the Sikhs. He conferred guruship on the scripture compiled by the fifth Guru, Guru Arjan (1563–1606), which he himself had revised, and which became known as the *Guru Granth Sahib* (*opposite*), and on the community, the *Panth*, which was to live by its teachings.

In investing the scripture as a Guru, Guru Gobind Singh was acknowledging the central Sikh teaching that God is the Guru of Gurus. Truth lies in the message, the voice of the Guru, not in the human personality of any of the 10 historical Gurus, however much they might be respected. In *gurdwaras*, Sikh places of worship, and anywhere else the scripture may be present, Sikhs bow toward it because of the Word it contains. But they should never bow to portraits of the human Gurus.

Since 1708, there have been many temporal leaders of the Sikhs. The best known was Maharaja Ranjit Singh (1780–1839), who established an independent state stretching from Peshawar in present-day Pakistan and the Himalayas south to the Sutlej River, one of the tributaries of the Indus. However, no one has claimed spiritual leadership, and there can be no one to usurp the authority of the scripture and the *Panth*. Perhaps in the future Sikhs may develop an organization that acts as a sort of "world council", but it will not be allowed to rival the *Guru Granth Sahib* and the God-centred *Panth*.

The Khalsa

In 1699, Guru Gobind Singh created a new order within the Sikh community, the Khalsa ("pure"), whose members were willing to arm themselves and serve the *Panth* militarily if necessary. According to the *Rahit Maryada*, a code of discipline of 1945, the Sikh ideal is to become a member of the Khalsa.

Members must vow to abstain from alcohol, tobacco and drugs, and to live moral lives. As marks of identity, they should also wear five symbols, known as the five Ks because each begins with the letter *K* in Punjabi: *kesh*, uncut hair; *kangha*, comb; *kirpan*, sword; *kara*, wristlet for protecting the sword arm; *kacch*, shorts (worn as an undergarment by women and also by men wearing western clothes). Men should wear a turban. Members of the Khalsa, and many other Sikhs, adopt the name Singh (Lion) or, if they are women, Kaur (Princess), instead of their caste name.

A Khalsa Sikh holds a ceremonial sword in the Akal Takht, the original palace of the Sixth Guru Hargobind situated opposite the Golden Temple at Amritsar.

World distribution of Sikhs

The world distribution of gurdwaras, *or Sikh places of worship, is shown here. Sikh communities outside India tend to be found in countries that were formerly part of the British Empire, such as Canada and Australia, or places, such as the United States, where English is spoken. Sikhs in the Middle East are usually migrant workers rather than settlers.*

Number of *gurdwaras*
(Sikh places of worship)

- Over 100
- 50 to 100
- 10 to 50
- 1 to 10

The *Guru Granth Sahib*

A **granthi***, or reader, acts as custodian of the Guru Granth Sahib in the Golden Temple of Amritsar. The feathered fan (chauri) is a symbol of authority. The book is installed in the temple and kept open from about 4 a.m. to 10 p.m.*

Sikhism's holy book, the *Guru Granth Sahib*, originally known as the *Adi Granth*, was compiled in 1604 by the 5th Guru Arjan and later revised by the 10th Guru Gobind Singh. It contains devotional hymns mainly composed by the first five Gurus – Nanak, Angd, Amar Das, Ram Das, Arjan – as well as the ninth Guru Tegh Bahadur. The *Guru Granth Sahib*'s value for Sikhs can be summed up by the following words, which are found near the end of the book: "In the platter are placed three things, truth, contentment and wisdom, as well as the nectar of the Lord's Name, the support of all."

The form of the *Guru Granth Sahib* is poetical, and printed copies of it – 1,430 pages in all – are identical. The book is essential in naming, marriage and initiation ceremonies, as well as in Sikh worship. Other occasions, such as festivals and the birth or death anniversaries of the Gurus (*gurpurbs*), are observed by a complete reading (*akhand path*) of the book, which lasts about 48 hours. Noncontinuous readings (*sidharan paths*) may be used before weddings, after funerals, or when moving to a new house and on other such occasions.

The *Guru Granth Sahib* is unique in containing compositions by a number of people not of the Sikh faith, such as Kabir (p.138) and a Muslim mystic, or Sufi, named Shaykh Farid. Their inclusion is taken by Sikhs to symbolize their openness to other religions – they have never claimed that their path alone is true.

An immortal keeps watch inside the Man Mo Daoist temple in Hong Kong. Daoism is, along with Confucianism and Buddhism, one of the three traditions that form the basis of Chinese spiritual history. Daoism developed from an abstruse philosophical system into a popular religion, absorbing many beliefs, customs and rituals from folklore.

The gods Man and Mo are both the deified forms of individuals who lived about 1,500 years ago. Man is the god of literature and patron of civil servants; Mo is the god of martial arts and is revered by both Hong Kong's police and underworld fraternity.

The paper motor car, the aircraft behind it (LEFT) and the fake money (ABOVE) are some of the objects that the Chinese transmit to the deceased in the afterlife through burning. Although replicas of more traditional objects such as figures riding horses are still burned, the trend now is to use those of modern goods.

The Ordered Cosmos

CHINESE PEOPLE RECOGNIZE THREE MAIN traditions in their spiritual history – Confucianism, Daoism (Taoism) and Buddhism. The first two reach back to the sixth century B.C.E. – the time of Confucius and Laozi (Lao Tzu), the traditional founder of Daoism. Confucius, the most influential thinker in Chinese history, inspired a movement that emphasized traditional values – appropriate behaviour, modesty, restraint and respect for rituals. Daoism began as a sort of mystical philosophy, stressing the importance of being "natural" and spontaneous, of living at one with the Dao, or "Way", the underlying principle of reality. In time, it developed into a popular religion, focusing on rituals and elixirs, as well as gods.

Buddhism reached China after the first century C.E. (pp.184–85) and gradually settled into a tripartite relationship with the other two indigenous traditions. The three traditions commingled and fused with Chinese folk beliefs and practices that had existed from earliest times. Other religions have also been transplanted into China – for example Islam and Christianity – and a considerable community of Chinese Muslims (pp.110–11) still exists in the country.

Death, ancestors and ghosts

The first Christians in China (pp.68–69), when trying to make converts, had to argue their view that each person has only one soul, since the Chinese believed that everyone possessed several. Today, the Chinese treat the souls of the dead in different ways, depending on whether or not they belong to family members.

Within the family, the deceased is transferred by funeral rituals of parting to the ranks of the ancestors. Paper models of desirable possessions – including paper money – are remitted to the spirit world by burning. Buddhist or Daoist clergy may also be hired to transfer religious merit. The ancestors are later commemorated through spirit-tablets – lengths of wood bearing their names (and housing their souls) kept on a family altar and honoured with constantly burning incense.

But the dead outside the family may appear as ghosts – strangers who will cause misfortune, especially if they are neglected. To deal with them, clergy are often brought in, either to placate hungry ghosts through annual rituals or to exorcise specific ones by invoking supernatural authorities. Keeping order in the world of the dead is the responsibility of greater and lesser gods arranged in a hierarchy like that of the old imperial bureaucracy. Criminals are imprisoned in hells and punished by grotesque versions of jailers and other officials.

From the distant past up to the present, the need to eke out some sort of living in a crowded and relatively small agriculture-supporting area has probably encouraged a practical and this-worldly streak in the Chinese character. Traditional Chinese art or literature also clearly reveals a religious influence from the time of the Shang dynasty in the second millennium B.C.E. right down to the modern era. But now, toward the end of the 20th century, it may be asked whether there is any room for Chinese religion in one of the last bastions of communism.

In the early 1970s, there seemed little hope for Chinese religion. In China itself, Chairman Mao's Red Guards were persecuting religious believers of every type and destroying their scriptures and places of worship. And among the Chinese overseas, the gathering pace of economic development seemed to herald a more prosperous, materialistic age equally ready to dismiss religious observance as superstition. In the early 1990s, however, the strength of Chinese religion is not so easy to dismiss.

During the 1980s, with the Beijing government relaxing its hostility, some seminaries opened to train Buddhist and Daoist clergy, while periodicals devoted to Daoism, Buddhism and the study of Confucius also started to circulate. Even more remarkable was the building or rebuilding of temples by local groups acting beyond the control of the authorities. Government officials have been known to speak with envy of the readiness with which some communities part with money for religious purposes, in marked contrast to their reluctance to pay taxes. Nor has this activity been directed purely to the nostalgic re-creation of past traditions: to meet new needs, completely new cults, such as that of the "God of Truck Drivers", have emerged.

Likewise, the increased prosperity of the countries along the Pacific Rim has led to greater spending on religion by laypeople, with the result that Daoist and Buddhist clergy from Singapore to Honolulu are not short of funds for their religious projects. In Taiwan, in particular, an upsurge in support for Chinese Buddhism has been shown by the number of Buddhist colleges offering education to laypeople. Where well-established Chinese religious traditions are prospering, a host of lesser-known cults – often based on fresh revelations from the spirit world, and mixing different Chinese and foreign elements – are also competing for those souls searching for meaning in a rapidly changing society.

Chinese religion has also spread to the west. For example, in the United States, new Buddhist monasteries and temples in the Chinese tradition are being added to the older Zen centres, first founded by Japanese masters. One of these is the Hsi Lai Temple in California, completed in 1988, which cost more than 30 million dollars and is the largest Buddhist temple in the western hemisphere.

Continuity and Change

Two important underlying themes in Chinese religion are those of continuity and change. On the one hand, the Chinese revere their link with the past and their ancestors. Conversely, their religion and philosophy emphasize the part played by the flux of existence and the need to predict it through divination or interpret it through various systems and concepts, such as yin and yang and the five elements.

The Chinese have always valued the continuity of the family and their indebtedness to their ancestors for life and prosperity. Ancestor worship is known to have occurred in prehistoric times. And the earliest written records, the oracle bones (*below*) of the Shang dynasty, show how the ancestors of the Shang kings were commemorated: not as an amorphous, anonymous group, but as individual family members, each with a specific place in a system stretching back over time.

This emphasis on the ancestral line still manifests itself. For example, there are the lineages of Chinese Buddhist masters and disciples, which, Chinese emphasize, stretch back to the Buddha himself (*c.* fifth century B.C.E.). And there are ordinary Chinese families who have a remarkable sense of their own lineages; for example, the descendants of Confucius are now headed by a member of the 77th generation from the sage.

The oracle bones also tell of respect for other spirits: timeless deities of rivers and mountains. Mountains came to have perennial importance in Chinese religion, and have been the favourite locations for Buddhist and Daoist monasteries.

By the first imperial period (221 B.C.E.), it was believed that as many as 72 kings over the course of centuries had performed sacrifices on Taishan, or Mount Tai, in Shandong province. Mount Tai and four other mountains of outstanding spiritual power watch over the whole landscape of China. But why five peaks in particular should be regarded with such importance is connected with Chinese concepts not of continuity but of change.

It is again the oracle bones which testify that divining the future was as important to the ancient Chinese as remembering the past. (For example, if a Shang king wanted to hunt, he might want to know whether he would be lucky or unlucky.) During the succeeding Zhou period (*c.*1122–256 B.C.E.), Chinese thinkers began to systematize the changing forces at work in the constant flux of the world.

The concepts yang, originally referring to the sunny side of a hill, and yin, its opposite, start to be used as terms expressing two underlying principles in perpetual interaction: yang, bright, hard and masculine, and yin, its dark, soft, feminine counterpart. In addition, by the late Warring States period (475–221 B.C.E.), the five elements or, more accurately "activities", earth, wood, fire, metal and water were felt to be significant. And each of these was associated with a number of correspondences – for instance, colours (yellow, green, red, white and black, respectively) and directions (centre, east, south, west, north). In turn, the five directions were associated with Mount Tai and the other four especially significant mountains.

Nor were these the only symbolic sequences of forces. The expert in divination, then as now, has to consider the complex interlocking systems that combine to make the 60-year Chinese calendrical cycle. This involves a smaller cycle of 12 years, each designated by an animal, such as the snake, monkey or tiger.

Finally, there are the Eight Trigrams of the *Book of Changes*, or *I Ching*, used in divination and well known in the west. These trigrams consist of various combinations of three broken (yin) and unbroken (yang) lines which, when doubled up, form 64 configurations or hexagrams. By using a procedure involving stalks of the yarrow plant, a diviner can arrive at a hexagram and interpret its meaning by referring to the *I Ching*.

Oracle bones

Until 1899, the Shang dynasty (*c.*1766–1122 B.C.E.) was little more than a name in Chinese history books. Then Chinese scholars started to pay attention to fragments of bone, inscribed with unfamiliar writing, which were being unearthed in Henan province. The writing proved to be an early form of Chinese characters, and once some progress had been made in deciphering the script, it became clear that the bones carried records of various divinations performed by the Shang kings and their subjects. Later systematic archaeological excavations have uncovered extensive remains of Shang burials, but the "oracle bones" still provide much of what is known about the earliest literate stages of Chinese civilization. In all, it has been estimated that about 100,000 inscribed fragments of bone have been retrieved.

To perform the divinations, a series of small hollows were scooped out of the shoulderblades of oxen or the lower shells of turtles, and heat was applied to them. The cracks that appeared on the other side of the bone or shell were then interpreted, and a written record of the question and answer engraved on the bone. Sometimes, it was also noted that the prediction came true.

Since the oracle questions covered such topics as the weather, warfare, hunting, agriculture and childbirth, it can be deduced that all these facts of life were thought to be subject to the influence of unseen powers, particularly the ancestors and a high god named Shang-ti. There were also many questions concerning sacrifices. In early China, this included human sacrifice, a practice abandoned during the first millennium B.C.E., just as the use of oracle bones was supplanted by consulting the 64 hexagrams of the *Book of Changes*, or *I Ching*.

To divine the future, the ancient Chinese made use of turtle shells and ox bones, such as the one above which dates from the Shang period in the second millennium B.C.E. A red-hot instrument was applied to the bone's surface, and the resulting cracks were then interpreted by an oracle expert.

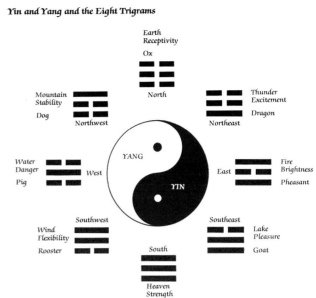

Yin and Yang and the Eight Trigrams

Earth
Receptivity
Ox
North

Mountain
Stability
Dog
Northwest

Thunder
Excitement
Dragon
Northeast

Water
Danger
Pig
West

YANG

Fire
Brightness
East
Pheasant

YIN

Wind
Flexibility
Rooster
Southwest

Lake
Pleasure
Southeast
Goat

South

Heaven
Strength
Horse

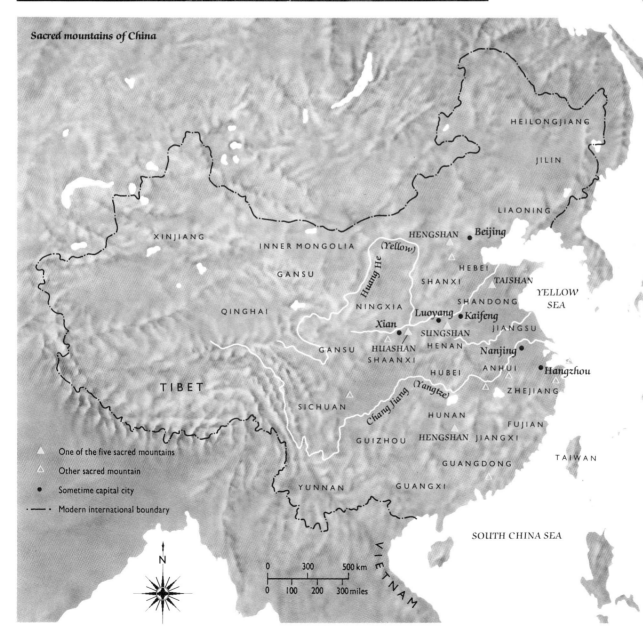

Sacred mountains of China

△ One of the five sacred mountains
△ Other sacred mountain
● Sometime capital city
–··– Modern international boundary

Yin and yang *represent two opposing but complementary natural principles. They are typically symbolized by a circle divided into two halves of different colours with each half containing a smaller circle of the opposite tone.*

Yin and yang can also be expressed as a broken line (yin) and a solid line (yang), and different combinations of three lines form the Eight Trigrams, which are used in divination in conjunction with The Book of Changes. *Each trigram expresses a particular quality, such as brightness or pleasure, and can be linked with a compass direction, an animal and other correlations. By this "correlative thinking", the Chinese sought to impose order on their universe, but at times the correspondences tended to become overelaborate and artificial.*

Five sacred mountains, roughly corresponding to the cardinal directions plus one for the centre, are particularly revered in China. This map shows these and other holy mountains, as well as Chinese capitals past and present and modern provinces. Taishan, or Mount Tai (ABOVE LEFT), is the most famous and most frequented of the holy mountains.

179

Confucius and Confucianism

Confucius, flanked by two disciples, walks away from a minor local ruler, seated at a table, having failed to impress him with his teachings, in this 19th-century engraving. Once Confucius had taken the decision to dedicate himself to teaching, he travelled around China for a while in the hope that some local ruler might put his ideas into practice, but without much success.

Before embarking on his career as a teacher, Confucius had attracted a small group of disciples, who were responsible for passing on the sayings that are his chief legacy. From these recollected fragments of conversation, often witty, it is clear that he impressed his followers as a man utterly dedicated to learning but not without a sense of humour.

Until you know about life how can you know about death?   CONFUCIUS

For more than 2,000 years, the people of China, and of Japan and Korea, have lived in societies profoundly influenced by the thought and ideals of the great Chinese sage Confucius (c.551–c.479 B.C.E.). Confucius was no prophet or mystic. Instead, he saw himself as a civilized gentleman and taught that benevolence toward fellow human beings, moral behaviour, and sound family relationships are the essence of a harmonious and well-ordered society. Although he was not overtly religious, his humane philosophy aspires to the highest ethical values of other religious systems.

Confucius himself avoided religious speculation, but recognized the importance of ancestor worship and believed that he was guided by a higher power that he called heaven. After his death, his followers preserved his thoughts and sayings and, over the next three centuries, a Confucian tradition evolved.

Born into a minor aristocratic family, Confucius lived at a time when China was starting to change rapidly as ancient states and their aristocracies gave way to larger new monarchies governed by men without strong family traditions. Confucius bitterly regretted the disappearance of earlier cultural traditions, which he thought had been formed under the influence of long-vanished heroic sage-kings.

Part of these traditions had been written down and would later form the nucleus of the Confucian canon of scriptures known as the Five Classics (*above*). But they also included rites and their accompanying music which, handed down from generation to generation, were now in danger of being lost.

Confucius's view of life was that resistance to all change was hopeless, and he saw it as his mission to keep alive an ideal of noble conduct, without which the world would descend into savagery. Thus he set himself up as a teacher of the old culture and its values, and by the time of his death, he had gathered a number of disciples.

The next three centuries saw a remarkable proliferation of philosophical thought in China. Indeed, this

The Five Classics

The Confucian canon of scriptures is centred on a core of texts known as the Five Classics, which were regarded as products of ancient times edited by Confucius. In fact, the texts contain much material that has now been placed at a later date. The usual enumeration of the classics is:

I Ching or **Yi Jing** (Book of Changes): originally a manual of divination, it has parts which may reach back into early Chinese history, although the philosophical portions that are ascribed to Confucius probably date from imperial times in the late third century B.C.E.

Shi Jing (Book of Odes): an anthology of 300 poems of popular and court origin. It was much used by Confucius as a record of the "better society" which had existed three centuries or more before his own day.

Shu Jing (Book of History): a collection of historical documents attributed to legendary and early rulers, it contains much material that dates from the Later Han dynasty (23–220 C.E.).

Li Ji (Record of Rites): consists of a large number of Confucian writings relating to ritual, probably put together in imperial times.

Chun Qiu (Spring and Autumn Annals): a chronicle of Lu, the home state of Confucius, supposedly edited by him to illustrate his evaluation of history.

burgeoning of intellectual ideas at times eclipsed the practical educational concerns of those who took up the work of Confucius. Among these later Confucians, Mencius (c.371–c.289 B.C.E.) and Xunzi (c.300–c.230 B.C.E.) in particular responded to the challenge of elaborating his ideas.

Mencius explored the Confucian understanding of morality and is famous for his conclusion that the seeds of goodness exist naturally in everyone, but have to be carefully nurtured if they are ever to grow and develop. Xunzi, on the other hand, believed that people were *not* innately good, and was more concerned with preventing morally unacceptable behaviour. Consequently, he thought that people needed the guidance of Confucian ritual established by the sage-kings.

During climactic warfare between local rulers which led to the victory of the First Emperor, Shihuangdi, in 221 B.C.E., the dominant themes of all Chinese thought centred on coercion and control. But political unification and peace in the second century B.C.E allowed later emperors time to see the benefits of basing a way of thinking on an ancient humanist tradition. By the end of the second century B.C.E., Confucianism was well on the way to becoming a state-supported official doctrine that only eventually, after more than 2,000 years, faded with the communist triumph in the 20th century.

This Confucian temple, with its winglike roofs, is situated in Kunming, a town in southwestern China. Confucius, who was born at the opposite end of the country, in Shandong province, would probably have been surprised to find his name known in an area that was far beyond the bounds of Chinese civilization in his day. He would also have been surprised by the elaborate temple ceremonies, involving music, dance and animal sacrifice, which grew up from the second century B.C.E.

Confucius, here depicted in the centre as a sage equal with the Buddha, on the left, and Laozi, the traditional founder of Daoism, on the right, was born a minor aristocrat in the ancient Chinese state of Lu. His early career was spent in a number of governmental offices. However, he did not achieve great prominence before forsaking public life to become a teacher at the age of about 50.

Jesuits and Confucians

It is no accident that Confucius (Chinese, Kong fuzi) and Mencius (Chinese, Mengzi) are known in the west by the Latin forms of their names. The first Europeans to come to grips with the religious traditions of China were the Jesuit missionary Matteo Ricci (1552–1610) and his colleagues (pp.68–69), whose writings made Confucius widely known in Europe as early as 1615. At this time, all missionaries wanted to determine the religious status of Confucianism to decide whether Chinese converts to Christianity could legitimately participate in practices such as ancestor worship.

In the end, the Jesuits felt that Confucianism and Christianity could be reconciled, and so they depicted Confucius as the "Chinese Aristotle". Their works of interpretation, chiefly the Latin rendering of Confucian texts in *Confucius Sinarum Philosophus* ("Confucius, Philosopher of the Chinese"), published in Paris in 1687, had a great impact on European views of China. The missionaries halted their policy of accommodation in the early 18th century, but their understanding of Confucius has remained influential up to the present despite the difference between the broadly humanist and ethical aims of Confucius and his followers, and the more metaphysical concerns of Greek philosophy.

The Jesuit missionary Matteo Ricci, the first westerner to send reports of Confucianism to Europe, is here pictured on the left next to the mandarin Paul Xu, one of his most famed converts, in a 17th-century Jesuit description of China.

Laozi and Daoism

Daoist philosophy stresses the harmonious relationship between the individual and the natural world, especially mountains, lakes, trees and waterfalls. This is reflected in Chinese art, which excels in landscape painting. The fantastic limestone pinnacles of the Guilin Hills in southwestern China (BELOW) have inspired countless works of art, including this watercolour (INSET) of the Ming period (1368–1644).

True to style, reality has been embellished with symbolism. Nature dominates the scene; for example, the people in the left foreground and the pagodas are insignificant against the grandeur of the scenery.

While Confucius and his followers were concerned with morality and society, Daoism, the other great Chinese religious tradition, has a more other-worldly flavour. Central to Daoism (Taoism is the older form of the word) is the concept of Dao, usually translated as "Way", but which really refers to the underlying reality in the world of nature.

The Dao and its ramifications are explored in the two earliest surviving and most important Daoist texts: the *Daodejing*, a short work ascribed to an older contemporary of Confucius named Laozi, but probably written in the fourth or third century B.C.E.; and a collection of writings named for its chief author, Zhuangzi, who lived in the fourth century B.C.E. Later Chinese drew upon these works for their wisdom and guidance, and for the structure they provide for understanding the universe which is still of value to many Chinese today.

The *Daodejing* and the *Zhuangzi* were composed at a time when Chinese life was becoming brutally regimented by local rulers struggling to conquer all their opponents. The Daoist writers responded with an eloquent defence of the individual, which looks beyond human society to the Dao. Their themes, which they illustrate with vivid parables or sum up in pungent aphorisms, form the heart of philosophical Daoism.

They include the importance of spontaneous action (*wu wei*); the relativity of all value judgments; the inevitability of change between polar opposites; and the benefits of obscurity, uselessness and, particularly, "doing nothing".

Yet Daoist ideas defy simple categorization. The main chapters of the *Zhuangzi* show a formidable intellect exploring the limits of language and thought. Some scholars have detected a note of mysticism and have suggested – despite the author's professed indifference to survival after death – that the scattered references to religious practices hint at the pursuit of religious goals.

In a similar vein, the *Daodejing* reads like a manual of survival for the weak and powerless. However, it leaves open a multiplicity of interpretations of this message; and in later ages, it has been seen variously as a political tract, a handbook of military strategy, a guide to mystical progress for the initiate, and a philosophical account of the workings of the universe. Its numerous foreign translations, which convey something of its insights without ever doing full justice to its concise, compressed language, simply mark the modern phase of a process of reinterpretation already ancient in China.

Two versions of the *Daodejing* written in the second century B.C.E. and discovered in 1973 have brought

modern scholars closer to understanding the way the text was read during the first phase of its existence. However, for most of Chinese history, readers of the text would have been influenced by the interpretations of outstanding commentators such as Wang Bi (*below*).

The way that can be called ''the way'' is not the constant way. The name that can be named is not the constant name.

FROM THE *DAODEJING*

The writings of both Zhuangzi and Laozi – and those of other early Daoists – were constantly read by all educated Chinese. Even so, they never achieved the same sort of endorsement from the imperial state that the Five Classics (p.180) and other Confucian literature attracted. Indeed, these Daoist works contain a note of individualism – even anarchy – which provided a necessary antidote to those suffering from the bureaucratic excesses of an imperial government whose declared Confucian concern for the welfare of its subjects was not always matched by its deeds.

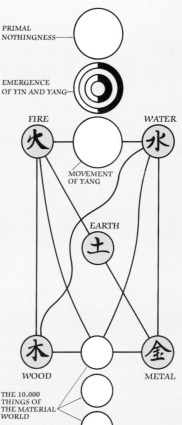

This bronze sculpture of Laozi on an ox illustrates one of the many legends associated with his life. The first recorded Daoist sage, Laozi is said to have been the historian in charge of the archives of the state of Zhou. When he realized that the state was falling into a decline, he headed for the mountains in the west on the back of an ox.

At a mountain pass, the guardian of the frontier asked him to write down his teachings. So Laozi wrote a book in two sections of 5,000 characters in total, setting down the ideas of the Dao, or "Way", which came to be called the Daodejing. He then vanished and was never heard of again.

Wang Bi and the Dark Learning

During his short life, Wang Bi (226–49 C.E.) brought about one of the most dramatic changes of direction in Chinese thought. Wang expounded a philosophy of "starting from scratch" because the value of much Confucian learning had been brought into question by the collapse in 220 C.E. of the Han, the first dynasty which had supported it. The collapse was so total that the new Wei dynasty (220–265/6 C.E.) relied on radical new policies for its rule. Wang's philosophy, influenced by the *I Ching* and the *Daodejing*, was based on the idea that all reality is derived from an undifferentiated state of "primal nothingness," or "original non-being" – as basic a background as silence is to speech.

Yet Wang Bi honoured Confucius above Laozi, who had said, "Those who know do not speak, those who speak do not know," thus, ironically, disqualifying himself in Wang Bi's eyes from true understanding. Conversely, Confucius, by discussing only mundane matters, had shown himself more in touch with non-being, a concept later compared with the superficially similar – but quite different – Buddhist *shunyata*, meaning emptiness or void, used to describe ultimate reality.

Wang, and those who subsequently commented on the *Zhuangzi* in a similar vein, are often termed Neo-Daoist. But since their aims were evidently different from those of the authors on whom they commented, the Dark Learning, a contemporary description of their thought, is preferable.

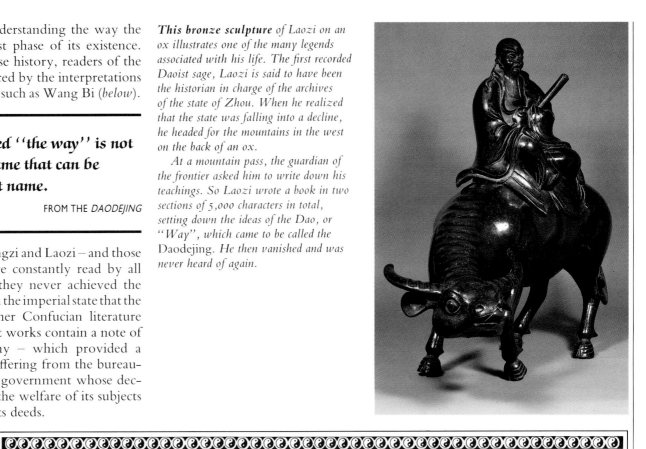

PRIMAL NOTHINGNESS

EMERGENCE OF YIN AND YANG

FIRE 火

WATER 水

MOVEMENT OF YANG

EARTH 土

WOOD 木

METAL 金

THE 10,000 THINGS OF THE MATERIAL WORLD

A cosmological scheme, first outlined by Wang Bi and widely accepted by Daoists and non-Daoists alike, is summarized in the diagram (LEFT). The blank circle at the top symbolizes the original state of primal nothingness underlying the cosmos. From this emerge the forces of yin and yang, symbolized by the half black and half white concentric circles, respectively.

The active yang principle then stimulates the appearance of the five elements, or forces, of fire, water, earth, wood and metal. These interact with each other to start the creation of the material world, termed in China the 10,000 things, symbolized by the series of smaller circles at the foot of the diagram.

The Coming of Buddhism

This rock-carved laughing Buddha in China's Hangzhou province is a figure based on an eccentric monk named Budai, who lived at the end of the Tang dynasty. The figure is still popular among Chinese today.

Buddhism in Chinese culture

Although Buddhism has had a significant impact on Chinese life, Chinese scholars have not always recognized the extent to which it has pervaded their culture. The great Confucian scholar Ruan Yuan (1764–1849), looking back on the impact of Buddhism in China, composed an essay "On Pagodas". Although pagodas were familiar to him, their shape still betrayed their alien, Indian origin. However, in the realm of language, Buddhist influences were less obvious to Ruan and his contemporaries. For example, they still spoke of human nature (*xing*) using the same term as Confucius and Mencius. But their understanding of this and other concepts had been modified by Buddhist thought.

Ruan also believed that only a few words of Indian origin, such as *seng* ("monk", Sanskrit *sangha*), were used in Chinese. But he had noticed that many more Chinese words convey Buddhist meanings, such as *karma* (*ye*) or Nirvana (*wu wei*), even though their users were often unconscious of their connections with ancient India.

At the end of the 20th century, the impact of India on China seems even more profound than Ruan suspected. Even the philological science which he recommended as a key to retrieving purely Chinese thought from pre-Buddhist times was probably stimulated in its early development by the translation of Buddhist texts. It was precisely because Chinese scholars had to translate and adapt Buddhism to suit their own culture, rather than accept its scriptures in their original language, as in Southeast Asia, that the outside influence became so all-pervading. It modified art, literature and thought at every level from the popular to the most elitist. And it furnished even Confucian and Daoist detractors of Buddhism with perspectives unknown in classical times.

For Ruan Yuan, the design of pagodas such as this one in present-day Xian was a reminder of their foreign origin. In fact, multistorey towers such as this were derived more from Chinese architecture than from Indian stupas.

The first Buddhists to arrive in China during the first and second centuries C.E. were probably traders from central Asia. In their wake came Buddhist monks, who brought with them the Mahayana form of Buddhism (pp.158–59). But these foreign visitors did not do much to pique Chinese curiosity: out of all the Buddhist doctrines that had developed by this time, only a few, mainly concerning practical skills such as meditation, were rendered into Chinese.

In the early fourth century C.E., northern China fell under the control of military leaders of Inner Asian descent, who were less prejudiced against foreign monks. At the same time, the Chinese who had been exiled to the south were sufficiently shaken out of their cultural complacency to accept the Buddhist message of impermanence. The apparent similarity between *shunyata* (pp.158–59) and "primal nothingness" in the Dark Learning (p.183) even led to the first serious discussion of Buddhist thought among the elite.

New Chinese translations of Buddhist philosophy by a central Asian missionary known as Kumarajiva (344–413 C.E.) at the start of the fifth century C.E. allowed Chinese intellectuals to gain a far greater grasp of the religion. At the same time, the notion spread that people could gain merit toward a better rebirth through donations to the Buddhist monastic community, and monasteries grew rich and powerful.

However, wealth sometimes meant that monasteries became lax and corrupt, and intensive study of Buddhist philosophy caused many monks to doubt whether Buddhism was really relevant to Chinese life. This intellectual uncertainty led a number of Chinese monks to go to India to seek out the wellsprings of Buddhism. One such was Xuanzang (602–64), who spent 16 years in India and returned in 645 with 520 cases packed with Buddhist texts and objects. But despite these monks' efforts, Buddhism, with its strong other-worldly dimension, still remained a relatively alien creed to the practical-minded Chinese.

During the Sui (581–618) and Tang (618–907) periods, however, Chinese Buddhists absorbed aspects of Buddhism felt to be compatible with traditional Chinese beliefs, and several schools arose. The Tiantai school (Japanese Tendai, pp.162–63) focused on the *Lotus Sutra* text, which says there are many "skilful means" that lead people to enlightenment, a notion that chimed with a Chinese tendency to harmonize competing ideas.

Pure Land Buddhism, later to become popular in Japan (pp.162–63), showed a typical Chinese practicality in its rejection of complex doctrines in favour of a method that ensured its adherents reached the "Pure Land" of the celestial Buddha Amitabha (Japanese Amida) simply by calling his name. And Chan (Japanese Zen, pp.162–63) Buddhism concentrated on what was said to be the Buddha's ultimate message. This was an enlightenment passed "from mind to mind" by a series of teachers until the last Indian bearer of this living truth, Bodhidharma (*c*.470–543), had brought it to China.

Over time, Buddhism's fortunes fluctuated. In 845, it suffered severe repression under the zealous emperor Wu Zong. And during the Song dynasty (960–1279) and later, it was eclipsed by Neo-Confucianism (pp.190–91). However, until its suppression by the communist authorities in this century, Chinese Buddhism has continued its transformation from an alien creed to being an integral part of Chinese society.

For, despite the disapproval of Confucian scholars, Buddhism was found to be too useful in promoting social order for the government to suppress it. Buddhist schools and hospitals which had come into being in the Sui-Tang period were replaced with Confucian equivalents. But it was more difficult to replace Buddhist doctrines. For example, Confucians found a belief in Buddhist *karma* – the force whereby people reap in their next life the fruits of their actions in this – so entrenched among the populace that they were reconciled to reinforcing this notion rather than denying it.

This image of the celestial Buddha Vairocana, embodiment of the highest form of Buddhahood, was carved out of rock at Longmen, not far from the ancient capital of Luoyang. The capital marked the final part of the silk road through central Asia, and Buddhist art in the area shows inspiration from sources outside China.

Over the centuries, sites sacred to Buddhism became established in other parts of the country. Certain mountains, shown on the map, assumed particular importance as · Buddhist pilgrimage sites, usually because of the manifestation of a Buddhist figure. Thus Putuo became associated with the goddess Guanyin, while the fame of Wutai as the dwelling place of the bodhisattva *Manjusri* became so well established that even today pilgrims come from as far away as Tibet to visit this and other sites hallowed by his presence.

Buddhist holy sites in China

MONGOLIA

DUNHUANG

GREAT WALL

YUNGANG · Beijing

WUTAISHAN

NORTH KOREA

SOUTH KOREA

YELLOW SEA

Huang (Yellow)

MAIJISHAN

LONGMEN SONGSHAN

· Luoyang

C H I N A

JIUHUASHAN

EMEISHAN

Chang Jiang (Yangtze)

TIANTAISHAN

Shanghai

PUTUOSHAN

HENGSHAN

/ One of the four Buddhist holy mountains
Cave-temple complex
Other important Buddhist site
— — — Modern international boundary

SOUTH CHINA SEA

N

0   250   500 km
0 100 200 300 miles

VIETNAM

185

The Development of Daoism

Although Daoists conventionally look back to Laozi (pp.182–83) as their founder, the Daoist tradition does not flow from a single source or period. However, over the centuries Daoism was transformed from a movement with a mystical basis to a loosely organized religion, and a crucial phase of this process can be pinpointed in the second century C.E. during Han rule.

This was a time of social and political disorder, and it led to the rise of a number of religious groups which believed they could set China to rights. One of these, the Yellow Turbans in eastern China, challenged the Han in 184 C.E. This led to a full-scale civil war, the Han emperor lost authority and his generals became warlords. And, in western China, a group known as the Way of the Celestial Masters (opposite) came to prominence.

The Celestial Masters took their name from a title said to have been conferred on their founder, Zhang Daoling (c.34–c.156 C.E.), by Laozi. (By this time, Laozi had become deified, a process that occurred with other historical figures and personifications, furnishing Daoist groups with their deities.) The regime of Zhang's descendants was so successful that in 215 Cao Cao, the warlord who was effective ruler of the Han Empire, accepted its surrender, but allowed its spiritual leadership to survive. As a result, the Masters spread throughout Cao Cao's power base in northern China.

Meanwhile, in southern China, where the rival Wu government (220–80) was established, older religious lore and traditions flourished in an atmosphere of cultural conservatism. Particularly popular here were alchemy, or the search for a chemical elixir of immortality, meditation and dietary practices, mastery of which was supposed to confer supernormal powers and finally the ability to become immortal (below).

In the late third century, the Western Jin dynasty (265–316) in the north incorporated the south into their empire. The succeeding Eastern Jin dynasty (317–420) moved its capital to present-day Nanjing in 317. This brought in a northern elite, who patronized the priesthood of the Celestial Masters and curtailed the influence of the southern aristocracy, who were keepers of traditional religious lore. This led to the emergence of

The quest for immortality

From at least the second century B.C.E., Daoists and others believed it was possible to discover an elixir which would confer immortality on them. This belief gained credence at the Han and later courts, and alchemical research flourished. Since cinnabar, traditionally the chief ingredient in the elixir, is highly poisonous, a number of imperial fatalities ensued. This had the effect of diverting attention toward the safer pursuit of the inner elixir, replacing the quest for a potion with the creation of an "immortal embryo" within, by mental and physical disciplines.

Such an approach may be prefigured in early Chinese texts, in which there are hints of yogic and meditational practices. Also, many Daoist sources concentrate on the concept of qi, which in some contexts means "breath". But it is also used for the primal energy believed to flow through the body, as well as through the universe, which the adept must learn to control. People can develop this energy through a form of exercise known as taiji (ABOVE LEFT), whose antiquity may be shown by figures (LEFT) recently found on a second-century C.E. Han tomb.

The emphasis on bodily control is also paramount in the description of certain sexual techniques conducive to immortality. These were definitely not for the fainthearted: a man is said in one source to require 108 women in succession to achieve 10,000 years of life, while for divine status, no fewer than 1,200 women were required.

new Daoist groups, usually originating as a result of spirit revelations from the gods, transmitted through human mediums. And these divine messages tended to emphasize the more magical practices of the south.

Meanwhile, by the late fourth century, Buddhism had won political influence in both the north and south, providing an impetus for the various Daoist groups to range themselves together. By about 450, Daoist scriptures, such as the meditational text called *The Canon of the Yellow Court*, derived from these different groups were ranked together in one unified order, just as the various teachings of Buddhism were.

From this time onward, however diverse the strands within it, Daoism became a distinctive movement with shared practices, such as priestly rituals and communal festivals; and common beliefs, for example, that the world (macrocosm) parallels the body (microcosm). Also, unlike Buddhism, which stressed a divide between religion and state, Daoism was compatible with traditional Chinese political theory. So it was favoured by emperors seeking religious justification for their rule.

With the collapse of the Tang in 907, new Daoist groups arose in the provinces, less dependent on imperial patronage. Even these provincial groups were supported from time to time by emperors of later dynasties. But despite its varied forms, from the 10th century on, the strength of Daoism remained what it was in the days of the first Celestial Masters. This was the ability of its priests to mediate between humans and the supernatural, and to give the reassurance that cosmic order can be upheld, whatever the uncertainties of daily existence.

The Celestial Masters

Organized Daoism has long been specially associated with the Zhang family, who trace their descent from the founder of the Celestial Masters, Zhang Daoling (*c.*34–*c.*156 C.E.). Zhang's importance in Chinese religion has always been well recognized. Pictures of him and charms ascribed to him have been used to deter evil forces and still appear in Chinese almanacs. His grandson, Zhang Lu, was responsible for maintaining the Celestial Masters as an independent regime for almost 30 years, but probably died soon after the surrender to Cao Cao in 215. Of his later descendants little is known until the ninth century. Then a family in Jiangxi province, far from western China where Zhang Daoling was well remembered, claimed to be heirs to an unbroken line of Celestial Masters stretching back over the centuries.

They in time came to be officially accepted by successive imperial governments as the Celestial Masters. This at times gave them great influence, but not the authority implied in the title Daoist Pope, coined by western observers in the 19th and 20th centuries. Indeed, under the Qing (1644–1911), their most important function was to be allowed to confer official ordination on Daoist priests. In the 20th century, the 63rd Celestial Master, harassed by the communist authorities, fled to Taiwan in 1959 and died 10 years later. In 1970, Zhang Yuanxian, son of a cousin, succeeded him in Tainan, Taiwan.

In Daoism, incense burners, such as the one inside a Daoist temple (BELOW) and the tiered structure (LEFT) outside a temple, were often made in the shape of mountains. This conveys the idea of incense wafting up as a token of devotion to the gods and of mountains being places of encounter with the divine.

The Religion of the People

From early imperial times, there has always been a popular or folk religion in China, coexisting with the organized religious traditions. This folk religion increasingly came to be dominated by diverse local cults whose adherents sought the help of particular gods (often the spirit of a charismatic person), to whom they would sometimes build temples. From the end of the Han (220 C.E.) to the start of the Song dynasty (960 C.E.), as Buddhism and Daoism became established, tension between locally based cults and organized religions grew.

Toward the end of this period, however, some forms of local religion gained wider acceptance and transformed the balance of Chinese worship. For example, by the 10th century, an entire class of local deities known as *chenghuang*, or city gods, who were publicly worshipped for, say, their powers to bring rain, came to be accepted by both Buddhists and Daoists. In the following century, a number of cults of local origin attracted support from the Song government and so became known nationwide. One of these was the western Chinese cult of a certain Zhang Ezi, famed as a dragon-slayer, who came to be honoured across the country as god of literature in the 13th century.

These were not the only developments. New folk deities arose that assimilated elements from Buddhism and Daoism. For example, Xu Jia, the reputed servant of Laozi (pp.182–83), became the patron god of religious functionaries who assisted Daoist priests with rites at religious festivals. There were also popular figures, such as the Eight Immortals (*below*), whose attributes became standardized as a result of the process of printing.

Scholars of Chinese religions are not yet able to generalize about all these trends. And there is debate as to whether they were directly linked with changes in Chinese society, such as the decline of the aristocracy and less direct government control, which started in the late Tang period (618–907). However, it has become apparent that the government at this time attempted to recognize certain forms of local religion, while restricting as far as possible the freedom of Buddhist and Daoist clergy to interact with society.

By embracing local religious groups, the state alienated those who disliked having their religion over-organized. To fill this vacuum, several cults, such as the 11th-century White Cloud, grew up, but were forced underground to escape state persecution. Some cults perpetuated religious teachings of long standing, but

The Eight Immortals

Popular in Chinese folk religion for the last 500 years, the Eight Immortals were formalized during the Yuan, or Mongol, period (1260–1368). Some of them, such as Han Xiang, who lived in the ninth century, were historical figures. Others are probably purely imaginary in origin.

Although there are variations, the immortals' typical artistic representations, shown on this Ming jade plaque, are as follows (CLOCKWISE FROM TOP RIGHT): Zhongli Quan, a stout, bearded figure carrying a fan; Han Xiang, a young man held to have power over nature, playing a flute; Zhang Guolao, often depicted with a white mule; He Xiangu, a young girl carrying a lotus, sometimes depicted upon a floating lotus petal with a fly-whisk in her hand; Lan Caihe, at first described as a man, who came to be represented as a young woman carrying a flower-basket; Lu Dongbin, an elderly swordsman; Cao Guojiu, an old man with a pair of castanets or wooden clappers; Li Tieguai, a skinny, grotesque figure usually depicted leaning on a crutch but here seated, holding a gourd.

Colourful figures in Chinese garb with Daoist symbols form part of a procession of a Hungry Ghosts festival in Hong Kong. This popular festival originated as a sort of Buddhist equivalent to the Christian All Souls', the day of prayer for souls in purgatory. The festival's function is to give the best protection against possible mischief from ghosts who might otherwise feel neglected.

Of all the rites introduced by Buddhism into China, this festival has been most readily compatible with the traditional Chinese concern for ancestors. Whatever its original associations with the conventional Buddhism of the monasteries, this festival has provided a vehicle for a popular expression of religion for more than a thousand years, with Chinese elements foreign to Indian Buddhism finding a place in its ceremonies.

others were led by adventurers, more interested in money and power, and aroused government hostility.

From the Song period onward, there began an intermingling among folk religion, Buddhism and Daoism. As a result, new forms of worship developed that were expressed in the language of the people, not the classical Chinese of old, tangible evidence of their debt to folk religion. Typical of this synthesizing process are Daoist movements of the 12th century that betray Buddhist borrowings, notably the Quanzhen school. And in the Ming era (1368–1644), a deliberate attempt by Lin Zhaoen in the 16th century to reconcile Confucianism, Daoism and Buddhism resulted in an amalgam known as the Three Teachings, which still flourishes in Chinese communities overseas.

It was also in the 16th century that Confucian scholars became worried about what they saw as a rising tide of superstition, which they linked with the proliferation of popular literature. Always suspicious of the irrational aspect of popular religion, the Confucians targeted colourful figures such as the Monkey King, who, in the tale *The Journey to the West*, accompanies a Chinese pilgrim travelling to India to obtain Buddhist texts. However, many modern scholars compare unfavourably the rather narrow, over-intellectual attitude of the Confucians with the exuberance and love of life with which Chinese folk literature and religion are imbued.

A fire walker shows his skill during the Monkey King festival in Hong Kong. Nothing illustrates the vitality of the popular religious spirit in Chinese civilization better than the cult of the Monkey King. In the best-known version of his story, the Monkey King is employed in the service of Buddhism to afford the Chinese pilgrim Xuanzang protection on his journey to India.

In fact, there is evidence that the cult of the Divine Monkey predates the Buddhist era in China and that it was always associated with the religion of the people, despite the attempts of the established religions to bring it within their orbit. Displays of power, such as fire walking, may have been repellent to the educated mandarins, but they formed a natural part of the Monkey King festival.

Challenge of the cults

The conviction that a new order is about to replace a corrupt, decadent world can be found in China as far back as the Han dynasty (206 B.C.E.–220 C.E.). Since Chinese governments down the centuries found this belief implicitly critical of their rule, they tended to suppress those groups that espoused it. During the Yuan, or Mongol, rule (1260–1368), a lay-Buddhist cult known as the White Lotus included members who desired a revolutionary change in the country. In the disordered times at the end of Mongol rule, the cult was involved in widespread violent rebellion.

Some cults, such as the Red Yang, founded in 1588, were unorthodox but pacific and posed no threat to the government unless they were first persecuted. Other cults were more aggressive, emphasizing physical meditation, martial arts and religious rituals. They often became involved in criminal activity. A well-known example is the Tiandihui, or Heaven and Earth Society, generally known as the Triads, which, during the Qing dynasty (1644–1911), was associated with anti-government activities. Triad gangs still exist in Chinese communities today and have maintained religious rituals (BELOW) like other Chinese.

Today, too, a host of heterodox cults, sometimes mixing Christianity and Islam with China's established religious traditions and often guided by divine revelations, are evident. One such, the Yiguandao, or Way of Pervading Unity, was suppressed in the People's Republic of China in the 1950s, but now has many thousands of adherents in Taiwan.

Neo-Confucianism

Confucian priests in their regalia stand outside Youngnung tomb in South Korea. Confucianism came to Korea well before the unification of the country in the seventh century C.E., but it only became a dominant force with the rise of Neo-Confucianism there from the 15th century onward.

Today, Confucianism in South Korea has a tradition of rituals unparalleled in the modern world, with many differing only marginally from those once performed in imperial China.

During the Song dynasty (960–1279 C.E.), Confucian scholars began to reevaluate their tradition in reaction to the strength of contemporary Daoism and Buddhism. The resulting movement, termed Neo-Confucianism in the west, developed into two distinct groups: the School of Principle, expounded in particular by Zhu Xi (1130–1200), and the School of Mind, developed by Wang Yangming (1472–1529).

On a philosophical level, both schools were trying to realize the vision of an idealized state of early China inherent in ancient Chinese texts. From these writings, they wanted to formulate a view of the universe, and the place of humans within it, that could rival, in particular, the other-worldly vision of Buddhism. But each school emphasized a different approach – intellectual study and intuition, respectively.

On a more practical level, Neo-Confucianism arose from a need of Confucian scholars to shape the political and cultural direction of the new Song dynasty. In particular, there was much debate as to whether the Song emperors should continue the social and cultural legacy of imperial times, especially the Tang and, earlier, the Han periods, with their well-defined state institutions, or re-create in its place an idealized China of remote antiquity. This debate provoked fierce infighting between different groups of scholars. From the conflict emerged the moralistic, backward-looking School of Principle of the brothers Cheng Hao and Cheng Yi, whose 11th-century work was completed by Zhu Xi.

Central to Zhu Xi's teaching was the assertion that the universe and all existence was composed of a material element patterned by an underlying principle known as

li. He also proposed that since humans had the potential to reach the desired state of sagehood, it was incumbent on all Confucians to study the ancient texts diligently to reach that goal. Four works (*opposite*) in particular were selected from the Confucian canon as being especially helpful for this aim, and Zhu Xi's commentary was used for the civil service examinations (*opposite*).

For those who sought a less academic or bookish approach to sagehood, an alternative way was put forward by Wang Yangming. A professional soldier and a profound thinker, Wang approved of the goal of sagehood but advocated a more intuitive approach to it through meditation and moral reflection, rather than relying solely on textual study. However, Wang's later followers were sometimes regarded as being aloof from Confucian book learning to the point of standing outside the tradition altogether. And after 1644, when the Manchu Qing successfully invaded China from the northeast, Wang's followers suffered a reaction. For Wang's emphasis on intuition as a way to sagehood was felt to be at the expense of the sort of down-to-earth qualities that might have helped repel the invaders.

The anti-Wang backlash also led to a renewed emphasis on the study of the Confucian classics. In the 18th century, however, this vogue for close textual analysis threw up some unexpected problems. Chinese scholars began to question not only the accuracy of Song commentaries on the classics, but also the authenticity of some of the classics themselves. Nevertheless, the state continued to support Zhu Xi's type of Neo-Confucianism, with its textual bias, and it was dominant in the country until the close of the imperial period in 1911.

A sage gives instruction on filial piety to a pupil in this 12th-century Chinese painting (RIGHT). This virtue was an essential part of the Confucian ethic and was drummed into young Chinese throughout imperial times. Even today, in many traditional Chinese families, acknowledgment of parental authority may be made on formal occasions by means of a kowtow, or respectful bow.

The promotion of filial piety before the 20th century was not, however, solely a domestic matter: illustrated texts of stories exemplifying filial piety were widely circulated. Exhortations to filial behavior were also included in the Sacred Edict, the text which, from 1670 onward, incorporated the emperor's basic instructions to his subjects.

召試縣令

Examination under a country magistrate, depicted here in an 18th-century painting, was only part of a process that could lead to more stringent tests at provincial centers. Here candidates would work in small cells to prevent cheating before proceeding to the imperial palace at Beijing.

The imperial examination system

One of the most distinctive features of Chinese governments up to the present century has been the need for prospective civil servants to take examinations based on the Confucian canon. Written tests for civil servants can be traced back to the Han period (206 B.C.E.–220 C.E.). Later, under the Tang (618–907), regular exams for which a knowledge of Confucian literature was assumed, became a prestigious, though limited, path toward government service. With the Song dynasty (960–1279), the heyday of Confucian-based exams began. However, it was not until the Yuan, or Mongol, emperors (1260–1368) that the officially accepted interpretation of Confucianism came to be based on the writings of Zhu Xi, whose commentary on the Four Books was officially recognized in 1315 as the approved interpretation for the civil service examinations.

Success in the examinations could transform a person's status in life, and some candidates continued to sit them, despite repeated failures, until well into old age. At times, the exam system may have allowed a certain measure of social mobility. However, in the long run, only those who were rich enough to enable them to afford to study for many years or, in some cases, cheat the system, could hope to succeed. Whether the exams stifled independent thought is still a matter of debate. The state was always particularly concerned to make them as objective a test as possible, sometimes at the expense of eliciting creative intelligence or originality. For example, the "eight-legged essay," the highly structured eight-part answer required by examiners, became notorious as a triumph of empty form over content.

By late imperial times in the 19th century, a whole hierarchy of examinations had to be passed. They consisted of local exams, triennial provincial exams, and metropolitan exams culminating in a final test, also held once every three years, in the imperial palace itself. Out of a total of several thousand would-be graduates, only about a hundred might expect to pass this final hurdle.

The Four Books

During the late Tang period (618–907), there were signs that Confucians were concentrating on the Four Books, listed below, as containing the essence of Confucian thought; and these books have retained their importance into the 20th century.

Lunyu (Analects): consists of the sayings of Confucius. It was treated as important from the start of the Confucian school, which began after the death of Confucius c.479 B.C.E.

Mengzi (Mencius): contains the collected sayings of Mencius (c.371–c.289 B.C.E.), the greatest exponent of Confucianism after the sage himself. The book had attracted commentaries by the time of the Han dynasty (206 B.C.E.–220 C.E.).

Daxue (Great Learning): ascribed by some to the disciple Zeng Shen, it was part of the *Li Ji* collection on ritual and one of the Five Classics (p.180). It outlined how individual spiritual development could help society.

Zhong Yong (Doctrine of the Mean): ascribed to a grandson of Confucius, this book was also part of the *Li Ji*. It deals with human nature and how it relates to the moral order of the universe.

The Imperial Cult

The official state cult of the emperor, by which he was regarded as the Son of Heaven and performed certain prescribed rituals, was part of the official Chinese religious tradition for hundreds of years before the start of the 20th century. In fact, this doctrine can be traced back to before the time of Confucius (c. 551–c.479 B.C.E.). However, the idea fell into abeyance until it was resurrected during the Han dynasty (206 B.C.E.–220 C.E.) by Confucian scholars, many of whom were keen to assert that the Han emperors conformed to what was known as the mandate of heaven.

After the collapse of the Han dynasty, some bureaucrats used Buddhist and Daoist ideas to support imperial rule. Later, however, from the Song dynasty (960–1279) onward, the Confucian notion of the emperor's role came to dominate Chinese thinking. According to this, the emperor had to pay great attention to ritual observances, and when opinions on these differed, the court

could be riven by major disputes. This happened, for example, when the Ming emperor Shizong (1507–66) succeeded in 1521 as the cousin of his predecessor and wished to grant full ritual honours to his own deceased father, even though the cult required that he treat his uncle as his immediate ancestor.

The full splendour of the imperial cult best known to westerners was that of the Manchu Qing dynasty (1644–1911). However, some of the early Qing rulers (below) privately drew greater solace from the very un-Chinese shamanistic practices, based around a shaman – a tribal figure who combined the roles of seer, healer and spiritual guide – of their Manchurian homeland in the northeast.

The Qing capital in Beijing had been laid out according to purely Chinese ideas of cosmic order. For example, the major buildings faced south, the direction of the sun's beneficence and therefore of holiness. Also,

The Qings' unofficial religion

Qing, or Manchu, emperors are widely regarded by scholars as great patrons of Chinese culture and Confucian scholarship, sponsoring the compilation of great scholarly works, massive encyclopedias and lectures on the Four Books (p.191), which they had translated into Manchu. They also privately practised a form of Tibetan Buddhism that the Chinese of the 17th century would have found unacceptable.

The Qing ruled not only China, but also Inner Asia, due in part to an alliance with some of the region's Mongol inhabitants going back to the 17th century. This alliance was made easier when the fifth Dalai Lama (1617–82), the leader of the Yellow Hat school of Tibetan Buddhism (pp.164–65), recognized the Qing emperor as a patron and later Qing rulers as incarnations of the *bodhisattva* ("buddha-to-be") Manjusri.

The emperors never referred to themselves as *bodhisattvas* in Chinese, or even in official Manchu documents, but were happy to see themselves described as such in Tibetan and Mongol documents. It is no wonder, then, that the Forbidden City, for all its Chinese design, incorporated a temple – the interior of which is shown (BELOW LEFT) – for lamaistic, or Tibetan Buddhist, worship.

This image of Tsong-Kha-pa (ABOVE), *teacher of the first Dalai Lama, was housed in the imperial palace in Beijing by the Qing emperors. In the 18th century, the Qing came to control Tibet through an arrangement which depended on the cooperation of the Dalai Lama.*

the Qing emperors fulfilled their ritual obligations to the letter. At the summer solstice, a sacrifice to Earth took place at a square altar north of the Forbidden City, the imperial inner sanctum in Beijing.

At the beginning of the four seasons, and at the end of the year, sacrifices were made to the imperial ancestors in a temple to the east side of the main axis of the Forbidden City. At spring time and harvest, sacrifices to the spirits of Soil and Grain were carried out at an altar west of the same axis. At the Temple of Agriculture the emperor personally engaged in a spring ploughing ceremony to mark the start of the year's agricultural work.

The architecture, as well as the timing and details of the sacrifices down to the colours of the silks and gems worn, conformed to the complex theories of yin and yang and the categories of five (pp.178–79), worked out over the centuries. But these solemn ceremonies were not intended as popular demonstrations of the Qing loyalty to Chinese tradition, since the common people were excluded from witnessing them.

What the people did receive was imperial support for the gods of their own communities, on condition that the gods exhibited worthy ethical values. Thus Guandi, the deified late Han general renowned for his loyalty, embodied a virtue much esteemed by the state. Gods who showed their efficacy by responding, say, to prayers for rain might be promoted in the order of sacrifices; gods who failed might be demoted or even chastized.

Yet this criterion of efficacy affected the emperor, the Son of Heaven, as well. From Han to Qing times, emperors responded to catastrophes like droughts or floods with much soul-searching, since they believed that such disasters might be signs of heaven's displeasure toward their rule. In recent times, the massive earthquake which preceded the death of Mao Zedong in 1976 could not but be interpreted in the same way.

This view of court ritual at the imperial palace in Beijing comes from Todo meisho zue, *a Japanese guide to China published in 1806. The scene shows a lecture on the Confucian classics being delivered in the emperor's presence.*

Japanese Confucians of the time were acutely interested in Chinese institutions, although their knowledge of them was derived more from Chinese texts than eyewitness accounts. Japanese publishers who prepared lavishly illustrated works such as this one could find a ready market among educated Japanese for whom, at this time, there was little possibility of travelling abroad.

The Temple of Heaven, with its richly carved stairway, is a ritual complex lying south of Beijing. Most of the buildings date from the 18th century, when large-scale renovations were carried out on the buildings that were originally built in the 15th and 16th centuries.

The two main features of the temple are the Round Mound, where the emperor would report to heaven on the state of the empire at every winter solstice, and the Hall of the Prayer for Good Harvests, which was used for prayers in the first month as well as at harvest time.

Revolution and Change

The first religious contacts between China and the west occurred when European missionaries went to China in the late Ming (1368–1644) and early Qing (1644–1911) periods. But the missionaries made little impact, especially after they lost imperial protection when internal disputes over the religious status of Chinese ancestor worship weakened their credibility.

In the 19th century, a new wave of Protestant missions arrived in China and encountered a government struggling to contain social problems such as overpopulation and opium addiction. The first great convulsion that this encounter precipitated was the Taiping Rebellion (1850–64). This revolt was led by a certain Hong Xiuquan (1814–64), a visionary who had read Protestant tracts and declared himself the younger brother of Jesus Christ. Hong launched an assault on all forms of idolatry, and the initial success of his rebellion brought him from the far south to Nanjing, which he made his capital. The rebellion was finally put down by imperial troops helped by the European powers.

The Taiping Rebellion resulted in a massive destruction of religious foundations. Although Buddhism and Daoism to some extent revived, they never recovered fully in the 19th century. In the first half of the 20th century, a modernizing, secular spirit pervaded government policy and undermined the institutional strength of China's organized religions, exemplified by the state's attempts to turn monasteries into schools.

In 1949, Mao Zedong's Communist Party came to power and the government of China became avowedly atheistic. The communists formed religious associations so that the major religions, such as Daoism and Buddhism, could be subjected to official guidance. Folk religion, however, had no means to defend itself from the charge of being mere superstition. Also, the standing of Confucius continued to fall, though there were times when he was commended as a figure of world importance (for instance, as an educator) from China's past.

The outbreak of the Cultural Revolution (1966–76) unleashed Mao's Red Guards against all relics of the past

The sutras say that all sentient beings belong to the Buddha, so I honour him: but why should I therefore reject the way of the Confucian sages? Gold and jade do no harm to each other.

MOUZI (FOURTH CENTURY C.E.?)

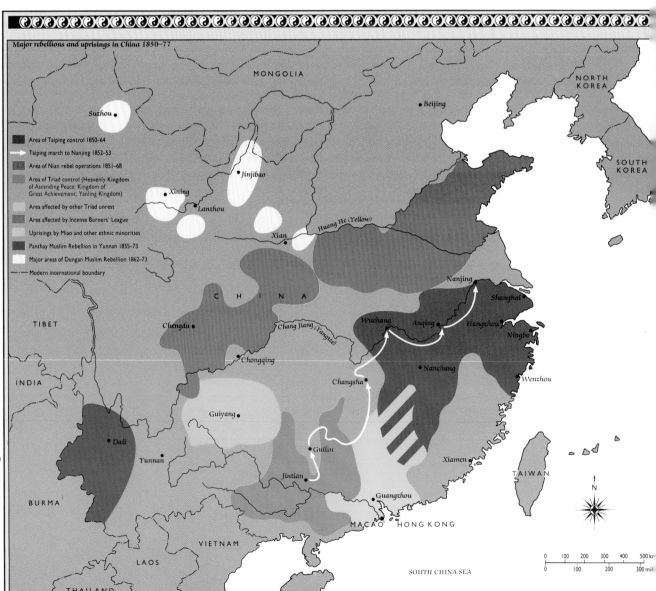

Major rebellions and uprisings in China 1850–77

Area of Taiping control 1850–64

Taiping march to Nanjing 1852–53

Area of Nian rebel operations 1851–68

Area of Triad control (Heavenly Kingdom of Ascending Peace; Kingdom of Great Achievement; Yanling Kingdom)

Area affected by other Triad unrest

Area affected by Incense Burners' League

Uprisings by Miao and other ethnic minorities

Panthay Muslim Rebellion in Yunnan 1855–73

Major areas of Dungan Muslim Rebellion 1862–73

Modern international boundary

and the religious heritage in particular. At the same time, Mao Zedong was, ironically, treated with a degree of adulation bordering on worship. However, Mao's death in 1976 led to a period of reassessment in the 1980s under Deng Xiaoping, which showed that 10 years of persecution had not broken the power of religious belief.

In the mid-1980s, elaborate ceremonies in honour of Confucius were revived at his birthplace in Shandong province. However, they were mainly for the benefit of tourists. Also, they were carried out by hired opera performers (traditionally despised in official circles), not by the government officials of old. Government attitudes toward religion in China itself remain cautious, and it is probably only among some overseas Chinese communities, such as in the United States, that religious observances may be openly performed without fear of government censure. Yet the consistent placing of political values above religious ones shows that, in one sense, the Chinese government of the 1980s and early '90s is true to one of the principles upheld by Confucius.

In this modern Chinese poster (BELOW RIGHT), *soldiers and peasants "advance under the victorious banner of Mao Zedong". Many foreign observers of the Cultural Revolution were impressed by the quasi-religious imagery surrounding Mao and by attempts made to use Mao worship as a substitute for earlier religious cults, a process illustrated by the use of his image on a local shrine* (RIGHT).

Many Chinese caught up in the fervour of Mao worship during this period now speak with disillusion of a blind faith which has since been discarded. Even so, Mao's image shows little sign of fading from use.

Religion and rebellion: the Marxist view

Since 1949, Chinese Marxist scholars have had to address themselves to the relationship between religion and rebellion in Chinese history, from the Yellow Turban uprising in the second century C.E. to the Taiping Rebellion in the 19th. Marxists have construed the various revolts against imperial authority as peasant rebellions that established a tradition of resistance crowned by the communist triumph in 1949. But it was more difficult for them to deal with the heterodox religious ideas often associated with these rebellions. The question was whether the religious elements were a genuine challenge to the religious and political status quo; whether they were simply used as rallying points by rebel leaders to help mobilize the backward peasantry; or whether they simply represented a stage of historically outmoded belief.

Since there have also been rebellions in China unconnected with religious movements, such as the great uprisings which extinguished the Ming dynasty in 1644, the safest course for the Marxists has been to play down the significance of religion altogether. For example, they have stressed the nationalist, anti-Qing side of what they call the Taiping Revolutionary Movement, rather than its religious aspect.

However, the 1980s saw some change in official Chinese attitudes to religious history. The religion of sectarian groups such as the 14th-century White Lotus is now studied as representative of popular religious thought separate from the major religions. This has not, however, in the early 1990s, led to a full acceptance of folk religious practice: much of it is still officially regarded as mere superstition.

The great rebellions from 1850 to 1877 show a broad spectrum of religious concerns, or the lack of them. Muslims and Taipings were both identifiable by their religion. The Triad and Nian cults, while using some religious symbolism, were more in the manner of bandits. The Miao were an ethnic minority reacting against oppression. Scholars are unclear to what extent religion was a motivating force in revolts involving other groups such as the Incense Burners.

Shinto's sacred shrines

In Japan, people can choose from about 80,000 shrines to venerate and petition the gods, or *kami*. Some are grand, others are more intimate. Almost all have a *torii* – the gateway to the sacred enclosure, consisting of two columns crossed by two beams.

Typical features inside the enclosure are a trough for ritual washing; an open-sided structure where visitors can hang wooden tablets (*ema*) inscribed with petitions and prayers; a raised, roofed platform (*haiden*), where offerings and petitions to the *kami* can be made; and a *honden*, the central building which houses a sacred object, such as a mirror, in which the *kami* are believed to reside.

Visitors to a typical shrine such as Izumo (LEFT), one of Japan's oldest shrines, proceed through the *torii* along a straight path. They purify themselves at the water trough and then hang up their *ema*. They then go either to the *haiden* or, in small shrines, straight to the *honden*, the central building. Standing before it, visitors throw coins or paper-wrapped rice into an offertory box and ring a bell to "summon" the *kami*. Veneration involves two bows, two claps to welcome the *kami*, and one final bow.

On special occasions, petitioners enter the *haiden* to be ritually cleansed by a priest. Offerings of food, wine and a twig from the sakaki tree are then placed on an altar. At the end of the rite, the wine, now fortified by the *kami*, is drunk by the petitioners.

This camphor wood torii, or ceremonial gateway, marks the entrance to the Itsukushijima shrine on Miyajima island, and is a famous symbol of Shinto. A feature of all Shinto shrines, the torii divides the sacred precincts from the ordinary world, and is often painted vermilion. The Itsukushijima shrine was probably founded in the late sixth century, but the present buildings date from the mid-16th century; this torii was erected in 1875, four years after Itsukushijima was designated a national shrine.

SHINTO

The Spirit of Japan

SHINTO, JAPAN'S INDIGENOUS RELIGION, means "way of the gods". It began in the mists of prehistory as a cult of the *kami*, the innumerable deities believed to inhabit the mountains, trees, rocks, springs and other natural phenomena. From the sixth century C.E. began the fusion of the *kami* cult with elements of Buddhism, Confucianism and Daoism, which had come from China, to create a Shinto religion based around the veneration of the *kami*.

From its outset, Shinto has consisted of two interdependent traditions, the popular and the political. In brief, popular Shinto remained a local shrine-based cult of the *kami*, while political Shinto, with its rituals and priests, served to legitimize Japanese rulers. After the imperial restoration in 1868 (pp.200–201), the government injected nationalistic elements into popular Shinto, fusing the two traditions. The result was "state" Shinto. After 1945, state Shinto was dismantled, leaving popular Shinto to go its own way.

Shinto lacks many characteristics familiar in the monotheistic religions of Judaism, Christianity and Islam. For example, although Shinto has its deities, rites, shrines and priests, it has no human founder or concept of a divine creator. It lacks a doctrine of the soul and has no Bible-like core text or a codified system of ethics.

The central concern of Shinto is with this world, and its most visible form of expression is in the ritual visiting of shrines – 95 percent of contemporary Japanese may be classified Shinto in that they go to shrines at some time in their lives. In short, Shinto is concerned more with community than with the individual, with performing rituals rather than with doctrines and believing. This is underlined by the surprising fact that only 20 percent of Japanese who venerate *kami* actually profess to believe in their existence.

The *kami* at the heart of Shinto are shadowy beings – usually not personified – possessed of supernatural power. Inari, or "Rice Provider", is the most popular *kami* in Japan today, venerated in some 30,000 shrines. Originally a guardian deity of agriculture, Inari is today petitioned for prosperity by a wide variety of businesses, many of which have Inari shrines on their premises. Spirits of great people and national leaders can also become *kami*. For example, the scholar Sugawara Michizane (845–903) is today revered as a *kami* in some 3,500 shrines by students about to take examinations.

Kami can also be worshipped at home. Many Japanese households have on their shelves wooden models of shrines, or *kamidana*. To these are attached paper amulets, renewed each new year, which bear the name of a favoured shrine and represent its *kami*. In some families, prayers and offerings of rice, salt and wine are made daily.

Shinto's emphasis on this world, rather than the afterlife, means that its focus falls on the life-cycle rites of birth and marriage; funerals follow Buddhist lines. Shrine rites in the annual cycle underline the same point. New Year (Hatsumode), Girls' Day (Hinamatsuri) in March, Boys' Day (Tango no Sekku) in May and Children's Day (Shichigosan) in November are all celebrations of birth and renewal, of youth and vigour. Participants make votive offerings, buy good-luck charms, and place written requests for good health and longevity in front of the enshrined *kami*.

Shinto also permeates the fabric of modern Japanese society in more secular ways. Shinto priests can be seen performing rites to pacify the earth on behalf of construction companies or blessing new automobiles for their owners. Businessmen and students pray to the *kami* for good returns on investments and success in exams.

The communal aspect of Shinto is borne out by annual shrine festivals, which serve to renew and consolidate the sense of local community. At these festivals, locals flock to the shrines to pay respects to the *kami*, drink wine and eat snacks, spend money at market stalls and generally make merry. The highlight occurs when men carry on their shoulders a portable enshrined *kami* around the community to guarantee that blessings are bestowed on all its households and enterprises.

A portable shrine, containing a local deity embodied in a mirror or other object, is borne aloft through a crowded street during a shrine festival. In this way, the deity's blessings are bestowed on the entire community.

From *Kami* Cult to Shinto

In prehistoric times, the Japanese believed that the *kami* inhabited a celestial plane, but that they also often resided in the earth's natural phenomena and had power over human life and natural forces. The ancestral spirits of powerful leaders were added to this *kami* pantheon probably between the third century B.C.E. and the third century C.E., when, as a result of the spread of rice cultivation, Japanese society became stratified.

At this time, it seems that the Japanese thought that all *kami* were offended by pollution from death, disease and blood from wounds, menstruation and childbirth. They performed purification rites, made offerings of rice, and worshipped communally to propitiate the *kami* and win their protection against drought, floods, pestilence and other natural disasters. These same rites later played a crucial role in endorsing the political authority of the local – and, in time, national – leaders who as priests presided over their celebration.

The *kami* cult developed in the sixth, seventh and eighth centuries in response to the threat to Japan of the advanced political and religious culture of its giant neighbour, China. For example, myths were composed to prove that the Japanese emperor was descended directly from Amaterasu, the female sun *kami*, and that she in turn was descended from the *kami* creators of the entire universe and Japan itself. From this time on, the *kami* cult was known as Shinto to give it its own identity distinct from the Chinese imports of Confucianism, Daoism and Buddhism.

It was Buddhism, in its Mahayana guise (pp.162–63), that was to influence Shinto most. Buddhism won court patronage, spread to the populace, and merged with elements of Shinto. The Buddhist preoccupation with rebirth, enlightenment and its ethical path proved more an aid than an obstacle to its coexistence with the earthly and pre-moral cult of the *kami*.

Also, a rapport between the two religions gradually emerged at a more metaphysical level: the *kami* were variously identified by Buddhists as sinful spirits in need of Buddhist salvation, as protectors of Buddhist divinities, and as the uniquely Japanese manifestation of those divinities. For example, the sun *kami* Amaterasu was identified with the celestial Buddha Vairocana. On a physical level, Buddhist temples were sited in Shinto shrine compounds, and shrine rites were supervised by Buddhist priests.

In the 15th century, however, the subordinate role that Shinto *kami* had in relation to Buddhism began to be reversed. Claims were now made that the *kami* were the ultimate expressions of reality, and that Buddhas

The spirit as a *kami*

The funeral cortège of Emperor Hirohito (1901–89) proceeds to the building known as the sojoden *where the Shinto funeral rites are conducted. Members of the Imperial Guard, clad in eighth-century court dress, carry the palanquin containing the coffin. In accordance with Shinto beliefs about the defiling nature of death, the* sojoden *is destroyed immediately after the funeral.*

Shinto's concern with this world makes it more suitable for performing birth and marriage rites than for funerals, which most Japanese today conduct along Buddhist lines. Nevertheless, there are well-established Shinto funeral rites, albeit based on Buddhist models – used by Japanese emperors and shrine priests and their families.

The early Japanese had a bewildering profusion of views on the afterworld. Some believed it was a gloomy, polluted nether realm known as *Yomi*, cut off from this world, and host to all but a few whose worldly power had enabled them to join the *kami* pantheon in heaven. Others thought it was *Tokoyo no kuni* – a land of eternal life and material abundance existing beyond or beneath the seas. Such views were superseded, but not wholly replaced, by a belief that the afterworld was much closer at hand in mountains or in the sky. In all cases, however, death was deemed to be defiling. People's ethical behaviour in this life did not affect their fate in the next; and at least a few spirits returned to earth and influenced human and natural life for better or worse.

These views, later shaped by Chinese Buddhism from the sixth century C.E., lasted until the mid-19th century, when Shinto scholars began to disentangle the strands and formulate an orthodox view of the afterworld. This was a mixture of Shinto myth and Jesuit-derived Catholic theology and held that at death, all spirits pass into an invisible realm where a *kami* passes judgment and determines the spirit's ultimate fate of paradise or hell.

Shinto funeral rites – suppressed in the 1880s and revived only after World War II – treat the spirit of the dead as a *kami*. The deceased is placed in a coffin, the face covered with a white cloth, in a front room of the house. Relatives stand guard throughout the night after death and offer sake (rice wine) and a sakaki branch to the corpse. The spirit is then ritually transferred from the corpse to a small portable shrine called a *tamashiro*.

Meals are prepared for the dead until the coffin is taken for burial the next day. The *tamashiro*, however, never leaves the home. The grave site is marked off by the same type of rope used in shrines to designate a particularly sacred spot. At the graveside, relatives again offer sake and a sakaki branch and end the ceremony by purifying themselves. Back home, the head of the family informs the *tamashiro* that the burial is over, and offerings are made. Memorial rites are performed before the *tamashiro* for the first 100 days of the spirit's return to the dark realm.

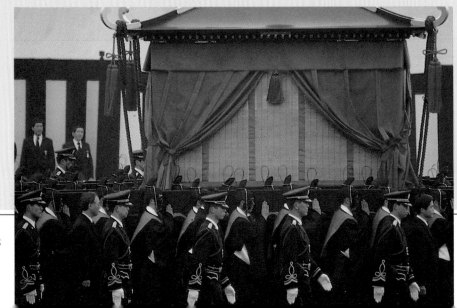

and other divinities were just *kami* in foreign dress and Buddhist doctrines were revelations of Shinto truth. As a result of this new trend, the *kami* cult selected and added a number of new metaphysical and moral dimensions from Buddhism.

Shinto's identity developed further from the 17th to the mid-19th centuries, a period when Japan was isolated as a nation and ruled by shoguns, or feudal overlords, of the Tokugawa dynasty. Influenced by Buddhism and even by Christian theology brought by missionaries (pp.68–69), Shinto imbibed concepts of creation, judgment, and heaven and hell. However, more crucial still was Shinto's powerful new ethical core of loyalty and filial piety, a debt it owed to the influence of Chinese Neo-Confucianism (pp.190–91).

Scholars of this new style of Shinto wanted to purify it from those foreign creeds that had shaped it, and to "return" to the "way of the *kami*" and to political rule by their descendants, the emperors. These ideas had minimal impact on popular religion. But in the 1850s, when Japan's national isolation was breached by the United States and other western powers, they fed a widespread nationalism and provided the rationale for the overthrow of military rule in 1868 and the restoration of imperial rule.

The inner shrine at Ise (ABOVE), *the most important Shinto shrine in Japan, is dedicated to Amaterasu, the sun* kami *and legendary founder of the imperial line. It houses the sacred mirror which, along with the jewel and sword kept elsewhere, form the three imperial regalia that legitimize the emperor's authority.*

According to a tradition thought to date back to the fifth century, the inner shrine is destroyed every 20 years and rebuilt on an adjacent plot in exactly the same style, but with fresh materials. The old wood is presented to other shrines that have helped finance the rebuilding.

Ice-cold cascades *from a waterfall, one of the many natural phenomena held sacred by Shintoists, purify a religious ascetic performing water austerities, or* suigyo, *and symbolize his regeneration. The thick rope, or* shimenawa, *stretched across the falls is made of rice straw and is a common Shinto symbol defining sacred and pure space. The lengths of folded paper suspended from the rope recall the paper strands attached to the purifying wands used in Shinto rites.*

Pilgrims trek to Ise (ABOVE), *as millions of Japanese have done since the Middle Ages, in this 19th-century Japanese print. Apart from its religious aspect, the pilgrimage to Ise also involved much festivity and merriment at Ise's taverns and brothels. In the late 18th and early 19th centuries, several million pilgrims are known to have converged on the shrine on at least three occasions.*

War and Peace

The period from 1868, when the new Meiji emperor was enthroned, until 1945 witnessed the establishment of Shinto as a state cult. Although there was nominal freedom of worship for other religions, this new political Shinto, stripped of its spiritual trappings, became part of state ideology and a dominant religious force in the country. After World War II, however, all this was to change. State Shinto was dismantled and a new breath of religious freedom was allowed to blow through Japan.

From the start of the Meiji period, Shinto was favoured by the state. Laws were passed to end the Shinto-Buddhist synthesis that had defined religious culture up till this point. The annual programme of imperial ritual was purged of Buddhist influence and politicized to stress the emperor as the descendant of the sun deity Amaterasu and as paragon of loyalty and filial piety – qualities now regarded as essentially Shinto. Buddhist priests and paraphernalia were barred from shrines, which were appropriated by the state.

The government also launched a pro-Shinto, anti-Buddhist propaganda campaign, in which shrine priests preached Shinto's new theology and ethic, and performed state-invented Shinto funeral rites. The state's recognition of Buddhism and new sects, such as Shinto-derived Konkokyo (p.208), was made conditional upon their full participation in the campaign.

However, stubborn resistance by these groups in the 1870s forced the government into an important re-appraisal: Buddhism and the new religions were freed from state control, and although state ritual continued to be Shinto in form, most Shinto shrines were deprived of state support, and priests were banned from preaching and performing funeral rites. With such overt religious manifestations stripped away, Shinto was reformulated as a state cult of loyalty to the *kami*-descended emperor.

Although the 1889 constitution guaranteed religious freedom, it also confirmed the emperor as sovereign of *kami* descent, thus guaranteeing state Shinto's dominance. One year later, the Education Rescript, the cornerstone of state ideology and education until 1945, defined loyalty to him as an absolute value binding all Japanese regardless of creed. And worship of the rescript document and the emperor's portrait was enforced throughout the school system.

Japan's military victories over China and Russia in the 1890s kindled a popular nationalism which helped to spread Shinto's loyalty ethic and turn shrines dedicated to the war dead, such as the Yasukuni shrine in Tokyo, into militaristic cult centres. The state reinstated financial support for other shrines between 1920 and 1945, and Shinto then became, in all but name, a state religion. Those sects that refused to cooperate were suppressed on charges of treason. This state Shinto was a key ingredient in the ultranationalistic spirit that pervaded Japan before and during World War II.

In 1945, after the war, the Allied occupation of Japan resulted in the rapid severance of ties between the state and Shinto. The emperor disclaimed his status as a *kami* and forbade worship of his portrait and the Imperial Rescript. Also, from this time on, all Shinto involvement in education was banned.

The separation of state and religion, as well as religious freedom, were guaranteed in the 1947 constitution. As a result, Shinto ceased to be used in Japanese state ritual, and state sponsorship of shrines was prohibited. Divested of military associations, shrines are protected by the constitution as independent "Religious Juridical

At the Yasukuni shrine (BELOW LEFT) *the spirits of those who have died fighting for Japan – some 2.5 million since the shrine was founded in 1869 – are venerated. Under military control until 1945, it is now independent. Since the war, it has courted controversy for its exaltation of 14 war criminals and the yearly visits of cabinet ministers despite the official separation of religion and state.*

Dressed in traditional wedding clothes, a woman prepares for her shrine wedding, a Shinto rite that began in the 19th century and still continues today. The white symbolizes a new beginning; the typical headpiece, or tsunokakushi, symbolically hides her "horns of anger" at her husband's possible infidelity.

Shinto weddings today usually take place before a portable shrine in a hotel or special wedding hall, and their popularity is being challenged by Christian-style nuptials.

Persons," a status which they now share with all other religions in Japan.

Since the immediate postwar years, Shinto has continued to develop. The state's interest in Shinto has revived, as shown by annual semi-official visits of prime ministers to the Yasukuni shrine to venerate spirits of the war dead. New Shinto-based religions, such as Sekai Kyuseikyo, Sekai Mahikari and Seicho No Ie (pp.208–9), are thriving. And local and national shrines, which seem to have suffered little from wartime associations with the state, today make a major contribution to Japan's vibrant religious culture.

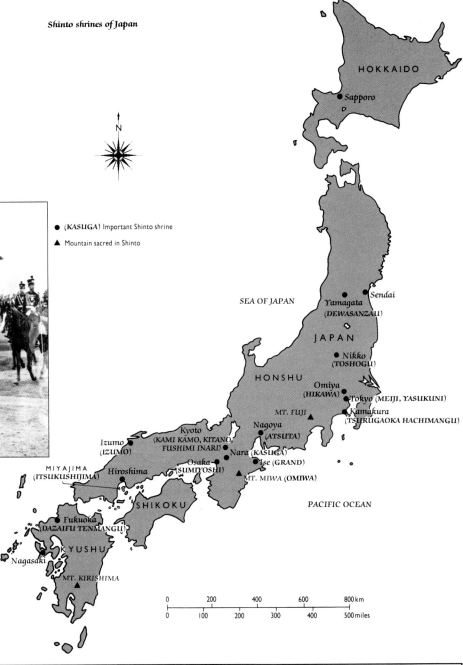

Shinto shrines of Japan

● (KASUGA) Important Shinto shrine

▲ Mountain sacred in Shinto

Emperor Hirohito *heads an army procession, in his capacity as commander-in-chief. At the same time, he was revered as a living deity. Japan was unique among nations in sustaining this belief into the modern era. However, in 1946, Hirohito renounced all claims to divinity in an historic address.*

Shinto shrines in Japan *tend to cluster on the island of Honshu, although there are important sacred sites in Hokkaido and Kyushu. Most shrines are found in areas of great natural beauty; and nature's importance is underlined in the sacredness that is invested in the three mountains of Kirishima, Miwa and Fuji.*

Rituals of state and emperor

With the restoration of the Meiji emperor in 1868, the private Shinto-Buddhist ritual of the imperial court was transformed into a public, exclusively Shinto, state ritual. Buddhist rites for the imperial ancestors ceased, the emperor was no longer initiated into esoteric Buddhism, and the five festivals based on the agricultural cycle were abolished. But harvest rituals were still performed for their political value, including the *Kanname* and *Niiname*. In the *Kanname*, the emperor "worshipped from afar" the shrine of Ise, dedicated to his ancestor

Amaterasu, while in the *Niiname*, the emperor thanked Amaterasu for the harvest and partook of its first fruits with her.

However, many more rites were created, including those that commemorated the death of the mythical first emperor Jinmu and that of Meiji's father, Emperor Komei. The annual cycle stressed not only the emperor's descent from Amaterasu but also the emperor as a paragon of filial piety. Thus the annual memorial rites for Meiji's father were especially important. Japan's national holidays were based on this ritual cycle,

and local shrines had to adjust their own festival programme to accommodate them.

With the separation of religion and state after World War II, Shinto state rituals became the prerogative of the imperial family only. Today, shrines no longer perform state rites, and national holidays are of a more secular nature. The five agricultural festivals have been reinstated, and the government has added others such as Adult's Day, Labour Thanksgiving Day, Culture Day and, somewhat controversially, the Emperor's Birthday and State Foundation Day.

Micropedia

The following section contains entries on some of the more significant movements, sects and philosophies that have branched off from or run alongside mainstream religions, or have evolved from the inspiration and teachings of charismatic individuals. Some movements, such as the Christian Hutterian Brethren, have been established for centuries, while others, such as the Sikh-derived Healthy Happy Holy Organization, are post-World War II phenomena. The entries are listed alphabetically, under their parent religion where appropriate. Cross-references to entries within the section are indicated by SMALL CAPITALS.

——— CHRISTIANITY ———

Aladura churches

Some of the largest and best known of the African Independent churches (p.74) are the Aladura ("praying people") churches. They are prophet-led healing churches that began to emerge in Nigeria after World War I. From Nigeria they spread throughout western Africa, where they are often known as "spirit" churches, and from there to the United States and Europe.

Among the pioneers of the Aladura movement were Moses Orimolade, also known as Baba Aladura; Christianah Abiodun Akinsowon, also known as Captain Abiodun; Pastor Shadare; and Sophia Odunlami. All came from southwestern Nigeria. They were influenced by religious ideas from the United States, in particular the divine healing principle of the Faith Tabernacle Church of Philadelphia. Dissatisfied with the lack of spiritual power in the established mission churches, the founders combined the idea of divine healing with their own indigenous beliefs. This was precipitated by the worldwide influenza epidemic of 1918.

The main emphasis at the outset was healing through prayer and blessed water, and the avoidance of western medicine. These churches were also concerned with making Christianity in Africa more African in character. Existing churches were mostly led by foreign missionaries and were European in attitude and in their patterns of worship.

The Aladura churches rejected little of the doctrinal content of Christianity; it was mainly in the area of ritual and church leadership that they differed from mission Christianity. They also allowed polygamy, although in general they were highly selective in what they took over from indigenous beliefs and practices.

By 1922, there were enough differences from Christian missionary practice to force the separation of a group that became known as the Faith Tabernacle. Major expansion occurred in the 1930s, generated in the main by Joseph Babalola's divine healing movement. Two of the larger and better-known Aladura churches dating from around this time are the Cherubim and Seraphim Society, founded by Moses

Orimolade, and the Church of the Lord, Aladura, started by Josiah Oshitelu, both of whom were Yoruba from southwestern Nigeria. Although some women, known as prophetesses, such as Captain Abiodun, had leading roles in a number of Aladura churches, they rarely became overall leaders of the churches' male and female sections, a position reserved for men.

Anabaptists

The Anabaptists, or rebaptizers, came together as a movement in Zurich in 1525 when George Blaurock, a former Catholic priest, espoused the principle of adult baptism. This was interpreted by the local civil authority and some of the religious leaders, among them Huldreich Zwingli (1484–1531), one of the Swiss protestant reformers, as a symbolic act of defiance. The movement appealed mainly to peasants, and some supported Thomas Münzer (1490–1525; p.60), who tried to link the movement with the Peasants' Revolt (1524–25). The Anabaptists spawned numerous subsects, including the MENNONITES, the largest surviving one, and the Hutterites, or HUTTERIAN BRETHREN.

Anabaptists looked forward to the imminent establishment of the kingdom of God. Some prophesied that the town of Münster in Germany would be the New Jerusalem and that it alone would remain standing when the earth was destroyed in the near future. Under Jan Mattys and Jan Brockelson (also known as John of Leiden), who proclaimed himself the King and Messiah of the Last Days, Anabaptists gained control of Münster and expelled the Catholic and Protestant residents who refused to join their ranks.

A reign of terror followed, during which common ownership of property and polygyny were introduced. Anabaptist rule continued for 18 months until 1535 when Münster fell to besieging forces led by the town's expelled bishop prince.

While awaiting the millennium – a 1,000-year period of peace and prosperity ushered in by Christ – members of the Anabaptist movement, which was never coherent or unified, advocated different forms and

methods of interim government. And while some groups accepted the use of force, others were resolutely pacifist in the pursuit of their goal.

Campus Crusade for Christ

One of the largest of the evangelical Christian mission organizations based in California, Campus Crusade for Christ is now represented on hundreds of university and college campuses throughout North America.

It began in the 1950s as a mission to evangelize college students. However, its founder, Dr. Bill Bright, was determined to extend its ministry overseas and realized that films could be a useful tool in helping him to achieve this goal. Bright developed the idea of the *Jesus* film, based on Luke's Gospel, and found an American tycoon named Baker Hunt to underwrite the $10 million necessary to make it. Over 100 foreign-language versions of the film have already been completed, and it is expected that one billion people will have watched it by the year 2000.

Confident, dynamic and rich, Campus Crusade has close to 20,000 full-time and associate staff members, all of whom are self-supporting, and is active in over 150 countries. It preaches a radically conservative Christianity and is the epitome of the modern American evangelical Protestant mission organization.

Christian Science
(Church of Christ, Scientist)

Founded by Mary Baker Eddy (1821–1910) in New Hampshire, the movement, like many other new religions of the 19th century, aimed to make Christianity "scientific". It developed a system of spiritual healing, which, along with Jesus' ministry of healing, was explained by Eddy in her *Science and Health with a Key to the Scriptures* (1875).

The basic principle of Eddy's teaching was that matter was an illusion and mind alone was real. This extended to the belief that suffering and death were both illusory: no one can die, Christian Scientists maintain, and once this notion is believed salvation comes. Christian

Scientists therefore deny the orthodox doctrines of creation, sin and redemption, maintaining they are unreal.

Eddy owed much to the Swedish philosopher Emanuel Swedenborg (1688–1772), in particular to his ideas that all things are mystically connected and that physical illness is a reflection of discord in a person's spirituality. She also followed Swedenborg in maintaining that the Bible had a meaning other than its literal one.

Christian Science worship is simple and centres on readings from the writings of its founder and accounts of cures from members. The movement has spread from the United States to Europe and parts of the third world, and a daily international newspaper, *The Christian Science Monitor*, is published in Boston.

Coptic Church

According to tradition, St. Mark the Evangelist was the founder and first patriarch of this church, some time in the first century C.E. The name derives from the Greek for Egyptians, *Aiguptioi*, which became *gibt* in Arabic, and was then westernized as Copt. The church has its own calendar of martyrs, which marks its persecution at the hands of Rome. Year one of this calendar (1 *anno martyri*) is 284 C.E., the beginning of the reign of Emperor Diocletian.

Present in Egypt before this time, the Coptic Church produced a number of prestigious centres of theological learning. Among them was the Catechetical School of Alexandria where much of early Christian doctrine was first expounded, including the doctrines of the Trinity and the incarnation. The list of great thinkers from this school, and others of its kind, includes Clement of Alexandria, Origen, Heraclas, Cyril of Alexandria, Apollos, and Athanasius, after whom the main creed used in the western church was named.

Once a powerful intellectual and spiritual influence on the Christian world, the church was curtailed by the Council of Chalcedon (451) which condemned its "monophysite" formula that suggested that after the incarnation Christ had only one nature – a divine one – not two, that is, one divine and one human.

Following Chalcedon, the Coptic Church was persecuted, severely weakening Christianity in Egypt and facilitating the later Muslim conquest of northern Africa in the seventh century. Many Copts moved to the desert to join some of the earliest Christian monastic communities, based on the rule of St. Pachomius (*c*.290–346).

Missionary work brought the Coptic Church to Ethiopia in the fourth century and to Nubia (western Sudan) in the sixth. It later spread to Khartoum in Sudan where there is now a large Coptic community. The Ethiopian Church remained in union with the Coptic Church in Egypt until the Italian conquest of Ethiopia in 1936. Thereafter it became an independent Orthodox church – in the tradition of the Eastern Orthodox Church – but retained the monophysite doctrine. There is no link between this church and the Ethiopian Churches similar to ZIONIST churches. About 30 million strong today, the Copts regard themselves as the true descendants of the ancient Egyptians.

House Church Movement

One of the fastest-growing new religions in Britain in the early 1980s, the House Church Movement consists of a collection of Christian fellowships ranging from hard-line fundamentalists to more liberal evangelical Christian organizations. It formed out of the charismatic renewal movement of the Protestant and Anglican churches, and its name derives from the fact that people initially gathered in their homes to worship. As numbers increased, fellowships moved into public auditoriums and small churches to accommodate members.

Much of the fellowships' teaching is derived from Pentecostalism (p.82). Many of them are, however, distinguishable by their emphasis on the controversial practice of "shepherding", or strict pastoral supervision. This is based on the belief that the leaders command the same authority as the New Testament Apostles, and should be strictly obeyed. The movement is also known by other names, such as the Pyramid Church, because of its rigid hierarchy of "shepherds"; and its adherents are sometimes termed "Restorationists", owing to their belief that God is about to restore his kingdom.

Many of the fellowships have grown into large groups with several thousand members who carry out street evangelism. Most of them are best understood as new churches outside the existing denominations.

Hutterian Brethren

This sect, founded in the 1530s by the former ANABAPTIST pastor Jacob Hutter from the Tyrol in Switzerland, is perhaps unique among Christian groups in having maintained a strict communitarian lifestyle from its beginnings. This has been preserved intact despite its many migrations – forced upon it by persecution – from its homeland in Moravia, through Russia, to North America. Here, it has become established among farming communities in western parts of the United States and Canada.

Hutterites believe that true Christianity can be practised only in communal living, sharing all possessions. Other fundamental beliefs are admission to the community through adult baptism and absolute pacifism. The language of everyday life is a Tyrolean dialect, whereas worship is conducted in German or English.

Hutterite communities take little interest in education beyond the primary level, except in the study of their own works and traditions. Once the membership of a community reaches 150, it is split. A new colony is then formed and handed over to the care of an elected minister, who becomes its moral guide and is assisted by a household steward.

Jehovah's Witnesses

Founded by Charles Taze Russell (1852–1916) in Pittsburgh, Pennsylvania, the Jehovah's Witness movement is an example of an American millenarian religion, that is, one believing in a future 1,000-year reign of blessedness. Russell was succeeded by Joseph Franklin "Judge" Rutherford (1869–1941).

The Witnesses believe that Armageddon, the final battle of the nations depicted in the biblical books of Daniel and Revelation, is imminent and that at its end Jehovah's Witnesses will reign with Christ. Other churches will be under the dominion of Satan. The Witnesses reject a number of beliefs held by mainstream Christian churches, including the belief in the Trinity, or three persons in one God. They also reject the belief that Jesus was God by nature and instead insist that he received the status of Son of God because of his perfect goodness.

The Witnesses have a simple lifestyle. They prohibit blood transfusion as well as stimulants. Their pacifism, hostility to secular political institutions, and professed allegiance to God alone have frequently brought them into conflict with civil authorities. They are aggressively evangelical and their magazine – *The Watchtower* – purports "to interpet world events as the fulfilment of Bible prophecy".

Kimbanguist Church

This church was founded in 1921 in the Belgian Congo, now Zaire, by a former Baptist, Simon Kimbangu (1889–1951). The church, whose full name is L'Eglise de Jesus Christ par le Prophète Simon Kimbangu (The Church of Jesus Christ by the Prophet Simon Kimbangu), was admitted to the World Council of Churches in 1969.

Great importance is accorded to the figure of the church's founding prophet, which is a controversial issue with some of the western churches. During the worldwide influenza epidemic of 1918, Kimbangu is said to have received several callings from God to tend the sick. After repeatedly ignoring these divine messages, he eventually, in 1921, healed a sick woman, and subsequent miracle cures brought him fame throughout the Belgian Congo.

Kimbangu was imprisoned for a short time by the Belgian colonial authorities, who feared an uprising. In spite of this, his following grew rapidly. Today the church has an estimated three million members in Zaire and the adjacent countries and is also found in western Europe and the United States.

Micropedia

Mennonites

Historically and theologically, the Mennonites are the direct descendants of the ANABAPTISTS, a radical reform group of the first quarter of the 16th century. The Mennonites, who espouse absolute pacifism, owe their name to Countess Anna of Friesland, who called them after their leader Menno Simons (1496–1561) in order to distinguish them from the more radical, militant Anabaptist groups.

The Mennonites have, over time, drawn up numerous "Confessions". One of the main ones is the Brotherly Union (1527), which decrees that the Bible is the final authority in all matters of faith and stresses that new birth, in the form of adult baptism and separation from the world, is an essential part of their faith.

Much persecuted by church and state alike for their so-called anarchic views and lifestyle, the Mennonites were forced to emigrate from northern Germany and the Netherlands across Germany, Poland, the Ukraine and Russia to North America. After a long period of isolation, an increase in missionary activity has now brought their numbers up to around 750,000 worldwide. Noted for their skill in farming, they are today becoming increasingly involved outside their own communities in peace and environmental issues, a trend which could lead to a conflict with their principle of separation from the world. A more conservative branch of the Mennonites, the OLD ORDER AMISH, is known to resist any involvement with world affairs.

Mormons (Church of Jesus Christ of Latter-Day Saints)

This movement was founded in New York in 1830 by the visionary Joseph Smith (1805–44), who claimed to have translated the revealed Book of Mormon. This purported to be an ancient text containing lost wisdom which supplemented the Bible. Smith also claimed that in 1842 he translated an ancient Egyptian manuscript, the *Book of Abraham*, which had fallen into his hands seven years earlier.

Mormon headquarters has been in Salt Lake City, Utah, since Mormons made their way there in 1846–47 under the leadership of Brigham Young (1801–77), who succeeded Joseph Smith. Although Mormons espouse a vigorous work ethic and are banned from smoking and drinking alcohol and caffeine-containing beverages such as tea and coffee, sports, recreation and education play an important part in their lives. They also place emphasis on missionary work.

In the early years, much about Mormonism, including polygyny, which was only made public in 1852 and was abandoned some 40 years later, remained unknown. Some practices, such as endowment – a ritual initiation ceremony – and baptism of the dead, were even kept hidden from the majority of members. Both baptism and marriage can be conferred on the dead to "seal" them in the faith.

Unlike other American new religions of its time, the Mormon Church built up an elaborate hierarchy. However, Mormonism provides a typical American form of millenarianism, or the belief, in its narrow sense, that Jesus Christ will reign for 1,000 years on earth during which time Satan will be subdued. According to Mormonism, Jesus Christ was revealed to early immigrants in America, and it is there that he will establish his millennium.

In the late 20th century, some 80 percent of the movement's five million followers live in the United States, with the rest in Canada, South America, Europe and Oceania.

Old Order Amish

This movement emerged as a distinctive branch of the MENNONITES in Switzerland in the 1690s. The Mennonite elder, Jakob Ammann (1644–1725), led a breakaway group which refused to have any social contact with excommunicated church members.

Amish communities, or colonies, which are not all entirely uniform in their beliefs, practice and lifestyle, endorse with varying degrees of rigour the principle of *meidung*, or separation, from society. They believe that salvation can be gained only within the community. Other central tenets and practices of the Amish are non-resistance; acceptance of Christ as the supreme model and exemplar of human conduct; obedience to the Bible and the church; and the avoidance of all worldly pleasures, amusements and vanities.

Many of the European Amish communities have returned to the mainstream Mennonite fold, and only those that have migrated to the United States have continued with their distinctive lifestyle. These communities – located mainly in Pennsylvania, Ohio, Delaware, Iowa, Indiana and Michigan – are distinguishable by their conservative dress, for example, they use hooks and eyes in preference to buttons and wear caped dresses and bonnets. Some, moreover, will not use "modern" inventions such as the rubber tyre or electric drill.

Seventh-Day Adventists

This group is the best known of the 19th-century Adventist ("believers in Christ's Second Coming") movements that grew up in the United States. These stem from the teachings of William Miller (1782–1849), who prophesied the imminent return of Christ.

Miller's prophecy of Christ's return some time between March 21, 1843, and March 21, 1844, based on his studies of the books of Daniel and Revelation, aroused considerable euphoria in its day. By 1843, a multitude of Adventist groups had sprung up, with some 100,000 members. This number, though, fell dramatically when both this prophecy and a revised prediction of October 22, 1844, based upon a reinterpretation of scripture, proved to be unfulfilled.

After "the great disappointment", as the failed prediction came to be known, the remaining groups joined to form the Seventh-Day Adventists under the leadership of Joseph Bates and James and Ellen White. The group keeps the seventh day of the week, that is, Saturday, as the Sabbath, instead of the first day, Sunday, hence the derivation of the name.

Seventh-Day Adventists believe Christ will return and inaugurate a millennial, or 1,000-year, reign in heaven, at the end of which the wicked will be annihilated along with Satan, while believers will lead a blessed new life on earth. Great emphasis is placed on cleansing the body and spirit of harmful elements in preparation for this. Alcohol, tobacco and meat are forbidden, and strictly no work is to be done on the Sabbath, which has sometimes resulted in job discrimination against members.

The movement now has a worldwide membership, and its evangelistic literature is translated into more than 500 languages.

Zionist and Ethiopian churches

Zionist churches emerged in southern Africa around the time that the ALADURA CHURCHES began to spring up in western Africa, after World War I. They did not begin as breakaway movements but grew up around a prophet-healer. One of the more remarkable and well known of these was Isaiah Shembe (d.c.1960), the Zulu prophet-healer who founded the Church of Ama Nazaretha.

Zionist churches derive their name from the Christian Catholic Apostolic Church in Zion, founded in Chicago in 1896, which sent missionaries to Africa at the beginning of the 20th century. Emphasis is placed on a continuing pentecostal revelation of the Holy Spirit, with its prophetic and healing power, and the imminent Second Coming of Christ. Exorcism and repeated baptisms are common healing rites.

The Zionist churches developed essentially as a protest against white control of the Christian church in Africa. They also stood against the lack of opportunity for black Christians to rise in the church hierarchy and assume positions of leadership and responsibility.

Similar to the Zionist churches were the Ethiopian churches that sprung up all over the African continent, but particularly in southern Africa, at around the same time. The fact that Ethiopia means "black" and that the country remained independent until 1936 made the name a powerful symbol of independence from foreign rule.

Ahmadiyya

A reforming and modernizing movement, the Ahmadiyya was established in 1889 by Ghulam Ahmad (c.1839–1908) at Qadian in the Punjab, India. As advances were being made in the Punjab by Protestant Christians and Hindus, Ghulam Ahmad attempted to revitalize Islam. He claimed to be the Mahdi, that is, the one sent by God to guarantee justice and peace on earth and the triumph of Islam, and also claimed to be the Christian Messiah, as well as an incarnation of the Hindu god Krishna.

Furthermore, he told his followers that he was a prophet and that the age of genuine prophecy had not ended with the founder of Islam, Muhammad, who is known as the "seal of the prophets" by orthodox Sunni Muslims. Other Ahmadi tenets, which Sunni Muslims regard as unorthodox, include their interpretation of *jihad* ("holy war") as a campaign by peaceful, rather than military, methods, and their belief about the death and resurrection of Jesus Christ. Ahmadis maintain that Jesus did not die on the cross but was taken down while unconscious and resuscitated. He then went to Kashmir to teach and died there at the age of 120.

The Ahmadiyya split into two factions over the understanding of Ahmad's status: the Qadianis, who accepted him as a prophet and followed his teachings, and the Lahoris, who accepted him only as a reformer, not as a prophet. Following the partition of India in 1947, the Qadianis settled in Rabwah and the Lahoris in Lahore. Both wings are strongly missionary and insist on the importance of combining western and Islamic education. Ahmadi communities can be found in western Africa, Asia and throughout the west.

Bahaism

Founded by Baha Ullah (1817–92) in Iran in the second half of the 19th century, Bahaism has its roots in Babism, a Muslim sect in Iran that claimed to have exclusive knowledge of final truth. Bahaism places emphasis on missionary work, the unity of all religions, world peace, education, equality of the sexes and monogamy. It has no set doctrines, no priesthood, no formal public ritual and no authoritative scriptures.

Baha Ullah, born Mirza Husayn Ali Nuri, was originally a Babi, a follower of Babism, who claimed to be a manifestation of God. He succeeded as co-leader Mirza Ali Muhammad (c.1819–50), who had proclaimed himself to be the Bab, or "gateway", to the Hidden Imam (p.109) and who saw himself as the beginning of a new cycle of prophets to follow the Prophet Muhammad. In 1850, however, he was executed for attempting to seize power in Iran.

Baha Ullah turned what was essentially an authoritarian offshoot within Shiism (pp.90–91) into a movement that sought to embrace all faiths in a nondogmatic way. After his death, his son Abdul Baha (1844–1920) led the movement, which spread beyond the Middle East. Currently an oppressed religion in Iran, Bahais are found mainly in North America, Europe and Africa.

Hizbollah (The Party of God)

Notorious for its role in hostage-taking in Lebanon in the 1980s, the Hizbollah movement came into existence in Lebanon in 1982 under Shaykh Muhammad Husain Fadlallah, known as al-Qaid (the "just jurist"). Until the triumph of the Islamic revolution in Iran in 1979 and the Israeli invasion of southern Lebanon in 1982, Hizbollah had been little more than an idea in Fadlallah's mind. By 1983, he had become the leading political and religious figure among Shiite militants and one of the three most prominent Shiite clerics in Lebanon. By 1985, he had reached the position of Ayatollah, a title held by high-ranking figures in Shiite Islam.

The organization of the movement consists of a consultative council of 12 members, the majority of whom are Muslim clerics; the others are military personnel. In the 1980s and early 1990s, when there was deadlock on major policy issues, the council appealed to Iran for a decision. There are also specialist committees dealing with specific areas such as finance, ideology, politics, military affairs, intelligence, and judicial and social affairs. When engaged in underground terrorist operations, the movement has used the code name Islamic Jihad ("holy war"). Some members of Hizbollah regard the ISLAMIC AMAL movement as part of the Hizbollah fraternity, or community.

Prominent figures in Hizbollah include Shaykh Muhammad Mahdi Shams al-Din, Ibrahim al-Amin and Subhi al-Tufaili, all clergymen from the Bekaa Valley. In June 1992, a new overall leader named Shaykh Hassan Nasrallah was appointed at the comparatively young age of 31.

Islamic Amal

The formation in 1975 of the Amal movement – an acronym for the Arabic for Groups of the Lebanese Resistance – by Imam Musa al-Sadr marked the beginning of the rise of militant Shiism in Lebanon. The Amal is the military wing of the group known as the Movement of the Oppressed. Amal members were trained by Palestinian guerrillas primarily to overthrow the powerful ruling land-owning families in southern Lebanon under the pretext of defending southern Lebanon from the Israelis.

By the beginning of the 1980s, four events in particular had radicalized the movement, turning it into a major military and political force in Lebanon. In 1978, the Amal imam, or religious head, disappeared in Libya, and Israel invaded Lebanon. The following year, the Ayatollah Khomeini's rule (pp.118–19) began in Iran; and in 1980, Nabih Berri took over the leadership of Amal. As a result of his close relations with Syria, Berri was provided with military training and weapons for his men.

Amal is run on a regional basis under the overall control of an executive committee. However, the movement lacks cohesion and suffers from intense rivalry at the top.

Ismaili Khojas

This group was originally composed largely of converts from Hinduism to Islam in what is now India and Pakistan in the 14th century. The name Khoja refers to the Hindu caste from which they came and is not a religious term. Today, Ismaili Khojas live mainly in western India, central Asia, eastern Africa, North America and western Europe.

The Ismaili Khojas believe their imam, or religious leader, is infallible and strive to follow his *firmans*, or instructions, which may be modern in content. One, for example, advises that "only education is of any use". For Ismailis, the mosque is known as the Jamat Khana; and the imam gives each member a *boll* (a secret word personal to them), which they meditate on daily.

Subdivisions have occurred among the Ismaili Khojas who are often not regarded in Sunni circles as orthodox Muslims, but a majority continue to follow the leadership of the Aga Khan, the title of the spiritual head of the Nizari branch of the Ismaili sect (pp.96–97).

Muslim Brotherhood

Egyptian Islamic activism in the 20th century has its roots in the Muslim Brotherhood, or Ikhwan, founded by the Egyptian schoolteacher Hasan al-Banna in 1928 to bring about an Islamic order in Egypt (pp.116–17). It aimed to purify Islamic society by rejecting western secular attitudes and demanding a return to original Islamic lifestyle as laid down in the Qur'an and the *hadith*, or Muslim tradition. In its most militant phase, from 1945 to 1954, the Brotherhood was implicated in the assassination of its political opponents, and it was outlawed by the government following an attempt on President Nasser's life in 1954.

The Brotherhood began to re-emerge in public with the defeat of Egypt by Israel in 1967; its older members endorsed a strategy of non-violence, something that the younger members generally opposed. Although, in the early 1990s, it is still banned, the Brotherhood has effectively enjoyed official recognition since the 1970s. It was critical of President Anwar Sadat's peace initiative with Israel in 1978, but it was not implicated in his assassination in October 1981. This was the work of al-Jihad, founded in 1978 and one of a number of militant Islamic groups to emerge in Egypt at the time.

Neo-Sufism

This term refers to the practice of Sufism (pp.98–99), a form of Islamic mysticism, in the west in the 20th century. One of the leading exponents of Neo-Sufism is Idries Shah (1924–) who, while using traditional Sufi methods of teaching such as story-telling, aims to relate these teachings in a way that the western mind can understand.

Deeply rooted in Islam, Neo-Sufis seek much of their inspiration from the Qur'an. However, many would claim that Sufism predates Islam. The oldest order in the west, established by the Indian Pir Valyat Inyat Khan, is linked to the Indian Khwaji Muinuddin Order. One of the central messages of the Neo-Sufis is that of universal religion, that "God is one", a notion found in New Age and other new religions.

Subud

This movement was begun in Indonesia in 1933 by a Javanese civil servant named Muhammad Subuh (1901–87), who claimed to have received a divine revelation of the power of God. A student of Sufism (mystical Islam) as a youth, he later became known to his followers simply as Bapak ("father"). Many miracles, including cures of sickness, were attributed to him.

The Subud movement sees itself as a symbol of the "possibility for man to follow the right way of living". Its principal ritual is the *latihan kejiwaan* ("spiritual exercise"), which purports to help the "outer" and "inner" person, heal, correct character defects, and foster love and compassion. In this ritual, which is practised communally twice a week, the individual surrenders his or her own will to the will of God. Members allow the divine power to express itself through spontaneous activity, such as singing, dancing and shouting, for purposes of personal and group therapy. Successful enterprises – and Subud has many – are considered proof of the efficacy of the *latihan*.

Bapak was invited to Cyprus and England in 1957 and later travelled to the United States, Australia and elsewhere in the western world. He died in Jakarta in 1987.

—— HINDUISM AND SIKHISM ——

Brahma Kumaris World Spiritual University

The Brahma Kumaris movement was founded in 1937 in Hyderabad, central India, by a diamond merchant named Dada Lekhraj (1876–1969), also known as Brahma Baba. The movement is mainly composed of women – the word *kumari* means "unmarried woman" – since they are believed to be more spiritual, sensitive and patient than men and therefore better suited for teaching.

The Brahma Kumaris begin their teaching by talking to new members about the Supreme Soul, known as Shiv Baba, who possesses all the attributes of perfection, love, purity, power, bliss and peace. Shiv Baba is the re-creator of the universe and enables souls to achieve perfection and entry into the "golden age", a paradise of endless happiness that will come about on earth.

The movement is dualistic, that is, it maintains that the body is merely the garment of the soul, and members recite "I am a soul, my body is a garment" many times a day. Its chief characteristic, which sets the movement apart from ordinary life, is celibacy. This is recommended even within marriage, since sexual activity of any kind is equated with lustfulness. The Brahma Kumaris maintain that celibacy also confers spiritual power and social advantage on women and provides the means for them to develop their spirituality.

On the death of its founder, the movement began to spread to the west. Today, it has numerous meditation centres in all the main cities of western Europe and North America.

Hare Krishna (International Society for Krishna Consciousness; ISKCON)

One of the more visible of the new religions of Indian origin, ISKCON was founded in the United States in 1966 by His Divine Grace A. C. Bhaktivedanta, also known as Swami Prabhupada (1896–1977). Although new to the west, ISKCON follows the devotional path taught by the Bengali guru Caitanya (1486–1533) who based his beliefs and practices on the Hindu scripture the *Bhagavad Gita*, which dates back to before the common era.

ISKCON followers practise a form of *bhakti* yoga, devotion to a personal god through love, in which the focus of worship is the god Krishna and not, as is the case in traditional Hinduism, Vishnu. Krishna is worshipped not as an impersonal force, but as a personal god who incarnates himself in living entities.

The principal form of devotion is the congregational chanting (*kirtana*) of the names of God. The main mantra, or sacred verse, is the *maha* mantra: "Hare Krishna Hare Krishna, Krishna Krishna, Hare Hare, Hare Rama, Hare Rama, Rama Rama, Hare Hare." The chanting of this by followers in many capital cities gave the movement the name Hare Krishna, by which it is best known. There is also devotional service (*sankirtana*), which involves worship as well as teaching, cooking, gardening and distributing literature in exchange for donations.

The Hare Krishna teach that the individual is a spark of Krishna, of the divine, and is of the same nature as, but separate from, God. The real self is the soul, which is immortal and is reincarnated successively until *karma* runs its

course, ending the cycle of birth and rebirth. Followers are initiated at a Hare Krishna temple in a ceremony which binds the disciple to a guru for life. The novice vows to observe the main principles of Krishna consciousness: abstinence from meat, fish, eggs and intoxicants; no sexual relations, except within marriage, and then only for procreation; no gambling; chanting for 16 rounds on *japa* beads each day and reading for an hour from the works of the founder. Male devotees also shave their heads except for a topknot, by means of which, they believe, Krishna will draw them up to heaven at the time of the deliverance of the world.

Healthy Happy Holy Organization (3HO Foundation)

A customs official and, later, an Interpol officer, Harbhajan Singh Khalsa Yogi (1929–), also known as Yogi Bhajan, started the 3HO Foundation in Los Angeles, California, in 1969. His aim was to teach traditional Sikhism combined with a form of yoga that aims to awaken and release *kundalini* energy, which underlies sexual energy and the higher forms of consciousness. The movement is the educational arm of the Sikh Dharma organization which Yogi Bhajan founded in Pakistan.

By 1975, an estimated 20,000 North Americans living in some 100 self-supporting, self-sufficient ashrams, or religious retreats, had adopted the Sikh lifestyle through contact with 3HO. All members are expected to become teachers. In the early 1990s, however, numbers of those living in a community dropped, to around 5,000 at most. Moreover, the links with

Indian Sikhism have been weakened because 3HO refuses to support the Sikh campaign for their own homeland in India.

Sathya Sai Baba Movement
Named for its founder, Sathya Sai Baba (1926–) of Puttaparti, India, the movement is one of the most successful of the new Indian religions. This is true both in India and in parts of Europe – including Great Britain – where it began to spread in the late 1960s, particularly among Hindu immigrants from the subcontinent. Sai Baba has acquired a reputation as a remarkable miracle worker and claims to be the reincarnation of the holy man Sai Baba of Shirdi (c.1856–1918), who had a large following by the time of his death.

The movement's teachings differ little from those of mainstream Hinduism, but it stresses four aspects in particular: establishing the faith on a firm foundation, fostering scholarship, preserving the Vedic scriptures, and keeping its adherents from materialism and secularism. Devotees are mainly concerned with venerating their founder and recounting his miracles. Most try at some time to attend a *darshan*, or audience, with Sai Baba at the movement's headquarters in Prasanthi Nilayam in India.

Swaminarayana
This movement originated in Gujarat, in western India, in the early 19th century. It teaches that its founder, Sahajananda Swami or Swami Naraya (1781–1830), a religious reformer in Gujarat, is the perfect manifestation of God. Swami Naraya taught that God exists in human form in his eternal abode and manifests freely when needed, possibly in more than one form. Among the images of God most worshipped and revered are Krishna and Rama.

There are various grades of Swaminarayana membership, with appropriate initiation rites for each one: entry into the ascetic state, for example, is symbolized through the rites of shaving, bathing and the putting on of new clothes. Members renounce the world and much of their time is given over to study of Vedic and Sanskrit religious texts. As a result of their belief in *ahimsa*, the doctrine of non-violence and non-killing, they are strictly vegetarian and animal sacrifice is prohibited. They are also opposed to the consumption of alcohol.

The Swaminarayana movement in the west has spread mainly through immigration and, since the 1960s, it has become one of the fastest-growing new Hindu movements, appealing mainly to immigrants of Gujarati origin.

Transcendental Meditation (TM)
One of the first and best known of the new religions – although it regards itself as more of a technique than a religion – Transcendental Meditation was started in India by a monk, Maharishi Mahesh Yogi (c.1911), in 1958. The following year he began teaching his philosophy in the west, his aim being to improve through meditation both the individual and society in general. The movement, known colloquially as TM, grew slowly in the west until it was popularized by the Beatles rock group in the late 1960s. Since then, it has developed its meditation-based programme known as the Science of Creative Intelligence and formed the political Natural Law Party, which contested several hundred seats during the British general elections in 1992.

TM has a simple rite of initiation, during which members are given a secret Sanskrit mantra upon which they meditate daily, to induce a feeling of deep relaxation, leading to greater vitality and creativity. TM also runs a number of courses in which various techniques and powers, including what TM instructors call levitation, may be acquired. The movement maintains that the effectiveness of its techniques can be proved scientifically.

— BUDDHISM —

Friends of the Western Buddhist Order (FWBO)
The FWBO aims to make Buddhist teachings and practices accessible to people brought up in western culture, irrespective of their association with a particular country or tradition.

The founder of the FWBO, the British-born Venerable Maha Sthavira Sangharakshita, formerly Denis P. E. Lingwood (1925–), was ordained a Theravada monk in 1950 and thereafter underwent various initiations of Tibetan Buddhism. When Sangharakshita opened the first Friends of the Western Buddhist Order centre in London in 1967, his aim was to create a Buddhist *sangha*, or spiritual community, in the west. The FWBO has refused to insist on the dominance of any one particular form of Buddhism with regard to hierarchy, ceremonies, social custom, lifestyle, dress and language.

By 1968, a number of committed members had been ordained by the Venerable Sangharakshita, and the FWBO began to found an ever-increasing number of FWBO centres that run courses not only on Buddhism and meditation, but also on business ethics. The FWBO also engages in a variety of social action programmes, both in the west and in India. While the number of full-time committed members is small – there is no active proselytizing – the number of Friends continues to grow at a steady pace.

Reiyukai (Association of Friends of the Spirit)
Begun in 1925 by Kakutaro Kubo (1892–1944) and Kimi Kotani (1901–71), this religion largely bases its teachings on the *Lotus Sutra* and so shares much in common with other Japanese new religions of the Nichiren tradition (pp.162–63). However, Reiyukai stresses ancestor worship, which it regards as crucial to its belief in the family as the centre of human life. Moreover, its followers believe that suffering and evil are the result of neglect of the ancestors to whom, along with all other buddhas and spirits of the universe, people are indissolubly linked. They also maintain that by reading the *Lotus Sutra* it is possible to obtain merit for their ancestors.

Reiyukai worshippers also believe that the scrolls produced by their founders and Nichiren contain spiritual power. Through reading them, believers can gain access to the buddhas and to the *bodhisattvas*, those enlightened beings who delay their entry into Nirvana in order to help suffering humanity.

Reiyukai, with its estimated two million followers, is deeply committed to social and welfare programmes. Its principal place of worship is the Shaka Temple in Tokyo.

Rissho Kosei Kai (Society for Establishing Righteousness and Friendly Relations)
A splinter group of REIYUKAI, Rissho Kosei Kai was founded in 1938 by Nikkyo Niwano (1906–), a milk dealer, who became its leader, along with a pious housewife, Myoko Naganuma (1889–1957). Its teachings, like those of its parent body, are based on the *Lotus Sutra* and so also resemble SOKA GAKKAI.

The society believes that religion is the basis for individual and collective growth, peace, stability and prosperity. This explains the movement's involvement in such organizations as the World Conference of Religion and Peace. The sect has an estimated five million members, and its headquarters and principal temple is the Great Hall situated in Tokyo, in which daily services are attended by up to 10,000 people, chanting in unison.

Micropedia

Soka Gakkai (Value Creation Society)
The largest of the Japanese new religions, Soka Gakkai was started in 1930 by Tsunesaburo Makiguchi (1871–1934), a teacher from Hokkaido in northern Japan. Makiguchi developed a theory of education that was based on the teachings of the 13th-century Buddhist monk Nichiren (pp.162–63), who regarded the text known as the *Lotus Sutra* as the final and supreme embodiment of Buddhist truth.

The religion has two main rituals. The first involves the worship of a mandala, or *gohonzon*, believed to have been inscribed by Nichiren on a sacred scroll which is housed in the main temple of the movement at Taiseki-ji near Mount Fuji. The second ritual, known as the *daimoku* invocation, consists of chanting twice daily before a shrine: "I salute the *Lotus Sutra*."

As with other Japanese movements, Soka Gakkai makes great use of art, music, dance and education to spread its message. It also lays emphasis on protecting the environment and establishing a lasting peace through inner spiritual growth.

Soka Gakkai is a lay organization and has legal recognition in over 150 countries, including the United States where it is known as Nichiren Shoshu of America. In 1964 it established its own political party, Komeito (Clean Government Party), which some 20 years later had become the third-largest political party in Japan.

— SHINTO —

Konkokyo (Golden Light)
This movement was established in 1859 by Bunjiro Kawate (1814–83), who received numerous divine revelations. One of these revelations disclosed that human prosperity was the principal concern of the Parent God of the Universe, who would be rendered morally imperfect if he failed to bestow wealth.

Konkokyo, like TENRIKYO, diverges from Shinto in teaching that there is a mediator between God and humans. Kawate believed that he was appointed mediator by the deity Konko to take on the pain and suffering of Kawate's followers and transfer them to God. Since the time of Kawate, the mediator – in whom the Spirit of God is believed to dwell – has always been a descendant of the founder. Konkokyo membership is estimated at about half a million, and its main temple is in Asaguchi city.

Omotokyo (The Great Origin)
The founder of this movement, a woman named Nao Deguchi (1836–1918), was at one time a member of KONKOKYO and preached a similar message. During the leadership of her "adopted" son Onisaburo Deguchi (1871–1948), Omotokyo began to develop its own distinctive character. Onisaburo Deguchi propounded the Three Great Rules of Learning: the body of God is nature; the energy of God is the source of the universe's movement; and every living creature possesses the soul of the true God. Thus from the last rule, it follows that every living thing is divine. Onisaburo Deguchi also preached the imminent arrival of the kingdom of God.

Frequently imprisoned for his opposition to government policy, Onisaburo Deguchi made peace a fundamental concern of Omotokyo. He also sought closer links with Christianity and stressed the indispensable connection between religion and art, insisting that the latter was the mother of the former.

Despite its relatively small membership – some 150,000 adherents – Omotokyo has had a strong impact on Japanese society and has been an inspiration for other Japanese new religions, including SEICHO NO IE and SEKAI KYUSEIKYO. It has two principal temples, one at Kameoka and the other at Ayabe in Kyoto prefecture.

Seicho No Ie (House of Growth)
Founded by Masaharu Taniguchi (b.1893), a former member of OMOTOKYO, Seicho No Ie's principal object of worship is known as the Great God of the House of Growth – that is, growth in both spiritual and material terms. In 1930, Taniguchi set up a publishing house and began publishing his teachings. His words are regarded as divine and are believed to have the power to heal, so they are frequently read aloud. His writings drew much inspiration from John's Gospel in the New Testament and from CHRISTIAN SCIENCE and NEW THOUGHT.

Seicho No Ie is concerned mainly with healing. It regards sickness as an illusion, or a "deceit of the mind", which can be overcome by spiritual means and by the healing power of the word.

Once an ultranationalist movement, and given over to emperor worship, Seicho No Ie has become more international in outlook. It has modified its stance toward the emperor whom it now regards as the centre of the Japanese nation only, not a living god. The movement emphasizes that self-development and self-transformation are vital if society is to be changed. It seeks to promote a deeper consciousness of the divine spark within and of the individual's almost unlimited potential for effecting change and bringing about the New Age.

Seicho No Ie is found in many countries. In Japan its following is about three million; its main temples are in Nagasaki and Uji in Kyoto.

Sekai Kyuseikyo (Church of World Messianity)
This movement, founded in 1934 by a former member of OMOTOKYO named Mokichi Okada, is, like SEICHO NO IE, concerned primarily with healing. Critical of western medicine, Okada developed a theory of healing which relates sickness to a phenomenon he called "spiritual clouds" and prescribed, among other things, the use of herbal medicine to remove such "clouds". The principal healing ritual is *jorei*, in which an authorized member, wearing an amulet called *ohihari*, raises the palm of her/his hand toward the patient to effect a cure.

Sekai Kyuseikyo has about one million members, a growing number of them in the west and the third world, especially Brazil and Thailand. Its main temples are in Atami and Hakore, situated between Kyoto and Tokyo, where it has built models representing paradise.

Sekai Mahikari Bunmei Kyodan (World True Light Civilization)
Mahikari was begun in 1959 by Yoshikazu Okada (1901–74) and, like SEICHO NO IE and SEKAI KYUSEIKYO, is a Japanese new religion whose main concern is healing. It focuses mainly on the transmission of healing Light in the purification ritual of *okiyome*, which all who have been initiated can perform.

In the *okiyome* ritual, the person administering the Light and the initiate receiving it kneel facing each other. The initiate then recites a prayer to awaken the disease-causing spirits, and the Light, which wakens the spirits, is transmitted for a full 10 minutes.

Mahikari maintains that spirits are the prime cause of disease and sickness. Restless spirits – ancestors, the victims of a person's ancestors, or enemies in a previous life – are believed to possess and afflict the living out of revenge or from ignorance. There is also a belief in reincarnation and that present pain may be due to activity in a past life.

The movement believes that the current world situation is one of crisis. In vivid biblical and Buddhist imagery, it admonishes people to embrace its teachings now if they wish to be saved, that is, to be healthy and wealthy.

Its membership is around 50,000, which is small compared to the size of most other Japanese new religious movements. Its headquarters is in Takayama city.

Tenrikyo (Heavenly Wisdom)

The largest and most successful modern Shinto sect in Japan, Tenrikyo was founded during a period of religious revival in the 19th century by Miki Nakayama (1798–1887), a peasant woman. From 1837 onward, Nakayama received supernatural revelations, which foretold the imminent advent of the kingdom of heaven and an end to sickness and poverty. The movement appealed mainly to those farming communities that had lost their property and status during the land reform programme under the Meiji government (1868–1912).

Tenrikyo is based on a belief in God the Parent, who is creator and sustainer of the universe and all life. Miki Nakayama is both the shrine of, and the mediator between, God and humanity. It is in this notion of a mediator that Tenrikyo diverges from Shintoism.

Like other Japanese new movements, Tenrikyo places Japan at the centre of the universe and depicts the Japanese as the original and supreme race – ideas compatible with the nationalistic outlook of the Meiji rulers. The movement's headquarters and main temple are in Jiba, in Tenri city, but churches have been established in other countries, including the United States, Brazil, Korea, China and the Philippines.

NEW THOUGHT, NEW AGE & MODERN "SECULAR" RELIGIONS

Church Universal and Triumphant (CUT)

A NEW AGE group inspired by teachings of the THEOSOPHICAL SOCIETY, CUT emerged in Washington, D.C., in 1958 initially as the Summit Lighthouse, founded by Mark L. Prophet. The Lighthouse exists today as CUT's education wing. Elizabeth Prophet, wife of the founder, took over the leadership in 1973 after the death of her husband. Under her direction, CUT has grown into a successful organization with tens of thousands of members.

Elizabeth Prophet, who has the titles Vicar of Christ and Guru Ma, claims to be, and is seen by her followers as, the spokesperson for the Great White Brotherhood, the spiritual hierarchy first made known in the 1880s by the theosophist Helena Blavatsky. The brotherhood is believed by New Age followers and occultists to guide individuals in their spiritual growth and the human race in its planned evolution back to the divine. Mark Prophet is now held to be a member of this brotherhood.

CUT has been dogged with controversy, with opponents claiming it brainwashes recruits. Also controversial were what were perceived as clandestine activities at its Montana headquarters. Here, in the second half of the 1980s, it embarked on a programme of building underground bunkers and allegedly stockpiled weapons, food and medical supplies as a precaution against what it believed was the coming nuclear destruction of the world.

Findhorn Community

The Findhorn Community was founded in the north of Scotland in 1965 by Eileen and Peter Caddy and Dorothy Maclean. It continues to be one of the most important centres of the NEW AGE movement.

The focal point of the founders' lives was their garden, which they believed to be under the tutelage of *devas*, or spirits, associated with various plants, species and landscape features. Its abundance, despite its relatively poor soil, became widely known. As a consequence, the community grew, guided by what were perceived as spirit messages channelled daily through Eileen Caddy.

In the 1970s, the fame of Findhorn took a great leap forward, and notable New Age publications followed such as the *East West Journal* and the *New Age Journal*. Eileen Caddy alone remains of the three founders. The community membership stabilized in the 1980s at around 250 people. Two important individuals associated with Findhorn have been former member David Spangler, a well-known theoretician of the New Age now active in the United States; and Sir George Trevelyan, founder of the WREKIN TRUST.

Neo-Pagan Movement

This movement has some ideas similar to those of the NEW AGE movement. A new interest in paganism began in the 1920s with the writings of the British Egyptologist Margaret Murray, in particular her work *The Witch Cult in Western Europe* (1921), which described the essentials of a witch cult. Gerald B. Gardner (1884–1964) and his colleagues set about creating such a cult in the late 1930s. They set up the New Forest Coven in southern England from where they attempted to "raise a cone of power" as a spell to prevent Adolf Hitler from invading Britain at the start of World War II. Gardner initiated priestesses for numerous covens in England, and in the 1950s a Gardnerian coven was established in New York.

New Age

Although it connects with a much older metaphysical, occult, spiritual tradition, the modern New Age movement unfolded as a relatively widespread popular movement in the late 1960s. New Agers are concerned with achieving a transforming, personal experience that will move them out of what they see as their old unacceptable way of life to a completely new future. This personal transformation, achieved by techniques such as meditation, yoga, alternative therapies and channelling, will, it is believed, transform humanity itself. Indeed, New Agers believe this is already happening as those who have been transformed help to transform others.

Although professedly undogmatic, New Agers share a common outlook and a number of common beliefs. These include reincarnation; the advent of a universal religion in the future New Age; the existence of a universal energizing force or power that supports and permeates all existence, and which could be called God; the belief in outstanding spiritual teachers, such as the Buddha and Jesus, as perfect vehicles for this universal energy; and the idea of a World Teacher who will be the catalyst for the advent of the New Age.

The New Age also has a social vision which is holistic, that is, it focuses attention on the universe as a whole and an ultimate reality that is more than the sum of all its parts. The movement sees the earth as the most important of the parts that make up this whole and is therefore preoccupied with ecological, environmental and peace issues. Moreover, since human beings are an integral part of the earth, their well-being and health are bound up with those of the planet. Although community living is the ideal form of New Age living, the movement is loosely organized, with networking the most common way of linking members.

New Thought

Opinion is divided over the beginnings of the New Thought movement. Some hold that it owes its origins to the teaching and writings of Emma Curtis Hopkins (1853–1925), while others trace it back to the mental healing practices and private tutorial sessions of the American clock maker Phineas Parkhurst Quimby (1802–66). The writings of Mary Baker Eddy (1821–1910), founder of CHRISTIAN

Micropedia

SCIENCE, are another possible starting point for this popular religious movement.

New Thought is found mainly in the United States but has also influenced other societies including Japan. It is basically a popular version of the philosophical position known as idealism, which claims that the highest reality, and the very foundation of existence itself, is mental. The mind is the basis of reality and the causal force behind material happenings. "Life is consciousness" is the key concept of the New Thought movement.

There is no set pattern of worship for adherents; services often include explanation of the movement's ideas, testimony to healing, and prayer for the sick. The movement has now divided into some 35 independent bodies, including the Shinto-derived group SEICHO NO IE, which has centres worldwide.

Rajneesh Movement

Begun by Mohan Chandra Rajneesh (1931–90), also known as Bhagwan Shree Rajneesh, former professor of philosophy at the University of Jaipur, the Rajneesh organization started off as the Neo-Sannyas International Movement in 1970. In order to accommodate the increasing numbers of newcomers, an ashram, or religious centre, was opened in Poona, India, in 1974.

During the second half of the 1970s, there were some 6,000 followers in Poona, the majority of them westerners. Full-time devotees wore orange robes and became popularly known as "the orange people". They were introduced to various forms of meditation, encounter groups and therapy sessions which aimed to help them discover their real selves and move away from their conditioned natures, which had been "imposed" upon them at home, in school and by society. Rajneesh's essential message was that everyone is divine, but that through conditioning, individuals have lost their natural divine qualities of spontaneity, freedom and detachment.

In 1981, Rajneesh left India for the United States to start a new, model ashram, Rajneeshpuram, in Oregon, where individuals could regain natural qualities. The way to achieve this was through dynamic meditation – that is, the witnessing and observing of all that is experienced – and group therapy, which was always conducted under the watchful eye of the guru or his deputies.

However, internal strife within the movement, provoked mainly by the authoritarian nature of the leadership, and hostility from outside led to the closure of the ashram in 1985 and the deportation of Bhagwan Shree Rajneesh, for tax offences, from the country. Since Rajneesh's death five years later, the movement has become much more decentralized and fractured.

Scientology (Church of Scientology)

The movement began life as the Hubbard Dianetic Research Foundation in Elizabeth, New Jersey, in 1950. This was an institution set up by L. Ron Hubbard (1911–88), whose main ideas are contained in his popular and best-selling book *Dianetics: The Modern Science of Mental Health*. Hubbard's activities became known as Scientology in 1952, the year he moved his headquarters to Phoenix, Arizona. The Church of Scientology was formally created in the United States in 1955, with Dianetics as its "gospel". It was later incorporated in Great Britain and other countries.

Hubbard claimed that human abnormalities and many illnesses were the result of "engrams". These are produced by what he termed the reactive, or unconscious, mind which comes into operation when the analytical, or conscious, mind is impeded by pain, drugs or excessive amounts of alcohol.

The activity of engrams is not confined to the present but can begin during conception or even in a previous life. Thus the individual, when encountering words or sounds similar to those recorded in the engrams, will possibly experience psychosomatic illnesses but without understanding why. Hubbard's treatment is expensive and takes the form of "auditing" sessions in which the patient, or "aberree", in a state of quasi-hypnosis, is guided by a trained Scientologist to recall the origins of the first, or key, engram.

Once this basic engram is discovered, the aberree has been returned to what is termed the state of "basic, basic". From there, the remaining engrams can more easily be unearthed, placing the individual in a state of "release", free of major neurosis and ready to move to the higher states of "pre-clear" and "clear". The latter condition is one of complete freedom from neurosis of any kind and one where the human intelligence functions at levels well above the average. However, evidence of "clears" is hard to come by.

Scientology calls itself "the common people's science of life betterment", but the movement has been criticized for its scientific and religious claims and for the financial demands it makes on its followers. In the early 1980s there were a number of lawsuits against Hubbard in the United States and elsewhere for misuse of funds paid to the movement.

Theosophical Society

The society, which combines esoteric Hindu and Buddhist thought, was established in New York in 1875 by the Russian aristocrat Helena Petrovna Blavatsky (1831–91) and the American journalist Colonel Henry Olcott (1832–1907). Four years later, following an exploratory visit, the founders settled in India and, in 1882,

moved their headquarters to Adyar, Madras, building up a strong following.

The Theosophical Society sought to combine the "wisdom of all past ages and religions" with the special revelation from a secret brotherhood, the "occult Mahatmas", thought to reside in Tibet. It has a number of basic teachings, among them the notion that a vital energy flows through all things and can be used by those who know its secrets to work wonders of a natural, but non-material, kind.

Theosophy also holds that the myths and legends of all religions contain a basic universal truth about the universe: that it is composed of spirit, matter and consciousness and is in a continual process of evolution in the form of rebirth and not natural selection, as the 19th-century naturalist Charles Darwin suggested.

Annie Besant (1847–1933), the Irish-born social reformer, was the society's president from 1907 until her death, during which time it reached the peak of its influence. In more than 300 books and pamphlets, including *The Ancient Wisdom* (1897), *Esoteric Christianity* (1901) and *Thought Power* (1912), she expounded the main perspectives of theosophy, some of which supplied the principal components of the New Age outlook. As a result of her teachings, many theosophical lodges were founded in Europe and the United States.

Despite its small following and its somewhat chequered history, the Theosophical Society has been influential in inspiring a number of religious movements in the United States, including sections of the NEW THOUGHT movement. Although its influence has declined since the 1930s, it is still strong in India and has followers throughout the world.

Unification Church

Founded in Korea in 1954 by the Reverend Sun Myung Moon (1920–), the Unification Church is one of the most controversial of the new religious organizations to enter the west since the 1960s. It is also known by other names, including the Holy Spirit Association for the Unification of World Chistianity, the United Family and Tong II.

Its teachings, which are known as the Divine Principle, offer their own unique interpretation of the Bible. Followers claim that Jesus' mission was in part a failure, because he did not marry and so was only able to offer spiritual and not physical salvation to the world. Now is the time, they claim, when the Lord of the Second Advent is alive on this earth – many members believe this is Moon himself – to provide this physical salvation, and in so doing creating the perfect family and saving the human race.

The movement started to become well known in the west after Moon arrived in the

United States in the early 1970s. Lecture tours by Moon, large rallies, mass weddings, international conferences and the takeover of daily newspapers in New York, Washington and Tokyo, and the launch of weekly newspapers in small towns throughout the United States and Great Britain gained the church much publicity. Widespread fears over the Moonies' alleged means of recruitment, involving brainwashing techniques, caused it to be popularly viewed as a sinister cult that broke up families.

As a result of this reputation, the church has come under attack, particularly in the United States, Britain and France, from the media and various anti-cult groups, such as the America-based Spiritual Counterfeits Project and the American Family Foundation. Many critics of this new religious organization also regard the church's leadership as corrupt, with scant regard for immigration and tax laws. To support this view they point to the fact that Moon himself was sentenced to 18 months in a Federal prison by a U.S. court in 1982.

Wrekin Trust
The movement was created in 1971 by Sir George Trevelyan, a British spokesperson of the NEW AGE, who later published *A Vision of the Aquarian Age* (1984). The Wrekin Trust's chief purpose was to organize esoteric study groups, which New Agers felt were needed. The trust also tried to promote a better understanding of the New Age phenomenon and to disseminate its teachings and practices. It also engaged in networking and forging links with other New Age organizations, such as the FINDHORN COMMUNITY.

— AFRICAN-MELANESIAN MOVEMENTS —

Black Muslim Movement
Previously known as the Nation of Islam, this movement had its roots in the United States of the 1920s. It became widely known under the leadership of Elijah Muhammad (1897–1975), who succeeded the movement's founder, Wallace Fard Muhammad (c.1877–1934), and his spokesman, the radical political activist Malcolm X (1925–65), who was assassinated.

Although it claims to be a Muslim movement, it diverges from orthodox Islam in its denial of an afterlife and in some of its beliefs, for example, that Fard was not only the authentic Mahdi (p.115) but also a prophet and the incarnation of Allah. Its strongly pro-African-American emphasis and its aggressive, negative attitude to whites have raised the question as to whether it is a racist political movement rather than a religious one.

Candomblé
Probably an onomatopoeic term referring to an African musical instrument, Candomblé was a movement brought by African slaves to Brazil. It began to establish itself as a religion in the first quarter of the 19th century in the states of Bahia, Maranhão and Pernambuco in northeastern Brazil, where – as an indication of its west African roots – it is also known by the name of the Yoruba god of thunder, Shango. In Belem in Paraguay, it is called Batuque.

Based on Brazilian versions of Yoruba myths and rituals, Candomblé mixes African beliefs in spirits and ancestor worship with mainstream Catholic beliefs and rituals and, to a lesser extent, Amerindian ones. Members are mainly Afro-Brazilians, and often the mediums of the Yoruba gods are women, especially in Bahia.

Cargo cults
The term refers to the several hundred new religious movements that emerged mostly in Melanesia in the late 19th century during the colonial era and proliferated from the 1930s. They all promoted belief in a New Age which would bring with it equality with white people and material well-being – the sign of which would be the arrival of ships and possibly planes bringing not only their ancestors but also cargo from the west. One of the best known of these somewhat ephemeral cults was the "Vailala Madness", which arose in Papua in 1919.

Rastafarian Movement
Inspired by Marcus Garvey's Back to Africa movement, which developed in the United States in the early 20th century, the Rastafarian movement took root in Jamaica. It saw the accession of Ras (meaning "Prince") Tafari, Haile Selassie I (1892–1975), to the imperial throne of Ethiopia in 1930 as the fulfilment of Psalm 68, that the black race had been singled out by God for special attention.

Rastafarians worship Haile Selassie and regard themselves as one of the 12 tribes of ancient Israel. They believe Haile Selassie will redeem them from white oppression and return them to their homeland, Africa. Elsewhere, in Dominica, they are known as "Dreads", meaning simply the power that lies within every individual.

Since the 1950s, the Rastafarian movement has increased in numbers, with branches established elsewhere in the Caribbean, as well as the United States, Great Britain and Canada. The lifestyle of members may include specific dietary rules – for example vegetarianism – the wearing of uncombed beards and hair, sometimes known as "dreadlocks", and the smoking of *ganja*, or marijuana.

Santería
The Spanish name given to an African-Catholic religion that originated in Cuba and then spread to Miami, Los Angeles and New York, where it is practised by Cuban immigrants and exiles and African Americans. In Santería, most of the African elements – the names and functions of the gods, and the types of sacrifice – are derived from the Yoruba traditional religion, which was brought to Cuba by west African slaves between the 16th and 19th centuries. The blending of Catholic and African beliefs enabled Africans to retain their own faith while appearing to convert to Catholicism.

Followers of Santería believe in one Supreme Being, as well as in spirits or saints known as *orishas*. These spirits have the power to mediate with God on a person's behalf, or even become part of their personality.

Umbanda
Formed chiefly in the south of Brazil, Umbanda emerged in the 20th century as a religion with no central unifying doctrine combining elements from, for example, Amerindian, traditional African and Roman Catholic beliefs and practices. Its membership is generally more affluent and more Euro-Brazilian than that of CANDOMBLÉ.

Voodoo
The name given to the African-Catholic religion found in Haiti. It combines Catholic ritual elements, brought to the island by French colonists in the 17th century, with African theological and magical elements brought by west African slaves. It resembles CANDOMBLÉ, SANTERÍA and other African-Catholic systems of belief and practice found in the Caribbean and North, Central and South America. In the late 20th century, Voodoo is the chief religion of at least 80 percent of the population in Haiti.

Loa is the term used to refer to the numerous African gods and Catholic saints on which this religion is based. Although it has retained fewer African myths than Candomblé, Voodoo also has special songs and dances performed in honour of each individual deity. Respect for the dead is extremely important, as it is in all other new world varieties of African-Catholic religion.

Bibliography

GENERAL

al Faruqi, Isma'il A. and Sopher, David E.
Historical Atlas of the Religions of the World
Macmillan Publishing Co., New York, 1974

Crim, Keith (ed.) *The Perennial Dictionary of
World Religions* Harper & Row, San
Francisco, 1989

Goring, Rosemary *Chambers' Dictionary of
Beliefs* Chambers, New York and
Edinburgh, 1992

Harris, Ian; Mews, Stuart; Morris, Paul and
Shepherd, John (eds.) *Contemporary
Religions: A World Guide* Longman,
Harlow, 1992

Ling, Trevor *A History of Religion East and
West* Macmillan, Basingstoke, 1988

Noss, David S. and Noss, John B. *A History
of the World's Religions* Macmillan
Publishing Company, New York, 1990

Hinnells, John (ed.) *A Handbook of Living
Religions* Penguin Books, London, 1991

RELIGION IN THE MODERN WORLD

Bellah, R. *Beyond Belief* Harper & Row, New
York, 1970

Clarke, P.B. and Byrne, P.A. *Religion
Defined and Explained* Macmillan,
Basingstoke, 1993

Hammond, P. (ed.) *The Sacred in a Secular
Age* University of California Press,
Berkeley, 1985

Sutherland, S. and Clarke, P.B. *The Study of
Religion, Traditional and New Religions*
Routledge, London, 1992

Wallis, R. *Religion Defined and Explained*
Routledge, London, 1984

Wilson, B.R. *Religious Sects* Weidenfeld &
Nicolson, London, 1971

— *Religion in Chronological Perspective* Oxford
University Press, Oxford, 1982

JUDAISM

Baeck, Leo *This People Israel* Holt Rinehart,
New York, 1965

Baron, Salo *A Social and Religious History of
the Jews* Columbia University Press, New
York, 2d ed., 1952–82

Ben-Sasson, H.H. *A History of the Jewish
People* Harvard University Press, Boston,
1976

Encyclopedia Judaica Keter Publishing,
Jerusalem, 1972

de Lange, Nicholas *Atlas of the Jewish World*
Phaidon, Oxford, 1984

Friedlander, Albert H. *Leo Baeck: Teacher of
Theresienstadt* Overlook Press, New York,
1991

Jacobs, Louis *A Jewish Theology* Darton,
Longman & Todd, London, 1973

Johnson, Paul *A History of the Jews*
Weidenfeld & Nicolson, London, 1987

Kueng, Hans *Judaism* SCM Press, London,
1992

Martin, Bernard and Silver, Daniel J. *A
History of Judaism* (2 vols) Basic Books, New
York, 1974

Orlinsky, Harry *Ancient Israel* Behrman
House, New York, 1980

Rayner, John and Goldberg, David *The
Jewish People* Viking, New York, 1987

Rivkin, Ellis *The Shaping of Jewish History*
Scribner's Publishing, New York, 1971

Sachar, Howard *The Course of Modern Jewish
History* World Publishing & Schocken
Publishing, New York, 1958

Seltzer, Robert M. *Jewish People, Jewish
Thought* Macmillan, New York and
London, 1980

Wiesel, Elie *Souls on Fire: Hasidic Leaders*
Random House, New York, 1973

CHRISTIANITY

Berardino, Angelo di (ed.) *Dizionario
patristico e di antichità cristiane* (English
edition: *Encyclopaedia of the Early Church*)
James Clarke, Cambridge, 1992

Brooke, John Hedley *Science and Religion*
Cambridge University Press, Cambridge,
1991

Chadwick, Henry and Evans, G.R. *Atlas of
the Christian Church* Phaidon, Oxford, 1987

Cross, F.L. and Livingstone, E.A. *Oxford
Dictionary of the Christian Church* Oxford
University Press, Oxford, 2d. ed., 1974

Dussel, Enrique (ed.) *The Church in Latin
America, 1492–1992* Burns and Oates,
Tunbridge Wells, England, 1992

Frend, W.H.C. *The Rise of Christianity*
Darton, Longman & Todd, London, 1984

Green, V.H.H. *The Young Mr Wesley* Arnold,
Sevenoaks, England, 1961

Haugh, Richard (ed.) *The Collected Works of
Georges Florovsky* Norland, Belmont, Mass.,
1979

Jones, Cheslyn; Wainwright, G. and
Yarnold, Edward S.J. (eds.) *The Study of
Spirituality* SPCK, London, 1986

Lange, Ernst *And yet it moves; dream and reality
of the ecumenical movement* Christian Journals,
Belfast, 1979

Lossky, N. *Dictionary of the Ecumenical
Movement* WCC, Geneva, 1991

The New Jerusalem Bible Darton, Longman &
Todd and Doubleday & Company, London
and New York, 1985

Penoukou, E.F. *Eglises d'Afrique* Karthala,
Paris, 1984

Raboteau, A.J. *Slave Religion* Oxford
University Press, New York, 1978

Rowland, Christopher *Radical Christianity*
Polity Press, Cambridge, 1988

Stevenson, J. (ed.) *Creeds, Councils and
Controversies Documented: Illustrating the
History of the Church, AD 337–461* SPCK,
London, 1966

ISLAM

Clarke, P.B. (ed.) *West Africa and Islam*
Edward Arnold, London, 1982

— *Islam* Routledge, London, 1990

Geertz, C. *Islam Observed* University of
Chicago Press, London and Chicago, 1968

The Koran Arberry, Arthur J. (trans.) Oxford
University Press, Oxford, 1989

Nasr, S.H. *Traditional Islam in the Modern
World* Kegan Paul International, New York
and London, 1987

Nicholson, R.A. *The Mystics of Islam*
Routledge, London, 1963

Nielsen, J. *Muslims in Western Europe*
Edinburgh University Press, Edinburgh,
1992

Rice, D.T. *Islamic Art* Thames and Hudson,
London, 1975

Robinson, Francis *Atlas of the Islamic World
since 1500* Phaidon, Oxford, 1982

Sutherland, S.R. (ed.) *The World's Religions*
Routledge, London, 1988

Williams, J.A. *Themes of Islamic Civilization*
University of California Press, Berkeley,
1971

ZOROASTRIANISM

Boyce, M. *Textual Sources for the Study of
Zoroastrianism* Manchester University Press,
Manchester, 1984; reprinted Chicago, 1990

— *Zoroastrians, Their Religious Beliefs and
Practices* Routledge and Kegan Paul,
London, 1979

— *A Persian Stronghold of Zoroastrianism* (based
on the Ratanbai Katrak Lectures 1975)
Oxford University Press, Oxford, 1977;
reprinted University Press of America,
Lanham, New York, and London, 1989

— "Zoroastrianism" in *A Handbook of Living
Religions* Hinnells, J.E. (ed.) Penguin Books,
New York and London, 1991

Dhabhar, B.N. (trans.) *The Persian Rivayats of
Hormazyar Framarz and Others* K.R. Cama
Oriental Institute, Bombay, 1932

Firby, N.K. *European Travellers and their
Perceptions of Zoroastrians in the 17th and 18th
Centuries* Reimer, Berlin, 1988

Insler, S. *The Gathas of Zarathushtra*, (*Acta
Iranica 8*) Brill, Leiden, 1975

Malandra, W.W. *An Introduction to Ancient
Iranian Religion, Readings from the Avesta and
Achaemenid Inscriptions* University of
Minnesota Press, Minneapolis, 1983

Mistree, K.P. *Zoroastrianism, an Ethnic
Perspective* privately printed, Bombay, 1982

Modi, J.J. *The Religious Ceremonies and
Customs of the Parsees* British India Press,
Bombay, 1922; reprinted Garland, New
York, 1980

Schmidt, E.F. *Persepolis I, Structures, Reliefs,
Inscriptions* University of Chicago Oriental
Institute Publications, LXVIII Chicago, 1953

Seervai, K.N. and Patel, B.B. "Gujarat

Parsees" in *Gazetteer of the Bombay Presidency*, Vol. IX, Part 2, Government Central Press, Bombay, 1899

West, E.W. *Pahlavi Texts (Sacred Books of the East*, vols V, XVIII, XXIV, XXXVII, XLVII) Clarendon Press, Oxford, 1880–97; reprinted Krishna, New York, 1974

HINDUISM

Babb, L.A. *The Divine Hierarchy: Popular Hinduism in Central India* Columbia University Press, New York, 1975

Bowes, P. *The Hindu Religious Tradition* Routledge, Boston and London, 1978

Brockington, J.L. *The Sacred Thread* University Press, Edinburgh, 1981

— *Christianity and Hinduism* Macmillan, London, 1992

De Bary, W.T. (ed.) *Sources of Indian Tradition* Columbia University Press, New York, 1969

Dumont, L. *Homo Hierarchicus* Paladin, London, 1972

Eck, D.L. *Banaras City of Light* Routledge and Kegan Paul, London, 1983

Hiriyanna, M. *Outlines of Indian Philosophy* Arthur & Darwin, London, 1967

Kinsley, D.R. *Hinduism* Prentice Hall, New Jersey, 1982

Mascaró, Juan (trans.) *The Bhagavad Gita* Penguin Books, Harmondsworth, 1973

Michell, G. *The Hindu Temple* Harper & Row, New York, 1977

O'Flaherty, W.D. *The Rig Veda: An Anthology* Penguin Books, Harmondsworth, 1981

Zaehner, R.C. (trans.) *Hindu Scriptures* J.M. Dent & Sons, London, 1966

Zimmer, H. *Myths and Symbols of Indian Art and Civilization* Harper & Row, New York, 1962

JAINISM

Caillat, C., Upadhye, A.N. and **Patil, B.** *Jainism* Motilal, New Delhi, 1974

Dundas, Paul *The Jains* Routledge, London, 1992

Gopalan, S. *Outlines of Jainism* Wiley Eastern Private Ltd., New Delhi, 1973

Jain, J.S. *Religion and Culture of the Jains* Bharatiya, Jnanpith, New Delhi, 1975

Jaini, P.S. *The Jaina Path of Purification* University of California Press, Berkeley, 1979

Ray, S. (ed.) *Gandhi's India and the World* Temple University Press, Philadelphia, 1970

Schubring, W. *Doctrines of the Jainas* Delhi, 1962

Talib, G.S. (ed.) *Jainism* Punjabi University, Patiala, 1975

Tatia, Dr. N. (trans.) *Tattrartha Sutra of Umasvati* Harper Collins, New York and London, 1993

BUDDHISM

Berchert, H.S. and **Gombrich, R.** *The World of Buddhism* Thames and Hudson, London, 1984

Carrithers, M. *The Buddha* Oxford University Press, Oxford, 1982

Conze, E. *Buddhist Scriptures* Penguin Books, Harmondsworth, 1959

Eppsteiner, F. (ed.) *The Path of Compassion* Parallax, Berkeley, 1985

Fields, R. *How the Swans Came to the Lake* Shambhala, Boston, 1981

Gombrich, R. *Theravada Buddhism* Routledge Kegan Paul, London, 1988

Gyatso, T. *Freedom in Exile* Abacus, London, 1990

Mascaró, Juan (trans.) *The Dhammapada* Penguin Books, Harmondsworth, 1973

Nyanaponika, Thera *The Heart of Buddhist Meditation* Rider, London, 1962

Pye, M. *The Buddha* Duckworth, London, 1979

Rahula, W. *What the Buddha Taught* Gordon Fraser, London, 1984

Robinson, R.S. and **Johnson, W.H.** *The Buddhist Religion* Wadsworth, Belmont, California, 3d ed., 1982

Saddhatissa, A. *Buddhist Ethics* George Allen & Unwin, London, 1970

Suzuki, D.T. *Zen and Japanese Culture* Pantheon, New York, 1959

Trungpa, C. *Cutting through Spiritual Materialism* Curzon, London, 1984

Williams, P. *Mahayana Buddhism* Routledge and Kegan Paul, London, 1989

SIKHISM

Barrier, N.G. and **Dusenbury, V.A.** *The Sikh Diaspora* Manohar, New Delhi, 1991

Cole, W.O. and **Sambhi, P.S.** *A Popular Dictionary of Sikhism* Glenn Dale, London, 1990

— *The Sikhs: Their Religious Beliefs and Practices* Routledge, Boston and London, reprinted 1992

— *Sikhism and Christianity: A Comparative Study* Macmillan, London, 1993

McLeod, W.H. *Textual Sources for the Study of Sikhism* Manchester University, Manchester, 1984

— *The Sikhs* Columbia University Press, New York, 1989

Macauliffe, M.A. *The Sikh Religion* Oxford University Press, New Delhi, reprinted 1976

O'Connell, J.T.; Israel, M. and **Oxtoby, W.G.** *Sikh History and Religion in the Twentieth Century* University of Toronto, Toronto, 1988

Singh, Harbans *Heritage of the Sikhs* Manohar, New Delhi, 1985

CHINA'S RELIGIOUS TRADITION

De Bary, W.T. *Sources of Chinese Tradition* Columbia University Press, New York, 1960

Ch'en, K. *Buddhism in China* Princeton University Press, Princeton, 1964

Ching, J. *To Acquire Wisdom: The Way of Wang Yang-ming* Columbia University Press, New York, 1976

Feuchtwang, S. *The Imperial Metaphor* Routledge, London and New York, 1992

Harrison, J. *The Communists and Chinese Peasant Rebellions* Athenaeum, New York, 1969

Jochim, C. *Chinese Religions* Prentice Hall, Eaglewood Cliffs, New Jersey, 1986

Overmyer, D. *Folk Buddhist Religion* Harvard University Press, Cambridge, Mass., 1976

— *Religions of China* Harper & Row, San Francisco, 1986

Robinet, I. *Histoire du taoisme* Cerf, Paris, 1991

Rule, P. *K'ung-tzu or Confucius?* Allen & Unwin, North Sydney, 1986

SHINTO

Aston, W.G. *The Shinto the Way of the Gods* Longman's, Green and Co., London, 1905

— (trans.) *Nihongi – Chronicles of Japan from the Earliest Times to A.D. 697* Charles E. Tuttle, Tokyo, 1972

Beardsley, Richard *et al. Village Japan* Phoenix Books, Chicago, 1959

Blacker, Carmen *The Catalpa Bow: A Study of Shamanistic Practices in Japan* Mandala, London, 1985

Breen, John "Shintoists in Early Meiji Japan" in *Modern Asian Studies* 24, 3, 1990

Crump, Thomas *The Death of an Emperor – Japan at the Crossroads* Constable, London, 1989

Grapard, Alan "Shinto" in *Encyclopaedia of Japan* vol. 8, Kodansha, Tokyo, 1983

Hardacre, Helen *Shinto and the State 1868–1988* Princeton University Press, Princeton, 1989

Holtom, Daniel C. *The National Faith of Japan* E.P. Dutton and Company, New York, 1938

Kurodo Toshio "Shinto in the History of Japanese Religion" in *Journal of Japanese Studies* 7, 1981

McFarland, H. Neill *The Rush Hour of the Gods: A Study of New Religious Movements in Japan* Macmillan, New York, 1967

Reader, Ian *Religion in Contemporary Japan* Macmillan Press, London, 1991

Swyngedouw, Jan "Religion in Contemporary Japanese Society" in *Japan Foundation Newsletter* 13, 4, 1986

Woodward, William *The Allied Occupation of Japan 1945–1952 and Japanese Religions* E.J. Brill, Leiden, 1972

Index

NOTE: **Bold** figures show main references; *italic* figures refer to information given in boxes or in picture captions. People are indexed under the name they are popularly known by. Many Islamic, and some Oriental, names are indexed under the first or second part of the name.

A

Abbas I *107*, *108*, 109
Abbas II 109
Abbasid dynasty 92, **94**, *94*, 95, 96, 100, 102
Abd al-Malik *92*
Abd ar-Rahman 94
Abraham 19, 20, 78, 88, *89*
Abu Bakr 91, *93*
Achaemenian Empire 121, *123*
Adam *88*
Adi Granth see Guru Granth Sahib
Advaita school 133
Afghanistan 97, 109, 116, 118
Africa, northern 85, 96, 114, 118; *see also* Algeria, Egypt, Morocco, Sudan
Africa, sub-Saharan 13; Hindus 125; Islam 82, 86, *99*, **112–13**, *113*; missionaries 69, **74–5**, 82; South Africa 80; *see also* African Independent Churches
African Independent Churches 10, 41, **74**, 75, 202
Aga Khan *91*, 205
Aglabid dynasty 96
Ahab 25
Ahaz 25
Ahmad ibn Tulun *95*
Ahmad Sirhindi, Shaykh 105
Ahmadiyya **205**
Ahura Mazda 121, *122*, *123*
Aisha (wife of Muhammad) *91*
Akbar *104*, 105, *105*, 147
Akiva ben Joseph 29
al-Abbas 94
al-Banna, Hasan 205
al-Basri, Hasan 99
al-Ghazali, Muhammad 30, *98*, 99, *101*
al-Hallaj 99
al-Jihad 118, 206
al-Ma'mun 94
al-Muhasibi 99
al-Mustali 96–7
al-Nizar 96–7

al-Qaid 205
al-Sadr, Musa 205
Aladura churches 41, **202**
Albert the Great *58*
Alexander the Great 26, *123*
Alexander IV, Pope 59
Alexander VI, Pope 68, *69*
Algeria 114, 116, *117*, 118
Ali al-Rida *109*
Ali (Muhammad's son-in-law) **91**, *109*
Allah 85, 86
Almohad dynasty 97, 100
Almoravid dynasty 97
almsgiving 150, *151*, *160*, 161, *169*, 174
Alvars 138
Amal, Islamic **205**
Amaterasu *198*, *198*, 200, *201*
America, Central and South *see* Latin America, Brazil
America, North 13, 14, 203, 204, 206; early Christian settlers **70–1**; *see also* Canada, Caribbean, United States
Amesha Spentas 121, *122*
Amida Buddha 163, *163*, 167
Amish, Old Order **204**
Amitabha 184
Ammann, Jakob 204
Anabaptists **202**; *see also* Mennonites
anathemas 55
Anawrahta 161
ancestor worship 177, 178, 180, 194, 207, 211
angels 86, 87, 88
Anglican Church 60, **70–1**, *72*, 75, 82, *82*
Angra Mainyu 121
Ansars 115
anti-Semitism *see* persecution
Antony of Egypt 64, *64*
Apocrypha 29
Apollos of Alexandria 51, 203
apostolic succession 55
Aquinas, Thomas *58*, *101*
Arab-Israeli conflict 38, *39*, 85, 118
Arabic language 32, *113*, 116
Aramaic language 48
Arafat, plain of 88, *89*
arhat 158, *159*
Aristotle *58*
Arius and Arianism 52
Arjan, Guru 174, *175*
Arnold, Sir Edwin 168
Arya Samaj 142
Aryans 128, **130–1**
Asa 25
Ashbury, Francis 73

Ashkenazi Jews 32, *32*, 38
Ashoka 135, **154–5**, *157*, 158, 161, 170
Asia, central **102–3**, 114; *see also* Commonwealth of Independent States
Asia Minor: early church **48–51**, 55, 56
Asia, north and east 149, 160; *see also* China, Japan, Korea
Asia, south *see* India, Sri Lanka
Asia, Southeast 42, 149, *159*, **160–1**, *160*, *171*; *see also* Burma, Indonesia, Malaysia
Asia, southwest *see* Middle East and its countries
Assassins 97
Assemblies of God 41, *82*
Athalia 25
Athanasius of Alexandria 203
Athanasius the Athonite 77
Athos, Mount 77
atman 126, 127, 129, *129*, 133
Atonement, Jewish Day of 23
Augsburg, Peace of 61
Augustine of Canterbury 53, *53*
Augustine of Hippo 52, 59, 61, 78
Augustinians **59**, 60
Aurangzeb *104*, 105, *105*, 174
Aurobindo 132
"Auspicious Incident" 106
Australia 121, 149, 175
Avalokiteshvara *159*, 164, *165*
Averroës 100, *101*
Avestan language *123*
Avicenna *98*, *101*
Ayyubid dynasty 96; *see also* Saladin
Azerbaijan 103, *107*, *108*, 109

B

Baal 25
Babalola, Joseph 202
Babur, Zahid al-Din 105, 174
Babylonia 23, 24, 25, *25*, 26, 28, *29*, *29*
Badaryana 133
Baeck, Leo *37*, 38
Baghdad 94, 99, 100, 104
Baha Ullah 205
Bahaism **205**
Bali *143*
Balak Singh, Baba 173
Balfour Declaration 36, *36*, 38
Bali *143*
Bandaranaike, Solomon 171
Bapak (Muhammad Subuh) 206
baptism 42, *71*, 76, 202, 203, 204

Baptists 71, *71*
bar mitzvah 19
Barmen Declaration 80
Barth, Karl (quoted) *79*
Basil of Caesarea 66
Bates, Joseph 204
Bayazid II 106
Beatles 125, 207
Begin, Menàchem 38
Beijing *192–3*, *192*, *193*
Bell, George *81*
ben Isaac, Solomon (Rashi) 32
ben Yochai, Simeon 31
Ben-Gurion, David *36*, 38
Benares (Varanasi) *132*, 140, 141, 153
Benedict and Benedictines 52, 126; his *Rule* 52, *59*
Benjamin, tribe of 24
Bernard of Clairvaux 59
Besant, Annie 125–6, 210
Bethlehem 44
Bhagavad Gita 129, **134**, 137, 138, 206
bhakti 126, 133, 138, 206
bhakti movement 132, 135, **138–9**
Bharatiya Janata 142
Bible: biblical scholarship 78–9; and Darwinism 66–7; modern interpretations 79; New Testament 42, **50–1**, *51*, 60, *see also* Gospels, Paul (St.); Old Testament 17, **28–9**, *44*, prophets 25, *25*, **28–9**, 86, Psalms 22, 46, 86, *see also* Torah
bishops 42, 43, 62, *63*
Black Muslim Movement **211**
Blaurock, George 202
Blavatsky, Helena 168, *168*, 209, **210**
Bodhi tree 153, 156, *157*
Bodhidharma 184
bodhisattva 158, *159*, *192*, 207
Bodhisattva (title) *see* Buddha
Bon religion 164
Bonhoeffer, Dietrich 80, *80*
Brahma *136*, 137, 143, 146
Brahma Baba 206
Brahma Kumaris **206**
Brahma Samaj 142
Brahma Sutras 137
Brahman 126, 127, 133, *136*
Brahmins 128, 135, 136
Brazil 10, 208, 209, 211; *see also* Latin America
Bright, Bill 202
Britain: Buddhists 12, 168; coming of Christianity 53, *53*; Reformation and after 60, 63; Revivalism 72–3; colonialism 74–5, *75*, 114,

114, *115*, 116, 142, 173; Hindus 125; Jews 18, 35, 36, *36*, 38; Muslims 118, *119*; Sikhs 173; Zoroastrians 121; new movements 203, 211
Buber, Martin *38*
Buddha, the (Gautama) **149**, 150, **152–3**, 158, *159*, 167, *181*; descendants 178; images 152, **156–7**
Buddhism **148–71**, 207–8; basic beliefs 149–52; expansion into Asia 149, 158–61; in China 177, **184–5**, *184*, 194; in Japan 162–3, 198–9, 200, *201*; in Tibet 164–5; in the west **168–9**; images 152, *156–7*; initiation rites 160; monks and laypeople *see sangha*; new movements 207; and other faiths: Chinese folk religion 188, 189, Christianity 171, 177, Hinduism 135, 136, 137, 171, Shinto 162–3, 198–9, 200, *201*; scriptures 154–8, *158*, *163*; symbols 156; today 9, 10, *12*, 13, **170–1**; Zen art and culture *162*
Buddhist Peace Fellowship 149, 170
Buddhist Society 168
Burma 149, 160, 161, *161*, 171
Buyid dynasty 94, 100
Byzantine Empire 89, 91, 92, 100; *see also* Constantinople

C

Caddy, Eileen and Peter 209
Caiaphas 46
Caitanya 138, 206
caliphates 90–7 *passim*; caliph's spiritual authority 94
Calvary 46, *47*
Calvin, John 61, *61*
Calvinists 71
Cambodia 149, 160
Camp David Agreement 38, 85, 118
Campus Crusade for Christ 10, **202**
Canaan 20; *see also* Palestine
Canada 82, 121, 125, *143*, 173, 203, 204, 211; *see also* America (North)
Candomblé 13, **211**
Cao Cao 186
Carey, George, Archbishop of Canterbury *82*
Cargo cults **211**

Caribbean 14, 125, 211
Carmarthian dynasty 97
Carmelites 65
Caro, Joseph 32
Cartier, Jacques 70
Casimir the Great 32
caste system 126, **128–9**, 136, 138, 141, 142, 169, 173
cathedrals 55, 58, 59, *68, 74, 77, 81*
Catherine the Great 76
Catholics *see* Roman Catholicism
Celestial Masters 186–7, *187*
Central Asian republics 103, 114
Cerularius, Michael 55
Chaghatay 102
Chalcedon, Council of 53, 203
Chalukya dynasty 137
Chan Buddhism 149, 184
Chandella dynasty *139*
Chandra Gupta II *135*
Chandragupta Maurya 135, 147
chaos theory 67
Charismatics *82*
Charlemagne 53, *53*, 58
Charles V (Holy Roman Emperor) 33, *60*, 61, 68
Cheng Hao 190
Cheng Yi 190
China's religious tradition **176–95**; ancestor worship *177, 178*, 180, *194*; art and culture *182, 184, 185*; Buddhism 177, **184–5**, *184*, *194*; calendar 178; Christian missions 69, *181*; communism 41, 69, 110, 177, **194–5**; Daoism **182–3**, 186–7, 188, 189, 194; emperor worship 192–3; exam system *191*; festivals *188*; folk religion 178, **188–9**, *193*; and Islam 110, *110*; rebellions *195*; today 110, *110*; *see also* Confucianism
"chosen people", Jews as 17–18
Christ (Anointed One) *see* messiah
Christian Broadcasting Network 41
Christian Science **202–3**
Christianity **40–83**; basic features and beliefs 42–3, 48, 53; beginnings 41–7; early church 48–51; expansion to Europe 53–4, *53*; to Asia 69, *69*; to New World 68, *69*, 70–1; and other religions: Buddhism 171, Hinduism 126, 142, Judaism 48, Shinto 199; Reformation and

Counter-Reformation 60–2; revivalist movements (18th C.) 72–3; Roman/Orthodox split 54–5, **76**; today 9–10, 14, **82–3**, new movements and minor sects 202–4; *see also* Bible, colonialism, Gospels, Jesus, missionaries, Orthodox Church, Protestantism, Roman Catholicism
church: defined 42
Church of England *see* Anglican Church
Church Universal and Triumphant **209**
circumcision 19, *19*, 20, 48
Cistercians **59**
Clare of Assisi 59
Clement of Alexandria 51, 203
Clement VII, Pope 58, *60*
Clermont, Council of 56
Clive, Robert 142
Clovis (Frankish king) 52
Codex Sinaiticus 50
Cohen, Hermann *38*
colonialism and religion **114**, *114*, 115, 116; Africa 74–5, *75*; India 142, 173; Latin America 68–9; *see also* missionaries
Commonwealth of Independent States (C.I.S.) 30, *40*, 41, 76, 86, *102*, 103, *103*
communism 9, *40*, **41**; Chinese 69, 110, 177, 194–5; Soviet 76, 103, *103*
Confessing Church *81*
Confucianism 177, **180–1**; distrust of folk religion 189; and exam system *191*; filial piety 190, *199*, *201*; and imperial cult 192; in Japan 180, *193*, 199; Neo-Confucianism 190; scriptures 180, 190, 191, 192
Confucius 177, 180, *180*, 181, *191*; descendants 178
Congregationalism 70, 71, 82
Congress of Vienna 34
Conservative Judaism 35
Constance, Council of 58
Constantine the Great 52
Constantine IX 55
Constantinople 55, 56, 57, 76, *106*; renamed Istanbul 106
Constantinople, Council of 52, *53*
Conze, Edward *150*
Copernicus 66, *67*
Coptic Church **203**
Cordovero, Moses *31*
Counter-Reformation **62**

"Covenant, Book of the" 25
cows: in Hinduism 127
creation stories 66, 78, 121, *122*
cross as symbol *40, 57*
crucifixion of Jesus 45, **46–7**, *46, 47*
Crusades 32, 55, **56–7**, *56, 57, 66*, 100, 102; and Assassins 97
Cyril of Alexandria 203
Cyrus the Great 26, *123*

D

Dalai Lama 164, *192*; 14th (present) *148, 149*, 164
dalit **128**, *129*
Dante 79
Daodejing **182–3**, *182, 183*
Daoism **182–3**, 186–7, *194*; and Chinese folk religion 188, 189; scriptures *187*; and Shinto 198
Dark Learning *183*, 184
Darwin, Charles and Darwinism 66–7
David, King 22, *22*
Davids, T.W. Rhys 168
Dayal Das 173
Dayan, Moshe 38
De Foucauld, Charles 65, *65*
deacons 43
Dead Sea Scrolls *27*
death and afterlife: Buddhism *150*, 167; Chinese beliefs *176*, 177, 186; Christianity 42, 87, *see also* Jesus (resurrection); Hinduism *126*, *143*; Jainism *145*; Judaism 19, *19*, *30*; Shinto 197, *198*; Sikhism *173*; Zoroastrianism *121*; other 204, 211; *see also* heaven and hell, reincarnation, resurrection
Deborah 21
Decalogue *21*
Deguchi, Nao and Onisaburo 208
Deists 72
Delhi: Red Fort 105, *105*
Delhi sultanate 104
Denmark 9
dervishes *98*
Deuteronomy 25, *28*
Devil, Evil One: Buddhist Mara 153; Satan/Shaitan 61, *86, 89*, 203, 204; Zoroastrian 121
dharam yudh (Sikh "just" war) 174
dharma: Buddhist 150, *151*; Hindu 125, 126
Diaspora 17, *28*, 32, 36, 38, *39*

Dibelius, Martin 79
Digambaras 147
Divine Truth cult *105*
diviners and divination, Chinese 178, *178*
Dogen 163
Dome of the Rock 92, *92*
Dominicans 58, *59*, 69
Donatus of Carthage 52
Dreyfus affair 36
Duns Scotus 58
Durga *137*, *143*; *see also* Parvati
Durkheim, Emile 9, 13, 14

E

Easter *40*, 47, 57; *see also* resurrection of Jesus
ecumenism 10, 80, 82
Eddy, Mary Baker 202–3, 209
edict pillars of Ashoka 155, *155*
Edwards, Jonathan 73
Egypt 85, 95, 96, 112, 114, 116; Coptic Church 203; Jews in ancient 20, *21*; Mamluks 102, 106, 112; Suez 114, *116*; *see also* Africa (northern), Sadat
Eight Immortals *188*, 189
Eightfold Path, Noble *152*, 153, 156
Einhorn, David 35
Eisai 163
Eli 21
Elijah 25
Elijah ben Solomon *34*
Eliot, T.S. 14, *79*
Elisha 25
Emerson, Ralph Waldo *168*
emperor worship: China 192–3; Japan 198, 199, *199*, 200, *201*, 208
Engels, Friedrich 9
enlightenment 162, 184; *see also* Nirvana
Enlightenment, Age of 34–5, 72
Ertugrul 106
Essenes *27*
Ethiopian churches **204**
Eucharist *40*, 43, 48, 61, 62
Europe: early Christianity 52–8; spread of Judaism 32–3; Islam in *see* Spain; Reformation and after 60–3; today 18; *see also* colonialism *and* separate countries
exile, Jewish Babylonian 23, *24*, 25, *25*, 26
Exodus 19, *19*, 20–1, *20, 21*; and Christian baptism 42
Ezekiel 24
Ezra the Scribe 26

F

Fa Xian 160
Far East: Islam in 110–11; *see also* China, Indonesia, Japan, Malaysia
Farid, Shaykh 175
Fatimah (daughter of Muhammad) *109*
Fatimid dynasty 96
Ferdinand II of Spain 100, *101*
Feuerbach, Ludwig 9
Findhorn Community 15, **209**
Finney, Charles 73
Five Classics 180, *180*
Florence, Council of 76
Four Books of Confucianism **191**, *192*
Four Lands, Jewish Council of the 32
Four Noble Truths 152, *153*
Four Signs, Buddha's 153
Fox, George 71
France 34, *63*, 65, 118
Francis of Assisi 59
Francis of Sales 65
Francis Xavier 69, *69*
Franciscans **59**, 68, 69
Frederick the Wise *61*
Freud, Sigmund 9
Friends, Society of *see* Quakers
Friends of the Western Buddhist Order (FWBO) **207**
fundamentalists: Christian 41, 43, 67, 78, *82*; Islamic 86, 91, 110, 114, *116*, 117, **118**

G

Gabirol, Solomon ibn 30
Galileo 66, *67*
Gandhi, Mahatma 125, 127, *127*, 141, 142
Ganesha *137*, 142, *143*
Ganges, River *126*, *140*, 141
Gardner, Gerald B. 209
Gathas 123
Gautama *see* Buddha
Gedaliah 25
Geiger, Abraham 35
Gelukpas (Yellow Hats) 164, *192*
Genghis Khan 102, *102, 103*
Germany *63*, 81, 118, 169; Jews in 36, *see also* Holocaust
Ghazali *see* al-Ghazali
Ghaznavid dynasty 97, 104–5
Ghulam Ahmad 205
Gita see Bhagavad Gita
Gnostics 51
Gobind Singh, Guru 173, 174
God, central idea of: Buddhist 149; Christian 53; Confucian

180; Hindu 126, 135; Islamic 86; Jain 145; Jewish 17, 18; Shinto 197, 209; Sikh 173, 174; Zoroastrian 121
Godfrey of Bouillon 56
Goethe 136
Gospels 42, 43, 46, 47, **50–1**, 51, 79; importance to Islam 86; John 45, 47, 47, 50; Luke 44, 47, 50; Mark 47, 50, 51; Matthew 44, 47, 50; "Q" 50
Graham, Billy 73, 73
Great Awakening 73
Great White Brotherhood 209
Greece 26, 114, 130; St. Paul in 48, 49; see also Asia Minor
Greek Orthodox Church see Orthodox
Gregory I (the Great), Pope 53
Gregory of Nyssa 64
Gregory of Tours 52–3
Gregory VII, Pope 58
Griffiths, Bede 126
Guandi 193
Gueth, Anton (Nyanatiloka) 169
Guiscard, Robert 55
Gupta dynasty 135, 136
gurdwaras 173, 174, 175
Guru Granth Sahib 173, 173, 174, 175
gurus 132, 206; Ten Sikh Gurus 173–5, 173, 174, 175

H

ha-Levi, Yehudah 30
ha-Nagid, Samuel 30
hadith 84, 91, 94
Hagar 89
Haggadah 21
Haile Selassie I 211
hajj (pilgrimage to Mecca) 86, **88–9**, 90, 113
Hammurabi 21
Han dynasty 183, 186, 189, 192
Hanafi school of Islamic law 94
Hanbali school of Islamic law 94
Hanukkah 26, 27
Hanuman 134, 137
Hardwar 140, 141
Hare Krishna movement 14, 125, 125, 138, **206**
Harris, Barbara 42
Harris Church 41, 74
Harris, William 41, **74**
Harun ar-Rashid 94
Harvey, William 66
Hasan (son of Ali) 91
Hasidic Jews 18, **34**, 35, 38
Hasmoneans 26, 27

healing 66, 74, 82, 202–10 *passim*
Healthy, Happy, Holy Organization 173, **206–7**
heaven and hell: Buddhism 150; Chinese religions 177; Christianity 42; Islam 87; Jainism 145, 146; Judaism 19; Shinto 198; Zoroastrianism 121; purgatory 60, 62, 188
Hebrew language 32, 38, 48; see also Bible
Heine, Heinrich 34
Henry IV (Holy Roman Emperor) 58
Henry VIII of England 60
Heraclas 203
Herod Antipas 46
Herod Antipater 26
Herod the Great 23, 26
Herodotus 121
Herzl, Theodor 36
Hesychasm 77
Hewavitarne, David 168
Hidden Imam **109**, 205
Hildegard of Bingen 65
Hinduism 9, 10, **125–43**; and Buddhism 135, 136, 137, 171; and Christianity 126, 142; culture and learning 135, 136; education 128; festivals 125, 140, 143; and Islam 99, 104–5, 105; and Jainism 145; pilgrimage 140–1; rituals 127, 127, 128, 130, 131; schools of philosophy 132–3; scriptures see *Mahabharata, Bhagavad Gita,* Upanishads, Vedas; new movements 206–7
Hirohito 198, 201
Hirsch, Samuel Raphael 35
Hisham 92
Hizbollah 86, **205**
Holcombe, Sir John 56
Holocaust 18, 19, 37, 38, 80
Holy Communion see Eucharist
Holy Land see Israel; Jerusalem
Holy Roman Empire 53, 53, 58
Holy Spirit: Christian 48, 53, 82, 204; Zoroastrian 121, 122
Honan 163
Hong Xiuquan 194
House Church Movement **203**
Hsuan Hua 168
Hubal 88
Hubbard, L. Ron 210
Hudaybiyyah, Treaty of 89
Huguenots 63
Hulagu Khan 102
Humbert, Cardinal 55
Humphreys, Christmas 168, 169

Hunas (White Huns) 135, 136
Husain the martyr 90, 91
Hutterian Brethren **203**
Hyksos kings 20
hymns and hymn-writers: Christian 73, 73, 79; Hindu see Vedas; Sikh 174, 175
Hystaspes (Vishtapsa) 121

I

I Ching (Book of Changes) 178, 179, 180, 183
Iblis 86; see also Satan
Ibn Battutah 103, 113
Ibn Khaldun 100, 113
Ibn Sina (Avicenna) 98, 101
icons 55, 77
Idries Shah 206
Ignatius of Loyola 53, **62**, 62, 69
Il-Khanid dynasty 102–3, 102
Imami school of law 94, 109
imams 94, 205; Hidden Imam 109, 205
Index of Prohibited Books 62
India: early history 128, 130, 130, 135, 154; Islam in 104–5; Jains 146–7, 146; Parsis (Zoroastrians) 122; pilgrimage sites 140–1, 144, 157, 173; postwar nationalism 116; Punjab and the Sikhs 173; today 82, 104, 142; new religions 205, 206–8; see also Buddhism, Hinduism, Sikhism
Indonesia 85, 110–11, 114, 116, 149
indulgences 60, 62
Indus civilization 130, 130
Inquisition 31, 62, 66
Iona 53
Iran: history 106, 109, 121, 122, 130; modern 13, 13, 84, 85–6, 90, 109, 116, 118, 205; Isfahan 108, 109; and Kurds 117
Iraq 100, 102, 106, 117, 118; see also Baghdad
Ireland 15, 63; Northern 13; Republic of 10
Isaac 19, 20, 78, 89
Isabella of Castile 100, 101
Isaiah 25, 25, 46
Isfahan **108**, 109
Ishaq Safi al-Din, Shaykh 108
Ishmael 78, 89
ISKCON see Hare Krishna
Islam 9, 10, 13, **84–119**; foundation 85, **88–9**; basic beliefs 86; expansion and

empire 85, 91–100 *passim*, 102–9 *passim*, 112–13; and Christianity 10, 56–7, 86, 100; culture and learning 92, 94, 96, 98, 100, 103–9 *passim*, 111; in Far East 110–11, 110, 177; and Hinduism 104–5, 105; and Judaism 30, 31, **38**, 39, 85, 118; numbers of adherents 85, 110, 113, 118, 119; religion and state 13, 84, 85, 94, 100, 109, 116–18; in Spain 30–1, 100; in sub-Saharan Africa 82, **112–13**; and women 107, 113, 116; offshoot movements 205–6, 211; see also Qur'an, Shiite Muslims, Sufism, Sunni Muslims
Islamic Amal **205**
Islamic Salvation Front 117, 118
Ismail (Safavid ruler) 108
Ismaili Khojas **205**
Ismailis see Seveners
Israel: ancient kingdom 22–7
Israel: modern state 17, 18, 27; founded **36**, 36, 116; Arab-Israeli conflict **38**, 39, 85, 118
Israel ben Eliezer 34
Isserles, Moses 32
Istanbul see Constantinople
Italy 10, 15, 59, 63; see also pope and papacy
Ithna'ashariyya see Twelvers

J

Jacob (aka Israel) 20
Jahangir 105
Jainism **144–7**
Jalal al-Din Rumi 98, 99
Janissaries **106**, 106, 114
Japan **196–201**; Buddhism 149, **162–3**, 162, 163, 170, 200; Christian missions to 69; and Confucianism 180, 193, 199; emperor worship 198, 199, 199, 200, 201, 208; new religions 207–9, 210; see also Shinto
jashan 120, 122
Jataka stories 153
jatis 126, 128
Jehoiakin 25
Jehoshaphat 25
Jehovah's Witnesses **203**
Jeremiah 24, **25**, 25
Jeroboam 25
Jeroboam II 25
Jerusalem 22, 22, 23, 24; Christian sites 46, 47, 57, 92; and Crusades 56, 56; Dome

of the Rock 92; Muslim sites 92; Solomon's Temple see under Solomon; under Roman rule 26–7, 26, 44–6, 44, 45, 50; Western (Wailing) Wall 23, 27, 39
Jesuits 46, **62**, 69, 69, 105, 181
Jesus: birth, life and death 42, 44–7; disciples 44, 46, 49, 51; as Lamb of God 50; Last Supper 43, 79, see also Eucharist; as Messiah 41, **44–5**, 50; resurrection 14, 40, 44, 45, **46–7**, 47; seen by other faiths 44, 52, 86, 125; as Son of God 14, 45, **53**, 78, 86, 203
Jesus Prayer 65
Jews see Judaism
Jezebel 25
jihad 86, 94, 100, 113, 115
Jin dynasties 186
Jinas 145, 146
Jinmu 201
jiva/ajiva 145
John the Baptist 42, 86
John of the Cross 65
John Paul II, Pope 83, 83
Joram 25
Josel of Rosheim 33
Joseph of Arimathea 47
Joseph (son of Jacob) 20
Joshua 21
Josiah 25
Judah (Judea) 24–5, 26–7; under Roman rule 44–5, 50; see also Jerusalem
Judah Maccabeus 26, 27
Judah the Prince 29
Judaism **16–39**; basic beliefs 17–19; early history 20–7; expansion into Europe 32–3; Enlightenment, Age of 34–5; festivals see Hannukah, Passover; influence on Christianity 42–3, 48, 78; and Islam 30, 31, **38**, 39, 85, 118; Kabbalists 31; neo-Orthodoxy 35; Orthodox 18, 18, 34, 35, 38; persecution 30–1, 31, 32–3, 89, see also Holocaust; Progressive 18, 18, 35; scriptures see Bible (Old Testament), Torah; in United States 17–18, 35, 36; see also Ashkenazi, Diaspora, Israel (modern), Jesus, Sephardi
Judas of Galilee 27
Judea see Judah
Judgment Day 87, 109, 115, 121, 121
Julian of Norwich 59, 65
justification, doctrine of 48

K

Ka'aba 88, *88–9*
Kabbalah *31*
Kabir 138, *138*, *175*
Kali 141; *see also* Parvati
Kalidasa 136
kami **197**, 198, *198*
Kant, Immanuel *38*
Karbala *90*, 91
karma 127, 129, 133, *145*, 146, *150*, *184*, 206
Kawate, Bunjiro 208
Kemal Atatürk 114, *115*, 116, *116*
Kerouac, Jack *168*
Khadija 88
Khalsa Sikhs *174*
Kharijites 91, *91*
Khazar kingdom 30
Khomeini, Ayatollah 85, *90*, *109*, 118
Kimbangu, Simon 41, **74**
Kimbanguist Church 41, *74*, **203**
Knights Hospitallers *66*
Komei *201*
Konkokyo 200, **208**
Koran *see* Qur'an
Korea, North and South 10, 82, 149, 160, 180, *190*, 209
Kotani, Kimi 207
Krishna *134*, 138, 140, 206, 207
"Ks", the five *174*
Kubo, Kakutaro 207
Kukai 162
Kumarajiva *184*
Kumarapala *147*
Kurds *117*
Kurukshetra 140

L

Ladino 32
Lakshmi *136*, 137
lamas 164, *164*, *168*; *see also* Dalai Lama
Laos 149, 160
Laozi 177, *181*, **182–3**, *183*, 186
Las Casas, Bartholomew de 68
Last Judgment *see* Judgment Day
Latin America: Spanish and Portuguese empires 68–9, *69*; today 10, 13, 41, 42, *46*, 80, *82*
Lebanon 13, 118, 205
Lefebvre, Archbishop 83
Lenin 41
Leo III (Byzantine emperor) 55
Leo IX, Pope 55
Lepanto, Battle of *107*
Lessing, G.E. 34

lex talionis 21
Lhasa *165*
liberation theology 42
limbo *42*
Lin Zhaoen *189*
Lindisfarne *53*
Little Brothers 65
Livingstone, David 75, *75*
Lodi dynasty 105
Lord's Supper *see* Eucharist
lotus *156*
Lourdes *11*
Luke, St. *51*; *see also* Gospels
Luria, Isaac *31*
Luther, Martin 33, 51, **60–1**, *60*, *61*, *62*
Lutheran churches 43, 71, 80

M

McGregor, Alan Bennett *168*
Maclean, Dorothy 209
Madhva *132*, **133**
Magi 44
Mahabharata 129, *132*, **134**, 135, *143*; *see also Bhagavad Gita*
Mahabhodi Society 168
Maharishi Maresh Yogi *132*, 207
Mahavira 135, *145*, **146–7**
Mahayana tradition 149, **158–9**, 160, 161, 162, 164
Mahdi *115*, 205, 211; of the Sudan *115*
Mahikari *201*, **208–9**
Mahinda 155
Mahmud Ghazan 102, *102*
Mahmud II *106*, 114
Mahmud (son of Mir Way) 109
Maimonides, Moses 30, *30*
Makiguchi, Tsunesaburo 208
Malaysia 110, 116
Malcolm X 211
Maliki school of Islamic law *94*
Mamluk dynasty 102, 106, 112
Man (Chinese god) *176*
mandalas *165*, 208
Manjusri *185*, *192*
Mansa Musa 113
mantras *126*, *128*, *143*, *164*, **165**, *167*, 206, 207
Manu-Smriti 135
Mao Zedong 177, 193, **194–5**, *195*
Marcion 51
Marco Polo 110
Mark, St. 203; *see also* Gospels
Marpa 164
marriage: Hindu *129*, 137, 142; Jewish 19, *19*, *34*; Muslim *103*; Shinto *200*; Zoroastrian *123*; other 202, 204
Martel, Charles 92

Marwan II *94*
Marx, Karl 9
Mary Magdalene 47, *47*
Mary, mother of Jesus 11, **44**
Masada 26, 27, *27*
Mass *see* Eucharist
Mathnavi 99
Mattathias 26
Mauryan Empire 135
Maximilian I *33*
Mecca 86, *87*, **88–9**, *89*, *90*, *93*
Mecktild of Magdeburg 59
Medina 89, 91, *93*, *96*
meditation 14, *15*; Buddhist *148*, 161, 162, 163, **166–7**; Islamic 88, 89, 99, 205; Jain *145*, *145*; Sikh 174; Transcendental 9, **207**; other 206, 210; *see also* mystics, prayer
Mehmed, Sultan 106
Meiji dynasty 200, 209
Meir, Golda 38
Mencius 180, *181*, 191
Mendelssohn, Felix 35
Mendelssohn, Moses 34, *35*
Mennonites **204**; *see also* Amish
menorah 16, 26
Merton, Thomas 65
Meshhed *109*
messiah: Jesus as 41, **44–5**; in Judaism 18, 22, 27, *30*, 33, *33*; in Zoroastrianism 121; *see also* Second Coming
Methodism 43, 71, 72, **73**, 82
metta 166
Michizane, Sugawara 197
Middle East: in Alexander's time 26; and Islam 85, 92, 114; in Muhammad's time *89*; postwar nationalism 116; Sikhs in *175*; *see also* separate countries *and* Islam
Milarepa 164
Mina 88, *89*
minarets *8*, *90*, *95*, *96–7*, 111
Ming dynasty 192, *195*
ministry, Christian 43, 62
Mir Way 109
Mirabai 138
Mirza Ali Muhammad 205
missionaries 68–9, *69*, 74–5, *83*, 181, *181*, *194*; modern movements 9, 10, 11, 205; Wesley's journeys 72, *73*; *see also* colonialism
Mo (Chinese god) *176*
Moggaliputta, Tissa 155
moksha *126*, 129, 133, 147
Molcho, Solomon 33
monastic orders 59; *see also* religious houses
Mongols 76, 100, **102**, 110, *192*; *see also* Yuan dynasty

Monkey King 189, *189*
monotheism 17, 18, 121, 135, 142, 173
Monte Cassino 55, *66*
Moody, Dwight L. 73, *73*
Moon, Sun Myung 210–11
Moonies *see* Unification Church
Moravian Brethren 72–3
More, Sir Thomas *60*
Mormons **204**
Morocco 97, 100; *see also* Spain (under Islam)
Morone, Cardinal *63*
Moses 20–1, *20*, *21*, *30*, *30*, 42
Moses de León *31*
Moses ibn Ezra 30
mosques **96–7**, *105*, 106, 107, 109, 111, 112; illustrated *85*, *95*, *96–7*, *103*, *108*, *112*, *113*
Mother Goddess, Hindu *136*, 137
mountains in Chinese religion 178, *179*, *185*, *187*
Mu'awiya 91, 92
Mughal dynasty 104, *104*, **105**, *105*, *107*, *147*, 174
Muhammad Abduh 114
Muhammad Ahmad (Mahdi of the Sudan) *115*
Muhammad Bello *113*
Muhammad, Elijah 211
Muhammad ibn al Hasan al Qummi *94*
Muhammad the Prophet 85, **88–9**, 91, *92*, *93*, *96*, 99, 114, 205
Muhammad, Wallace Fard 211
mujahedin 118
Münzer, Thomas *60*, *61*, 202
Musadeqq, Muhammad 116
Muslim Brotherhood 116, 117, **205–6**
Muslims *see* Islam
Mustapha Kemal *see* Kemal Atatürk
mystery plays *79*
mystics and mysticism: Christian 59, **64–5**, *77*; Hindu *132*, 142; Islamic *99*, *105*; women 59, 65, 99; *see also* Sufism

N

Naganuma, Myoko 207
Nakayama, Miki 209
Nanak, Guru 138, 173, *173*, **174**, *175*
Napoleon 34
Naraya, Swami 207
Nasrid dynasty *100*
Nasser, Gamel Abdul 85, *116*

Nathan of Gaza *33*
Nathan (Old Testament prophet) 22
nationalism *see* state
Nebuchadnezzar 25
Nehemiah 26
Nehru, Jawaharlal *154*
Neo-Confucianism 190
Neo-Pagan Movement **209**
Neo-Sufism **206**
Neumann, Karl 169
New Age 14, *15*, **209**
new religions 12, 13, 14, **202–11** *passim*
New Testament *see under* Bible
New Thought **209–10**
New Zealand 149
Nicaea, Council of 52, *53*
Nichiren Buddhism 163
Nicholas II, Tsar 41
Niemöller, Martin 80
Nietzsche, Friedrich 9
Nirvana 149, 150, 156, *156*, *159*, 161, *184*
Niwano, Nikkyo 207
Nizaris 96–7
non-violence *see* pacifism
Normans 55, *55*
Nyanatiloka (Anton Gueth) 169

O

Oberammergau *79*
Okada, Mokichi 208
Okada, Yoshikazu 208
Olcott, Henry S. 168, *168*, 210
Old Testament *see under* Bible
Oldenberg, Hermann 168
Omotokyo **208**
Omrid dynasty 24, 25
Opus Dei movement 43
oracle bones 178, *178*
Origen 203
Orthodox Church 41, 43, **54**, *57*, 65, **76–7**, *76*, *77*, 203; and ecumenism 82, *82*; Roman/Orthodox split **54–5**, 76
Osman (Othman) 106
Oswald, King of Northumbria 53
Ottoman Empire 76, **106–7**, 109, 112, 114, *114*, *115*, 116

P

pacifism and non-violence: Buddhist 149; Husain *90*; Jain *145*, *147*; Jesus' attitude 45; Quakers 71; new movements 203–10 *passim*

Index

Padmasambhava 164
pagodas 157, 161, 184
Pahlavi language 123
Pakistan: created 104; pre-1947 see India
Palestine 26–7; and Crusades 56–7; religious academies 27, 29; see also Israel (modern), Judah
Palestinian Arabs **38**, 116; see also Arab-Israeli conflict
Pali Canon 149, 158
Pali language 149, 155, 168
Panth 173, 174, *174*
Parshva 146
Parsis 122, *123*
Parthian Empire 121, *123*
Parvati (Amba, Durga, Kali, Shakti) *136*, 137, 141
Paryushan 145
Pascal, Blaise 65
Passover 19, *19*, 21, 32, 46, 50
patriarchates 55, 76
Paul III, Pope 62
Paul, St. **48–9**, *49*; letters 49, 50–1, 60, 82
Peasants' Revolt 60, 61, 202
Penn, William 71
Pentateuch 20, 28, *28*; see also Torah
Pentecost 48, 82
Pentecostalists 9, 10, *82*
persecution: of Buddhists 185; in China (all faiths) 177, 194–5; of Christians 41, 46, 52, 69; of Jews 30–1, *31*, 36, 89, Holocaust 18, *19*, 37, 38, 80, modern reconciliation *30*; of Muslims 103; of Zoroastrians 122
Persia 92, 94, 100, 102–3, 108–9; modern see Iran
Peter, St. *49*
Pharisees 26, 27, 48, 50
Pilgrim Fathers 70, *71*
pilgrims and pilgrimages: Buddhist 153, 157, 165, 185; Christian 11, 56, 58; Hindu 140–1; Islamic 88, *109*, 115, see also hajj; Jain *144*; Jewish 23
pillars of Islam 86
Poland 13, 32, 37, 40, 80
Pompey 26
Ponsak, Ajahn *171*
Pontius Pilate 44, 45, 46
Poor Clares 59
pope and papacy 55, 58–9; present pope 83, *83*; other popes 53, 55, 56, 58, 59, 60, 62, 68, 69; see also Reformation
Portugal: missions and imperialism 68–9, 75

Prabhupada, Swami 206
prayer and contemplation 13; Christian 64–5, *77*; Islamic 85, 86, *86*, **96**, 113; Shinto 197; Zoroastrian 122; see also mantras, meditation, mystics, worship
Presbyterianism 43, 70, 71, *74*, 75, 82
priests: Buddhist see lamas, sangha; Christian 42, 43, 82; Hindu see Brahmins; Jain 145; Shinto 197; see also women
"projectionist" theory 9
"Promised Land" 20, 21; see also Palestine, Israel
Prophet, Mark and Elizabeth 209
prophets *44*; Old Testament 25, *25*, 28–9, 86; see also Muhammad
Protestant Buddhism 171
Protestantism **60–1**, *60*; and biblical scholarship 78–9; goes to America 70–1; revivalism (18th C.) 72–3; today 9, 10, 41, 82, *82*; see also missionaries
Psalms, Book of 22, 46, 86
Ptolemy 26
puja 126, **127**, *139*, 145, 150
Puranas 136, 137
Pure Land Buddhism 149, 163, 167, 184
purgatory 60, 62, *188*
Puritans 70, *71*
purpose of religion 13–14

Q

qi 186
Qing dynasty 187, 189, 190, **192**, 192–3
Quakers 43, 71, *71*
Quanzhen school 189
Qumran 27
Quraish tribe 88, 91
Qur'an 10, 85, 86, *87*, 91, **93**, 94, 113; as basis of education 106, *113*; and Sufism 99

R

Rabi'a al-Adawiyya 99
Rabin, Yitzhak 38
race v. religion in Islam 94
Radhakrishnan *132*
Rajneesh, Bhagwan Shree 210
Rajneesh Movement **210**

Rajputs 105
Ram Mohan Roy 142
Ram Singh, Baba 173
Rama (Vishnu) 140, 207; see also Ramayana
Rama Khameng 161
Ramacaritmanas 138
Ramadan 86
Ramakrishna 142
Ramananda *138*
Ramanuja 132, **133**
Ramayana 132, *134*, 135, 140, *141*, 143
Ranjit Singh 174
Rashi (Solomon ben Isaac) 32
Rashid Rida 114
Rashtrakuta dynasty 137
Rastafarianism 14, **211**
Red Yang cult *189*
Reformation **60–1**; in England *60*
Rehoboam 24
reincarnation 14, 208, 209; Buddhist 150, 153, 160, 161, 184; Hindu 126, *129*, 133
Reiyukai **207**
relics, Christian medieval 58
religious academies 27, 29
religious houses 53, 55, 59, 60, 66, 75, 203
resurrection 27, 121; Islamic view *87*; of Jesus 14, *40*, 44, 45, **46–7**, *47*, 205
Reubeni, David *33*
Revelation, Book of *50*
Ricci, Matteo 69, *181*
Richard I of England 56, *57*
Rig Veda 126, 128, 130, *131*, *132*
Rimpoche, Chogyam Trungpa *168*
Rissho Kosei Kai 149, 170, **207**
Robertson, Pat 41
Robinson, John 14
Rolf (Rollo) 55
Roman Catholicism: and Celtic Church 53; and ecumenism 82, *82*; ministry and worship 43, 82; in New World 68–9, 70; Roman/Orthodox split 54–5, 76; today 9, 10, 13, 15, 41, 82–3, 211; see also Counter-Reformation, missionaries, pope and papacy, Reformation
Romans as rulers 26–7, 27, 44–5, *44*, 50, 52–3
Rosenzweig, Franz *38*
Rothschild family *33*, 34
Roy, Ram Mohan see Ram
Ruan Yuan *184*
Rudra see Shiva
Rushdie, Salman 118, *119*

Ruskin, John 125
Russell, Charles Taze 203
Russia, former Soviet Union see Commonwealth of Independent States
Russian Federation 40, 41
Russian imperialism 114
Russian Orthodox Church see Orthodox

S

Sabbath, Jewish 19, 47
sacrifice 50, 89, 130, 131, 135, 178
Sadat, Anwar 38, 118, 206
Sadducees 27
Safavid dynasty 106, *107*, **108–9**
Sai Baba 207
Saicho 162
Saladin 30, 56, 57, *96*
salat see prayer (Islamic)
Samaria 24, *25*
Samarkand 103, *103*
samsara 126, 129, *129*, 133, 150
Samson 21
Samuel 21, 22
Sandinistas 43
sangha (Buddhist monk/lay community) **150**, 151, 154, 155, *160*, **161**, *161*, 167, 169
Sanghamitta 155
Sangharakshita, Maha Sthavira 207
Sangtsen Gampo 164
Sankey, Ira D. 73, *73*
sannyasins 126, *128*
Sanskrit language 130, 136, *143*, 149, 158
Santería 13, **211**
Santoshi Mata 142
Sarasvati, Dayanandi 142
Saraswati *136*, 137
Sasanian Empire 89, 121, *123*
Satan (Shaitan) 86, 89, 203, 204
Sathya Sai Baba Movement 207
sati 137, 138, 142
Saudi Arabia 85, *90*, 94, 116, 118, *119*; see also hajj, Mecca
Saul, King 22
Sayyid al-Nahdi al-Sanussi *115*
Scandinavia 9, *63*
Schechter, Solomon 35
Schopenhauer, Arthur 132, 169
science and technology 9, 13, 114, *118*; Darwinism 66–7; modern technological aids 10, *11*, 41, 202; see also social and ethical concerns

Scientology 13, **210**
scriptures: Buddhist 149, *154*, 155–8, *158*, 163; Christian see Bible, Gospels; Confucian 180, 190, 191, *192*; Daoist 182–3, *187*; Hindu: *Gita* and epics 129, *132*, 133, **134**, 135, 137, 138, *143*, 206, Upanishads 131, **132–3**, *137*, 138, Vedas 126, 130, *131*, *132*, 142; Islamic see Qur'an; Jain 145, 147; Jewish see Bible (Old Testament), Torah; Sikh 173, *173*, 174, *174*, 175; Zoroastrian *123*
Second Coming 50, 204, 210; Hidden Imam *109*, 205
Second Isaiah 24
Second Vatican Council 10, 80, 82
Seicho No Ie 201, **208**
Sekai Kyuseikyo 201, **208**
Sekai Mahikari **208**
Seleucids 26
Seleucus 26
Selim I 106
Selim III *106*
Seljuk Turks 56, 94, *98*, **100**, 102
Sen, Ramprasad 141
Separatist Puritans 70, *71*
Sephardi Jews 30–1, *31*, 32, *32*, 38
Seveners (Ismailis) *91*, 96
Seventh-Day Adventists **204**
Shafi'i school of Islamic law *94*
Shaftesbury, Earl of 73
Shah Jahan *104*, 105, *105*
shahada 86, *87*
Shaitan see Satan
Shakyamuni see Buddha
Shang dynasty 178, *178*
Shankara 132, **133**
shari'a 94, 113
Sheba, Queen of 22
Shembe, Isaiah 204
Shiite Muslims 13, **90–1**, *90*, *91*, 92, 94, *94*, 97, 108–9; Seveners and Twelvers *91*, 96, *109*, 109; new movements 205
Shingon Buddhism 162
Shinran 163
Shinto **196–201**; and Buddhism 162, 198–9, 200, *201*; and Christianity 199; and Confucianism 198, 199; and Daoism 198; shrines and festivals *196*, 197, *197*, *199*, *200*, *201*; new movements 208–9
Shiv Baba 206
Shiva 130, *131*, 133, 135, *136*, 137, 140, 141, *143*
Shizong 192

shunyata 158, 184
Shvetambaras 147
Sigismund Augustus 32
Sikhism **172–5**, *175*, 206–7
Simons, Menno 204
Sinan (architect) *107*
Singapore: and Islam 110
Six Day War 38, *39*
slavery 68, *70*, 74, 75, 112
Smith, Joseph 204
Snyder, Gary *168*
social and ethical concerns 66, *66*, 73, 75, 83, 170, *171*, 174; *see also* science and technology *and* war ("just")
Society of Jesus *see* Jesuits
Soka Gakkai 13, 14, 149, 163, 170, **208**
Sokoto caliphate *113*
Solomon **22–3**, *22*; his Temple 22, *23*, 23, 26, 27, *27*
Son of Heaven 192, *193*
Song dynasty 185, 188, **190**, *191*
Song of Songs 29
South India, Church of 82
Spain: Jews *28*, **30–1**; mission and imperialism 68–9; mystics 65; under Islam 92, 94, 97, 100, *100*
Spangler, David 209
"speaking in tongues" *82*
Sri Lanka 149–50, 155, 158, 160–1, *168*, 171
Stahl, F.J. 34
Stalin, Josef 41
state, religion and the 13, 14; Buddhism 185; China *191*; Chinese religions *183*, 187, 188–9, *189*, 193, 194–5, *195*; Christianity 52–3, *53*, 58–9, 76; Islam 13, 84, 85, *94*, 100, 109, 114, 116–18, 121; Judaism 30; Shinto 197, 198, 199, 200–1, *200*; Zoroastrianism *123*; *see also* colonialism, communism
Stations of the Cross *47*
Stephen (first Christian martyr) 46, *46*
Sthanakvasis 147
Strauss, David *79*
stupas 155, 156, **157**
Subud 206
Sudan 112, 114, *115*, 203
Suez Canal *114*, *116*
Suffering Servant 45, 46, *90*
Sufism *98*, **99**, *99*, 108, 109, 110, 114; influence on Hinduism 138; Neo-Sufism **206**
Sui dynasty 184, 185
Suleiman I (the Magnificent) *106*, *107*

Sunni Muslims *90*, **91**, *91*, *94*, *103*, 108, 109, 205; al-Ghazali *98*; Kurds *117*
sutras 133, 137, 158, *158*, 163, 184, 207, 208
Suzuki, Daisetsu T. *168*
Swaminarayana 12, **207**
Sweden 9, *63*
Swedenborg, Emanuel 203
synagogues 23, *31*, 35, *37*

T

Tagore, Rabindranath 142
Taiping Rebellion 194, *195*
Taishan (Mt. Tai) 178, *179*
Taiwan *189*
Taj Mahal *104*, 105, *105*
Talmud 19, 27, 29, *29*
Tamerlane (Timur Lenk) 103, *103*
Tang dynasty 184, 185, 188, *191*
Taniguchi, Masaharu 208
Taoism *see* Daoism
Tathagata *see* Buddha
"televangelists" 41
temples: Buddhist *161*; Confucian *181*; Daoist *176*, *187*; Hindu *139*; Jain *144*, *147*; rebuilding in China 177
Ten Commandments 18, *21*, 23
Ten Precepts of Buddhism *161*, *161*
Ten Sikh Gurus 173–5, *173*, *174*, *175*
Tendai Buddhism 162
Tenrikyo **209**
Teresa of Avila *64*, 65
Thailand 149, 160, 161, 208
theological studies 29, 32, *38*, *58*, 82, 203; Islamic *109*; *see also* mysticism; religious academies; religious houses
Theosophical Society 168, **210**
Theravada tradition *148*, 149, 155, **158–9**, **160–1**, 167
Thich Nhat Hanh 149, 170
"Third Rome" 76
Thomas à Kempis *59*
Thoreau, Henry *168*
3HO Foundation 173, **206–7**
Tiantai 184
Tibetan Buddhism 149, 150, *151*, **164–5**, 170, *170*; Qing version *192*; in United States *168*
Timur Lenk (Tamerlane) 103, *103*
Timurid dynasty *103*
Tirthankaras *144*, *144*, 146
Titus (Roman emperor) *26*
Tokugawa dynasty 199

Tolstoy, Leo 125
Torah 19, 20–1, 26, 27, **28–9**, *28*, *29*, *30*; importance to Islam 86
torii 196
Transcendental Meditation 9, **207**
transubstantiation 43
Trent, Council of 62, *63*
Trevelyan, Sir George 209, *211*
Triads *189*, 195
Trigrams, the Eight 178, *179*
Trimurti 136
Trinity, doctrine of 53, 203
Tripitaka 158
triratna (three jewels of Buddhism) *151*
Tsong Khapa 164
Tukaram 138
Tulsi Das 138
Tulunid dynasty 95
Turkey: and Kurds *117*; today 118; *see also* Ottoman Empire, Seljuk Turks
Twelvers *91*, 96, **109**, *109*

U

Ubadayyah al-Mahdi 96
Ukraine 30, 41
Umar 91, *93*
Umayyad dynasty *90*, 91, **92**, *92*, 94, *94*, 99, 104; of Spain 97
Umbanda 13, **211**
Unification Church (Moonies) 13, **210–11**
unifying effect of religion 13–14, *13*
United States: Buddhists **168**, 177; coming of Christianity 70–1, 18th-century revival 72, 73, today 9, 10, 11, 14, 15, 41; Hindus 125; Jews 17–18, *18*, 35, 36; Muslims 118; Sikhs 173, *175*; Zoroastrians 121; other or new religions 12, 13, 202–11 *passim*
"untouchable" *see dalit*
Upanishads *131*, **132–3**, 137, 138
Urban II, Pope 56
Urban VI, Pope 58
Usuman dan Fodio *113*
Uthman 91, *93*

V

Vairocana 162–3, *185*, 198
Vajrayana 164

van Buren, Paul 14
Varanasi *see* Benares
Vardhamana *see* Mahavira
varna 126, 128, *128*, *134*; *see also* Brahmins, caste system
Vedanta philosophy 99, 132, **133**, *133*
Vedas 126, 130, **131**, 132, 142
Vedic tradition **130–1**, 135; *see also* Vedas
Vietnam 149
Virgin birth **44**
Vishnu 135, *136*, *137*, 140, *143*; *see also* Krishna
Vishtaspa (Hystaspes) 121
Visigoths 52
Vivekananda 125, 142
Vladimir, Grand Prince 76
von Dohm, Wilhelm 34
Voodoo **211**

W

Wali Allah, Shaykh 105
Wang Bi 183, *183*
Wang Yangming 190
war, "just": Christian **80–1**, *see also* Crusades; Islamic *jihad* 86, 94, 100, *113*, *115*; Sikh 174
Warring States period 178
Watts, Isaac *79*
Wei dynasty *183*
Weizmann, Chaim 36
Wesley, Charles *72*, 73, *79*
Wesley, John **72**, **73**, *79*
wheel as symbol 155, *155*, 156, *157*, 164
Whitby, Synod of *53*
White Cloud cult 188
White Huns 135, *136*
White, James and Ellen 204
White Lotus cult *189*, 195
Whitefield, George *72*, 73
Whitman, Walt *168*
Wilberforce, William 73
William of Occam 58
Williams, Roger 71, *71*
Wilson, Woodrow 36
Wise, Isaac M. 35
Wise, Stephen 36
women: and Buddhism 160, *161*; and Hinduism 125; and Islam *84*, 88, *107*, 113, *116*; and Jainism *147*; and Sikhism *174*; and Zoroastrianism 122; mystics 59, 65, 99; priests/ministers 42, 43, 82, in new movements 202, 206, 208, 209, 211
Worms, Concordat of 58

worship: Buddhist 149, 150, *152*; China, emperor (and Mao) worship 192–3, 195, *195*; Chinese folk religions 188, *189*; Christian 42–3, *82*; Hindu 126, **127**, 137, *139*; Jain *144*, 147, *147*; Sikh 173, 174; *see also* House Church Movement; prayer
Wrekin Trust **211**
Wu dynasty 186

X

Xu Jia 188
Xuanzang 184
Xunzi 180

Y

yatra 140
Yavneh 27
Yazid I *90*, 91
Yellow Hats (Gelukpas) 164, *192*
Yellow Turbans 186, 195
Yemen 118
Yiddish 32
Yiguandao cult *189*
yin and yang 178, *179*, *183*, 193
yoga 127, 130, *131*
Yogi Bhajan 206
Yom Kippur 23
Yom Kippur War 38
Young, Brigham 204
Young Turks 114
Yuan (Mongol) dynasty 110, *189*, 191
Yugoslavia (former) 54, *63*, 106

Z

Zarathushtra (Zoroaster) 121, *123*
Zealots 27, *27*, 44–5, *45*, 46
Zedekiah 25
Zen Buddhism 10, 149, **162–3**, 167, *168*
Zhang Daoling and family 186, *187*
Zhou dynasty 178
Zhu Xi 190, *191*
Zhuangzi (texts) 182–3, *183*
Zhuangzi (writer) 182–3
Zinzendorf, Nicholas von 72
Zion *24*
Zionism **36**
Zionist churches **204**
Zoroastrianism 99, **120–3**
Zumárraga, Juan de 68
Zvi, Sabbatai *33*
Zwingli, Huldreich 61, 202

Acknowledgments

The publishers would like to thank the following people and organizations for their help in the making of this book:

Editorial: **Maggi McCormick**, **Tim Probart**, **Dorothy Groves** (index), **Pennie Jelliff**, **Shirin Patel**, **Eleanor Nesbitt**, **Ram Krishnan**, **Geoffrey Parrinder**, **John Hinnells**, **Fred Gill**
Design: **Millions Design**
Picture research: **Richard Philpott**
Production: **Kate Waghorn**, **Nikki Ingram**

Biblical extracts taken from the New Jerusalem Bible, published and copyright by Darton, Longman and Todd Ltd. and Doubleday & Co Inc., are used by permission of the publishers.

Extracts from *The Koran*, translated by A. J. Arberry, first published 1955 by George Allen & Unwin Ltd., first published in the World's Classics by Oxford University Press 1964, are used by permission of HarperCollins Ltd.

PICTURE CREDITS

l = left; *r* = right; *c* = centre; *t* = top; *b* = bottom

1 Piers Cavendish/Impact Photos; 2–3 Mark Cator/Impact Photos; 6 William Strode/Susan Griggs Agency; 8 Abbas/Magnum Photos; 10 Mary Evans Picture Library; 11 Steven McCurry/Magnum Photos; 12*t* & *bl* Mohamed Ansar/Impact Photos; 12*br* Moradabadi/Impact Photos; 14*tl* Homer Sykes/Impact Photos; 14*r* Fred Mayer/Magnum Photos; 14*b* Paul Fusco/Magnum Photos; 16 R. Bond/ZEFA; 16–17 Geoffrey Hiller/Black Star/Colorific!; 18 & 19*t* ZEFA; 19*b* Fred Mayer/Magnum Photos; 20 Sonia Halliday Photographs; 21*t* Ancient Art and Architecture Collection; 21*b* ZEFA; 22*l* Sonia Halliday Photographs; 22*r* ZEFA; 23 ZEFA; 24*l* Christie's, London/Bridgeman Art Library; 24*r* Eric Lessing Culture and Fine Arts Archive/Magnum Photos; 25 Scala; 26 C.M. Dixon; 27*t* & *c* ZEFA; 27*b* J. Catling Allen; 28 Oriental and India Office Collections/British Library; 29*t* David Harris/Israel Museum; 29*b* Rachel Morton/Impact Photos; 30*l* Zev Radovan; 30*r* Marcos/Gamma/Frank Spooner Pictures; 31*l* Fabrice Rouland/Rapho; 31*c* & *r* Oriental and India Office Collections/British Library; 33*tl* & *tr* The Mansell Collection; 33*b* Alfred Rubens Collection; 34 Arlene Gottfried/Contact Press Images/Colorific!; 35*l* The Mansell Collection; 35*r* Bridgeman Art Library; 36 Britain Israel Public Affairs Centre; 37 & 38*t* The Wiener Library; 38*b* Hulton Deutsch Collection; 39 Cornell Capa/Magnum Photos; 40*t* Michael MacIntyre/Hutchison Library; 40*b* Shepard Sherbell/SABA/Katz Pictures; 41 Bruno Barbey/Magnum Photos; 42*t* Jean Williamson/Mick Sharp; 42*b* Sobol/SIPA/Rex Features; 43 David Alan Harvey/Susan Griggs Agency; 44 Magyar Nemzeti Galeria, Budapest/Bridgeman Art Library; 45 British Library/Bridgeman Art Library; 46 Bridgeman Art Library; 47 Musée Condé, Chantilly/Bridgeman Art Library; 48 Adam Woolfitt/Susan Griggs Agency; 49 Michael Holford, 50*t* Bible Society/Bridgeman Art Library; 50*b* Cathedral of St Bavo, Ghent/Giraudon/Bridgeman Art Library; 51 Trinity College, Dublin/Bridgeman Art Library; 52 Penny Tweedie/Impact Photos; 53*t* Brian Harris/Impact Photos; 53*b* Aachen Cathedral/Angelo Hornak; 54*l* Ron Haviv/SABA-REA/Katz Pictures; 54*r* Tim Megarry/Robert Harding Picture Library; 55 Adam Woolfitt/Susan Griggs Agency; 56*t* Bibliothèque Nationale/Bridgeman Art Library; 56*b* Michael Holford; 57 Mark Cator/Impact Photos; 58 Museo de Bellas Artes, Seville/Index/Bridgeman Art Library; 60 English Heritage; 61*t* National Museum, Stockholm/Bridgeman Art Library; 61*b* The Mansell Collection; 62 Château de Versailles/Giraudon/Bridgeman Art Library; 64 Michael Holford; 65*t* Johnny Van Haeften Gallery, London/Bridgeman Art Library; 65*b* Courtesy of the Gethsemani Abbey Archives; 66*l* James Kamp/Black Star/Colorific! 66*r* Forest McCullin/Black Star/Colorific!; 67*t* Bridgeman Art Library; 67*b* Ann Ronan Picture Library; 68*l* Walter Rawlings/Robert Harding Picture Library; 68*r* Roger Kohn; 69 Museu Nacional de Arte Antiga, Lisbon/Michael Holford; 70 Peter Newark's American Pictures; 71*t* Graves Art Gallery, Sheffield/Bridgeman Art Library; 71*b* J. Alex Langley/Aspect Picture Library; 72*t* National Portrait Gallery, London; 72*b* Bridgeman Art Library; 73*t* Richard Baker/Katz Pictures; 73*b* Hulton Deutsch Collection; 74 Christopher Cormack/Impact Photos; 75*t* Public Record Office; 75*b* Bridgeman Art Library; 76 Robert Harding Picture Library; 77*t* Hans Schmied/ZEFA; 77*b* Ignatiev/Network; 78*t* Keystone, Hamburg; 78*b* Bavaria Bildagentur, Munich; 79 IPC; 80*l* Imperial War Museum; 80*r* Keystone, Hamburg; 81*t* Kohlhas/ZEFA; 81*b* Ursula Benker-Schirmer/Dean and Chapter of Chichester Cathedral/Woodmansterne Picture Library; 82*t* Jon Hoffmann/Frank Spooner Pictures; 82*b* Homer Sykes/Network; 83 Giansanti/Sygma; 84 Rex Features; 84–5 Abbas/Magnum Photos; 86 M. Ascani/Hoa-Qui; 87 Mohamed Ansar/Impact Photos; 88*t* Mohamed Lounes/Gamma/Frank Spooner Pictures; 88*b* Mohamed Amin/Robert Harding Picture Library; 89 Abbas/Magnum

Photos; 90*t* Roy Miles Gallery, London/Bridgeman Art Library; 90*b* S.P.A./Gamma/Frank Spooner Pictures; 92 Michael Holford; 93 Robert Harding Picture Library; 95 Angelo Hornak; 96*tl* Mohamed Ansar/Impact Photos; 96*tr* Jàmes Harpur; 96*b* Robert Harding Picture Library; 97 Carl Purcell/Colorific!; 98 Peter Keen/Susan Griggs Agency; 100 Ronny Jaques/Colorific!; 101*t* Michael Holford; 101*b* Ancient Art and Architecture Collection; 102 Bibliothèque Nationale/Bridgeman Art Library; 103*t* Robert Harding Picture Library; 103*bl* Robert Harding Picture Library; 103*br* Abbas/Magnum Photos; 104*l* Angelo Hornak; 104*r* Michael Holford; 105*t* Michael Holford; 105*b* Chester Beatty Library, Dublin; 106 Sonia Halliday and Laura Lushington; 107*l* British Library/Bridgeman Art Library; 107*c* Victoria and Albert Museum/Bridgeman Art Library; 107*r* Angelo Hornak; 108*t* British Library/Bridgeman Art Library; 108*b* Robert Harding Picture Library; 109 Roger Wood; 110 Christophe Bluntzer/Impact Photos; 110–1 Alain Everard/Impact Photos; 111 Robert Harding Picture Library; 112 John Hatt/Hutchison Library; 113 M. Renaudeau/Hoa-Qui; 114 The Mansell Collection; 115*l* Hulton Deutsch Collection; 115*r* Hutchison Library; 116*t* Hulton Deutsch Collection; 116*b* Associated Press; 117*t* Hulton Deutsch Collection; 117*b* Mark Cator/Impact Photos; 118 Abbas/Magnum Photos; 119*l* John Arthur/Impact Photos; 119*r* Abbas/Magnum Photos; 120 Jehangir Gazdar/Comstock; 122*l* Robert Harding Picture Library; 122*r* Jehangir Gazdar/Comstock; 124 Raghu Rai/Magnum Photos; 125 Adam Woolfitt/Susan Griggs Agency; 126 Robert Harding Picture Library; 127*t* Robert Harding Picture Library; 127*b* Mohamed Ansar/Impact Photos; 128 Mohamed Ansar/Impact Photos; 129*tl* Mohamed Ansar/Impact Photos; 129*tr* K. Rodgers/Hutchison Library; 129*b* Ben Edwards/Impact Photos; 131*t* Victoria and Albert Museum/Michael Holford; 131*b* E. Bouvet/Odyssey/Impact Photos; 131 Ann and Bury Peerless; 132*t* Robert Harding Picture Library; 132*b* Gulbenkian Museum of Oriental Art, University of Durham/Bridgeman Art Library; 132–3 Bob Davis/Aspect Picture Library; 134*l* Ronald Grant Archive; 134*r* British Library/Michael Holford; 134–5 Michael Holford; 136*l* Victoria and Albert Museum/Bridgeman Art Library; 136*r* Duncan Maxwell/Robert Harding Picture Library; 137–9 Michael Holford; 140*r* Kim Naylor/Aspect Picture Library; 140*b* & 141 Roderick Johnson/Images of India; 142 Popperfoto; 143*l* Michael MacIntyre/Hutchison Library; 143*r* J.G. Fuller/Hutchison Library; 144*l* Ann and Bury Peerless; 144*r* Jehangir Gazdar/Comstock; 146 Ann and Bury Peerless; 147 J.H.C. Wilson/Robert Harding Picture Library; 148 Luca Invernizzi Tettoni/Photobank/BKK/Robert Harding Picture Library; 149 Tom Stoddart/Frank Spooner Pictures; 150 Alain Everard/Susan Griggs Agency; 151*l* Alain Le Garsmeur/Impact Photos; 151*r* Robert Harding Picture Library; 152*t* Ancient Art and Architecture Collection; 152*b* Select; 153 Ancient Art and Architecture Collection; 154 Graham Harrison; 155–6 Robert Harding Picture Library; 157 Liba Taylor/Select; 158*t* Ancient Art and Architecture Collection; 158*c* & *b* Robert Harding Picture Library; 160*t* Liba Taylor/Select; 160*b* Graham Harrison; 161 Jean Leo Dugast/Sygma; 162 Graham Harrison; 163*t* Graham Harrison; 163*bl* Jean-Paul Nacivet/Colorific!; 163*br* Sygma; 164*t* Graham Harrison; 164*b* Alain Le Garsmeur/Impact Photos; 164–5 Graham Harrison; 165 Ancient Art and Architecture Collection; 166*t* Tibor Hirsch/Susan Griggs Agency; 166*b* Robert Harding Picture Library; 167 Graham Harrison; 168 Martin Janowitz/Vajradhatu Archives; 169*t* Hulton Deutsch Collection; 169*b* Mohamed Ansar/Impact Photos; 170 Tibet Image Bank; 171 Irene R. Lengui/LIV; 172 Robert Harding Picture Library; 174 Ann and Bury Peerless; 175 Dilip Mehta/Contact Press Images/Colorific!; 176*t* & *b* Sally and Richard Greenhill; 176 inset *b* Tim Barrett; 178 Ancient Art and Architecture Collection; 179 Peter Carmichael/Aspect Picture Library; 180 Bibliothèque Nationale/Giraudon/Bridgeman Art Library; 181*t* Robert Harding Picture Library; 181*bl* Collection of the Nelson-Atkins Museum of Art, Kansas City, Missouri (Gift of Bronson Trevor in honour of his father, John Trevor); 181*br* The Mansell Collection; 182 Victoria and Albert Museum/Bridgeman Art Library; 182–3 Luc Girard/Explorer; 183 Gulbenkian Museum of Oriental Art/University of Durham; 184*t* Tony Waltham/Robert Harding Picture Library; 184*b* Robert Harding Picture Library; 185 Werner Forman Archive; 186 Sally and Richard Greenhill; 187*l* Rolf Richardson/Robert Harding Picture Library; 187*r* Sally and Richard Greenhill; 188*t* Victoria and Albert Museum/Ian Thomas; 188*b* Robert Harding Picture Library; 189*l* Robert Harding Picture Library; 189*r* Patrick Zachmann/Magnum Photos; 190 Philip J. Griffiths/Magnum Photos; 191*l* Bibliothèque Nationale/ET Archive; 191*b* ET Archive; 192*l* Robert Harding Picture Library; 192*r* Commercial Press; 193 Robert Harding Picture Library; 195*t* G. Corrigan/Robert Harding Picture Library; 195*b* ET Archive; 196*t* Michael Holford; 196*b* Yuzo Yamada/Q Photo International Inc; 197 The Image Bank; 198 J. Griffiths/Magnum Photos; 199*t* Orion Press; 199*bl* Asai Collection/Orion Press; 199*br* Geoff Howard; 200*l* Elly Beintema/Robert Harding Picture Library; 200*r* Geoff Howard; 201 Popperfoto.

ILLUSTRATION CREDITS

Stephen Conlin: 23, 59, 97, 130, 139, 157
Maxine Hamil: Decorative panels throughout
Technical Art Services: Maps throughout
Roger Wade-Walker/Kathy Jakeman Illustration: 34, 156